The Quest for
NONSUCH

NONSUCH FROM THE NORTH-WEST

Painting by an unknown Flemish artist, c. 1620

The Quest for Nonsuch

John Dent

London Borough of Sutton Leisure Services

First published April 1962 by Hutchinson & Co. (Publishers) Ltd
Second edition (revised) August 1970

1st paperback edition (reprinted from 2nd edition)
November 1981
Reprinted 1988

LONDON BOROUGH OF SUTTON LEISURE SERVICES
Central Library, St Nicholas Way
Sutton, Surrey, SM1 1EA
Telephone 01-661 5050

ISBN 0 907335 04 7

Title page and cover design: Shirley Edwards

Printed and bound in Great Britain by
Anchor Brendon Ltd, Tiptree, Essex

For
ANNA

Acknowledgements

For all the information based on the excavations of 1959 and 1960 which I have incorporated, and for permission to use it, in printed, pictorial and diagrammatic form, I am deeply indebted to the Nonsuch Palace Excavation Committee under its Chairman, Sir John Summerson. I have naturally drawn only selectively on the detailed and specialized archaeological information now available to that Committee, on which Mr. Martin Biddle, the Director of the excavations, is preparing a full report. This will deal comprehensively with the archaeology, history and art-history of the Palace and will include contributions by specialists in various fields. Copyright illustrations reproduced by permission of the Committee are Plates 2, 8(a), 9, 10, 12(a), (b), 13, 14, 15, 17 and 18; the Line Drawings on pages 29, 77, 87, 97, 127 and 247; and all the Tail-pieces except those on pages 53 and 90. Much of the printed and documentary material which I have used was discovered by Mr. Martin Biddle and generously placed by him at my disposal. He has kindly read through my manuscript and has made many valuable suggestions.

I also owe a debt to Mr. C. L. Quinton, formerly Borough Librarian of Sutton and Cheam, for his research into books and manuscripts mainly concerned with the Restoration period and particularly for his location of one of the most important of the 'new' documents, that relating to the demolition of the Palace. Miss J. M. I. Griffiths, Deputy Borough Librarian of Epsom and Ewell, has helped in many ways, notably by drawing the pre-excavation reconstructed plan of the Palace and assisting with the transcription of the Building Accounts. Mr. Herbert Dunk, of Cheam, has checked my details of the history of the Lumley family; Mr. C. G. Dobson, also of Cheam, and Miss E. M. Myatt-Price, Assistant Registrar at the London School of Economics, helped to clear obscurities in the Building Accounts; and Mrs. C. F. Winmill, of Banstead, has helped in the checking of printed and pictorial sources.

Unpublished Crown Copyright material in the Public Record Office has been reproduced by permission of H.M. Stationery Office, and the Burghley and Popham documents in Appendix II are reproduced by permission of the Trustees of the British Museum. Extracts from Anthony Watson's *Description of Nonsuch* are given by permission of the Librarian of Trinity College, Cambridge, and also of the Nonsuch Palace Excavation Committee, for whom the translation was made by Mr. C. F. Ball and Mr. A. Carr. The Loseley Manuscripts in the Guildford Muniment Room have been used by kind permission of the owner, Major James More-Molyneux, and with the valued assistance of Miss E. M. Dance, the Archivist. Dr. B. Lawn, of Barnes, kindly made available the 1374 Inventory of Cuddington, through Miss M. Gollancz, County Archivist of Surrey, and the extract which appears in Appendix II is from a full transcription checked in her office. Mr. Philip Shearman has kindly allowed me to paraphrase information from his transcription of the so-called Cartulary of Ewell. Information on a number of documents in the Grafton (Wakefield) Collection has been supplied by Mr. P. I. King, Archivist at the Northamptonshire County Record Office.

In many cases the photographs and plans have been specially printed from borrowed negatives by Mr. Stan Witkowski, who has also newly photographed for me a number of items, and his wife has given valuable assistance in many ways. The tail-pieces and the tracing of the 1731 map are the work of Mr. Terry Ball.

Information on John, Lord Lumley, extracted from *Records of the Lumleys of Lumley Castle*, by Edith Milner, is quoted by kind permission of the Earl of Scarbrough and of Messrs. G. Bell and Sons, Ltd., the publishers. Quotations and information from *Thomas Platter's Travels in England, 1599*, edited by Clare Williams, are given by permission of Messrs. Jonathan Cape, Ltd.

Many more people than I could hope to acknowledge by name have contributed in one way or another to this adventure of rediscovery. I hope they will accept the story of the adventure which I have tried to tell in my Introduction and final chapter as a record of, and a tribute to, the part they played.

Contents

Illustrations

PLATES

Frontispiece   Nonsuch from the north-west

LINE DRAWINGS

TAIL-PIECES

A NOTE ON TYPOGRAPHY

Single 'quotes' have been used to indicate paraphrased or translated quotations. Verbatim quotations are given in double "quotes".

In the interests of readability, no index figures have been given in the text as a guide to notes. The notes appear at the end of the book, and they are printed in the same order as the text, with subject catch-words to facilitate reference.

NOTE TO PAPERBACK EDITION

No revisions have been made to the author's text in this facsimile reprint, and, whilst he himself might have made some additions now, after eleven years, few corrections would have been needed. One point, however, has been made locally more than once in connection with Chapter 12: "Whereabouts Unknown". There were, in fact, accurate pinpointings of the Palace site earlier than that by Cloudesley S. Willis in 1948: for instance that of the Cheam historian, Charles Marshall in his *History of Cheam and Sutton*, 1936 (p 19); and this should, perhaps, be recorded here.

FOREWORD TO PAPERBACK EDITION

We are proud to make available this first paperback reprint of John Dent's well-received standard work on the history of Nonsuch Palace. Since the excavations on the site, no other work has detailed so comprehensively or explained so readably the discoveries made and the history of which they form part.

John Dent was a highly regarded local historian, a knowledgeable amateur archaeologist and above all a professional librarian of great skill. It is entirely appropriate therefore that his great contribution to the story of Nonsuch should be kept alive in popular format by his neighbouring public library service.

Our thanks are due to the original publisher Hutchinson of London, for permission to use the second edition text and to Mrs Anna Dent, John's widow, whose full co-operation is gratefully acknowledged.

Roy Smith
Borough Librarian

Introduction

The Quest for Nonsuch

Until the summer of 1959 the royal palace of Nonsuch was almost a myth. Even a hundred years ago, a century after its despoiled ruins had been levelled off and buried under a thin covering of loam, the memory of its existence had faded so completely that one of the few contemporary pictures of the building had been labelled 'St James's Palace', and another, first 'Richmond Palace', then 'Henry V's Monastery at Richmond' and finally 'Theobalds'. After another century, in 1956, a reputable author had moved the palace site to Sheen: a more courageous, albeit more misguided, transposition than that made by many thousands of people who visited Nonsuch Park each year. To very many of these the nineteenth-century Mansion House was 'Nonsuch Palace', and they walked over the hidden site of the Palace, half a mile away, without realizing that they were doing so.

This state of affairs was all the more surprising in view of the widespread fame of Nonsuch. Known throughout Europe for its splendour and magnificence, it brought into the neighbourhood kings and queens, officers of state, the Court and its servants of high and low degree, and influenced the life of the countryside for miles around. To make way for its erection, the village of Cuddington was wiped off the map, and fields which had been tilled for centuries were turned into deer parks. Ancient highways were closed because they passed too near the site of the Palace, and the new roads which had to be made are still used today. The nearby town of Ewell, a place of some size and consequence in mediaeval times, was quite overshadowed by its new neighbour, the outpost of which, a timber Banqueting House, stood on top of a hill only a few hundred yards from Ewell Church. For the actual building work, supplies and workmen came from far and near, and during the 150 years of the life of the Palace many of the people at work in field, township and village, particularly in Ewell and Cheam, must have been working to supply the needs of Nonsuch. When the end came, and the building was pulled down, the materials were dispersed, and the few surviving 'relics' of Nonsuch are, so far as I have been able to discover, undocumented.

With scarcely a vestige of the Palace left, even in local tradition, and with only a handful of people who were prepared to say where it had stood, I felt that Nonsuch presented a challenge which could not be ignored. On a cold windy day in the winter of 1957–8 I spent the afternoon in Nonsuch Park, going over the site-indications described by Cloudesley S. Willis in his *Short History of Ewell and Nonsuch*, published in 1948. Scratched and slapped by saplings, muddy and chalk-marked, I came away accepting his statements on the siting of the building, and determined to do all I could to expand the work he had done and to interpret it in a more digestible form; to end the obscurity surrounding Nonsuch and to restore the Palace, in words and pictures, to its present owners, the general public.

I began collecting for the Epsom and Ewell Library copies of every relevant book, manuscript and picture I could find. The printed descriptions of Nonsuch were never more than single chapters in books dealing with wider subjects, and the realization that there were discrepancies between the various accounts of the Palace soon led me back to original sources. My first objective at the Public Record Office was the Parliamentary Survey of 1650, of which a transcribed version made in 1778 had proved unreliable. A corrected version had been printed in 1871, but this had been overlooked by most later writers. Errors in the earlier transcription included an inaccurate rendering of the punctuation which had led to the Banqueting House being thought ever since to have had three storeys and cellars, whereas in fact the three storeys included the cellars. From this beginning, documentary research ranged far and wide.

The search for pictures of Nonsuch led me, in correspondence, as far as the Eastern Transvaal for what was then the only known view from the north-east; but in the late autumn of 1959 a visitor to Berkeley Castle noticed a similar painting wrongly titled (Plate 5). Some coloured prints were added to the collection and copies of portraits of people connected with Nonsuch came from various sources, but principally from the National Portrait Gallery and the British Museum. The museum also supplied copies of the only three maps I could discover which were of any assistance in fixing the site of the Palace;

two of these, dated 1675 and 1790, showed the site as being somewhere near where we now know it to be, and the other, a Survey drawn in 1731, although showing no building still standing, named the field next to the Palace site 'Nonsuch Field'. Apart from these, there were no plans of the site in existence, and the only plan of the Palace building was a modern theoretical reconstruction made by Mr. Sydney R. Turner in 1948.

By May, 1958, I felt ready to apply the evidence left by Cloudesley Willis, which was mainly based on his observations in trenches dug for sewers in 1933 and 1945, to the task of plotting the exact position of the building on a large-scale Ordnance map. This led to a discussion with Mr. R. P. Brownjohn, Deputy Borough Engineer of Epsom and Ewell, who enlarged, to the same scale as my map, a tiny discoloured area which appeared on an Ordnance Survey 'aerial mosaic' photograph. The area of discoloration almost exactly matched the area which I had plotted on the map.

For a detailed plan of the Palace itself Mr. Turner's reconstruction was an invaluable starting point but, after checking every detail against my own interpretation of the available evidence, I decided that it would be better to start afresh and build up a new plan. This was drawn by Miss J. M. I. Griffiths.

Early in 1959 I met Mr. Martin Biddle who was acting as an archaeological consultant to the Ministry of Works. The Ministry was interested in the excavation of Nonsuch as an important source of material for the projected *History of the King's Works*. An Excavation Committee was formed, with representatives both of the Ministry and of local interests, and Sir John Summerson, Curator of Sir John Soane's Museum, agreed to act as Chairman. The excavations were to be directed by Mr. Biddle who had been conducting his own research into the history of the Palace. In July 1959 he and I pooled our resources and since then a great amount of new documentary material has been found and old material checked, so that even without the excavation our knowledge of the Palace would be far more detailed today than it was three years ago. Although he and I have borne the brunt of this intensive research, we have had the valued assistance of a number of volunteers.

In a *Guide* for the visitor to the excavation site I had made some fairly dogmatic statements about the siting of the building, and had included maps and the reconstructed plan. During June, 1959, I had been conducting parties over the area explaining what was to be dug for and where it would be found. Consequently, the weeks preceding the actual start of the dig on 6th July were a time of anxiety as well as great excitement. The only really definite information I had had was Cloudesley Willis's observations on about two-thirds of the north-south axis. I had assumed that the modern roadway ran through the centre of the site, and it was with some relief that I saw, on the first day, evidence that the roadway was in fact only a few feet off-centre.

For three short months Nonsuch Palace came to life again. The obscurity surrounding it had been due to three main causes. The obvious one was the destruction of the Palace after it had been sold as building materials by Barbara Villiers, Countess of Castlemaine and Duchess of Cleveland. Even with the buildings gone, the foundations would have been of the greatest interest to succeeding generations; but, to the farmer, any rubble which interfered with his ploughing was an unmitigated nuisance, and so the topsoil was gradually cleared of fragments which were at one time scattered over a wide area. Finally, the rapid building development during the past fifty years all but completed the destruction which the Duchess of Cleveland began; the whole of the Great Park and more than half of the Little Park have been built upon. One railway cuts straight across the "fine prospect about the house", and another runs through the Great Park. The area surrounding the site of the Palace has fortunately been spared, but the foundations of the separate Banqueting House vibrate to the heavy traffic of a modern by-pass road.

Yet, despite the obliterating hands of time and progress, and despite the unavoidable filling-in of the foundations after so much time and effort had been spent on uncovering them, there is abundant evidence to enable us to obtain a clear picture of the past glories of the Palace. We can read the accounts of those who visited Nonsuch, and can study detailed pictures of the building in its prime; but to bring to life these pictures fashioned by pencil, brush and writer's pen we must visit the Park itself. There we can stand on the site of the Palace and of Cuddington Church and walk in the Privy Garden; and with us may walk the spirits of Henry VIII and Elizabeth, the first two Stuarts and their queens, Essex, Salisbury, Arundel and Lumley, Francis Bacon, Evelyn and Pepys, and a host of others, known and unknown, whose voices and footsteps once filled the air where even now the whispering of trees seems to shut out the noise and bustle of a busy world.

As I put down my pen at the end of the four years' work which went into the first edition of this book, I expressed the hope that I had been able to communicate some of the enthusiasm and pleasure which came from helping in the excavation, and the interest which had been mine in the documentation of the history of Nonsuch. In the intervening years this hope has been amply fulfilled. The book has brought correspondence from all parts of the world; I have lectured to audiences totalling several thousands and have had the pleasure of feeling their response to the interest of the subject, and have helped a great many students with theses and projects connected with the Palace and its parks.

Little has been discovered during these years to add to what I wrote in 1961. Through the vigilance of Mr. Peter Klein, one of the volunteers of 1959 and now at the City of Birmingham Museum, a version of the Hoefnagel drawing which appears to ante-date the British Museum drawing has been located at Fonthill House, Tisbury, Wilts, and photographed by Mr. Biddle by kind permission of the owner, Mr. James Ian Morrison. My attention was drawn by Miss E. Johnson, of New York, to James Cleland's *The Institution of a Young Noble Man* (1607, reprinted New York 1948). This was almost certainly written at Nonsuch, and describes the "courtly college" established there for Prince Henry Frederick and the sons of noblemen. The 1962 volume of *Architectural History* reproduced a plan of about 1609 by Robert Smythson entitled "Iner Courte of my Lo' of Wosters house at nonesuche". This is the plan for the re-building of the Keeper's House after the enlargement of the Great Park in 1605–7.

The excavation, apart from its main purpose of discovering the ground plan of the Palace, produced a great deal of evidence to add substance to the mental picture of life at Nonsuch, in the shape of a large collection of 'finds'. In the years following the excavation, the custody of the finds presented a problem: there was no museum in the immediate neighbourhood, and some of the materials called for the most expert conservation treatment. Accordingly, in 1962, the Excavation Committee recommended the Park Management Committee to offer the whole collection to the London Museum, and the transfer was effected in 1963, on the understanding that when proper accommodation became available in the vicinity of Nonsuch, a selection of the finds would be sent from the London Museum for local display.

In 1970 this promise was carried out. In February of that year a new building was opened on the site of Bourne Hall in the centre of Ewell. It houses a public library, halls, meeting rooms and a Museum and Exhibition Gallery. One part of the gallery is devoted to Nonsuch material, consisting of some of the finds on loan from the London Museum, displays of maps, pictures and documents, and a Nonsuch Chest, purchased by the Corporation in 1968. In the Library part of the building there is a large collection of photostats of documents relating to Nonsuch, and seven volumes of typed research material; as well as a large file of photographs of the excavation and copies of portraits and prints. A collection of 35mm. colour slides is available on loan.

The London Museum, owing to acute shortage of space, was unable to make a permanent display of Nonsuch material; but a special Nonsuch exhibition was staged from November, 1969 to April, 1970.

A large display of framed pictures has been provided by the Park Management Committee in the Committee Room at the Nonsuch Mansion House. The pictures include portraits in oils presented by members of the Farmer family, as well as enlargements of photographs of excavation scenes and plans and of the four contemporary pictures of Nonsuch.

Hopes are now high that the plan of the Palace will shortly be marked out on the site, so that it should never slip back into oblivion. I hope that this book will help the visitor to recreate in his mind's eye some of the splendour of the life of Nonsuch and to see in imagination, as he stands on the site, "Towers and battlements . . . Bosom'd high in tufted trees".

I

'A Healthful Place Called Cuddington'

THE SITE chosen by Henry VIII for his last and most remarkable palace was near the centre of the parish of Cuddington. Here, at the foot of the North Downs, a narrow belt of Thanet sand separates the chalk of the Downs from the London clay, and, as in Ewell, there are traces of human habitation going back into Mesolithic times.

A fine tranchet axe of the late Mesolithic period was found in Nonsuch Park in 1938, and is illustrated in Volume 50 of the *Surrey Archaeological Collections*. Iron Age pottery and pot-boilers were found by Mr. S. S. Frere, in 1939, when work was proceeding on the new road which was intended to link Ewell and Cheam. The Roman road, Stane Street, which ran from Chichester to London Bridge, forms for a considerable distance the London Road boundary of the present park. Another Roman road, which has been excavated at Purberry Shot in Ewell, appears to have crossed Stane Street in the old Fair Field behind the 'Green Man' Inn in Ewell, and continued in the direction of Cuddington, passing Roman sites at Staneway House and on the Nonsuch Court Estate. The *Gazetteer of Anglo-Saxon Surrey*, by John Morris, records the finding of an Anglo-Saxon spearhead at Cuddington.

The first written record of Cuddington is a deed, of doubtful authenticity, which survives in a thirteenth-century cartulary. It purports to be a copy of a deed of A.D. 675 by which Frithwald, Sub-King of Surrey, and Bishop Erkenwald gave a number of 'mansas' or dwellings in various places to the recently founded Abbey of Chertsey. Among them were thirty "*apud Euuelle cum Cotintone*". This gift was confirmed by King Athelstan in the year 933, when the name was spelt Cudintone. In 1062 Edward the Confessor confirmed the Abbey in its possession of six dwellings at Cudintone. At that time two-thirds of the manor was held by Earl Leofwine, brother of Harold.

The remaining land was held by 'allodial' tenants, who were not tied to the lord of the manor, as were the majority of their contemporaries, but were free to choose any overlord they wished.

After the battle of Hastings William the Conqueror sent part of his army through Sussex into central Surrey, whilst he himself drove through Kent to London. Finding the city well defended, he did not attempt to take it, but turned westwards to join the rest of his forces near Dorking, and may well have travelled along Stane Street through the middle of the manor of Cuddington. William gave the manor to his half-brother, Odo, Bishop of Bayeux and Earl of Kent.

At the time of the Domesday Survey in 1086 Ilbert de Laci, Lord of Pontefract, held the manor from Odo. Its value had gone down since Edward the Confessor's time, from £11 to £5, but had afterwards been restored to £9 12s. The manor was twice forfeited for treason: by Ilbert de Laci's son Robert, when Henry I gave Cuddington to Hugh de Laval, and in 1203, when Guy de Laval supported the French against King John and lost his English estates. In that year John gave the manor to William de St. Michael, whose descendants later adopted Codyngton or Codington as a family name.

A few glimpses into the life of the mediaeval village may be obtained from the so-called Cartulary of Ewell. This is in fact a cartulary of the subordinate manor of Fitznells, a 'member' of the manor of Ewell but with its own manor house near the centre of the village of Ewell, and with lands in both Ewell and Cuddington. Many of the documents included in the cartulary are undated, but they range from about 1215 to 1466. Their chief interest centres upon Walter de Merton, his family connections and his office of Rector of Cuddington Church.

First we see Master Robert, Rector of the Church of Cudintone, paying 25s. for 2½ acres of land in 1218. He also bought 8 acres and 1 rood from John, son of Roger de Cudinton, and a curtilage to the south of John's house near the public road; and 7 acres from Martin, son of Gilbert de Cudinton. In one deed to which he was a party there is a reference to the highway to London, to the north of the 'vill' of Cudinton, which seems to indicate Stane Street, or the route of the present London Road parallel to Stane Street. Master Robert gave lands in Ewell and a house, barn and land in Cudinton to Gilbert 'son of Osbert de Wiredesburi, my nephew and foster-child'.

During the middle years of the thirteenth century Gilbert acquired several pieces of land. On the Morrow of the Feast of St. James, 1236, the dowry of Gotha, widow of Martin Barat, was quitclaimed to him, but it was indeed a widow's mite, for it consisted of a third share in 4 acres and a croft in the common field, called Barrattescrofte. From William of Butailes or Batailles (another subordinate manor of Ewell) he received ten acres of land in Cudintone; 7½ acres came from John, son of Roger; 2 acres from Matilda, daughter of Moses de Cudintune; 2 from Gonnora, daughter of William Clenhant de Codentone; and 6 acres from Laurence, son of William de St. Michael.

Gilbert married Agnes, sister of Walter de Merton, who came to Cuddington as Rector as soon as he had taken Holy Orders in about the year 1238. Walter bought the lands of Henry Ballard and John le Blanch in Ewell, and made them over to Gilbert and Agnes jointly, with the proviso that if he should decide to share his inheritance with his sisters these lands should go to Agnes as her share, as that was his purpose in buying them. Every Michaelmas, John le Blanch was to receive from Gilbert and Agnes a pair of gloves or a penny. Walter was one of the witnesses to another deed whereby his sister and her husband obtained 5½ acres and other lands and tenements from Philip le Jouene of Ewell; but if Philip's brother, Adam Faukes, who was presumed to be dead overseas, should return to claim any of the lands, Philip would pay Gilbert 2 marks for surrendering them.

The confusion which must have resulted from the almost complete absence of surnames is well illustrated by Gilbert. He is described at various times as being 'son of Osbert de Wiredesburi', 'son of Osbert de Eytune', 'nephew of Master Robert', 'of Cuddington' and 'of Ewell', and matters come to a head when Martin, son of another Gilbert of Cuddington, surrenders to the present Gilbert a croft in Cudinton, to the north, between the common pasture of Sparfelde on the north, the acre of the Church of Cudinton on the south and the road to Malden on the west.

The gift of lands from Walter de Merton to Gilbert and Agnes was made very soon after he came to Cuddington, for at Easter in the year 1239 the three of them were parties to an agreement with John le Blanch whereby John undertook to give full seisin of the lands and the capital messuage which went with them. On another occasion Walter paid 15s. to be quit of his obligation to pay a quarter of wheat annually to Cecilia, daughter of William le Frylond, which he owed her for a house and land which she had granted to him. On the 'Sunday next after the Feast of St. John before the Latin Gate' (i.e. on 13th May), in the year of grace 1274, Walter granted to God and the Blessed Mary and the Church of Codinton all the 'services' due to him from Philip Hereward. These services had been granted to Walter by Laurence de St. Michael. Out of the 18*d.* annual rent due to Walter for a house in the village, Philip was to provide and maintain a wax candle in the chancel of the church, to burn daily before the altar during Divine Service. The candle was to be renewed three times a year with a pound of wax, or more if more could be bought for 6*d.*, and the remaining wax of the old candle was to be incorporated in the new. If Philip failed to renew the candle, Walter could use whatever means he thought fit to make him do so, and as a penalty could double the amount of wax demanded. One copy of the deed recording the gift was to be kept in the sacristy of the church.

Walter de Merton received the manor of Malden from Peter de Codinton in 1240. He was made Lord Keeper of the Great Seal in May, 1258, and Chancellor of England in 1260. By 1263 he had founded Merton College, Oxford, supporting it out of the revenues of his manors of Malden and Farleigh, and the foundation charter of the Scholars of Merton was written in the following year. He became Bishop of Rochester in 1274 and on his death, on 27th October, 1277, left twenty marks to the poor of Cuddington. Walter de Cuddington, who was probably the same as Walter de Portsmouth, Vicar of Cuddington, who was related to Walter de Merton, was elected a Fellow of Merton College in 1284, was Bursar in 1308 and was in charge of the important building operations at the college from 1287 to 1311.

The name of Laurence de St. Michael occurs in a number of the documents in the Fitznells Cartulary, between 1290 and 1315, usually as a witness to transfers of property in Ewell and Cuddington. In one of them he is "Laurence de Seynt Michell"; in another an acre of land in Codyngton is let for a rent of a rose, to be paid annually on the Feast of the Nativity of St. John the Baptist.

Gradually the name 'de Cuddington', in its various spellings, ceased to be applied to the entire population of the village, and became the recognized surname of the St. Michaels as lords of the manor. Laurence, nephew of Laurence, held the manor in 1337, and used both 'St. Michael' and 'de Codington' as a surname; but after his death 'St. Michael' was rarely used.

Sir Simon de Codynton, who was Sheriff of Surrey in 1353 and 1362, held manorial courts at Cuddington in 1355. He held lands in the common fields in Ewell, and was one of the witnesses to a Ewell deed of 1372. On his death on 12th April, 1374, an inventory (of which an abstract is given in Appendix II) was taken of all his goods, and, even allowing for the fact that the valuation placed on each article would have to be multiplied many times to convert it into modern money, the general impression the inventory gives is one of spartan frugality bordering on poverty. The rooms of Simon's house which are mentioned are the Chamber, Hall, Pantry and Buttery, and the Kitchen. There was also a Bakehouse and Brewhouse and a Grange. The frugality is illustrated by the contents of the Hall: hangings, bench covers and cushions, bowls with ewers, trestle table and two forms, andirons and a fire fork and rake. The impression of poverty comes from the frequent occurrence of items which, although a value is given them, are described as being much worn or broken, or even both worn and broken.

Simon's funeral did not take place until thirty-one days after his death, and the ceremony cost £21 10s. This included the provision of mourning for his widow and children, and the expenses of the Abbot of Chertsey, the Prior of Merton and others on the day of the burial. During these thirty-one days the household subsisted, and paid the expenses of various other persons, on £5. The business of clearing up her husband's estate took the widow and her family to Southwark, Westminster, St. Paul's and the Marshalsea, involving her staying in London on various occasions. Payments out of the estate, apart from the expenses of Lady de Codynton and the administrator, amounted to £131 7s. 9d. Simon's physician received £1 13s. 4d. for his services, and the steward collected four years' arrears of wages amounting to £2 13s. 4d. Most of the assets of the estate were made up of livestock and crops. With geese at 4d. each, pigs at 1s. 4d., lambs at 10d. and cows at 6s. 8d. the stock was valued at £58 6s. 4d., and the Prior of Merton bought the standing corn in the fields at 4s. an acre. Simon seems to have been the last member of the family to style himself 'de' Codynton. His son appears simply as Ralph Codynton.

The manorial lands included part of a large common called Sparrowfield, which stretched from Cuddington to Morden, and from Cheam to Malden. For centuries this common was the subject of disputes, as one after another of the lords of the manors bordering

Sparrowfield tried to deprive the people of the neighbouring villages of the right to graze cattle and gather wood on the common land. In 1403 Ralph Codynton brought an action against William Curson of Malden for trespass on his land in "Sparwefeld".

Ralph's two sons, Simon and Thomas, were the aggressors in a dispute with the lord of the manor of Malden, Henry Abyndoun, Warden of Merton College. On the 10th January, 1427, after it had been shown that Thomas had taken the Warden's cattle and deprived him of the tenants' services due to him at harvest time at Pistelhill in "Sparewfelde", the parties were bound in sureties of £100 to keep the peace. They were directed to be "gode frendes" and to share rights of pasture over the whole area between Malden Town, the arable lands of Cuddington, Worthfield on the Ewell border and a path called Fishersway on the east. The Warden was ordered to give Thomas, each Christmas, either a robe of gentleman's livery, with a livery fur, or a silver mark. However, the Codingtons were still making trouble in 1509, when the Court Roll of Malden records that John Codington would not allow the Malden tenants to have their common rights on Sparrowfield.

By this date, however, the end of the long connection of the St. Michaels and their descendants the Codingtons with the manor of Cuddington was not far off. In an unfortunate moment for them, their quiet country retreat found favour in the eyes of Henry VIII, at a time when his increasing corpulence was leading him to plan, on a grandiose scale, a great hunting estate based on Hampton Court, so that he would be able to indulge his favourite sport without the fatigue and discomfort of long journeys on horseback. Once Henry decided that he wanted it, it is difficult to believe that Richard Codington, the lord of the manor, had much choice in the matter. However, at least on paper, the proprieties were observed, and a "Vewe and Survey" of the manor, drawn up before Henry acquired it, sets out the attractions of the place in such laudatory terms that it almost succeeds in giving the impression that the king had to be coaxed into taking it. The part of the survey which described the house is given in Appendix II.

Putting the important things first, the surveyors began by describing the high and dry ground to the south of the manor house, where there was a warren for coneys, well stocked, and a keeper's lodge. This land joined Banstead Downs, which already belonged to the king and which were 'hale and lively' for sheep and coneys; here there was great plenty of partridges, hares and coneys in coverts of fir and juniper. Beyond, to the south, were forty square miles of 'commodious country' with pheasants, partridges, foxes, hares, badgers and 'all kinds of vermin'. There were arable lands to the south of the manor house; and meadows and pasture to the north, bounded by hedges of trees and coverts of thorns in which were pheasants, partridges and hares. Of these northern fields, 140 acres were in the common of "Sparrowfelde".

The manor house itself, rebuilt since Simon's day, stood on the western part of the manor, near the churchyard, surrounded by great trees. A courtyard measuring 140 ft. by 100 ft. had buildings on three sides, the fourth side, to the north, consisting of a wall with a small gatehouse. The manor house had a hall (measuring only 24 ft. by 18 ft.), three parlours and chambers, seven chambers for servants, pantry, buttery, two cellars, kitchen, pastry house, two larder houses, a well outside the kitchen door to the west and a dove-house. A barn and stable lay on the west, and on the east was a great barn, newly built of timber and with a tiled roof, 155 ft. long and 36 ft. wide. A garden and orchard occupied an acre and a half to the south of the house. Four farmhouses, with their barns and stables, were visible from the manor house; these were let, with land, to four 'honest men and tall persons, meet and able to do the king's service' who were able to live 'wealthily' upon them.

Henry's intention of erecting new buildings must already have been made clear, for the surveyors mentioned that there were quarries of freestone five miles away, presumably those at Merstham, from which stone could be carted at 1s. 4d. a load; and that, for 4d. a load, chalk could be carted from the great pits which were within a quarter of a mile of the site, and which must have been those on the south side of Ewell through which Cheam Road passes before it reaches Ewell By-Pass. For water, they suggested that a hidden spring in the side of a hill half a mile to the south, which they believed was the head of the springs in Ewell, should be opened up, and the water conveyed in conduits to the manor site. But, although they realized that the king had in mind certain 'edifying and building', they cannot have realized that he intended to sweep away the existing buildings, for they were at pains to point out that the structures they described were 'well-builded and without decay', 'newly and lately builded', or 'in good repair', and that the manor house itself had 'bay windows cast out, very pleasant in the view and show'.

The church of Cuddington, dedicated to St. Mary the Virgin, is not described in the "Vewe and Survey", for its compilers may not have known that the land it stood on was, for Henry, the most attractive part of the site. Nor could they have foreseen that, with the suppression of Merton Priory only a week before the building of the Palace began, the church was to be deprived of its patron and left defenceless, to be immediately demolished as part of the site-clearance work. The building which was thus ruthlessly flattened had a long history, but, until the excavation, little was known of it except an incomplete list of incumbents. Early in the twelfth century Hugh de Laval gave the church and its lands to Bernard the Scribe in trust for the Prior and Convent of Merton. The revenues of the church were appropriated to the Prior and Convent in 1284, and this was confirmed by Letters Patent in 1309. The terms of the appropriation stipulated that an adequate amount was to be reserved to provide a living for a vicar and to pay dues and other burdens. The vicarage was endowed in 1311, and Low Thomas of Kingston was appointed as the first vicar. The balance of revenue available to the Prior and Convent was very small: at the time of the "Vewe and Survey" the parsonage lands were let to a farmer, who paid £8 to the vicar and 40s. to the Prior.

The village of Cuddington seems to have been quite small even by mediaeval standards. From the Domesday Survey of 1086 we learn that there were then seven villeins, who were peasants occupying houses and cultivating land, and subject to the lord of the manor; nine bordars, or villeins of the lowest order, rendering menial service to the lord of the manor in return for a cottage which they held entirely at the will of the lord; and four serfs, who were little better off than slaves, except that their conditions were to some extent regulated by established custom. Four villeins and four bordars worked on the 'demesne' land, which the lord of the manor farmed for his own use. In 1428 there were fewer than ten inhabited dwellings and the church was exempted from taxation on that account. Yet the foundations of the church revealed by the excavation (opposite page) showed it to have been a fairly sizeable building, sufficiently used to justify its adaptation and extension on four separate occasions. There is no mention of a church here in the Domesday Survey, but that may only mean that the church was exempt from taxation. The finding of several post-holes below the level of the earliest floors indicates the strong possibility that there was, in fact, a wooden church, dating from before

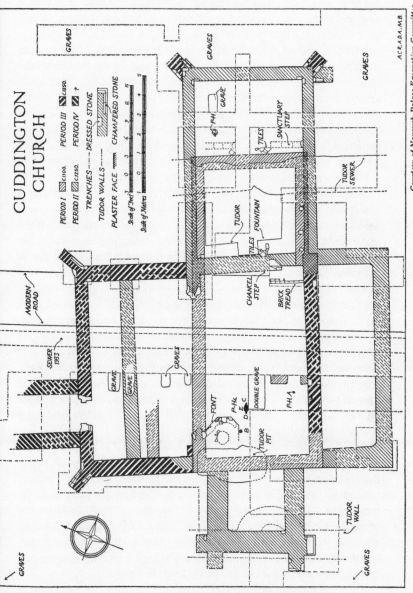

CUDDINGTON CHURCH

PERIOD I — c1100. PERIOD III — c1250.
PERIOD II — c1250. PERIOD IV — ?

TRENCHES —— DRESSED STONE
TUDOR WALLS ——— CHAMFERED STONE
PLASTER FACE

Scale of Feet
0   3   6   9   12   15

Scale of Metres
0   1   2   3   4   5

GRAVES

GRAVES

GRAVES

SANCTUARY STEP

TILES

TUDOR SEWER

F·H

GRAVE

TUDOR
TILES
FOUNTAIN

CHANCEL STEP

BRICK TREAD

MODERN ROAD

SEWER 1933

GRAVE

GRAVE

GRAVES

FONT

P·H·c

E   C
B   D

DOUBLE GRAVE

P·H·A

TUDOR PIT

TUDOR WALL

GRAVES

GRAVES

A.C.R., A.D.A., M.B.

Courtesy of Nonsuch Palace Excavation Committee

the year 1100. The first permanent building, consisting of a simple
nave and chancel, was erected about that year, and this was demolished
after a little over 100 years and replaced by a much more ambitious
building. This had a longer chancel, north and south aisles entered
through arcades, and a tower at the west end. In the middle of the
fourteenth century the south aisle was demolished, the north aisle
greatly enlarged, and buttresses were added. At a later date another
porch was added, possibly to provide easy access for the members of
the household of the adjacent manor house. At all stages, building was
carried out in flint with stone dressings. The floor, which had been
raised at least twice, was paved with glazed tiles 9½ in. square and
over an inch thick, set in a chalky mortar. The font was at the north-
west corner of the nave, at the junction between the north aisle, nave
and tower. Burials were found below the floor, and the skeletons may
well have been those of the Codington family. Surrounding the church
was an extensive graveyard, so full for so small a village, and with what
seemed such a high percentage of children among the burials, that it
provided gruesome evidence of the heavy odds against survival to a
ripe old age in mediaeval times. In the part of the churchyard near the
south-east corner of the chancel, young people had been buried right
up to the wall of the church, one above the other and close together.

On this spot, sanctified by the devotions of Cuddington villagers
for at least five centuries, and over the last resting place of all who died
there before April, 1538, Henry built the Inner Court of his Palace.
The royal apartments surrounded a flagstoned courtyard laid over the
graves; sewers were driven through burials and the foundations of the
church. The footings of the west wall of the church tower were
merged into a palace wall, and a fountain played where the chancel had
been. The village and, later, the manor house were also swept away, and
the farm lands were turned into deer parks, except for a small area in
the common fields to the south of the village. Both manor and rectory
continued to exist, at least on paper, and eventually came into the
possession of John, Lord Lumley; the manor was subsequently
administered with the manor of Ewell. But Cuddington was, by then,
a manor without a village, a rectory without a church, and a parish,
nominally four miles long and a mile wide, of which the greater part
lay within the so-called parish and manor of Nonsuch.

Uprooted and dispossessed, Richard and Elizabeth Codington were
given the manor of Ixworth in Suffolk in exchange for Cuddington.

RICHARD AND ELIZABETH CODINGTON
Memorial brass in Ixworth Church

Richard died at Ixworth on 27th May, 1567, and Elizabeth on 8th September, 1571. They surrendered Cuddington to the king by charter on 20th July, 1538, three months after the building of the Palace had begun, and the legal formalities were completed by November of that year. The property which the king acquired consisted of six messuages, 600 acres of arable land, 50 acres of meadow, 600 acres of pasture, 40 acres of wood, 600 acres of heath and furze and 20s. in rent; some of the land lay outside the parish boundary, in Malden.

The Great and Little Parks of Nonsuch covered nearly seven times the area of the present Nonsuch Park; their approximate boundaries are shown on page 33. They were enclosed by a close fence or pale, and many Ewell property deeds of the period take their bearings from Nonsuch Park Pale. The line of the Pale is still preserved in various rows of trees and in the wide curve of Cheam Road, Ewell. The fencing of the Parks must have been erected at a remarkable speed, for on the 17th November, 1538, £166 13s. 4d. was paid on a warrant to Sir Francis Bryan for collecting a thousand deer from various parks belonging to the king 'for the replenishing of the parks of Nonesuch and Kinton'. The parks were separated by the present London Road, Ewell, the Great Park extending from that road over the whole of modern Stoneleigh and parts of Worcester Park as far as Old Malden Lane and Church Road, Old Malden. On the east the Park Pale ran roughly on the line of Malden Road and Central Road, Worcester Park, and diverged in a south-easterly direction from Cheam Common Road, to reach London Road where it was blocked by a gate on the Ewell side of the present 'Queen Victoria'. The boundary on the west was Ewell Common: that part of it which lay to the right of the present main road from Ewell to Kingston. The area of a thousand acres included a separate piece of ground, Great Park Meadow, on the south.

The Little Park, which included the site of the Palace, lay between London Road and the present Cheam Road. On the west, the Park extended into Ewell, a little beyond the line of Ewell By-Pass. On the east, the position of the Pale is shown by the boundary between Nonsuch Park and Cheam Park. The boundaries of both the Great and Little Parks were altered from time to time, but in 1650 the Little Park contained 671 acres. On a map drawn during the reign of Edward VI, to which reference is made in Chapter 3, the Great Park is

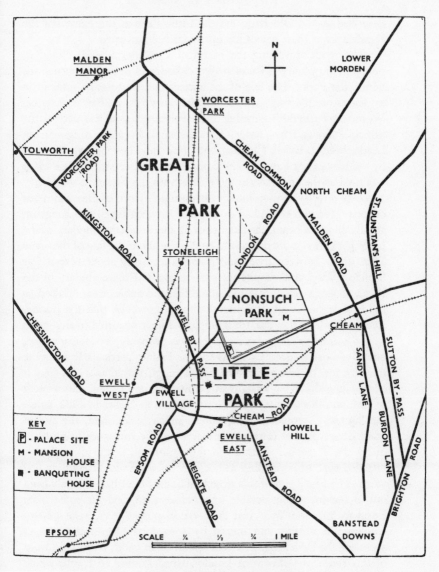

THE PARKS OF NONSUCH
In the Modern Landscape

described as the Old Park and the Little Park as the New; but the significance of these names has not so far been revealed.

The roads traversing the parish of Cuddington were closed to public traffic when the Parks were enclosed, and became private roads within the Parks. The line of the ancient highway from Cuddington to Kingston by way of Old Malden survives in Royal Avenue, Worcester Park; during the life of the Palace this road was part of the principal approach to Nonsuch from the north. Portway, running from Leatherhead to Ewell, Cuddington, Cheam and beyond, was blocked by the Little Park Pale near the Banqueting House; within the Park it was used as the approach to the Palace from the Cheam Gate. Henry was thus directly responsible for the position of two of the main roads of today, for new roads had to be made between Ewell and Kingston and Ewell and Cheam, the latter skirting the southern boundary of the Little Park. It is more difficult to be definite about the fate of the Stane Street route between Ewell and North Cheam. By about 1550 it was 'London Way' and, despite the gate across it at the boundary of the Parks, it seems reasonable to assume that the public were allowed to use it to some extent. It is most unlikely, however, that the Roman road itself was still in use, for it would not have occurred to anyone to keep a country road in repair, and it was probably, by Henry's time, buried almost as deeply as it is today. Traffic, particularly after the introduction of coaches in Elizabeth's reign, would move as best it could along the 'King's Highway', consisting of a rutted, miry stretch of turf; and in this case, from North Cheam to Nonsuch Park gates, the 'highway' would include, but be much wider than, the site of Stane Street. It thus came about that when the ruts were being filled in by the Turnpike Trustees in the eighteenth century, to make a metalled road of reasonable width, they missed Stane Street by a few yards. The Ewell end of this stretch of Stane Street had certainly been out of use for a considerable time before 1538, and the route from Ewell to 'London Way' had been via what is now Vicarage Lane to Cuddington village, and thence by a road parallel to the present avenue in the Park leading to the London Road gate. With the closure of this route, the stretch of London Road leading to Ewell, which today crosses Ewell By-Pass at the 'Organ', was laid down. This passed out of the confines of Nonsuch near Woodgate, and it is tempting to think that the Turnpike Gate which later stood there was the successor to a gate in Nonsuch Park Pale, similar to the gate near North Cheam.

By November, 1538, the estate had become "The Manor of Nonesuche otherwise Codingtonne". A survey of 21st November of that year indicates that, in addition to the site of the manor house, 1,901 acres had already been taken into the king's park. 153 acres were in the parish of Ewell, including 100 acres which had belonged to the "late monastery of Marten", and 145 acres in Malden, of which 72 acres belonged to "marten Colledge in Oxforde". If the surveyor's arithmetic was correct, the Parks must later have undergone some reduction in size.

The manor of Nonsuch was annexed to the Honour of Hampton Court in 1540. The Honour had been established in the previous year, and included the manors of Hampton Court and Walton-on-Thames. The manors added with Nonsuch were those of Ewell, East Cheam, West Cheam, Banstead, Walton-on-the Hill, Sutton, Epsom, Bedding-ton, Coulsdon, Wimbledon, Mortlake, Brixton, Putney, Rokehamp-ton, Dunsford, Balham, Wandsworth, Battersea and others in Middle-sex. The whole of this area was turned into a veritable New Forest, with the king's officers acting as stewards and bailiffs of the constituent manors. For what it was worth, a clause was inserted in the Act of Annexation, safeguarding the rights of the tenants of the manors. Henry thus provided himself with a hunting estate large enough to satisfy his modest requirements in his later years, and in it two princely hunting lodges, large enough to house an adequate entourage, were rapidly taking shape at Oatlands and Nonsuch.

2

'The Kinges Workes'

Over the ruins of Cuddington there grew, between 1538 and 1547, 'the most remarkable of Tudor buildings': remarkable in its own right as a building; remarkable for its influence on later Tudor architecture; almost equally remarkable for the number of misconceptions to which it has since given rise.

The first of these misconceptions concerns the identification of the architect responsible for Nonsuch: a fruitless exercise, for at this time the profession of architect in the modern sense was virtually non-existent. Vasari said that Antonio Toto del Nunziata was responsible for Henry's 'principal palace', but it is most unlikely that he had anything to do with the building in its early stages. The king must have indicated in general terms the kind of building he wanted, but the plan would almost certainly have been worked out in detail, in committee, by the chief officers of the King's Works, who included the king's master carpenter and master mason, together with specialist consultants. An actual plan or 'plot' may or may not have been drawn; certainly none has survived, and it was by no means unusual for a building, even of this size, to be set out directly on the site without a drawn plan.

On the ground plan of Nonsuch, as set out on the site, a building could have grown up which was just one more palace, and a fairly small one at that. Instead, through the king's desire that there should be no other palace such as this, there emerged a building of unrivalled splendour, lavishly decorated to the point of vulgarity, a monument of princely ostentation. The twenty-year-old rivalry between Henry and Francis I was the driving force behind the whole conception of Nonsuch. From the accession of Francis in 1515 vanity led the two into one extravagance after another in an attempt to outdo each other in magnificence. At a much lower level the struggle would have been

36

childish; between kings it was both disastrous and enriching: disastrous because so much money and labour were diverted·from other
channels and devoted to vainglory, enriching because the royal
patronage made possible the spread of the art of the Renaissance
in France and England on a scale which otherwise (despite such semi-
private works as Wolsey's at Hampton Court) could never have been
achieved. Although the feud continued until the two kings died,
within three months of each other, in 1547, it reached its height of
costly absurdity in the Field of Cloth of Gold in 1520. Henry's
temporary 'palace' for this meeting with Francis was put up by 3,000
workmen. It was a Gothic structure, made of boards painted to look
like brick, square in plan and with corner towers, and with a gatehouse
in the middle of one of the 328 ft. sides. Although it was thus traditional in its general plan, much of its decoration was in the Renaissance style, described as 'antique' or 'Romayne' work.

Eighteen years later another show place was begun. This time it
was to be permanent, and it was to incorporate the best that Henry's
money could buy. Again a Gothic building was erected, but one half
of it was so overlaid with Classical decoration that the building itself
has often been described as 'Renaissance' or 'Italian'. We may seek
parallels for individual features of Nonsuch: the five-storey towers on
the south front have been compared both with those at Chambord
and with the tower in the sketch of the Castello Sforzesco at Milan in
a corner of Leonardo's drawing of St. James Major, and the origin of
some of the decoration is discussed in a later chapter; yet the fact
remains that it was unique and that it was a basically English building
to which was added a great deal of Classical ornamentation.

The planning and building of Nonsuch, then, were in the hands
of the Tudor forerunner of the Ministry of Works. The Surveyor-
General of the King's Works throughout most of the Nonsuch
building period was James Needham, who was by training a carpenter.
Under him were the Comptroller and the Accountant. A separate
section of the King's Works was based on Hampton Court; this was
responsible for works in Surrey and for the fortification of castles in
Kent. The Hampton Court group or circuit was under the control of
Richard Bennyce, Surveyor, and Davy Marten, Comptroller. The
Prior of Newark held the office of Accountant or Paymaster until
14th September, 1538, when he was replaced by Robert Lorde. The
master carpenter, William Clement, and the master bricklayer (later

described as a master mason) Christopher Dickenson, made up the hierarchy. Whatever general instructions they may have had from higher authority, Clement and Dickenson, with the assistance of the chief artificers on the site, will have been responsible for setting out the foundations; and, as we shall see when we come to examine the building in detail, the work was not particularly well done. They were also responsible for supervising the plundering of stone from Merton Priory. Their journeys from Hampton Court to Cuddington were not, however, sufficiently numerous to indicate anything like daily super-vision of the site. For this, the Warden of the masons would at first be responsible, and he probably later had to take second place to the more highly paid Chief Warden of the carpenters.

The volume of information about the building of Nonsuch which has survived is lamentably small, in comparison, for example, with the thousands of pages of Building Accounts which exist for Hampton Court. The principal documents for Nonsuch are the Building Accounts for the period from 22nd April to 14th September, 1538, and a summary of the accounts for 15th September, 1538, to 14th November, 1545. The first of these is summarized in Appendix I. The original gives details of every single payment made during the period. The second document, under any particular heading, gives only the total expenditure for the whole seven years. The loss of the detailed accounts for the later period means that the answers to many important questions connected with the building can only be surmised. The 1538 accounts give a vast amount of information about the army of workmen who swarmed over the site during this first summer and the great quantities of materials which converged from all points of the compass. It is unfortunate that they end just as the work was getting under way, and that they contain only a few passing references to particular parts of the building.

Building began towards the end of April, 1538. Two clerks began work on the 22nd, the day on which Henry's reign entered its thirtieth year, and a week later the craftsmen and labourers began to arrive: the Warden of the freemasons and five lodgemen, two bricklayers and five labourers. From this modest beginning the labour force grew daily, and by the 12th August the masons consisted of a Warden, thirteen setters and thirty-five lodgemen; the carpenters included a Chief Warden, a Warden and 120 men and apprentices; the bricklayers, who by mid-June had been redesignated 'rough-layers', comprised a Chief

Warden, a Warden (both of whom were later demoted) and 100.men
and apprentices. By this time there were thirty sawyers, all but four of
whom had a 'fellow' or mate, and fourteen carters in addition to scores
who were hired for specific jobs; there were eleven chalk-diggers, 183
labourers, a scaffolder and a hodmaker, and the administrative section
had grown to three clerks and an under-purveyor. The scaffolder
arrived on 17th June, and two thatchers on 22nd August. Three servitors worked as such for only a few weeks, after which two of them
became apprenticed to the rough-layers. A plasterer worked from 5th
June to 13th July, and although large amounts of plaster and hair were
paid for after that date his name does not reappear in the accounts.

The Warden of the masons was paid 4s. a week, which was increased to 5s. on 15th July. During the sixth and seventh weeks five of
the lodgemen were designated *Positors* (setters), and by the eighth
week there were eleven setters at work. The setters received 3s. 8d.
a week, 4d. more than the lodgemen.

Right from the start the Chief Warden of the carpenters, who took
up his duties on 20th May, had a weekly wage of 5s. The Warden
received 9d. a day and other carpenters 8d., 7d. or 6d. according to
their skill, and the apprentices 4d. to 6d. Most of the rough-layers had
7d. a day, some 6d., the Warden 8d. and the Chief Warden 10d. From
17th June to 10th August the labourers had their wages increased from
4d. to 5d. a day, reverting to 4d. on 12th August. Other wages ranged
from the servitors at 5d. to the plasterer at 7d.; the carters were paid
1s. 2d. a day to include the hire of horse and cart.

The working day was, in theory, from dawn to sunset. A Statute
of 1495 had laid down that, from the middle of March to the middle
of September, the day should last from 5 a.m. to between 7 and 8 p.m.
The men were to have breaks for breakfast and mid-day meal, and, in
the summer, a short siesta. Other short breaks were allowed for
drinking. As the days lengthened, and the tempo of work on the
Palace increased, more and more overtime was called for. The temporary increase in the wages of the labourers during the height of the
summer probably indicated that they worked as long as daylight
lasted; others had to give up part of their dinner break and their
drinking breaks, and the times thus worked were aggregated and paid
for at approximately one day's wage for every ten hours' overtime.
Where this calculation led to a fraction of a penny, the workman
usually lost it and found that he had worked an hour or so for nothing.

Occasionally an extra half-day's pay was awarded, presumably as payment for overtime. Many of the public holidays on saints' days and at Whitsun were worked, particularly by the skilled men such as the masons, who, for example, received an extra half-day's pay on the eve of St. James' Day and double pay on the day itself.

The establishment and maintenance of a labour force some 500 strong was not easy. There was a good deal of coming and going, especially among the labourers, some of whom worked for only a few days. Thus, at the August peak there were 214 labourers on the register, but only 183 were actually at work on the 15th. There was more stability among the skilled men, most of whom came to stay. Whether they came willingly is another matter, for many of them were pressed into service. We read of journeys made to places between Dorking and Edenbridge, and in Gloucestershire, Wiltshire, Hereford-shire, Worcestershire, Northamptonshire and Bedfordshire, by crafts-men armed with the king's commission to arrest and take up workmen. The help of the Master and Wardens of the carpenters of London in arresting workmen for Nonsuch was rewarded by a payment of 5s. Compensation was paid to the "prested" men at the rate of 6d. for every twenty miles of their journey. Only forty-one payments are recorded, and these are limited to freemasons and rough-layers. Very many more men than this must have been forced from their homes, and the short list of payments is probably due to the Pay Clerk's being once again on the side of the king, so that those who came less than twenty miles received nothing, and others, including the carpenters, were kept wait-ing for their money. Although the maximum payment recorded was 2s. the appearance in the pay-lists of names such as Matthew Morgan, John Jones, Davy Welsh, John Gwyn, John A'Powell, Robert Griffiths, Benet Federyg, Hugh A'Parry and Morgan Kidwalder seems to indicate that some of the workmen may have been appreciably more than eighty miles from home.

In addition to these journeys in search of workmen, many other journeys were made, chiefly in Surrey, to select materials. The master carpenter and master bricklayer spent between ten and thirteen days each month after the first two in riding between Hampton Court, Cuddington and Merton and into the woods from place to place for the provision of timber. For this they received 1s. a day for themselves and their horses. During the second month they rode 'from one place to another of the king's works to set out certain works'. Various

ERECTING A TIMBER-FRAMED BUILDING
(From *Ein schön Nützlich Buchlin*, by Hieronymus Rodler. 1531)

carpenters spent a total of eighty-two man-days in choosing and marking timber in woods at Horley, Newdigate, Leigh, Banstead, Merstham, Cobham, East Horsley, Godstone, Bookham Common and Epsom Common. Throughout this first summer, trees were crashing down in woods all over central and eastern Surrey and over the Kent and Sussex borders, and the rough roads were choked with carts taking the spoils to Nonsuch. For the 80 ft. 'pieces' for the five-storey towers, a special wain was made, but even that broke down and had to have a new axletree and the wheels mended. Quite apart from this newly hewn timber, which would be prepared on the site by the sawyers and carpenters, and over 600 loads of fencing to make Nonsuch Park Pale, great quantities of prepared timber were bought. This included squared timber, planks, laths, wainscot and scaffolding. Some of the green timber may have been stacked near the site to allow it to become seasoned, but there is no reason why much or even all of it should not have been used as soon as the builders were ready for it, for the mediaeval carpenter had no qualms about using unseasoned wood even though it might later shrink and warp.

Whilst this timber was being acquired, processed and used, other materials of all kinds were pouring on to the site. Very little newly quarried stone was paid for during the summer, but 3,600 tons were carted from Merton Priory, the carters being paid 8d. for their four-mile journey with a ton of stone. Although the surrender of the Priory was not signed until 16th April, demolition must have begun earlier in the year, for carting of the stone to Nonsuch began in late April or early May, and at this time 13s. 4d. was paid to a Merton tiler for stripping the roof from the nave of the Priory church. The carved pieces of stone from Merton, unsuitable for use above ground, were put into the foundations, where they were mixed in with blocks of chalk quarried by the chalk-diggers. These men, in addition to working in what had hitherto been 'the great chalk pit of the Lord Prior' at Ewell, may well have been responsible for the pit which is now a turfed dell in front of Nonsuch Mansion House. With chalk and stone available at no cost except for labour and carriage, and thirty-five loads of Liége and Caen stone already 'in stock' and brought down river from London to Ditton and thence by road to Cuddington at a cost of 8d. a load for each stage of the journey, it was only necessary to buy ninety-six loads of stone during the first five months. These came from a Reigate quarryman, and cost 3s. 6d. a load.

Ironwork of many kinds came from the surrounding towns and villages, as well as from farther afield. A quarter of a million nails of all sizes came from a London ironmonger appropriately named Ketell, and from Rainolde Warde of Dudley, who, a few years earlier, featured in the Hampton Court building accounts. Another Hampton Court supplier, John Agilders of The Wyke, was the only tradesman to get more than £50 worth of business during the period: a fairly considerable sum when it is compared with the £2 which one of the labourers on the site would have received in wages for the same twenty weeks. Most of the £50 was spent on stay-bars and standards for the windows.

Bricks and lime were burnt in kilns a short distance from the site, near the Banqueting House and near the present Mansion House. Some of the bricks used for making the kilns were carted from Hampton Court. The lime burner received 8s. per kiln of ten loads and during the summer 460 loads were carted from the kilns to the site at a little more than 2d. a load. By September, 600,000 bricks had been dug, moulded and burnt, the brickmakers receiving 2s. a thousand. On the Ewell side of the Park the burning of lime and bricks caused damage to crops, and compensation was paid to four farmers for the loss of 6½ acres of rye, wheat, barley and tares. The water needed by the masons and bricklayers came from a well, presumably the one to the west of the manor house; water was carried from the well to the tubs at the mortar heaps in cowls, which were large tubs with 'ears' through which a cowl-staff was passed to enable each tub to be carried by two men.

One of the most surprising features of the organization on the site was the smallness of the office staff available to record and pay for this many-sided operation. There were never more than three clerks and one under-purveyor. The four clerical workers at Nonsuch were accommodated in the Pay House, where their days were spent in disbursing sums large and small, for materials supplied or work done, obtaining dockets for each payment. These were later copied into the 'Particular Books' which constitute the Building Accounts, and in which the register of workmen was kept ready for the next monthly pay parade. The large sums of money needed to meet their commitments were kept in a locked chest in the Pay House. Calculating was done by means of an 'abacus', the table in the Pay House being divided up into compartments by bands of silk ribbon, and the reckoning being done by counters placed in these compartments. This age-old and seemingly cumbersome method was, in the hands of experts, as quick as the numerical method of calculation which later replaced it. Apart from this, their needs were simple: paper and ink, sealing wax, dust for use as blotting-paper and two hour-glasses to enable them to act as time-keepers for the workmen. In addition to the Pay House, two other temporary buildings were erected: a Masons' Lodge, thatched with six and a half loads of straw, and a working house for the carpenters, which took five times as much straw.

It is quite wrong to suggest, as has been suggested, that the summer of 1538 was a period devoted only to the amassing of supplies and their preparation for use, and that building did not start until later. The accounts for the period, lacking any positive statement in the nature of a dated progress report, abound with inferential evidence that construction was in full swing by about the middle of June. Whatever the responsibilities of the masons for preparing stone in advance of use, the rough-layers are not likely to have had any such duties, but would be employed solely on brickwork, foundations and the mortared rubble in-filling between the two outer faces of a stone wall. Yet by 17th June there were fifty rough-layers on duty. By that date, too, the scaffolder was at work: not, we may be sure, engaged solely on checking in the supplies of alder poles and the ready-made hurdles which were used for platforms, but in erecting them for use. Even if, so soon after building began, it is unreasonable to suggest that any part of the main structure had reached scaffold height, scaffolding would be needed for the cellar (so far advanced by mid-September that an iron step and two window frames had been purchased). It may also have been needed for the 'miners' engaged on the demolition of Cuddington Church, for whom a number of tools were serviced by a blacksmith during August and September.

Before 15th June there were two purchases of equipment for use at the mortar heaps, and extra tools (to supplement those which the tradesman was expected to supply himself) had been bought for the masons, setters and rough-layers. Twelve hundred stone-axes for the masons and rough-layers had been sent to the smith for sharpening by 10th August, as well as more than twice that number of small tools for the masons. And the masons, whose prime concern would be with the parts of the building which showed above ground, were almost up to full strength by 15th July.

The Inner Court, therefore, first specifically mentioned during the third monthly pay period, which ended on 13th July, was not a hope for the distant future but something which was already taking shape, and fittings were being bought, not to be put into store but because they would soon be needed. Ironwork was bought for the windows of the 'nether lodgings' and spiral staircases, and eight of these window standards were cut down to make them fit. During the next two months well over two tons of stay-bars and standards were bought for timber windows round the Inner Court, and twenty bars of old iron were reworked for stone windows. Also in the third pay period, twenty-three pairs of 'stone hooks' were bought for the doors of the Inner Court to hang on. The fact that the digging of the foundations for the Inner Gatehouse was not paid for until some time between 12th August and 14th September need not mean that the work itself was not done until then. This was a special job, done by an outside workman at a negotiated price, and he would not be paid until after (and possibly some time after) he had completed the work.

By the time that the detailed Building Accounts came to an end, on 14th September, it would seem safe to assume that a progress report on the following lines could have been presented: The site for the Inner Court has been cleared, by felling trees and demolishing Cuddington Church. The foundations of the same court are virtually completed, the building of the actual walls has begun and in places they are up to window level, and the cellar walls are finished. Supplies of materials of all kinds are stacked conveniently near the foundations, and are being augmented, prepared and used at a very rapid rate by some 500 operatives. The great barn of Cuddington has been pulled down, but a new, smaller barn has been built to hold the king's corn; another barn has been underpinned with flint. The hall and other parts of Cuddington manor house have been retiled. Workshops and an office have been erected on the site, and arrangements have been made for an adequate supply of well water, lime and bricks. The financial arrangements are working smoothly; expenditure, which averaged £16 a week during the first three weeks, rose to £138 a week in July–August, and fell slightly, to £127, in August–September. Total expenditure to date is a little over £1,900. Of this total £1,010 has been spent on wages and overtime (the latter has fallen considerably during the past five weeks); £559 on the purchase of supplies (on which the expenditure would have been several times as great but for the fact that much of the basic material has come from the king's own woods, chalk-pits and from Merton Priory), and on journey-money and specific tasks carried out by outside labour at agreed prices; and £334 on the carriage of materials by land and water.

Robert Lorde took up his duties as 'Paymaster in the repairing and new buildings at the King's Majesty's house and houses of Hampton Court, Nonsuch and others' on Monday, 16th September, 1538, although his appointment officially dated from 15th December and was confirmed by Patent dated 19th April, 1539. He was responsible for disbursements in connection with works at Hampton Court, Nonsuch, Oatlands, Mortlake and Sion House, Guildford, Hanworth and Woking, the Paling of the Chase in the Honour of Hampton Court and the Parish Church of Esher. For the next seven years he drew the handsome sum of 6s. 8d. a day for travelling and subsistence and for his book-keeping expenses. He was also allowed the wages of two clerks and two servants, and 4d. a day each for five horses. For every £1,000 of 'treasure' which had to be carried from the various places from which he drew his cash, to his house and thence to the buildings where it was being spent, he was allowed 'portage' costs of 40s.

With the addition of other duties, connected with the provision of armaments at Mortlake and Sion and the fortification of castles on the Downs in Kent, he was responsible during his seven years as Paymaster for over £65,000. More than one-third of this money was spent on Nonsuch, the exact figure being £22,631 14s. 11½d. At Hampton Court, where the first stages of Henry's rebuilding and new works were nearing completion when the building of Nonsuch began, £16,686 6s. 0⅝d. was spent. Oatlands came next with £14,345 0s. 4d., and the only other item reaching four figures was Mortlake and Sion with £1,951 4s. 1d. The translation of these sums into terms of modern money would involve taking many factors into account; there is no simple way of arriving at such a comparison, for every factor involved has undergone a radical change since the time of Henry VIII. Even the obvious comparison of wage-rates tells us very little, if we ignore such considerations as the length of the working day, productivity, the tools and other equipment available, changes in building materials affecting output per man and changes in differentials between labourers and skilled men.

The lion's share of Lorde's disbursements, then, came to Nonsuch. The summary of his accounts which has survived gives no clue as to the rate of expenditure, either in total or as regards individual items, at any particular period during the years 1538 to 1545; such clues as we have on the progress of the building operations come from other sources. However, as an indication of the size and scope of the work at Nonsuch, Lorde's totals are not without interest. Labour of all kinds accounted for over £16,000; the purchase of supplies, and journey-money, £3,739; and the carriage of materials £2,764, of which sum £353 was for transport by water. Comparing these figures, for the seven years from 1538 to 1545, with the figures for the first five months of building, we find that sixteen times as much was spent on labour during the seven years as had been spent during the five months, less than eight times as much on materials and a little over eight times as much on carriage. From this, we see that, with seasonal fluctuations, the work went forward for most of the seven years at about the same average pace as it had begun; but a proportion of the labour was expended in a way which did not involve expenditure on materials, that is, upon decoration.

Although great quantities of timber, ironwork, bricks, tiles, stone, plaster and paving tiles were bought, there are some rather curious omissions from the list of purchases. There is no specific mention of the slate which was used so extensively on the decoration of the outside walls of the Inner Court. No wainscoting was bought, and only twenty-five loads had been delivered before the beginning of Lorde's accounts; yet we know from later descriptions that both the Palace and the Banqueting House abounded in wainscot, and the conclusion is that it was made on the spot and accounted for some of the £3,183 paid for 'joiners and carvers to carve and garnish images and wainscots as also sundry other kinds of timber and panelling of chambers'. £184 was spent on the wages of plumbers, yet no lead was bought for them; no doubt Merton Priory was able to supply all that was needed of this valuable commodity. The burning of bricks (costing £522) and lime (£200) went on, but no firewood had to be bought to supplement the supply from the king's own woods. If the bricks cost the same as those paid for in September, 1538 (2s. a thousand), the £522 represents 5,220,000 bricks, in addition to the 600,000 mentioned in the earlier accounts. Glass for the windows of Nonsuch cost £162 to buy and £184 to fit.

The changing composition of the labour force, as the work progressed from construction to fitting out and embellishment, can to some extent be adduced from the totals of expenditure on the different trades. Masons cost £1,194, Bricklayers, Slaters and Tilers £1,772, Plasterers £125, Carpenters £2,670, Sawyers £1,298, Joiners and Carvers £3,183 and Painters £550. The trifling expenditure on plasterers cannot possibly include work on the magnificent moulded plaster panels which covered the outside walls of the Inner Court, which were described elsewhere as 'white works' made by 'mould-makers'. It seems likely that the joiners and carvers included the 'mould-makers' and the artists who carved the slate panels to which reference has already been made. The painters would be responsible for 'painting and decorating' in the modern sense, for it was the fashion to paint not only ironwork, doors and walls, but also exposed beams and other woodwork, and much of the 'old-world' timber we see today has been cleaned of its original paint. With such a large amount of utilitarian painting to be done, the £550 is unlikely to have covered the work of any artists engaged on decorative panels, and we have, in fact, only one reference, in Pepys' Diary, for the existence of such painted panels. No paviors are recorded as having worked at Nonsuch, although there were two large courtyards to be paved, and although paviors were being employed at Hampton Court. No gardeners are included for Nonsuch, yet the Nonsuch gardens are mentioned in other contemporary documents.

Lorde's disbursements, added to those of the Prior of Newark during his Paymastership, brought the total known expenditure on Nonsuch, up to 15th November, 1545, to £24,536 7s. 7d. We must remember that this figure is far less than the actual value of the building; for a great deal of the material did not have to be paid for.

Before leaving this question of the cost of Nonsuch, it may be of interest to draw a comparison, not between Tudor prices and modern prices but between Nonsuch and another Tudor building which is still standing. Loseley House, near Guildford, was in building from 1562 to 1570. It cost £1,640 19s. 7d., that is, less than was spent during the first five months at Nonsuch, and only one-fifteenth of the total recorded cost of the Palace.

Against the general background of the Building Accounts and Lorde's accounts can be set other fragmentary records which give an indication of work in progress at various dates during the building of the Palace, and so help towards the dating of the different stages of construction. It is clear, from the 1538 Building Accounts, that the

Inner Court was built before the Outward Court, but it is equally clear that the Outward Court was planned right from the start, and was not, as some writers have suggested, an afterthought by Arundel or Lumley; for the frequent references in 1538 to the Inner Court would be meaningless if that court had been the only building Henry intended to erect. Whilst the work on the Inner Court went on, the manor house of Cuddington was repaired and used for living quarters, but there is nothing to show whether these quarters were ever used by the king during his hunting expeditions, or were simply lodgings for some of the men working on the site.

The actual building work on the Inner Court was probably completed by 1541, and the decoration of the exterior, which took at least four years, had begun. An estimate for five weeks' work ending on 4th June in that year includes £6 to be paid to Moden (that is, Nicholas Modena) and his company working upon slate, and £20 for William Kendall and his company (twenty-four in number) occupied in the making of moulds for the walls. Six carvers were also busy on pendants and barge-couples. The completion of the panelling of the interior was probably, by this time, the main preoccupation of the seventy carpenters and twenty sawyers, and £16 was to be spent on wainscot, although no wainscot appeared in the final summary of Lorde's accounts. No masons were at work, but £16 was to be spent on Caen stone and there were still labourers at Merton Priory 'occupied in setting forth stuff to be carried'. In addition to bought and plundered stone, bricks were being burnt by thirty brickmakers at a rate far in excess of the rate at which they could be used by the 'establishment' of six 'plasterers and bricklayers'. These factors may indicate that, whilst the decorating of the Inner Court went on, stocks of materials were being accumulated, during the summer of 1541, for use on the Outward Court, the foundations of which had, in all probability, been laid at the same time as those of the Inner Court.

Henry's predilection for employing skilled foreigners is well illustrated at Nonsuch. Nicholas Bellin of Modena had worked with Primaticcio on the stucco and painted decoration of the Galerie François Ier at Fontainebleau. He is referred to, in a letter which Sir John Wallop wrote to Henry in 1540 describing the Galerie, as "Modon" who "maketh your Majesty's chimneys". His work at Nonsuch consisted of carving and gilding the panels of slate which covered the timber-framing of the Inner Court building. The work, which was under way in June, 1541, continued at least until May, 1544, but by July of that year Modena was engaged on the King's Works at Westminster. A copy of his bill presented to Davy Marten, Comptroller, for the years 1542 to 1544, survives among the Loseley Manuscripts in the Guildford Muniment Room and is reproduced in Appendix II. In the first of these years he was paid for mastic, varnish, oil and other necessaries for polishing, setting and varnishing gilded slate to preserve it from the weather. In the following year he worked on the gilding of various devices cut and carved in slate for 'garnishing the timber work of the King's manor of Nonesuche,' the devices including forty-eight batons and thirty-one great roses. He was paid 1s. 4d. a square foot, for a total area of 64 sq. ft. The work done between November, 1543, and May, 1544, is not specified, but the carvers and gilders worked for 204 days during that period.

The name of Antonio Toto del Nunziata has long been associated with Nonsuch. He came to England in 1511 with Torrigiano, with whom he worked on the tomb of Henry VII and his queen, Elizabeth. He stayed on in the king's service, and was naturalized in 1538. In March of that year the king's payments include £12 10s. to Antony Toto and Bartilmewe Pen, painters; the latter was Bartolomeo Penni, a portrait painter. There are many other references to Toto, who painted scenery and masks for the Revels, decorations for temporary banqueting houses and pictures for Hampton Court, where he received his first payment in 1530. Two years later he was paid for a long list of materials for making his own paint, for badgers' tails, swan and goose quills and glovers' waste for making size. Toto became Serjeant Painter to Henry VIII in 1543. As such he would undoubtedly be concerned with both utilitarian and decorative painting at Nonsuch, but there is unfortunately no documentary evidence whatever to connect him with the Palace. Even the painted panels preserved at Loseley, which are attributed to him, are linked to Toto and to Nonsuch by a chain of surmise.

A German, Stefan von Haschenperg, supposed to be a fortification expert, who was classed as a 'Deviser' of buildings, was dismissed for incompetence in 1544. He attempted to restore himself to favour by writing to the king in 1545 about a number of projects, including the water supply at Nonsuch. All attempts to tap the spring in the hill four furlongs to the south seem to have failed, for Stefan said that he had seen the aqueduct which had been begun but was not producing a water supply. He offered to finish the work, so that all who saw it would agree that it lived up to the name of the Palace. However, he is unlikely to have been given the work he asked for. It is, in fact, quite possible that the elaborate plumbing, the washbasins, the fountains and the sewers of Henry's dream palace never carried during his lifetime the gushing waters for which they were designed; for when Guzman de Silva, the Spanish Ambassador, visited Nonsuch in 1565 he reported that the Earl of Arundel had 'brought water thither which King Henry could not find'.

William Cure, a Dutch stone-carver, was said in 1571 to have been in England thirty years, having been sent for 'when the king did build Nonesutche'. Six French clockmakers were working 'upon the clock at Nonsuch' in July, 1544. They were Mathewe Bachlatt or Bathlatt, John Brisborough, Dedie Colls, Charles Durrant, Robert Lamberd and Peter Mare.

Work on the moulded plaster decoration continued at least until well into 1545. Henry's letter of May, 1545, printed in Appendix II, shows that by Christmas, 1544, William Kendall had been replaced by Giles Gering as 'overseer of certain of our white works', to whom an annuity of £20 was granted in September, 1545, under the style of 'the mouldmaker at Nonesuche'.

Dating evidence for the laying-out of the estate round the Palace is very scanty indeed. The wonderful gardens, which were later to be described in such glowing terms, had been under the care of a keeper since before the building of the Palace began; for when Sir Thomas Cawarden took over the Keepership, in 1544, the preamble to his deed of appointment declared that Sir Ralph Sadler had held the office since March, 1538, although he was not officially made Keeper until 1541. Sadler certainly drew his keeper's pay of 4d. a day for the gardens for the whole of the year beginning 29th September, 1541. There is nothing to indicate the date at which the 'gardens' ceased to be the gardens, orchard and churchyard of Cuddington, were cleared of builders' rubble, and became gardens worthy of the Palace. Many of their features seem to have been inspired by Italian gardens of the early sixteenth century; the actual work of constructing them is likely to have been done by Frenchmen, for many French gardeners became 'denizens' in 1544, and some of them are known to have been in the service of Henry and of various noblemen, including the Earl of Arundel.

There seems no reason to doubt that later writers on the gardens
at Nonsuch were describing the matured and mellowed results of the
work done in Henry's reign in landscaping, ornamentation and
planting, with only minor additional work by Arundel or Lumley. For
the gardens, orchard and wilderness were all parts of the original layout designed to connect the Palace and the Banqueting House, which
lay some 300 yds. to the west. The latter building is nowhere mentioned during Henry's reign, but we can be certain that it was built at
the same time as the Palace. It was standing in 1550, and cannot have
been built between 1547 and that date as the total expenditure on
Nonsuch during the reigns of Edward VI and Mary was only
£190 11s. 11¼d.

With the closing of Robert Lorde's accounts on 15th November,
1545, the documentary evidence on the building of Nonsuch comes to
an end. He left £1,020 in ready money to be handed over to Nicholas
Bristowe, his successor in the office of Paymaster, whose accounts for
the period from 15th November, 1545, to 1st May, 1547, have not
survived. Even after Davy Marten, the Comptroller, had sold off
surplus supplies to 'divers persons inhabitants thereabouts', Lorde was
found to have drawn £2,274 more than he could account for. This
was unfortunate for his daughter Alice and her husband, Henry
Polstede, for they were required to make good the discrepancy. They
made over to Edward VI a number of properties in Rotherhithe,
Southwark and St. Martin-in-the-Fields, with an annual value of
£113 14s. 5d.

Henry did not live to see the completion of the building of
Nonsuch. The extent of the work necessary to complete it after his
death has long been a matter of conjecture. Evelyn tells us that the
whole of the Outward Court was built by John, Lord Lumley, and the
sixteenth-century biographer of Henry Fitzalan, Earl of Arundel,
claims that Arundel's completion of Henry's work comprised 'buildings, reparations, pavements and gardens'. One writer even asserted
that Arundel built the whole Palace and presented it to Henry, who
then added the embellishments which gave it its name. There is,
however, sufficient inferential evidence in the accounts, and sufficient
direct evidence from a hitherto unnoticed source, to affirm that the
building was well-nigh complete when Henry died. Anthony Watson,
Rector of Cheam and Bishop of Chichester, was a protégé of John,
Lord Lumley, owner and later permissive Keeper of Nonsuch. To-

wards the end of the sixteenth century he wrote a description of Nonsuch, and his description, unlike the writings of casual visitors, is based on years of first-hand contact with the building, gardens and, above all, with the people who lived there and had been there ever since Arundel acquired the Palace from Mary Tudor. It is difficult to imagine more favourable circumstances for ensuring authenticity, and, even though he was fulsome in his praise of Arundel and Lumley, he tells us that Henry VIII laid down the foundations of the three courts and enclosed them with towers and walls, and that Arundel was responsible for the addition of 'built-in pictures' on the Outer Gatehouse and for the cupola over the Inner Gatehouse. Another cupola stood over the junction of the Kitchen Court and the east wall of the Inner Court, and as this was in the same style as the one over the Gatehouse it was probably also added by Arundel, although it is not mentioned by Watson. In Hoefnagel's view of the Palace, drawn in 1568 (Plate 1), there appear to be two incomplete towers, one at each end of the central block between the two courtyards; but these structures may well be the staircases which, in later views from the north, can be seen protruding into the Inner Court from the sides of the two known towers. The theory has been advanced that Henry intended to have towers at each corner of the Inner Court, that he did not complete them, and that Arundel took them down; but the evidence of the excavation did not support this view. Watson tells us that, in addition to the things which he mentions specifically, Arundel added various embellishments, and Lumley devised the most exquisite delights of pleasure, honour, prosperity and wonder; but he makes no suggestion whatever that the building he describes and its magnificence were due to anyone but 'the invincible King Henry'.

3

Pearl of the Realm

WHAT manner of building was this upon which so much labour, skill and money were lavished? It has earned, over the years, a whole range of adjectives, from 'magnificent' to 'monstrous'. Was it an important landmark in the history of English art and architecture, or the wholly regrettable origin of an excessive use of decoration on the outside surfaces of Elizabethan and Jacobean buildings? Obviously, there can be no final assessment of it, and each new generation will judge it by its own standards. We can do no more than record the effect it had on those who saw it, and then attempt to arrive at a dispassionate description of the building by piecing together contemporary accounts and archaeological evidence.

It is significant that, in all contemporary writings on Nonsuch, there is scarcely a hint of adverse criticism; and these writings cover a period of 120 years of rapid change in all aspects of our national life, not least in art and architecture. Some of the descriptions were obviously intended to please, and some were shameless plagiarisms, but in all of them, from Leland to Evelyn, there was a sense of wonder at the magnificence of the Palace and its gardens.

The first to describe it was John Leland, librarian and antiquary to Henry VIII. Leland made an antiquarian tour of England, spreading his researches over the years 1534 to 1543. He died whilst his projected *History and antiquities of this nation* was still in note form, and the results of his labours were not published until 1710, when *Leland's Itinerary* came out in nine volumes, and 1715, when six volumes of *Collectanea* were issued. From Part VIII of the 1909 edition of the *Itinerary* we learn that he came to Cuddington whilst the king was building Nonsuch. He mentions, incidentally, that there was at Cuddington a close, held by Crompton of London, which contained a vein of earth from which crucibles were made for goldsmiths and casters of metal, that there was none like it in all England, and that a load of this earth was sold for a crown or two crowns. His Latin description of Nonsuch, *Nulli Secunda*, is in the *Commentarii in Cygneam Cantionem*, in Volume IX of the 1769 edition of the *Itinerary*. It tells us little about the details of the building, but is clearly the fountainhead from which later writers drew their gushing streams of extravagant praise, both of the building which easily carried off the palm, with its emulation of Roman antiquity and all kinds of ornament, and of the most magnificent prince who had spared no cost to make the Palace a wonder in the minds and eyes of men. We may quote here the Latin couplet ascribed to Leland, but which does not appear in his published works:

'Hanc quia non habent similem, laudare Britanni
Saepe solent, nullique parem cognomine dicunt.'

The next observer was Joris Hoefnagel, a Flemish artist and engraver, whose drawing of Nonsuch, reproduced on Plate 1, was made in 1568. He described the Palace as the Royal Palace (although it was by this time in the hands of the Earl of Arundel), and was almost certainly responsible for the details which appeared in the account of Nonsuch in *Civitates Orbis Terrarum*, by George Braun and Frans Hogenburg. This six-volume work was published at Cologne from 1572 to 1618, and in Volume 5 there appeared an engraving based on Hoefnagel's drawing, and a letterpress description of '*Palatium Regium in Angliae regno Noncivtz, hoc est, Nusquam Simile, dictum*'. On this, John Gough Nichols, writing in the *Gentleman's Magazine* in August, 1837, commented:

"It is remarkable that Houfnagle should have taken home the impression that it was then a royal palace, and the description commences with a romantic but much perverted story, that the palace had formerly belonged to the Earl of Arundel, and that he, having sumptuously entertained there King Henry the Eighth, made it a present to his Majesty. It then proceeds to state that—

" 'The King, having graciously accepted it, declared that he would take care it should always deserve to retain this name of Nonciutz. With this in view he procured many excellent artificers, architects, sculptors, and statuaries, as well Italians, French and Dutch, as natives, who all applied to the ornament of this mansion the finest and most curious skill they possessed in their several arts, embellishing it within and without with magnificent statues, some of which vividly represent the antiquities of Rome, and some surpass them. There is a great court very large and spacious, capable to receive all the nobility of the king, and horsemen in great numbers; in the midst of which there is a marble fountain which raises water in abundance for various purposes for the use of the mansion, and remarkable for the exquisite ornament of the various statues which surround it. At the entrance of the mansion the artificers have created an echo which is admirable, having ingeniously made so many cavities and holes in the arches, that they return the voice and the sound of trumpets, not merely one time, but four or five, very distinctly.' "

Shortly after the death of the Earl of Arundel, which occurred on 24th February, 1580, a member of his household (possibly a chaplain) wrote the *Life* which is now in the British Museum. The only reference to Nonsuch is:

"Among the number of whose doings, that past in his tyme, this one is not the least, to showe his magnificence, that perceivinge a sumptuous House called Nonesuche to have bene begon, but not finished, by his first maister Kinge Henry, the eighte, and thearfore in Quene Maryes tyme, thoughte mete rather to have bene pulled downe, and sold by peacemeale, then to be perfited at her charges, he for the love and honour he bare to his olde maister, desired to buye the same house, by greate of the Quene, for which he gave faire lands unto her Highnes. And, havinge the same, did not leave, till he had fullye finished it, in buildings, reparations, paviments, and gardens, in as ample and perfit sorte, as by the first intente and meaninge of the said Kinge, his old maister, the same should have bene performed, and so it is nowe evident to be beholden, of all strangers and others, for the honour of this Realme, as a pearle thereof. The same he haith lefte to his posterity, garnished, and replenished, with riche furnitures, amonge the wich his lybrarie is righte worthye of remembrance."

The most important eye-witness account of Nonsuch is that of Anthony Watson, mentioned in Chapter 2. A translation of his Latin 'Brief and true description' of the Palace is, at the time of writing, still in draft. It is, in any case, too long for extensive quotation, and I have therefore given here only a short paraphrased selection from his twenty-five-page manuscript, leaving further extracts until they are needed to illustrate the next three chapters, on the building and its surroundings. The selection robs the original of much of its character, for Watson thought and wrote in superlatives, and the form of many of his sentences was governed by his desire to work in an appropriate classical allusion or quotation. There is, however, still sufficient colour left to convey his enthusiasm, and his descriptive details are better in many ways than those given in what has hitherto been the main authority on Nonsuch, the Parliamentary Survey of 1650. He wrote of a building which he had known intimately for a number of years; in a style almost as flamboyant as the Palace itself but with the authority of first-hand knowledge.

Watson, Rector of Cheam from 1581, became Bishop of Chichester in 1596 through the influence of John, Lord Lumley. He continued to hold the Rectory of Cheam *in commendam* until his death in 1605. His description is not dated, but it was written after the second marriage of Lumley in 1582, and it makes no mention of the surrender of the Palace to the Crown, which took place in 1592. Stripped of many of his flowers of rhetoric, his picture of Lumley's royal home is as follows:

'The site of the Palace is on a small elevation in a rolling plain. To the north are extensive pastures. On the east there is arable land for five miles, but on the west the delights of hunting may be enjoyed. The south wind is calmed by a gentle hill and a belt of trees. The wind from the west is repelled by the natural defences round the site and by the strength of the building.

'Before the lower court, a large gatehouse, lying between west and north, looks inwards on the beauty of the building; outside are fields and a plain of grass, about 140 acres. In the middle of a field a silver spring bursts forth with sparkling waters, and flows through broad plains into the majestic River Thames. Nearby are an ancient leafy grove and wooded hillocks.

'This gatehouse of which I speak, most beautiful in its size and appearance, is adorned with the double support of a stone window, bearing the insignia of king and kingdom worked with exquisite art. Remarkable for its four towers, it rises nobly to four storeys. On the right and left front, at the expense of the Earl of Arundel, built-in pictures increase its grandeur and add a new point to its brilliance.

'On entering the house itself, one sees long paths of smooth stone, and everywhere else is paved in rougher stone. Notice the size of the rooms, the splendid windows, the manifestly royal style of the building, the high pinnacles, which at the bottom are held up by small animals and at the top have dogs, griffins and lions resting on decorated shields.

'To the east a way lies open to a somewhat hidden court, which you would say is most appropriate for the shutting off of the noise of the kitchens and household offices. To the west is the way to the stables.

'An archway leads, by the ascent of eight steps, to the royal court. In the middle gatehouse (which outdoes the first gatehouse by a tower, a clock, chimes and six golden horoscopes), the projecting windows might be thought to have been hewn from the heart of the rock. Since King Henry, either because he had greater problems on his mind, or because he despaired of having an adequate water supply, or because he was prevented by fate, did not give this tower a top, Earl Henry, last of the Fitzalans, set up a lofty open tower fully worthy of such a building.

'The quadrangular space, laid with square stones brought in from Newcastle-on-Tyne, has nowhere anything that displeases; its fountain gives much delight and is the very perfection of art.

'A huge mass of stone, brought by an army of wagons, was used for the foundations, which will endure for all time.

'From the powdered ashes of stones, carefully moistened, a substance was made which was suitable for taking any kind of impression, and in the natural process of drying became harder than adamant. Much skill was lavished on this material, and everywhere there are kings, Caesars, sciences, gods. Since the whole edifice is royal, it is divided into a king's side and a queen's side, on either side of the square. The king's way is guarded night and day by Scipio, clothed in bronze garments, and the queen's way by warlike Penthesilia.

'Setting foot, with Scipio's permission, into the royal quarters, you will first see the spacious chamber of the royal guard. From there the way goes up by generous winding steps, leading to the most glorious precincts of the royal presence. The precincts look out one way on the riches of the courtyard, and the other way on the perplexing twists of the maze and the scented beauty of the garden. From there, leaving the closets on the right, extends the dignified approach to the king's privy chamber, which has most pleasing windows and suffers no disturbance either from the wind or from the view outside or from noise.

'A somewhat narrower room leads, to the right, to a lofty tower if you go up, to a richly planted garden if you go down; while to the left it leads into two fine chambers exclusively reserved for the king. Adjoining these is the royal bedchamber. At the back is sited a gallery. From the king's quarters we go across to the queen's, which are accorded the unrestricted benefit and use of the gallery and are marked by the same spaciousness and ornamentation as the king's, as far as the gate of Penthesilia.

'Throughout the rest of the whole house, dukes, marquises, counts, viscounts, barons, knights, soldiers, noblemen, each according to his rank, sojourn, and are frequently pleased to stay the night.

'If Ptolemy could come back to life, he would die again of envy when he saw this library with its books on the arts, philosophy, jurisprudence, medicine, mathematics, theology and history, and spheres, globes, bronze and paper instruments of all kinds.

'The wardrobe is worthy of description in rich language, but out of deference to the most honourable Lumley, a master I am bound to revere on many grounds, my reticence may be pardoned if I suffer all ears to be deprived of this great pleasure, and all knowledge of those riches to stay within the privacy of the walls.

'The door which opens to the right of the king leads into the garden. From there, if you turn your gaze to the lofty towers, the turretted walls, the projecting windows, the plaster-work, the exquisite statues, you will wonder whether you are walking in courtyard or garden, for the face of each has the same splendour and majesty.

'Leaving the garden, we enter the wilderness, which is, in fact, neither wild nor deserted. The land, which is naturally somewhat hilly and is plentifully watered, is set out with lofty and magnificent tree-lined walks to the south and west. At the end of the path to the south, the trees have been trimmed to form canopies. Through the heart of the wilderness there are three paths, the middle one worn and sandy and the others turfed. There are trees for shade and for fruit: almost countless young apple trees, shrubs, evergreens, ferns, vines. To the north is a widespreading circular plane tree, its branches supported on posts, so that many people can sit beneath it, talking, listening to the calls of animals and birds, or gazing at the wire-fenced aviary.

'An ancient oak shows the way straight into the shady grove of Diana, where there are places arched over by the skill of topiary, walls and sandy walks. Diana herself, guardian of the groves, lurks in the shadows, near the Vale of Gargaphy with its icy spring. Actaeon's misfortune is well known; Diana put out the flames of unlawful love with sprinkled water, from Actaeon she made a stag, from the noble hunter a wretched prey to dogs. Now the divine virgin enjoys the pleasures of the rock-well in peace, washes her limbs in the icy water and regards the absurd shade of her foe. The path leads on to a stately bower for Diana, over which the hero Lumley caused an inscription to be set up in praise of the goddess and as a warning to youths to avoid the fate of Actaeon.

'On a lofty arch is an eagle, a pinnacle is topped with a pelican, and on another pinnacle stands a phoenix. In a grassy space of the orchard a handsome pyramid rises, set off with divers heads which, while counterfeiting dryness in the mouth, discharge small streams of water. In the thickest parts of the orchard, in the more open wood, and in the bare plain, there is pleasure and refreshment: the timid steps of the deer, the flight of fowls, the harmonies of the birds, the gentle breezes and the scented plants. If we climb the winding steps by the Pelican, there are brought together delightful promenades and handsome elms in the most perfect order, with grape-vines adjoining the elms.

'On a small hill neighbouring these pleasant places a most sumptuous banqueting house was erected. In its most peaceful views, most agreeable windows, the spaciousness of its rooms and hall, it is worthy of King Henry—of Diana herself. No ornaments of prosperity or honour are lacking here.

'Watercourses run hidden through the inmost parts of the wilderness and grove, and break out gently in a neighbouring valley. Here there is a pond with shoals of trout.'

In marked contrast to Watson's original and vivid description are the three accounts which follow. They were the results of short visits, by an Englishman, a German and a Swiss. The Englishman, William Camden, borrowed from Leland. The two foreign visitors, like many of the early writers on travel, made notes during a few weeks' whirlwind tour of the country, wrote them up when they got home, and then read up anything they could find to enable them to expand their notes into a travel book. It would therefore be unwise to accept unreservedly the results of their hasty observation, written partly, at least, from memory and partly culled from the writings of others.

William Camden, in his *Britannia*, published in 1586 and translated by Philemon Holland in 1610, described Nonsuch; but it was Holland who inserted the reference to Leland in the following extract:

"About foure miles from the Tamis within the Country, Nonesuch a retiring place of the Princes putteth downe, and surpasseth all other houses round about: which the most magnificent Prince King Henrie the Eighth, in a very healthfull place called Cuddington before, selected for his owne delight and ease, and built with so great sumpteousnesse and rare workmanship, that it aspireth to the very top of ostentation for show; so as a man may thinke, that all the skill of Architecture is in this one peece of worke bestowed, and heaped up together. So many statues and lively images there are in every place, so many wonders of absolute workmanship, and workes seeming to contend with Romane antiquities, that most worthily it may have, and maintaine still this name that it hath of Nonesuch according as Leland hath written of it:

" 'The Britans oft are wont to praise this place,
For that through all The realme they cannot show
the like, and Nonesuch they it call.'

"As for the very house it selfe, so environed it is about with Parkes full of Deare, such dainty gardens and delicate orchards it hath, such groves adorned with curious Arbors, so pretty quarters, beds, and Alleys, such walkes so shadowed with trees, that Amenitie or Pleasantnesse it selfe may seeme to have chosen no

other place but it: where she might dwell together with healthful-
nesse. Yet Queen Marie made it over to Henrie Fitz-Alan Earle of
Arundell for other lands; and he, when he had enlarged it with a
Librarie passing well furnished, and other new buildings, passed
over all his right when he died to the L. Lumley, who for his part
spared no cost, that it might be truly answerable to the name: and
from him now it is returned againe by compositions and con-
veiances to the Crowne. Neere heerunto (and worth the noting it
is) there is a vaine of potters earth highly commended and therfore
the deerer sold, for the making of those crucibles and small vessels
which goldsmiths use in melting their gold."

The *Travels* of Paul Hentzner, a German who visited this country
in 1598, owe nearly as much to Camden and to Braun and Hogenburg
as they do to Hentzner. His remarks on Nonsuch are in part a direct
copy of the foregoing extract from Camden, and in part the result
of his own observation. The translation is that of Horace Walpole,
printed at Strawberry Hill in 1757:

"Nonesuch a royal retreat, in a place formerly called Cuddington, a very healthful situation, chosen by King Henry VIII
for his pleasure and retirement, and built by him with an excess of
magnificence and elegance, even to ostentation: one would imagine
every thing that architecture can perform to have been employed
in this one work. There are every where so many statues that seem
to breathe, so many miracles of consummate art, so many casts
that rival even the perfection of Roman antiquity, that it may well
claim and justify its name of Nonesuch, being without an equal;
or, as the poet sung,

" 'This, which no equal has in art or fame,
Britons deservedly do Nonesuch name.'

"The Palace itself is so encompassed with parks full of deer,
delicious gardens, groves ornamented with trellis work, cabinets of
verdure, and walks so embrowned with trees, that it seems to be
a place pitched upon by Pleasure herself, to dwell in along with
Health.
"In the pleasure and artificial gardens are many columns and

pyramids of marble, two fountains that spout water one round the other like a pyramid, upon which are perched small birds that stream water out of their bills. In the grove of Diana is a very agreeable fountain, with Actaeon turned into a stag, as he was sprinkled by the goddess and her nymphs, with inscriptions.

"There is besides another pyramid of marble full of concealed pipes, which spirt upon all who come within their reach."

An alternative translation of the Latin 'song' in praise of Nonsuch appeared in 1792 in Lysons' *Environs of London*. It ran:

"Unrivalled in design the Britons tell
The wondrous praises of this Nonpareil."

The Swiss visitor was Thomas Platter, who spent a day at Nonsuch on 23rd September, 1599, during a five-week stay in England. He wrote up his notes the following year and, six years later, incorporated extracts from his reading. His *Travels in England, 1599* was translated by Clare Williams and published in 1937. His interesting account of a day in the life of Elizabeth's Court at Nonsuch is given in a later chapter; of the Palace itself he says:

'Nonsuch is a fine royal residence; it takes its name from its magnificence, for None Such is equivalent to *non pareille*, without equal, for there is not its equal in England.

'The Palace exterior is built entirely of great blocks of white stone on which are represented numerous Roman and other ancient stories. Above the doors of the Inner Court, stone statues of three Roman emperors are erected. Then, in the Inner Court, I noticed a very handsome and elaborate snow-white stone fountain, showing a griffin angrily spewing water with great violence.

'At the entrance to the garden is a grove called after Diana, the goddess; from here we came to a rock out of which natural water springs into a basin, and on this was portrayed with great art and life-like execution the story of how the three goddesses took their bath naked and sprayed Actaeon with water, causing antlers to grow upon his head, and of how his own hounds afterwards tore him to pieces. Further on we came to a small vaulted temple, where was a fine marble table, and the following mottoes (in Latin) were inscribed here thus—on the nearest wall: "The goddess of chastity gives no unchaste counsels; she does not counsel disgrace, but avenges it; they are the fruits of an evil mind and an evil spirit." On the right is written up: "From an impure fountain impure springs, from an unpleasant mind a sight defiled." On the left is: "Shade for the heated, a seat for the weary; in the shade thou shalt not become shady, nor sitting grow serpent-eyed."

'Then I beheld a pointed tower spurting out water, and a rock from which issued water. We next entered an arbour or pavilion where the Queen sits during the chase in the park. Here she can see the game run past. Then through a wood in the gardens, with fine straight long alleys through it, fashioned in this wise:

'In the very densest part of the wood about here a great many trees are uprooted and cleared, within a breadth of some eighteen to twenty feet, along a straight course, so that there is a vista from one end to the other. And here and there they are partitioned off on either side with high boards, so that the balls may be played in the shade of these same alleys very pleasantly, as in an enclosed tennis court, and other amusing pastimes may also be pursued, while the delicious song of the birds in the tall trees, densely planted along the sides in ordered array, afford one great delight.

'From here we came to a maze or labyrinth surrounded by high shrubberies to prevent one passing over or through them. In the pleasure gardens are charming terraces and all kinds of animals— dogs, hares, all overgrown with plants, most artfully set out, so that from a distance one would take them for real ones.'

It has been suggested that Francis Bacon had Nonsuch in mind when he was writing two of his essays, those 'Of Building' and 'Of Gardens'. These essays are readily accessible, so that it seemed unnecessary to reproduce them here; and it is unlikely that 'Of Building' has much, if anything at all, to do with Nonsuch. It is a mosaic of ideas gathered from many places, a composite picture of a 'princely palace'; and the pieces are fitted together in such a way that the model building he describes could scarcely differ more, in individual features and in layout, from Nonsuch.

"God Almightie," writes Bacon, "first planted a Garden." He then

goes on to make "a Platforme [i.e., plan] of a Princely Garden, Partly
by Precept, Partly by Drawing, not a Modell, but some generall Lines
of it; And in this I have spared no Cost". He wishes to see a 4-acre
"Green" at the entrance, a "Heath" of 6 acres made like a natural
wilderness and a "maine Garden" of 12 acres; as well as alleys, both
open and covered, fountains, arbors and seats. He could certainly have
noted these features during his visits to Nonsuch, and also the statues
and topiary which he condemns; but he could equally well have seen
them in other places. However, his "Lelacke Tree" may well have
been inspired by the six lilacs at Nonsuch, for they were still sufficient
of a novelty in 1650 to be commented on by so prosaic a body
as a Parliamentary Commission. And even if we have no external
evidence to prove that his conception of a perfect garden was in fact
based on Nonsuch, we can at least learn from his essay a great deal
about the appearance and contents of the Nonsuch gardens and others
in late Elizabethan or early Stuart times.

John Speed, cartographer and historian, published in 1611 his
Theatre of the Empire of Great Britaine, an atlas designed to accompany
his *History of Great Britaine.* On the back of the Surrey map, first
printed in 1610, he says:

> "Albeit the County is barren of Cities or Townes of great
> estate, yet is shee stored with many princely Houses, yea and five
> of his Majesties, so magnificently built, that of some shee may well
> say, no Shire hath none such, as is None-such indeede."

During 1650 surveyors were sent out by Parliament to report on
the "honors, manors and lands of the late King Queene and prince",
and to evaluate them for sale and demolition. They were at Nonsuch in
April of that year. They faithfully carried out their task, but the place
so fired their enthusiasm that their report, far from being a terse
valuation, is written in glowing terms. The full Survey is given in
Appendix II, and, with Anthony Watson's description, it has provided
much of the information on which the next three chapters are based. It
will therefore be sufficient here to extract a few quotations to illustrate
the theme with which the present chapter began: that contemporary
observers had nothing but praise for Nonsuch.

The Outward Gatehouse is "very strong and graceful", and its
top storey is "a very large and spatyous roome very pleasant and

delectable for prospect". The Inner Court is "richly adorned and sett forth and garnished with variety of statues pictures and other Antik formes of excellent art and workmanshipp and of noe small cost". Its rooms are "very fayre and large many of them being waynscoted round and matted and adorned with spatious lights both inwards and outwards". The Inner Gatehouse is "of most excellent art and workmanship and a very speciall ornament to Nonsuch House". The five-storey turrets "command the prospect and view of both the parkes of Nonsuch, and of most of the Country round about, and are the chiefe ornament of the whole house". Even the Bowling Green is "neate and hansome". They made bold to say that the buildings were "in very good repayre" and "not fit to bee demolished or taken downe", and even suggested that 200 trees near the Palace, already marked for felling, should not be cut down, as it would "very much impayre the magnificence of the structure".

John Evelyn, on 3rd January, 1666, records a visit to Nonsuch:

'I supped in Nonsuch House . . . at my good friend's Mr. Packer's, and took an exact view of the plaster statues and bass-relievos inserted betwixt the timbers and puncheons of the outside walls of the Court; which must needs have been the work of some celebrated Italian. I much admired how they had lasted so well and entire since the time of Henry VIII, exposed as they are to the air; and pity it is that they are not taken out and preserved in some dry place; a gallery would become them. There are some mezzo-relievos as big as the life; the story is of the Heathen Gods, emblems, compartments, etc. The Palace consists of two courts, of which the first is of stone, castle-like, by the Lord Lumleys (of whom it was purchased), the other of timber, a Gothic fabric, but these walls incomparably beautified. I observed that the appearing timber-puncheons, entrelices, etc., were all so covered with scales of slate, that it seemed carved in the wood and painted, the slate fastened on the timber in pretty figures, that has, like a coat of armour, preserved it from rotting. There stand in the garden two handsome stone pyramids, and the avenue planted with rows of fair elms, but the rest of these goodly trees, both of this and of Worcester Park adjoining, were felled by those destructive and avaricious rebels in the late war, which defaced one of the stateliest seats his Majesty had.'

The description given by Pepys a few months earlier, on 21st September, 1665, differs in some of its details. He tells us that he saw:

"A great walk of an elme and a walnutt set one after another in order, and all the house on the outside filled with figures of stories, and good paintings of Rubens' or Holben's doing. And one great thing is that most of the house is covered, I mean the posts, and quarters in the walls, covered with lead, and gilded."

These paintings mentioned by Pepys remain a mystery, for nowhere else is there any suggestion that there were paintings on the outside walls of the Inner Court. He also falls into the same error as the Parliamentary surveyors, mistaking for lead the carved slate panels covering the timber frame of the building.

The earliest picture of Nonsuch is a "thumbnail sketch" in the margin of a map of the country between Nonsuch and Morden. The map was drawn up, during the reign of Edward VI, by commissioners appointed by the Court of Augmentations, during yet another dispute over common rights on Sparrowfield. This time the contestants were the tenants of Morden and Cheam. A copy of the marginal sketch is reproduced on page 90. It is too roughly and hastily drawn to have any great value so far as matters of detail are concerned; it is an approximation, just as are the houses, churches, trees and the Park Pale on the map itself. What is significant about it, however, is the central portion, which clearly represents the north frontage of the Outward Court, with its flanking towers, at a date at least three years before the Palace was acquired by Arundel in 1556. On this evidence alone, it is impossible to accept the theory that Arundel or Lumley built the Outward Court; and the fact that the flanking towers are of unequal height is, I believe, only due to the carelessness of the drawing, and does not mean that one of them was unfinished; for each of them is shown as having windows in the top storey, and only in that storey.

Hoefnagel's drawing of the Palace has already been mentioned. The original is in the Prints and Drawings Department of the British Museum. It is a sketch in ink which has faded to brown, and has faint washes of water colour. The 1582 engraving based on the drawing (Plate 6) has been redrawn on a number of occasions for use in books of smaller format than the original, and Hoefnagel's is undoubtedly the best-known view of Nonsuch. The artist was standing to the south-east of the building; his landscaping is conventionalized, but the foreground may be fairly accurate, for considerable changes have taken place since his visit. Running across the middle of the picture is the wall of the Privy Garden, and a straggling cavalcade is conducting Elizabeth's cumbersome coach towards the south-west corner of the garden, where there may be an invisible gate leading to two small buildings, possibly coach-house and stables, the roofs of which can be seen over the wall.

The garden wall unfortunately hides the lower part of the Palace building, and when we come to compare the parts which can be seen with Speed's view of the same frontage (Plate 4(a)) we realize that there are many differences of detail. This brings up the question of authenticity and reliability, and, quite apart from the archaeological evidence, it seems reasonable to assume that Speed, with his curious draughtsmanship, is even less likely to be correct than Hoefnagel. The latter probably took away with him some sketches and notes, and did not produce the finished drawing until later, when he had to rely on his memory for some of the details. He shows a building rather longer from east to west than in Speed's view, and this effect is exaggerated because the lower storey is hidden by the garden wall; a building poorly equipped with windows and decorated with pennants on masts instead of with the king's beasts. A curious quirk on the part of the engraver has caused the wind to blow from right to left instead of the other way, as in the drawing; but the flag on top of the right-hand tower is defying nature and streaming out into the wind.

Despite these reservations, Hoefnagel's picture is, of course, invaluable. We will return to its points of detail when we attempt to 'reconstruct' the building in the next two chapters. In the meantime, we may note the general impression of the timber-framed frontage of the Inner Court with its octagonal flanking towers and a central, half-octagonal bay; the moulded plaster decorations between the timber-framing; what appear to be clerestory or attic windows but are in fact the embrasures in battlements made of timber covered with lead; above the central bay, the clock-tower and the roof of the central block separating the Inner from the Outward Court; and, to the extreme right, a return wing of the kitchens, linking the main kitchen building, of which the roof and chimneys can be seen, with the east side of the Inner Court. To the left of the clock-tower, and partly obscured by it, is a roof which may be intended to represent the Outward Court Gatehouse, although no corner turrets are visible. The mystery of the two structures visible near the inner faces of the twin towers, above the main roof level, has already been touched upon. The back of the right-hand tower in Hoefnagel's view can be seen in the painting by Danckerts (Plate 5), which clearly shows a fairly large addition (probably containing the staircase) to the face of the otherwise octa-gonal tower. Yet in the Hoefnagel these two structures appear to be separate from the octagonal towers; in fact, to be rising above the roof of the central block.

Speed's familiar view of Nonsuch appeared in the corner of his map of Surrey, printed in 1610. Obviously it is not meant to be an artist's impression of the building, but is the work of a surveyor packing as much information as he can into two superimposed eleva-tion drawings, and almost certainly compressing his drawings laterally to make them fit inside the ruled border of the engraving. For the first of these drawings he has imagined himself to be about twenty feet above the Privy Garden wall which we saw in Hoefnagel's drawing; and from there he looks down on the Privy Garden with its walks, shrubs and ornaments, and on the outside wall of the south front, where he depicts the plaster decorations with greater clarity than did Hoefnagel, but exaggerates their size.

Once he had delineated the frontage of the Palace nearest to his imaginary viewpoint, Speed projected himself another twenty feet or so into the air, so that he could see right over the roof and across the 134 ft. 6 in. of the Inner Court to the far wall, that is, the south wall of the central block. Here he overdoes the size of the Inner Gatehouse, but we can see the clock, the chimes under a cupola, a large sundial and three projecting windows. Below them is the archway leading down into the Outward Court. The rest of this wall shows the same arrange-ment of timber-framing and plaster panels as was used on the outside walls.

Returning to the garden, we see on the right the prancing horse which Watson tells us was on the Queen's side of the Palace. Near the bottom edge of the picture are the three mounds, the central one, according to Watson, being adorned with Lumley's fountain with a nymph, and the outer pair, according to the 1650 Survey, being falcon perches. On the extreme left is part of the pyramid mentioned in the Survey.

The two principal oil paintings of Nonsuch are in such marked contrast to the views given by Speed and Hoefnagel that it is not surprising that they were, until comparatively recently, thought to be pictures of other buildings. The painting in the Fitzwilliam Museum, Cambridge, by an unknown Flemish artist (frontispiece) was reproduced as an engraving by James Basire in *Vetusta Monumenta* with the title 'Richmond Palace from the Green', in *Richmond and its inhabitants* as 'The Monastery in Richmond Gardens, erected by Henry V', and it has also been described as a picture of Theobalds. Sir Alfred Clapham, writing in 1913 or 1914, in *Some famous buildings and their story*, claimed to be the first to recognize it as a view of Nonsuch. It was for a time attributed to David Vinckeboons, but it is no longer thought to be by him. The style of dress dates it at about 1620, and it is a view of the Palace from the north-west, painted from a position on the edge of the present London Road, on the Ewell side of the Park gate.

The high wooden gate can be seen at the extreme left, and from it a tree-lined roadway leads to the Bowling Green and to the Outward Court Gatehouse. Farther to the right stands the Inner Gatehouse with its clock-tower, and, behind it, and also to the extreme right, are the five-storey octagonal towers on the south frontage. On the Bowling Green a game is in progress, and in the meadow beyond are four coaches. In the foreground, in what is now the ploughed field of Cherry Orchard Farm, three brave huntsmen with their dogs are cornering a singularly docile-looking victim.

The Fitzwilliam picture gives the only known view of the west side of the Palace. The east side can be seen in a painting which was only re-identified in 1959 as representing Nonsuch. The artist was Hendrik Danckerts (*c.*1630 – *c.*1678) who was commissioned by Charles II to paint a series of views of royal palaces. His picture of Nonsuch is now at Berkeley Castle, and it is reproduced on Plate 5. At some time it has been lettered "St. Jame's Palace" but it is clearly Nonsuch. The artist was to the north-east of the Palace in the vicinity of the main stables. On the right of the building is the north frontage with the Outward Court gatehouse, and near the centre is the clock-tower. Below that, and nearer the observer, the building juts out to form the Kitchen Court. To the extreme left is the south-east tower, joined to the east wing of the Inner Court. Signs of neglect are visible: the coping of the garden wall is damaged, near the coachman's head and after turning the corner, and the pinnacle on top of the hidden south-west tower is bent.

Possibly copied from the Danckerts is another painting from the same viewpoint and with the same sunlight and shadow. Although this picture lacks sharpness of detail, the appearance of the building is the same as in the previous view, the only difference being in the treatment of the foreground and sky. However, the Danckerts was not discovered until after the excavation of the Palace, so that a photographic copy of this present picture, the original of which is in the Eastern Transvaal in the possession of W. J. Kynnersley-Browne, Esq., was invaluable at that time.

Apart from a tiny sketch of the ruins as seen from Epsom Downs in 1702, there are no other known pictures of Nonsuch. It is difficult to believe that it was not sketched and painted on many occasions, or that no artist was sufficiently interested in the remarkable Banqueting House to want to depict it. So that there is every hope that, as knowledge of the Palace spreads, other wrongly attributed or unidentified pictures will be recognized as views of Nonsuch.

Having seen how Nonsuch appeared to the writers and artists who visited the building in its lifetime, we can use this evidence to supplement and interpret the discoveries made by the archaeologists, and do our best to repair the damage caused by my Lady Castlemaine nearly 300 years ago.

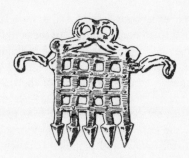

4

The Outward Court and Kitchens

Much of the evidence on which our knowledge of the Palace is based has been given in Chapter 3. The two most important documentary sources remaining to be considered in detail are Anthony Watson's *Description* and the Parliamentary Survey made in 1650 when the building was threatened with destruction. These two can now be examined together and correlated with the information obtained as a result of the excavation of 1959; and the results can be further illumined by reference to the foregoing chapter and to small items gleaned from many different sources, particularly the accounts for the repair of the building, which exist for some sixty years. This will give as clear a picture of the Palace as is possible, unless some really startling new evidence comes to light.

Obviously, the excavation plan of the foundations, given on page 247, is essential to an understanding of the layout of the building. To facilitate the detailed consideration of the building in this and the following chapter, the plan has been adapted and divided to form separate reconstructed ground-floor plans of the three courts. These appear on pages 77, 87 and 97, and in the text the relevant key-numbers on the plans are given in parenthesis. As to the appearance of the various parts, the excavation added immeasurably to what could be gathered from documents and pictures. It is when we try to get down to the actual use to which particular rooms were put that we run into difficulties, for all too rarely do our sources enable us to be specific. Rooms are mentioned, but not their position or their relationship with each other. The same applies to the many outbuildings associated with the Palace, the position of which is indicated only vaguely, if at all.

The approach to the Palace from the direction of London, the present London Road parallel with Stane Street, was known at various times as London Waye, London Lane and Elm Lane. As it neared the boundary between the parishes of Cuddington and Ewell, it curved sharply from the Stane Street line to the left and then to the right. At the first of these curves it joined another Nonsuch approach road, that which ran past Worcester House in the Great Park, from Hampton Court, Kingston and Old Malden; and the avenue inside the Little Park leading to the Palace was in fact a continuation of this second road. At the entrance to the avenue was the gate already noticed in the Fitzwilliam Museum picture. This was replaced in 1639 by 'a great pair of new gates and a pale at the side thereof, in London lane entering into the Park before the house'. The material of which the gates themselves were made is not mentioned, but they were set in a stone archway between pillars 27 in. square, on which rested the 22 in. square springers of the arch. The posts for the pale or fence were 9 in. square, the rails 6 in. and 3½ in., and the boards 1 in. thick. Incredible as it may seem, the work was no sooner finished than it was covered, including the stonework, with oil paint in timber colour.

Inside the gates the meadow to the left of the avenue is today fulfilling the same function as it did when Thomas Platter came through the gates in 1599. Here the visitor must leave his carriage and proceed on foot; the twentieth-century visitor will merely lock his car, whereas Thomas and his contemporaries doubtless left their horses to be led away to be fed and watered at the great stables which, I believe, lay in the next field and were reached by the footpath which crosses the meadow diagonally in the direction of the present Mansion House. Half-way along the path to the stables stood Queen Elizabeth's Elm, where the queen is said to have stood to shoot at the deer. The elm, of great size, hollow but still in leaf, was destroyed about sixty years ago: burnt down, according to a Sutton writer, by some boys from Ewell.

The position of the stables is nowhere precisely described. In the 1650 Survey they are said to be 'a little remote from Nonsuch house upon the north-east'. On the survey plan drawn in 1731, reproduced on page 233, one of the fields to the north-east of the Palace site is lettered "Old Stable Ground". And in a corner of this field, ploughed during the winter of 1959–60, there were many surface indications of fairly extensive buildings, as well as evidence of human and animal life, in the shape of Tudor and Stuart pottery fragments, charcoal, teeth and bones. The great stable, built partly of wood and partly of stone, and with a tiled roof, had stalls for thirty-two horses, with two saddle rooms in the middle, and at each end was a smaller building; one of these was a stable for six horses, and the other, on two floors, consisted of lodgings and a forge. Nearby was another building, of timber, used as a stable for eight horses, with a hay-loft. The structure actually known as the 'Stable Buildings' was in fact a lodging house for the grooms of the stable and lower officers of the Court. It had eighteen rooms, of which two on the ground floor were the Palace bakehouse.

The stables thus described by the Parliamentary surveyors were not the original stables of the early years of the Palace. Early in 1599 materials, including 250 trees and 573 loads of flints, were collected for building new stables, barn, privy bakehouse and "skalding house". In the following year labourers trenched the ground for the founda-tions of the long stable and other buildings adjoining, and some 440 square yards of flint wall were built, presumably continuing the foundations above ground. Lathing and tiling of the long stable with an adjoining building and porch covered 520 sq. ft. The pavior laid 477 sq. yds. of paving in the long stable, the 'upper stable, the porch and Court without'—at 2d. a square yard—and the 'privy bakehouse and skalding house and Poultry' were paved with bricks. The new buildings comprised long stable, upper stable and saddle-house, barn and two returns, and bakehouse with staircase and lodging; but, of these, only the upper stable was entirely new, the rest being 'taken down, new framed and set up again', presumably, because of the need to dig new foundations, on a slightly different site or on a larger scale. Surrounded by thirty-eight perches of brick wall was a "Sincke" for the stables.

After this date, although the bakehouse was frequently in need of attention, the stables themselves were found by Cromwell's men just as Elizabeth had left them, except for minor repairs carried out in 1607, 1615 and 1626, when planks were pinned down, the racks and mangers mended and the walls "Quartered upp".

The position suggested as the probable site of the stables is a short distance to the north of the upper or free end of the wide, deep ditch known as Diana's Dyke. The purpose of this channel, coupled with its name, has given rise to a great deal of conjecture, and the general feeling hitherto has been that it was the site of the Diana and Actaeon statues mentioned by Watson and others, and that it was here that Elizabeth I bathed in a marble bath. This idea, and even the name of the Dyke, must now be abandoned: a careful reading of Watson and Platter undoubtedly places the Grove of Diana well to the west of the Palace, confirming a local tradition which Cloudesley Willis mentions in some unpublished notes. On the 1731 survey map of the Park, the name 'Long Ditch' is faintly pencilled alongside the Dyke, and the words 'Diana's Dyke' appear in the position suggested for the Grove of Diana.

A trench was dug across the Long Ditch in 1961, and no traces were found of any artificial lining to what appeared to have been a conventional ditch. The land slopes towards it from all directions, and at the Ewell end the water in the Ditch passed through a brick culvert parallel with the avenue, and eventually entered the Hogsmill river near Ewell Court. The Ditch is now dry, but within the past twenty years the bourne which used to rise every few years in both Ewell and Cuddington filled the trench to overflowing, and in the 'thirties the whole area lay under water for a time, part of the avenue itself being washed away. The Ditch is undoubtedly the 'silver spring' which 'bursts out with sparkling waters' mentioned by Watson in his description of the landscape outside the Outer Gatehouse.

Having been sidetracked in our intention of visiting the Palace by this detour to the left, we are back again at the Park gate. From the gate we look down the avenue—'a fair and straight path betwixt two fair ranks of trees', say Cromwell's surveyors. Platter described it as 'a long grassy avenue enclosed by wooden palings'. The palings, or rather posts and rails, can be seen in the Fitzwilliam picture; they were renewed or repaired from time to time, but had disappeared by 1660. The trees are described by Evelyn as rows of fair elms, but Pepys says that they were elms alternating with walnuts.

As we pass down the avenue, the field on the right, now a part of Cherry Orchard Farm, was formerly known as the Plain; this is the field which forms the foreground of the Fitzwilliam picture. On the left of the avenue, the meadow in which Thomas Platter left his coach would, whenever the Court was in residence, have been the scene of great activity. A large retinue travelled round with the monarch, and, except in the few places where there were lodgings near at hand, tents had to be used to accommodate all except the higher officials. In the summer of 1599 the meadow was full of tents, both round and 'elongated like a church', and here lived not only servants and retainers but many of the noble lords in the train of the Court.

The modern roadway continues, not quite on the line of the original avenue, past the end of the Long Ditch and eventually two slight rises in the road surface can be seen. These mark the approximate positions of the Outer and Inner gatehouses.

To reach the Outer Gatehouse the visitor had to cross the bowling green. In the central part of the Fitzwilliam picture the paling of the avenue can be seen opening out to enclose the green. Between 1613 and 1615 the posts, rails and latticing round the bowling green were extensively repaired, for they were "rotten and decayed and some stollen away". They, and the seats there, were painted timber colour in oil. The 1650 surveyors were much impressed by the 'neat and handsome bowling green, well ordered, lying muchwhat upon a square, and railed with good posts, rails and lattices of wood'. Between it and the Palace was a cobbled promenade eight yards wide, split by the ragstone-paved approach to the gatehouse. Each half of the promenade was enclosed by a stone balustrade, and was entered through an archway, the archways facing each other across the path to the gatehouse. For some reason, this balustrading was constantly in need of repair. Payments, such as that made in 1607 to John Rotheram for turning twenty-one "ballister" of stone at 1s. each for the rails before the gate, were numerous.

The frontage of the Palace shown in the Fitzwilliam painting and, foreshortened, in the Danckerts, faces north-west. I propose, however, to continue a practice which grew up during the excavation, when, to simplify explaining the ground plan, we described the building as having had a true north-south axis instead of keeping strictly to fact. This north front, then, was, as shown on the plan, sadly out of alignment. In many parts of the building the right-angles were fractionally wrong; but on this frontage the error is clearly visible.

From a position in front of the gatehouse (1), facing the building, the two-storey battlemented stone wall of the Outward Court stretched to left and right. The wall jutted out at either end, but the resultant effect of flanking towers was a purely decorative feature, produced by thickening the walls without increasing the size of the 'tower' rooms in relation to their neighbours. On the east face of the north-east 'tower', in the thickness of the wall, was a garderobe (3). Beyond, in line with the frontage, was a brick wall with two gates (see (4) on page 87), giving access to the kitchen yard. This brick wall

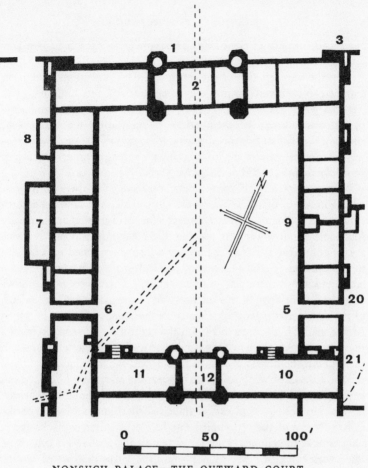

NONSUCH PALACE—THE OUTWARD COURT
(Based on the Excavation Plan on page 247)

KEY

1. The 'north' wall of the Gatehouse, at the point where the modern roadway
   passes over the foundations.
2. The entrance archway.
3. North-east corner, with garderobe.
5. Archway leading from Outward Court to Kitchen Court.
6. Archway leading to stables.
7. Three-gable building (see Fitzwilliam painting).
8. Single-gable building.
9. Entrance porch.
10. Wine-cellar.
11. Cellar, probably the Buttery.
12. Inner Gatehouse.
    (Dotted lines indicate sewers)

continued, turning at right-angles, enclosing the kitchen garden and joining the wall of the Privy Garden.

On the western side of the gatehouse the foundations had been completely removed during the demolition of the building. The trenches where the walls had been ('robber trenches' to the archaeologist), were cleared of their rubble filling during the excavation, enabling the plan of this missing wing to be drawn. Beyond the north-west corner the gate in the brick wall gave access to an area which is probably that described as the wood yard.

The gatehouse itself, seen in detail on Plate 7 (a), dwarfed the rest of this north frontage. It was some 58 ft. wide, and contained three storeys, according to the 1650 Survey; Watson claimed that there were four storeys. However this may be, the gatehouse was nearly twice the height of the two-storey building which surrounded it. Through the central arch (2) ran a flagstoned path. Over the arch were the royal arms, and above them was an oriel window. There were no windows at ground-floor level in this outside wall of the gatehouse, or, indeed, of the whole of the frontage. Watson's *contabulatae formae*, of which I have made 'built-in pictures', on the right and left front, remain a mystery. At each corner of the gatehouse was an octagonal turret, and the two outside turrets contained garderobes: the foundations of these turrets, instead of being solid like those at the rear, were hollowed out to a depth of 6 ft. and the resultant circular pits were lined with bricks.

Garderobes were placed at intervals all round the walls of the Palace. Many of them occupied one-half of a chimney-stack, and it may be that the chimneys served as ventilating shafts. The pits were lined with brick or stone or both; into them was discharged sewage from the 'stoolhouses' above; into them too were thrown many articles broken or discarded during the ordinary daily life of the Palace, possibly to get them out of sight of someone in authority. By 1959 any unpleasant associations of the garderobes had long since disappeared, and they yielded a perfectly wholesome compost and a remarkable collection of 'finds'.

Of the internal arrangement of the gatehouse little is known. One-third of the ground floor was taken up by the arched entrance, the ceiling of which produced the acoustic effects mentioned in Braun and Hogenburg. The rooms on either side of the arch, measuring 16 ft. by 20 ft., may have been the two rooms which the Parliamentary surveyors noted as being for the Groom Porter. The second storey may also have contained three rooms; it had three outward-facing windows, and no room on this floor caught the attention of Cromwell's men sufficiently to merit the description they gave of the 'large and spacious' room on the floor above. The battlements and turrets surrounded a flat roof covered in lead.

Passing through the entrance arch, the visitor entered the court-yard. Round him were the two-storey Outward Court buildings, and straight ahead was a central block separating the Outward from the Inner Court. The inward-facing walls of the outer court were probably of brick with stone facings, for in 1645 some of the stone battlements and tops of chimneys over the west side of the gatehouse were 'ready to fall', and there were other loose stones there, because the fascia of stonework beneath the battlements had 'cleft from the *brickwork* and fallen away'. No pictures of these inside walls exist, and the 1650 surveyors' information is that the whole Outward Court building was 'of free stone, well wrought and battled with stone and covered [i.e., roofed] with blue slate'. Much of the plain stone ('ashlar') used for the outer face of the walls came from Merton Priory. In the founda-tions, the space between the two faces of a wall was filled with un-shaped pieces of chalk and stone mortared together. Above ground level the core was probably of brick. In using the Merton stone, the masons weeded out the carved pieces, unless they had at least one plain surface enabling them to be set in the wall so that the carving did not show. The 'rejects', consisting of sculptured heads, intricate mouldings, window tracery and the like, were incorporated in the foundation rubble; mixed with blocks of chalk, they were held together by a lime mortar so strong, in places, that it was appreciably harder than the stone. It is significant that a large part of the foundations of the Outward Court seen in 1959 contained little or no Merton stone. The demolition workmen had done a thorough job, but they had been selective. Here and there, notably in the middle of the Outward Court Gatehouse, they had carried out trial digs right through the foundations to the soil beneath. Where they found only chalk foundations they abandoned the spot and tried elsewhere. This 'robbing' was well illustrated in the kitchen area, where a huge bite had been taken out of the foundations, and pieces of Merton stone could be seen in the sloping edges left when the 'quarry' was for some reason abandoned. The complete disappearance of the foundations of the west wing of the Outward Court, however, was probably not due to their high stone content but to the fact that this area of the Palace was demolished at a later date than the rest of the building, and that the materials were needed for a different purpose.

The absence of Merton stone from a large part of the Outward Court foundations might be thought to support the legend that this court was built after Henry's death. It was more probably the result of better organization as the work progressed. The carved stones were not actually needed as foundation material, for there were abundant supplies of perfectly adequate chalk close at hand. It was, in fact, wasteful to cart them all the way from Merton, taking up space in the carts which could have been occupied by ashlar. In the first rush of starting the building, when the walls of the Priory were crashing down, the stone was thrown into the carts indiscriminately and hurried off to Nonsuch as fast as the clumsy wagons and rough roads would allow. By 1541, however, there were men at Merton employed in sorting the plunder before it was carted, and it seems feasible that the need for this sorting was realized during the first few months, after which only squared stone was sent to the Palace. If this is so, it would explain why Henry's builders had little carved stone left to get rid of by the time they reached the north wing of the Outward Court.

Subsequent owners of the Palace may at times have wished that Henry had left the Merton stone at Merton. By 1608 they were 'squaring, hewing and setting new stone into the walls about the gatehouse which were decayed with weather'; in 1611 'setting up of stone about the porch before the court where it was decayed', and in 1614 'working and setting up 31½ ft. of base and 58 ft. of ashlar'. The foundations of the two northern towers of the Outer Gatehouse had to be repaired in 1615. Ashlar had to be set into the foundations of the stone walls 'in divers places in the first and second courts' in 1616, and "porteland ashlerstone" was set on the east and west sides of the outward gates in 1633. The fairly extensive repairs on the west of the gatehouse in 1645, to which reference has already been made, were only carried out after '18 foot square' had 'broken down through two roofs into the Lady Carlisle's lodgings and driven down one pair of rafters and some ceiling joists and ceiling there'.

Stone from many other sources was used, for moulded doorways and windows, paving, steps, balustrading and the like; in fact, for all the places in which salvaged stone would have been unsuitable. Although there are only references in the Building Accounts to

1. NONSUCH PALACE

A drawing by Joris Hoefnagel, 1568

2. CUDDINGTON CHURCH

Courtesy of Nonsuch Palace Excavation Committee

(a) Burials below floor of nave

(b) Nave floor tiles, and base of font to left of base of respond leading to north aisle

(c) East end, from the north-east, showing buttresses

3. MERTON PRIORY STONE USED FOR BUILDING NONSUCH

(a) Lion gargoyle found next to carved boss (c). Height 10 in.

Courtesy of S. Witkowski

(b) Female head. Height $10\frac{1}{2}$ in.

Courtesy of S. Witkowski

(c) Carved, painted and gilded keystone boss from Priory Church vaulting. Weight $4\frac{1}{2}$ cwt.

Courtesy of C. Yardley

(d) Twelfth-century roundel built into cellar wall. Diameter 8 in.

Courtesy of C. G. Dobson

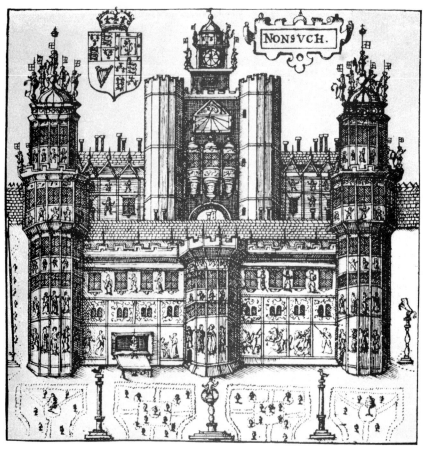

4. THE SOUTH FRONT OF THE PALACE
(a) Engraving from the corner of Speed's Map of Surrey, 1610

(b) A Nonsuch chest reflects the design

St JAMES PALACE. TIME OF CHARLES 2^D BY DANCKERT.

5. NONSUCH FROM THE NORTH-EAST

Painting, at Berkeley Castle, by Henry Danckerts, c. 1660

PALATIVM REGIVM IN ANGLIÆ REGNO APPELLATVM NONCIVTZ,
Hoc est nusquam simile.

Effigiauit Georgius Houfnaglius Anno 1582.

6. NONSUCH PALACE

Engraving, dated 1582, based on Hoefnagel's drawing

(a) The Outer Gatehouse

7. OUTWARD COURT DETAILS

(b) The north face of the Inner Gatehouse

(a) Gatehouse, from inside the cobbled courtyard

Courtesy of Nonsuch Palace Excavation Committee

(b) North-east corner, looking so
One of many rectangular gardero

Courtesy of C. G. I

8. OUTWARD COURT FOUNDATIONS

(c) North-east corner, showing demolition damage and line of chalk dust and chips dropped by builders on the original soil level

Courtesy of D. Cousins

Reigate, Caen and Luke stone, the Repair Accounts also mention Oxfordshire stone, Kentish pace, Purbeck, hardstone and ragstone, and no fewer than twenty-seven different types of stone were identified during the excavation. Among them were Tudor mouldings skilfully executed and as perfect as when they were first carved. Some of these stone dressings can be clearly seen in the Fitzwilliam picture.

To revert for a moment to the foundations of the Outward Court, these were remarkable in two respects: in their massive size in comparison with those of the more lightly constructed south front, and in their height in relation to the soil level of the site. For the north front wall, a great raft of unshaped chalk blocks was sunk into the soil and continued above it. On top of this a narrower foundation wall of several courses of shaped chalk was built, and above that, and narrower still, came the ashlar and core of the wall itself. After the foundations had been laid, 'imported' soil was tipped round them to raise the level of the courtyard and the ground outside it well above the natural soil level. By the Outward Court Gatehouse the natural soil was buried to a depth of nearly 5 ft.; the depth tapered off towards the east. The old soil level was clearly visible during the excavation, partly because of its colour and partly by a white line showing where chips and dust had fallen from the chalk blocks whilst the foundations were being built (Plate 8 (c)). This raising of the level of the ground may have been done to avoid an unduly long stairway between the Outward courtyard and the higher Inner Court, or because the ground to the north of the Palace was liable to flooding. It was a part of the operation of shaping the gradually rising ground into the two 'terraces' on which the courts were to be built, but the 'imported' soil did not come from the parts of the hillside which were dug away during this process.

On one of the inward-facing walls of the Outward Court was a 'dial' covering nearly 8 sq. yds. We are not told which wall it was on, or whether it was a sundial or a clock dial; but assuming, as its description suggests, that it was a sundial, a fitting place for it would have been the inner face of the gatehouse. When it was repainted in 1622 the signs of the Zodiac were done in colour, the letters painted gold and the groundwork of light blue-green ("byce"). There was a pilaster on each side, a semicircle on top, and the whole was surrounded by a frieze. In the centre of the dial was a picture of Time painted in stone colour.

The interior walls, separating the rooms of the Outward Court, appear to have been of brick, and most, but not all, of the ground-floor rooms had brick floors. The flooring was in some cases laid in a herring-bone pattern, and in others it was like ordinary bonded brickwork. Parts of it were found only about 5 in. below the turf of the Park, where, until a few years earlier, cereals and potatoes had been grown; and it was deeply scored in places where the ploughshare had run across it. The rooms shown on the plan, and those on the floor above, are nowhere described in such a way as to enable us to identify any of them except the wine-cellar (10). The 1650 Survey lists the various occupants before the execution of Charles I. The House-keeper had six rooms on the ground floor and two on the first; Lady Holland occupied three rooms on the first floor and her servants three rooms on the ground floor. Also on the ground floor were three rooms for the Gentlemen Ushers and Quarter Waiter; two for the Groom Porter; one used as the buttery; and one for Henry Jermyn, a favourite of Henrietta Maria, who accompanied her to France as her secretary and Captain of Bodyguard in 1644, was created Earl of St. Albans in 1660 and at the Restoration received many rewards for his services. Lady Denbigh, Groom of the Stool, had three rooms on the first floor, where Lady Carlisle had a dining-room, a withdrawing room, a bedchamber and two rooms for her servants. On the same floor the Lord Chamberlain, Lord Dorset, had four rooms and the Queen's Almoner two. Several staircases would be needed to make it possible for such a varied collection of people to live peaceably together, for corridors were rarely incorporated in Tudor buildings and one room opened into the next. Thus, there were probably entrances (9), each with its staircase, and with doors to right and left on each floor, each door giving access to a separate suite of rooms, as may be seen in some Oxford and Cambridge colleges.

Hazarding a guess as to the occupiers of the rooms shown on the ground-floor plan, we may perhaps give the Housekeeper the six rooms which constituted the whole of the west wing. The Groom Porter, as suggested earlier, may have had the two rooms in the gatehouse, and Henry Jermyn the single room at the cellar end of the east wing. This leaves seven rooms to accommodate the buttery, to which we will return later, and two suites of three rooms each, but here even guesswork breaks down.

The courtyard itself was found to measure 135 ft. from north to south and 114 ft. 9 in. from east to west, as against the 132 ft. by 115 ft. given in the 1650 Survey. It was cobbled, with the pebbles ranging from two to four inches in diameter. As finally cleaned up during the excavation, the cobbles stood very high above the groundwork in which they were set; but it is extremely unlikely that they ever had such a careful brushing during the lifetime of the Palace, for, with such deep spaces between them, they would have been most uncomfortable to walk on. Even so, flagstone paths of Purbeck paving stone, frequently in need of repair or replacement, were laid across the cobbles. One path led straight across the courtyard to the Inner Gatehouse (12), and others ran to left and right, towards the openings which can be seen on the excavation plan near the bottom of the east and west wings of the Outward Court (5, 6). These openings were brick-walled archways, paved with cobbles. That on the left, or western, side of the plan led, according to Anthony Watson, to the stables; but it can only be assumed that there were privy stables on this side of the Palace, for the main stables were some distance to the north-east. The archway on the east led to the Kitchen Court. It may also be assumed that another path led to the entrance, shaped like a horseshoe on the excavation plan of the foundations, but probably rectangular above ground, in the middle of the east wing (9), which may have had its counterpart on the west. Surface water from the cobbles and flagstones drained into a sink, which was covered by an iron grating with a stone surround.

Leaving the Outward Court for a moment, by means of the archway through the western wing, the Palace visitor found himself outside that part of the building which looks out towards the artist's right in the Fitzwilliam picture. On this side two buildings are shown abutting on the Palace wall, one with three gables (7) and the other with a single gable (8). These may be two of the buildings mentioned in the 1650 Survey as 'standing and being in the yard called the woodyard'. They were 'commonly called the gardener's house, the rush house, the privy buttery and the bottle house'. Some of these functions may, however, have been carried out by another building, not visible in the picture; for in 1600 a timber frame was erected for 'a new range of offices and lodgings round about the woodyard'. This was for a two-storey building, 20 ft. wide.

This western wing was, to the layman, the big disappointment of the excavation, owing to the thoroughness with which it had been robbed. Yet in another sense it was one of the most interesting parts of the site, for it was here that considerable remains of buildings associated with the manor house of Cuddington were found. Foundations of flint walls had been cut through by the Palace foundations. One massive wall, believed to be a wall of the 155 ft. barn which stood to the east of the manor house, ran along the west wing between the Palace foundations, but lying at an angle a little to the west of the Palace alignment. Near it, several superimposed floor-levels were found, two of them being of carefully laid pebbles. In one of these two floors the pebbles were very small, rarely exceeding half an inch in diameter; in the other their diameter averaged one inch. Near the central block, earth floors were discovered, as well as mediaeval pottery and roofing tiles.

To obtain further information about the great barn of Cuddington, another trench was dug here during the 1960 excavation of the Banqueting House. Below the Palace and Cuddington rubble, a large mattock was found where it had been dropped by the demolition workmen in 1538. The wooden handle had rotted away, leaving a line of discoloured earth to show its shape; but the business end, although heavily encrusted with rust, was in excellent condition. It was nearly half as big again as its modern counterpart.

The fourth side of the Outward Court building consisted of the central block dividing the two courtyards. This block contained the Inner Gatehouse flanked by two cellars. The Parliamentary Survey treats the "wineceller" as belonging to the Outward Court and the gatehouse and rooms over the cellar to the Inner, and the same plan may be followed with advantage here.

The Parliamentary Survey mentions only "the wineceller", yet there were two cellars, separated by the foundations of the Inner Gatehouse, and with no connection between the two. So far, there is no documentary evidence of the use to which the smaller, western cellar (11) was put; it had been badly damaged during demolition, and was filled with normal demolition rubble, so that the excavation yielded no conclusive evidence as to its purpose. It could have been used for cool storage of any kind, but it was more probably the buttery (a place for keeping ale as well as butter), for the repairs carried out in 1605 included 'setting up stands for wine and beer in the Cellar and buttery'.

The wine-cellar, seen in Plate 9, was, for the visitor, the most striking feature revealed by the excavation; for here there were actual walls to be seen, instead of foundations and 'robber trenches' which needed explaining before the walls above them could be envisaged. The walls of the western cellar, half robbed away during demolition, had suffered further extensive damage during the laying of the sewer trench in 1933, so that only a few feet of the north and south walls remained. The wine-cellar, however, was comparatively little damaged. It was filled with demolition rubble, from which many fragments of bottles and flasks were recovered. It measured 68 ft. by 18 ft.

Stone steps, as seen on the right in Plate 9, led into each cellar from the Outward courtyard, and no other means of access was discovered during the excavation; but it seems reasonable to assume that there may have been a wooden staircase from the floor above. The cellar steps were extensively repaired in 1620, loose stones being reset and worn stones replaced, and a new door was fitted. During the same year the pavement of the Outward Court round the top of the cellar steps was taken up, the ground raised and the pavement re-laid "with a better currente". The cellar walls, still standing, in places nearly 7 ft. high, were mainly of Merton stone, interspersed with shaped blocks of chalk and with bricks. Many of the blocks of stone, although they presented a smooth surface to the cellar, were in fact carved, the edge of the smooth surface showing the shape of the hidden moulding. In two cases the masons had set Norman roundels with the carved surface outwards; one of these is illustrated on Plate 3 (d). Masons' marks abounded, and on one stone was a roughly scratched caricature of a head with a hat, or possibly a crown, perched on top. Holes in the walls showed where the racks had stood; the new installation of 1605 was augmented in 1620 by "shelfes" and stands for beer, and in 1626 the stands in the buttery and wine-cellar were mended and new shelves put up. Except round the walls where the racks had been, the wine-cellar floor was cobbled, and gulleys ran down the sides and middle to a soakaway at the eastern end. Provision was made for washing vessels, running water being taken to the cellar in a lead pipe, with a tap by the cellar door. The hole in the wall near the cellar steps through which this pipe ran, and the channel in the cobbles of the Outward Court from which the pipe had been removed during the demolition, were seen during the excavation.

The excavation revealed a few rectangular spaces in the facing stones of the cellar walls, at about the same level as the Inner Court paving: and these will have held beams supporting the floor above. Unfortunately, the cellar walls had been 'robbed' to a depth which was, in most places, greater than the depth at which these rectangular spaces were found, so that it was not possible to establish a regular pattern of spaces; but, either as complete rectangles or as flat stones on the same level in some of the more heavily robbed parts of the walls, sufficient remained to show their purpose. On the same level, in the west wall of the cellar (that is, the side wall of the gatehouse), was the base of a fireplace belonging to a room over the cellar.

Steeply sloping brick window-sills were found, almost on a level with the cobbles of the courtyard outside; and the Building Accounts of 1538 included the purchase of "lawnslet" windows for the cellars. The windows looked out into the Outward Court and the Kitchen Court, both of which were at a lower level than the Inner Court.

The lower 'lodgings and offices' included the Kitchen Court. The comparatively small area occupied by the Palace kitchens presented more than its share of problems, both during the research leading to the drawing of the reconstructed plan before the excavation and during the excavation itself. It is poorly documented, and pictorially, until the Danckerts painting became available after the excavation, there was little guide to the position and extent of the Kitchen Court.

Speed's view helps not at all, for where the southern face of the kitchens should be, to the right of his right-hand tower, he shows only a garden wall. In the Hoefnagel, a wall, the roofs of the three wings of the kitchens, and chimneys can be seen. Using the excavation plan and the Danckerts painting in combination gives meaning to Hoefnagel's roof pattern, even though it is not strictly accurate; but the point at which he shows the nearest wall of the kitchens joining the main building could previously only be surmised. The Kynnersley-Browne painting, from the same viewpoint as the Danckerts, the north-east, was the most useful piece of evidence then available; but it lacked contrast, making it extremely difficult to form an accurate estimate of the location and length of the walls it showed. In these circumstances it is perhaps not surprising that the main discrepancy between the pre-excavation reconstructed plan and the excavation plan should have been found here.

The kitchens were approached, from outside the Palace, by either of two doors in the 14 ft. brick wall near the north-east corner of the Outward Court (4). These gave access to a yard containing two small outbuildings, one of which can be clearly seen in the Danckerts picture, against the wall between the two doors; the other is in shadow, beyond the tree which adjoins the first outbuilding. Food supplies for the

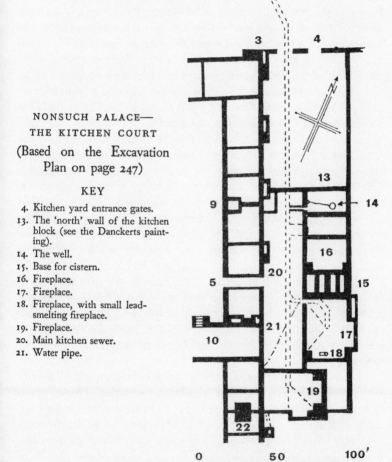

NONSUCH PALACE—
THE KITCHEN COURT

(Based on the Excavation
Plan on page 247)

KEY

4. Kitchen yard entrance gates.
13. The 'north' wall of the kitchen block (see the Danckerts painting).
14. The well.
15. Base for cistern.
16. Fireplace.
17. Fireplace.
18. Fireplace, with small lead-smelting fireplace.
19. Fireplace.
20. Main kitchen sewer.
21. Water pipe.

Palace would doubtless be delivered through this yard, and thence through an archway in the north wing of the kitchens into the court-yard beyond. This north wing, in heavy shadow in the picture, added its quota to the complexities of the area from the archaeological point of view. Although the foundations were perfectly normal (though heavily 'robbed') in the part of the wing below the flat-topped gable, the rest of the wing, to the right in the picture, was found to have existed at first-floor level only, the missing ground floor being represented by the archway. Moreover, although foundations were found for the front wall through which the archway ran (13), no trace was ever discovered of a rear wall or even of supports for an arch. Yet it does not seem feasible for this rear face to have been entirely open, at ground-floor level, to the kitchen courtyard, without at least some thickening of the walls down to foundation level to support a 25 ft. arch. Such an arrangement, without supports, can be seen in kitchen yards in mansions built fifty or a hundred years ago; but in these the weight of the first floor is carried on a girder.

The ground both inside and outside the north wall of the kitchens contained a deposit in which small animal and poultry bones, oyster shells, charcoal and small metal objects of various kinds were found. The kitchen courtyard was cobbled, and below it ran a main sewer: a brick-and-stone-lined tunnel 2 ft. 6 in. high (20). The upper end of this sewer-vault, near the cellar, had been broken in during demolition, and only the floor remained. The generous size of the tunnel was not due to the need to accommodate a great flow of water. A good deal of solid kitchen refuse would find its way into it. Liquid sewage would wash some of the solids away, but from time to time the sewers had to be cleared out, by workmen with the delightful title of "mazer-scowrers" who on at least one occasion employed a boy to crawl into the sewer. No doubt arrangements would be made for the sewer to collect rainwater from nearby roofs as an additional means of flushing it.

The main wing of the kitchens was that behind the gable, already mentioned, which can be seen in the Danckerts picture. This wing ran from north to south for a distance of 135 ft. Its eastern wall is the long, sunlit wall nearest to the observer in Danckerts' view. In the most northerly room (14) a remarkably fine well was discovered quite late in the excavation. It had lost about 3 ft. of its upper courses, but there remained a 27 ft. shaft of Caen stone, as smooth and perfect in its symmetry as when it was new. The bottom consisted of a large disc of stout oak, with a circular hole in the middle. Water was drawn from the well by means of a pump in the kitchens, and a length of the perforated lead pipe feeding the pump was found in the well. On demolition the shaft had been filled up, partly with soil and partly with

Palace building stone. The stone included a number of large pieces of balustrading and mullions, as well as decoratively carved blocks. Below this filling was an interesting collection of occupation rubbish, which must have given the water a subtle flavour all its own: several pewter plates, pierced with square holes as though the kitchen lads had used them as targets and then taken fright and slipped them into the well; animal and poultry bones; pieces of leather; a tiny toy book made of wood, and several pieces of black, rotting oak.

The well, however, was a secondary water supply, the main supply being piped from the cistern in the south-west tower, described in Chapter 5. The channel for the pipe was found crossing the southern part of the cobbled kitchen courtyard at an angle (21), and entering the main block of the kitchens near the middle. Here the excavators found a complex series of 'robber trenches' which, when they had been cleared, were interpreted as the trenches where the foundations of supports for a storage cistern had been (15). In the next room, on the southern side, was a subsidiary drain, feeding into the main kitchen sewer, and a recess for a great fireplace (18). At right-angles to this, another fireplace backed on to the outside wall (17). In the first recess was found a stone bowl set in a circle of bricks, with a short, 1 ft. wide brick channel leading from it. The bowl still contained ashes, and fragments of lead mixed with them suggested that the structure had been used for smelting the lead salvaged from the building, and that it might well have been specially made for that purpose. Two of the walls of the last room on this side, at the south-east corner of the kitchens, consisted of the fire-backs of the cooking ranges in other rooms. The room was L-shaped, the 5 ft. wide cross-piece of the L being an entry from the kitchen courtyard. The southern wing of the kitchens (19), linking the main kitchen block with the outside wall of the Inner Court, contained only one large room on the ground floor. Under the floor of this room the main kitchen sewer began. The function of the various rooms is mentioned only by the Parliamentary surveyors, and once again it is impossible to tell whether they are following any particular order in listing the rooms. However, it may perhaps be assumed that they begin with the last-mentioned room, in the southern wing, and work back towards the well. They found 'a fair and large livery kitchen, a pastry room, a boiling house'; they make no mention of the cistern, but continue with 'a bottle house, a "Cole" house and seven rooms for officers of the kitchen and

pastry'. The 'seven rooms' would be living and sleeping quarters on
the first floor. In earlier years, one of the kitchens, presumably the
'livery kitchen', was referred to as the 'great' kitchen. In 1600 some of
the paving stones on the floor were renewed and others were replaced
by bricks. At the same time the 'mouths' and 'roofs' of the ovens in
the Pastry were repaired with bricks, and they were re-paved with
160 square feet of Reigate stone; but the bottoms of the ovens in both
the Great Kitchen and the Pastry had to be taken up again seven years
later.

In the Danckerts picture, above the near corner of the garden wall,
chimneys can be seen. These appear to be on the outside wall, and
would doubtless serve first-floor rooms and the kitchen fireplace
which backed on to this wall (17). In the position where chimneys
might be expected for the two main cooking ranges, backing on to
the L-shaped room (18, 19), there is a domed turret, similar in architectural style to the bell turret over the clock. Unlike the bell turret,
however, the sides of this turret are closed. It is difficult to know what
purpose it served. It may have been merely decorative, or a means of
access to the roof for repairs and cleaning out gutters; it may have
been farther away from the observer than it appears to be, near the
junction of the east and central wings of the main building, in which
case it could possibly have been over the Chapel.

From the long, narrow kitchen courtyard, the passageway through
the east wing (5) led back to the Outward Court. On the left was the
central block of the main building, containing the cellar. This block
belonged to the Inner rather than to the Outward Court. The north
wall of the central block, then, was the back wall of the Inner Court;
and in a very real sense the Inner Court was turning its back on its
neighbour. The Outward Court was built in a style with which
Englishmen had been familiar for generations, but the Inner Court was
the real 'None such', the nonpareil. The mediaeval atmosphere of the
Outward Court gave little hint of the Renaissance splendour of the
royal apartments, which were approached by climbing the "assent of
eight stepps" to the north face of the Inner Gatehouse, illustrated on
Plate 7 (b).

5

The Inner Court

THE royal apartments were reached through the Inner Gatehouse, a striking edifice in the centre of the whole area covered by the Palace, built and adorned with such art and skill that Cromwell's men considered it to be a special ornament to the Palace. The eight steps up to the northern face of the gatehouse led to an archway, which could be closed by folding gates. It may have been here, 'above the doors of the Inner Court', that Thomas Platter saw statues of three Roman emperors. The far end of this archway is just visible in Speed's engraving, which shows the southern face of the gatehouse (Plate 11 (a)). The gatehouse was of stone, three storeys high, with octagonal turrets at the corners. It was appreciably smaller than the Outer Gatehouse, being only 35 ft. wide. In the Speed engraving its width is much exaggerated, whereas Hoefnagel considerably reduces its height in relation to the visible roof of the central block. Hoefnagel's view is, in fact, so much at variance with the other pictures of the gatehouse that some explanation ought to be attempted. He shows the octagonal turrets so dwarfed that they cannot be seen, although in fact they were higher than the ridge of the adjacent roof, a Muscovite dome instead of a cupola, and a huge rosette surmounted by battlements where the clock should be. It is possible that Arundel increased the height of the gatehouse after Hoefnagel's visit in 1568; yet all that Anthony Watson, anxious as he was to give praise where it was due, could say of Arundel's work was that he had set up a lofty hollow tower on top of the gatehouse, and he gives no hint of any addition to the main structure of the gatehouse itself. It seems more likely that Hoefnagel's sketches and memory failed him when he came to complete his drawing, so that he had to guess the height and to repeat, on the gatehouse, the dome and windowed turret which topped each of the towers on the main south front.

The gatehouse was roofed in lead, and on the roof stood the clock chamber covered with lead. In 1607 the 'Clockhouse' was in a bad state of repair, and had to be 'forced up with screws to set it upright'; as well as needing new lead in various places. Of the clock itself we have no information, except for the names of the six Frenchmen working on the clock at Nonsuch in 1544. From the Fitzwilliam picture and the repair accounts we know that the clock dials were painted a light blue, and the hands and figures were gilded. The clock chimed each half-hour. Arundel's 'hollow tower', which Anthony Watson and Speed lead us to believe held a chime of bells, seems to have contained only one large bell when the Fitzwilliam picture was painted, and the 1650 surveyors saw only one. Above it was a weather-vane, which was painted during the reign of James I in blue and gold, with the letters 'J R' and a crown, three knots and three acorns. Hoef-nagel shows a mast and pennant at each corner above the level of the clock. Speed replaces the masts by king's beasts, and adds another tier of them round the bell-chamber. The Fitzwilliam picture, probably painted about ten years after the publication of Speed's engraving, shows neither pennants nor beasts on the gatehouse.

The corner turrets so clearly seen in Speed's version of the gate-house rested on solid bases, but the other two, facing into the Outward Court, stood, like those in the northern face of the Outer Gatehouse, over garderobe pits (Plate 12 (b)). From these many interesting objects were recovered during the excavation, including three completely undamaged sack bottles.

The southern face of the gatehouse was in marked contrast to the northern face, which matched the castle-like appearance of the Out-ward Court. Below the battlements on the southern face was a sundial, covering an area of $8\frac{1}{2}$ sq. yds. The figures were on a rectangular stone surround, and above this rectangle was a triangular compartment of stone containing a carved or painted death's head. The figures were gold, the face of the dial light blue and the rest 'stone colour shadowed'. The three oriel windows below the dial were much admired by Anthony Watson. The stonework above and below the lights was carved with the 'living image' of plants, trees, deer, birds, lions and men, and with the insignia of Henry VIII, Arundel and Lumley. The insignia would presumably have been on the corbels, although Speed contrives to make these look remarkably like faces.

Anthony Watson, standing with his back to the gatehouse, was well-nigh 'struck senseless' by the splendour of the scene in front of him. The inward-facing walls of the ground floor of the Inner Court were of stone, and the storey above was of timbered construction. Between the main timbers the spaces were occupied by plaster panels, decorated with a tremendous variety of Classical motifs which Watson describes at great length. The decorative panels on these inner walls appear to have been in three bands or orders, two of which can be seen on either side of the gatehouse in the Speed engraving. These two orders contained figures of gods and goddesses, the labours of Hercules, floral panels and insignia. Below them were panels representing the arts and virtues. Cromwell's surveyors found the Inner Court a 'fair and very curious structure' with the higher storey 'richly adorned'. Neither they nor Anthony Watson describe the outside walls, facing the gardens, in detail, but the Hoefnagel and Speed engravings show that the description of the inner walls applies equally to the outer, except that here the panels extend almost to ground level, even though the walls behind them, up to first-floor level, may have been of stone.

Thousands of fragments of these panels were found during the excavation, confirming some of the things which have been written about them and correcting others. The panels themselves averaged 2 in. in thickness and were as hard as stone, as, indeed, some contemporary observers, including Thomas Platter, thought they were. The backs of the panels still showed the impression of wood-grain from planks; this, and the fact that the stucco-workers were known as 'mouldmakers', might be thought to indicate that the panels were cast in wooden moulds on the ground and put up in position when they were dry. It seems more likely, however, that they were moulded *in situ*, with planks forming a backing sheet for the wet plaster instead of using wattles or laths. This would make some form of fixing necessary, and many dowel-holes were in fact found in the plaster fragments. Some of the dowels had undoubtedly been used as supports round which the thicker parts of the designs had been moulded, and square-section wood and very large nails had also been used as rudimentary 'armatures'. In the thicker parts the plaster, which, even with retarding agents, dried very quickly, had been put on layer by layer until the desired thickness was obtained. Some of the final shaping was almost certainly done by carving after the plaster had set. A few of the pieces found had a quarter-inch coating of fine plaster, free from coarse sand.

The designs on the panels could not be described as 'bass-relievos' or 'mezzo-relievos', as Evelyn called them, but as 'alto-relievos'. A Roman soldier was in such high relief that the plaster was in places over 9 in. thick, and the leg and hoof of a fawn were so nearly in the round that the next stage would have been complete separation from the background. The Roman, although only about half of him was found, was not, as Evelyn recorded, 'as big as the life', but about three-quarters life-size. Cherubs, angels' wings, beautifully slender hands and feet, rams' heads in very high relief, the head of a horse, fragments of lettering and swags of flowers and fruit, all 'of excellent art and workmanship', were found, smashed and used as filling-in rubble when the foundations were levelled off after the destruction of the building. They, more than anything else, drove home a full realization of the ruthlessness and wantonness of those who pulled down the Palace; for, whatever we may think of the building as a whole, the Nonsuch stuccoes were unique and priceless treasures, as works of art, as a colossal three-tiered decorative scheme covering at least 900 ft. of wall, and as the most important and striking component in the adornment of the first English building to be decorated largely in the Renaissance manner.

The Nonsuch plaster decorations were undoubtedly inspired by the stucco in the Galerie François Ier at Fontainebleau, although we have no record of any transfer of craftsmen from there specifically to work on the plaster at Nonsuch. Kendall and Giles Gering are the only two supervisors or overseers mentioned in the accounts, but it seems highly probable that the person responsible for the whole design and for its similarity to the work at Fontainebleau was the painter, carver and stuccatore, Nicholas Modena. With Kendall, Gering and their 'companies' of 'mouldmakers' interpreting in plaster his ideas for the decorative panels, Nicholas kept in his own hands the delicate work of carving, in slate, motifs similar in style to woodcarvings at Fontaine-bleau, to be hung as frames round the plaster panels.

Slate has been carved since the Archaic period of Egyptian history; in this country, during the eighteenth and early nineteenth centuries, it was very much in vogue for tombstones. The Nonsuch slate, how-ever, was in a class of its own, for nowhere else is carved slate known to have been used at any time on such a scale for the exterior decoration of a building. Unusual, at this date, as a decorative medium; unusual, at any time, in the method in which it was employed at Nonsuch; and new and striking in the manner of its decoration: it is not too much to claim that the Nonsuch slate, like the stucco work, was unique. The main timbers of the Inner Court building, both vertical and horizontal, were hung with panels of slate, primarily as a protection from the weather. The fragments of the panels which were found during the excavation were in some cases as much as an inch in thickness, and they were deeply carved within a moulded edging similar to the moulding of a picture frame. Some of the designs had been in such high relief that they appeared to have necessitated the use of two thicknesses of slate; in some cases this effect may merely have been due to lamination caused by dampness during their long burial in the demolition rubble; but in others the outlines of designs were found scratched on thick background panels, from which the added layers bearing the designs themselves had become separated during or after demolition. On some panels, instead of a design carved in relief, the motif had been incised in the flat surface. Many of the designs had been gilded, and traces of gilt were still discernible on some of the pieces recovered during the excavation. Guide lines, and written instructions, for those who would actually do the work of fixing the panels after they had been carved, were scratched on the edges and backs of the panels. The instructions were written in French, and among the fragments found was one inscribed *Troisiesme pillier* and another . . . *le masson*. As with the plaster, the style of decoration of the slate was entirely Renaissance. Trophies, birds, fruit and flowers, crowns, grotesques, flaming torches and small scrolls were much in evidence, as was the *guilloche*, an ornament much used in Classical architectural decoration and consisting of intertwining ribbon-like bands giving the effect of a flat chain of circular links. Of equal interest, however, from the point of view of architectural history, were the heavy timbers at the angles of the octagonal towers, and some of the timbers at intervals along the south front. In the Hoefnagel view, these have at first glance the appearance of rainwater pipes with ornamental hopper-heads; but Martin Biddle has pointed out that they may have been carved timbers designed to give the effect of pilasters. From the decorative use of these possible imitation pilasters at Nonsuch, it would be but a short step to their architectural use on later Renaissance buildings in England.

The general effect was that of a continuous gallery of high-relief pictures in dazzling white (the white plaster was even whitewashed on occasion). There is no evidence to support the statements which have appeared from time to time to the effect that the panels were painted, or that there were amongst them, as Pepys recorded, flat painted panels. The panels were framed in gilded slate, which was carved in the workshop of a master craftsman. The tools he used were almost certainly those of the woodcarver, and the slate has been identified with reasonable certainty as being imported from France, possibly from the great slate-quarries near Angers.

One other decorative medium must be mentioned: pieces of terra-cotta were found, two of which fitted together to form a chin surmounted by a very Roman nose. The effect was closely similar to that of the terra-cotta roundels or medallions at Hampton Court, which contain likenesses of Roman emperors. The Nonsuch terra-cotta fragments could have come from the three 'statues' of Roman emperors which Thomas Platter saw 'above the doors of the Inner Court'. The so-called statues could have been medallions or relief busts; or, conceivably, terra-cotta could have been the medium used for the thirty-one Roman emperors whom Anthony Watson saw portrayed as part of the 'highest order' of the decoration of the Inner Court.

To turn now from the magnificent scheme of exterior decoration to a consideration of the building itself, the walls surrounding the Inner courtyard had a deeply serrated roof-line, formed by a continuous series of gables. Some of these may be seen in Speed's engraving; there were in fact thirty-two of them, painted white, each of them measuring 26½ sq. yds. The wings of the building to left and right each had two semicircular bay windows, at the middle and the farther end of each wing (23). Symmetry demands that there should have been a third bay on each side near the junction with the central block, but here its place was taken by a doorway. Straight across the courtyard from the gatehouse, at first-floor level (24), was a closed balcony, painted in 1631 'fair blue', the knobs and "Bentalles" gilded, the cartouches partly coloured and partly painted in blue and gold, the groundwork white with 'antique' decoration and the window frames stone-coloured. Near the balcony, and possibly below it, was the likeness of Henry VIII, enthroned and with his foot resting on a lion, which Watson saw. This may have been a statue or part of the plaster mural decorations; certainly, for Watson, it was the centrepiece which gave meaning to the whole decorative scheme. 'Can harm befall the body politic,' he asks, 'when its most sagacious king, wielding

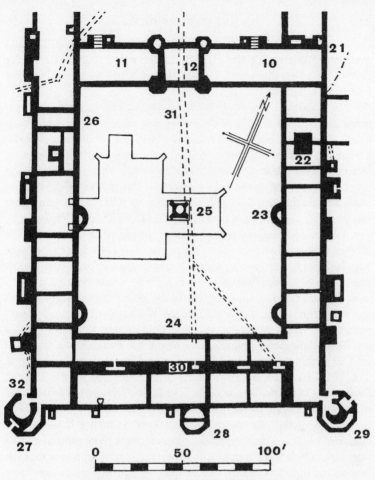

NONSUCH PALACE—THE INNER COURT

(Based on the Excavation Plan on page 247)

KEY

10. The wine-cellar.
11. Cellar, probably the Buttery.
12. Inner Gatehouse.
22. Base of staircase, Queen's Side.
23. Bay window.
24. Position of Balcony (first floor).
25. Fountain.
26. Probable position of entrance to King's Side.
27. South-west tower.
28. Central bay.
29. South-east tower.
30. Thick internal wall containing garderobes and fireplaces.
31. Sewer.
32. Door giving the King access to garden.

the sceptre, is protected, on the right, by the arts and virtues and avenging goddesses, on the left by the feats of Hercules and the tender care of the gods; that he may act always in affairs without danger, in leisure with dignity?'

The courtyard which the 1650 surveyors had recorded as measuring 137 ft. by 116 ft. was shown by the excavation to have been 134 ft. 6 in. from north to south and 115 ft. 6 in. from east to west. Unlike the Outward Court, it was entirely paved with flagstones. In Watson's time the stones were from 'Newcastle that graces the river Tyne'. Some of the stones were replaced by Purbeck stone in 1615 and 1616, and further repairs were carried out in 1622. Seven years later the whole of the paving was taken up; 8,585 sq. ft. were replaced by new Purbeck paving and 6,792 sq. ft. of the old stone were re-laid. It is to be wondered whether the people who trod these stones, or those who laid them, ever gave a thought to the gruesome 'hard-core' below the soil on which the flagstones rested; for the whole courtyard stood over the graveyard of Cuddington. In the centre of the courtyard was the magnificent fountain described by Watson (25). The 1650 surveyors are more mundane in their description: Watson's golden griffins become brass dragons, and below the fountain is a cistern of lead set within a frame of white marble, with an ascent of three steps. Yet Watson's account of it tallies with a picture in the Lumley Inventories in the possession of the Earl of Scarbrough; it is reproduced in the sixth volume of the publications of the Walpole Society. The inventories, listing the contents of all Lord Lumley's houses, were compiled in 1590. They begin with nineteen pages of pictures of marble furniture. These were thought, in general terms, to represent items at Nonsuch; but it was Martin Biddle who, when the pictures first came into our hands shortly after we had been working on Anthony Watson's manuscript, recognized one sketch as agreeing with Watson's description of the Inner Court fountain. From there it was an easy step to link up Watson and the 1650 Survey with several of the other sketches.

Interesting though the picture is, it hardly lives up to Watson's glowing phrases, and fails to convey an impression of great size or magnificence. He tells us that it excels Arethusa (a fountain on the island of Ortygia, near Syracuse) in richness of marble and height of jet. At the top is a noble horse (emblem of the Arundels) holding a graven stone with one hoof. The bowl over which the horse stands is supported by a stone held by three slender maidens with milk-white bodies; in this stone are little water-pipes which produce a pleasing murmur. The bowl below the maidens is held by two golden griffins, and a great force of water pours from their mouths into the lead cistern, which is surrounded by ivory marble.

The water-pipes feeding this and the other fountains were constantly under repair, and in 1623 Nicholas Stone was paid £22 for completely dismantling the fountain, polishing the marble, repairing it where necessary and re-erecting it. Below ground level was the brick-built base shown on the plan, with its circular cavity for the lead cistern. This base was below what had been the floor of the chancel of Cuddington Church, and the sewer into which waste water from the fountain discharged cut through the north and south walls of the chancel.

The outside walls of the Inner Court are shown in the four pictures of the Palace. In the Fitzwilliam painting (frontispiece) we have the only view of the west wall. The detail is not sufficiently clear to show whether there were plaster and slate decorations on this wall. The blue-slate pitched roof ran down to purely ornamental overhanging battlements; they were made of wood covered with lead, and supported by strong bars of iron which were also covered in lead. The battlements were surmounted by the king's beasts with vanes. In 1624 John de Creete painted ninety-one 'beasts' on the battlements and Banqueting House, eighty-three of which had been cleaned and set upright by a carpenter in the previous year. Brick chimney-stacks were built at intervals on the outside face of the west wall; in most cases these coincided with garderobes. The Nonsuch skyline bristled with chimneys; there were at least eighty-five of them.

The south front, depicted by Hoefnagel and Speed, is the most familiar aspect of Nonsuch. Flanked by two octagonal towers (27, 29), it had a total length of 200 ft. The towers, the 'chief ornament' of the Palace, were five storeys high, and were surmounted by a lead-covered turret or lantern. In all the views except that by Hoefnagel, and in the 1650 Survey, the towers are battlemented. Their height is nowhere recorded, and the listing of 80 ft. timbers hewn for their 'principal pieces' must refer to cubic rather than linear measure. Not all of the exposed timbers in the towers were covered in slate. We read of the painting 'white lead colour' on one occasion and 'lead colour' on another, of the pedestals, columns and plates on the turrets. Unfortunately,

the compilers of the repair accounts used the words 'turret' and
'tower' indiscriminately, so that repairs which at first sight appear
to have been minor operations on the lanterns may in fact have
involved major structural work on the main towers. Between 1607 and
April, 1609, carpenters made four pedestals and six columns 'canted
8 ways' for the 'staying and strengthening of the timberwork in the
turret on the queen's side', but a few months later both turrets had to
be remade. Below the turrets, presumably on the widest part of the
towers, there was wainscot painted 'lead colour in oil' adjacent to the
plasterwork. The weather-vane and lion on the west turret, seen in the
Danckerts painting to be leaning at a perilous angle, had given trouble
thirty years earlier, when they had to be set upright and strengthened
with timber and iron. From Speed's view, there appear to have been
no windows in the outside walls of the ground floor of the towers, and
even on the rest of this frontage the ground-floor windows are small
and set very high. Both Speed and Hoefnagel have taken a permissible
liberty with the half-octagonal bay in the middle of the frontage (28),
by placing it, as it ought to have been, in the centre. In fact the
excavation showed that it was some 9 ft. to the right of the central
point. In both views the battlements, with their masts and pennants,
can be clearly seen. Speed makes the slates on the roof look like tiles.

The degree of accuracy of these two views of the Palace has
already been discussed, but may now be considered further. In relation
to both the Speed and the excavation plan, Hoefnagel's view appears
to exaggerate the length of this frontage, but this is because the Privy
Garden wall hides the whole of the ground floor. The excavation
showed that the total length of this frontage, including the towers, was
200 ft. If we assume that the ground-floor level roughly coincided with
the lowest level of the ground outside the garden wall in the Hoefnagel
view, we find that the height from that level to just below the battlements is 5/32 of the length of the frontage. This is equivalent to 30 ft.,
which seems reasonable. A similar calculation makes the approximate
height of the towers to the base of the domes, that is, the five storeys
plus the lanterns, 75 ft. The proportions in Hoefnagel's view thus
appear to be reasonably accurate. This may perhaps be regarded as
making it all the more regrettable that he appears to have allowed his
imagination to run riot when he drew the domes on top of the towers,
since none of the other three views shows this type of dome.

Apart from the evidence revealed by the excavation, our authority

for the appearance of the eastern wall is the Danckerts painting
(Plate 5). In general, it matches the west wall, except that the masts
and pennants have not survived the Commonwealth. One noticeable
feature is, however, that no brick chimney-stacks are shown against the
face of the wall, although there were five on the west wall of this court.
The few chimneys which are shown rise from inside the battlements.
The plan shows that the arrangement of garderobes with chimney-
stacks, and chimney-stacks alone (the solid blocks protruding from the
wall-line), was roughly the same on the east and west walls. So that, if
the accuracy of this part of Danckerts' picture is accepted, it can only
be assumed that the flues were in their more usual place, inside the
walls, and that this was done to improve the appearance of the Palace
on its more exposed side facing the avenue leading from Cheam.

The foundations of the Inner Court building were, like those of
the Outward Court, a mixture of chalk blocks and carved stone,
although the foundations of the south wall were altogether lighter and
shallower in construction. In the south-eastern corner the outside east
wall had been completely robbed for a distance of 20 ft., and only the
lower part of the foundations of the south-east tower remained. The
southern part of its perimeter was partly edged with curved pieces of
stone window tracery. Many pieces of moulding, a huge carved boss
painted red and gilded, a lion gargoyle and a female head, all assumed
to have come from Merton, were found and added to the collection of
more portable 'finds'; they are illustrated on Plate 3. The boss, estimated to weigh 4½ cwt., would once have adorned the vaulted roof
of Merton Priory church. Next to it in the Palace foundations was the
lion, carved in the late fifteenth century; after the unceremonious
treatment it received in 1538, and after spending more than four
centuries resting on the flattened top of its head, it was in a remarkably
good state of preservation, even its teeth being intact. Everywhere the
exposed tops and sides of foundation walls showed pieces of Merton
stone, and the amount removed for record purposes in 1959 was only
a small fraction of the whole.

The smaller rectangles on or near the outside walls on the
excavation plan, particularly those on the south wall, were brick-lined
soakaways for rainwater. In the one nearest the south-east tower the
first of the carved slate fragments were found. On the solid bed below
the central bay the mason's inscribed setting-out lines could be clearly
seen, marking a half-octagon for the outside face of the wall and a

circle for the inside. The south-west tower foundations (27) were virtually complete up to ground-floor level; in fact some of the flooring itself remained: tiles on the area at the foot of the main staircase, where doors led into the garden and into the main building, and bricks on what appeared to be the below-stairs approach to a garderobe. On the western side of the Inner Court the remaining foundations were in marked contrast to the 'robber trenches' found on the corresponding side of the Outward Court. They stood so high, so near the surface, that the chalk blocks were deeply incised by the ploughshare, the plantation which at present covers this part of the site being of comparatively recent date.

Along the middle of the south wing ran the foundations of a massive wall (30), thicker than any other wall in the Palace. The wall which stood on these foundations divided the ground floor into 'front' and 'back' rooms. In the thickness of this internal wall four garderobe pits were discovered, and there may have been a fifth under the modern roadway. This seems an extraordinary place for such necessary evils, which would have to be emptied from time to time; but they would have been even more out of place either on the southern façade or on the inside wall of the court. Three of the four shown on the plan have an outlet channel, and in two cases the brick-lined drains from them were found; but the outlets were some 2 ft. above the floor level of the pits. The drain in line with the central bay continued past the fountain, where it widened (31), through the middle of the Inner Gatehouse, across the Outward Court, through the Outer Gatehouse and so down the avenue, as a brick vault, to join the outflow from the Long Ditch.

The functions of the various rooms in the Inner Court building raise just the same difficulty as do those of the Outward Court: it is known what rooms there were, but in most cases their location is far from clear. After examining the existing evidence, there is still considerable scope for conjecture. Neville Williams, in *The Royal Residences of Great Britain*, gives an excellent account of the layout of a typical palace, and of the duties of the various officers; but it would be unwise to fill in the gaps in the Nonsuch evidence from this source, for there can be no doubt that the comparative smallness of Nonsuch led to a number of departures from the usual layout.

The royal apartments were on the first floor, the 'King's side' being on the west and the 'Queen's side' on the east, with the privy gallery in the southern wing. On the ground floor most of the accommodation was occupied by people in the service of the queen. Apart from the guard chamber and two rooms for the Master of the Horse, there were, in the years before 1650, two rooms for Madam Nurse; two for Madam Vautlet, the queen's dresser; two rooms for the queen's priests; two for the queen's robes; and two for the queen's equerries. One room was "called the Queenes backstayres". Lady Cary, Dr. Myerne, Madam Conget and Madam Cyvet each had two rooms.

Statues guarded the entrances to the east and west wings of the Inner Court. On the king's side (26) was Scipio, outside the guard chamber (presumably where the west wing joined the central block), and Penthesilea faced Scipio across the courtyard, guarding the entrance to the queen's side. On the plan, a little below the junction between the central and eastern wings, the solid rectangle (22) marks the foundations of the queen's staircase. On the king's side, a wide, winding staircase led from the guard chamber to a waiting room adjoining the presence chamber. The 'Presence' was a large room where, in 1599, Thomas Platter, waiting for Elizabeth to appear, noted the contrast between the tapestried walls and the straw covering the floor, and the carpeted path in 'Turkish Knot' leading to the queen's red-damask chair under a canopy fixed to the ceiling. Farther on were the privy closet and the privy chamber, the closet being a small room for private interviews; it and another small room not mentioned by Watson occupied only part of the width of the wing, leaving a wide space between it and the wall on the courtyard side as the 'dignified approach' to the privy chamber. In the privy chamber, where the king would normally take his meals, was a fountain described by Watson, and presumably used as a drinking fountain. Water trickled from the mouth of a silver serpent, which was under the foot of a lion; the water fell into a decorated black bowl.

In his tour of the building Watson has now travelled down the west wing to a point near the south-west tower. From the privy chamber onwards, however, his description of the sequence of rooms is impossible to follow unless all preconceived ideas about the size of the privy gallery are abandoned; for he appears to put the king's bedchamber, and possibly two other rooms, in the south wing, with the gallery behind them. The gallery has always been assumed to have occupied the entire length and width of the south wing, which would have made it abnormally wide (35 ft.) for its length, the distance

between the inner faces of the towers being 160 ft. The Queen's
Gallery at Hampton Court in Henry's time measured 180 ft. by 25 ft.,
and this was wider than most galleries. Watson may be interpreted as
placing the bedchamber and other rooms in the front of the south
wing and the gallery at the back of the wing, overlooking the courtyard, and the gallery would extend, not between the towers but
between the inner faces of the east and west wings, a distance of
120 ft. Assuming that the thick interior wall along the ground floor of
the southern wing (30) supported a wall on the first floor, the gallery
could have been upwards of 12 ft. wide, leaving 23 ft. for the thickness
of the wall, for one dimension of the royal bedchamber and the outer
wall. The reason for the thick interior wall would be the need to
accommodate garderobe chutes (the 'Stoolhouses about the privy
lodge' were provided with new mats in 1600) and chimney-breasts for
both floors; and, in both the Hoefnagel and Speed views, chimneys
appear behind the ridge of the roof over the southern wing. Further
evidence in support of this arrangement of the gallery and bedchamber
is provided by the repair accounts: in 1620 there is an entry for 'mending the slating over the long roof of the privy lodging and the gallery'
(i.e., the long roof covered both). Finally, it may be noted that the
Parliamentary surveyors describe the privy gallery as being 'over
against the south side' of the Inner Court fountain, a description which
has hitherto seemed strange but which is perfectly sensible if the
gallery is reduced to the size suggested.

Next to the privy chamber Watson describes a 'somewhat narrower
room' which gave access to the spiral staircase of the tower, on his
right as he faced south. The stairs led down to the garden or up to
the top of the five-storey tower. Each storey contained one room, and
the staircase was probably the additional structure which can be seen
in the Fitzwilliam picture, on the face of the tower nearest to the corner
of the courtyard. On the second storey was a large lead cistern, fed,
according to the Parliamentary Survey, by several pipes of lead
conveying water from a conduit some distance away.

From Watson's 'narrower room', a turn to his left took him to two
fine chambers 'more exclusively reserved for the use of the King'. He
could have reached them only by turning his back on the tower, so
that he was facing along the south front in an easterly direction.
Beyond them was the royal bedchamber, with a 'magnificent' gallery
at the back and, in front, 'a new paradise' on a small hillock, with a

marble fountain, ivory columns, painted vases of flowers and plants. It is impossible to decide whether he is here referring to the view of the garden from the front windows, or whether there was an indoor 'Paradise' similar to that in Henry's Long Gallery at Hampton Court. The wainscot in the gallery, measuring 216 sq. yds., was renewed in 1629, after two "joyners" had spent a day in 'taking the measure of the gallery'. This figure for the area of wainscoting fits in quite well with the suggested size of the gallery based on Watson's description. A modest estimate of the height of the wainscot would be 12 ft., and the 216 sq. yds would give a continuous run of 162 ft. at this height. Allowing 120 ft. for the unbroken interior wall, the remainder would be adequate for the walls surrounding the doors at the two ends of the gallery and the spaces between the windows.

The queen's apartments were dismissed by Watson in one sentence; from this, however, it can be gathered that they were adjacent to the gallery. The 1650 Survey apparently does not list all the rooms on the first floor (the waiting room and the two private rooms near the king's bedroom are not mentioned); for those which are listed, there appears to be far more space left than they could have taken up. The first-floor rooms over the wine-cellar, the east wing, and such of the south wing as was not occupied by the king, remain to be accounted for; and it is known only that in this space were the queen's bedchamber, the queen's backstairs, the queen's chapel and two rooms for the Marquess Hambleton.

To Anthony Watson, the staircase on the king's side was 'magnificently built'. The approach to the presence chamber was 'the most glorious precincts of the majestic presence'. To the bowl of the lion-and-serpent fountain had been added 'especially fine ornamentation by a perfection of art and nature'. The gallery was 'magnificent with every device and the most sumptuous appointments', comparable with the best of the 'Greek galleries'. The Parliamentary surveyors found that all the rooms in the Inner Court building were 'very fair and large', most of them wainscoted and with spacious windows guarded by iron bars.

For the rest of the interior decoration, apart from wainscoting, there is no positive evidence. It may be confidently assumed that the interior matched the exterior in magnificence, but probably not in its style and treatment; for if it had been anything like the outside it would certainly have been commented on by contemporary observers. On the assumption, then, that the interior was typical of the best of its period, the walls would be covered with richly carved wood, with pictures or with tapestry. Most of the rooms would have moulded plaster ceilings; the fireplaces would be of carved stone, with chimney-pieces of moulded plaster, carved stone or wood. Some, but by no means the majority, of the decorative motifs would be Renaissance in character.

Of all this splendour scarcely a vestige remains, even on paper; apart from the few details in Watson's manuscript, there is nothing, written, pictorial or tangible, of which it can be said with complete certainty that it describes or is part of the interior decoration of Nonsuch. Because of this, we have to fall back on evidence which ranges from the circumstantial but reasonable to the traditional and wishful.

Pride of place must be given to a few items from the excavation finds-trays. One piece of stucco was found which might well have come from an interior wall. It was only half the thickness of the exterior stucco, and, from the slight markings of wood-grain on one edge and in a narrow strip down the side of the front, it could have been adjacent to wainscoting. The beginnings of a raised design appeared at the broken edge. The ordinary plaster used for walls or ceilings was a light-grey lime mortar, containing a gritty aggregate of up to $\frac{1}{4}$ in. diameter. This plaster was $\frac{3}{4}$ in. thick, and was laid over $1\frac{3}{4}$ in. laths with $\frac{1}{4}$ to $\frac{3}{8}$ in. spaces between them. The fine white finishing coat was nearly $\frac{1}{4}$ in. thick. The windows may perhaps be included in the interior decorative scheme, for many of them were of stained glass and thus enhanced the appearance of the furniture and decoration. Many pieces of stained or painted glass were found, including fragments which together almost completed the motto *Dieu et mon droit*. Much window-lead was collected, and a great deal of plain glass. Every piece of this was carefully scrutinized, for it was known that a fragment recovered from the sewer trench in 1933 had been inscribed, presumably with a diamond ring, with a message so censorable that it had been heavily scratched out; but it still managed to embarrass the archivist who eventually deciphered it. However, nothing quite like this was discovered in 1959, although small fragments of several inscriptions were found.

The most important piece of pictorial evidence to be considered is a drawing, formerly in the Louvre but now lost, showing a design for the carved wood and stucco decoration of an interior wall. It is not known whether this design was intended for use at Nonsuch, and, if so, whether it was in fact used there, with or without modification. Attention was first drawn to this sketch by Dr. Otto Kurz, writing in the *Burlington Magazine* in April, 1943. The caption under his reproduction of the picture stated that the wall was 'probably' in Nonsuch Palace, but in the accompanying article he was less definite: "There is no way of determining for which one of the numerous residences of Henry VIII it was destined." He inclined towards Nonsuch on the grounds that it was the favourite building of Henry's last years. Sir John Summerson, in *Architecture in Britain*, was more positive. "This design," he said, was "almost certainly connected with Nonsuch"; and it was reproduced with the caption "Nonsuch Palace. Design for the decoration of a Throne Room or Presence Chamber."

The drawing, in pen and ink, can definitely be assigned to the years 1543 to 1547, as it contains Henry's name and the badge of Catherine Parr. It is clearly a design, and not a drawing of something already in existence, for it shows the left-hand half of a wall; it would be copied in reverse to complete the right-hand half. The lower half represents carved woodwork, and the upper plaster stucco. In the middle of the completed wall was to be a bench capable of seating three people. This was to be inscribed 'HENRICVS VIII' on the back of the left-hand seat and 'DIEU ET MON DROIT' on the central one. Above the central seat, a stucco coat-of-arms, surrounded by the Garter and supported by a lion on the left, filled the space between the carved woodwork and the cornice. To the left of the bench, in the carved woodwork, was the badge of Catherine—a maiden's head, crowned, rising from a Tudor rose. Beyond this was a doorway. Many of the decorative motifs which have already been described in connection with the external stucco and carved slate at Nonsuch were embodied in the design. This is, said Dr. Kurz, no mere slavish imitation by Henry VIII of the famous gallery of his royal adversary: harmony, lacking at Fontainebleau, is achieved between the two 'storeys' of the decorative scheme; the upper part is more sober than the Fontainebleau stuccoes, and the woodcarving is richer.

Yet it seems unlikely that a three-seated wall-bench would be used as a throne, which was usually 'free-standing', and Platter, writing of the Presence Chamber at Nonsuch fifty years after the design was drawn, made no mention of a wall decorated in so impressive a manner.

The apartment, he said, was hung with fine tapestries; he must surely have added 'except on the wall behind the throne' if that had been the case. Moreover, Elizabeth sat in the Presence Chamber on a seat covered with damask, the seat being so low that the cushions almost lay on the ground. On balance, it seems unlikely that this design was ever carried out at Nonsuch. It is obviously intended for a royal chamber which was being decorated during the Nonsuch building years; but the little evidence we have suggests that the Nonsuch audience chamber, the 'Presence', did not look like this.

Another drawing, in the Victoria and Albert Museum, by Etienne Delaune, shows an ornate fireplace which would not have been out of place at Nonsuch. The fireplace is very lofty, being nearly four times as high as the width of the recess for the fire; it is decorated with angels holding shields, female figures, pilasters, pinnacles and a great deal of tracery similar to that on some of the Loseley panels. Someone at some time has written, at the bottom of the drawing, "Fire Place in Council Room at Queen Elizabeth's Palace of Nonsuch", but with what authority is not known. Certainly the bold statement in similar vein in Manning and Bray's *Surrey*, in the caption to their picture of an ornate carved chimney-piece at Reigate Priory, is no longer accepted. At Loseley there is carved panelling and a series of painted canvas panels, both supposed to have come from Nonsuch; but it has never been explained how and when they could have been removed from the Palace and installed at Loseley. The connection between the Mores of Loseley and Nonsuch was through Sir Thomas Cawarden, who ceased to be Keeper of the Palace six years before the building of Loseley began. Sir William More was Cawarden's executor, but it seems too much to suggest that Sir Thomas' effects included panelling taken from a building for the safe-keeping of which he was being paid a salary. Whatever may have been the origin of the carved wooden panels at Loseley (and they are very fine, the carving, only a quarter of an inch deep, producing a remarkable 'vista' effect), the painted canvas panels could have come from Cawarden, but not from him as Keeper of Nonsuch. He held the important office of Master of the Revels, and in this capacity frequently had to commission painted canvases for use on temporary banqueting houses or as stage properties for masques. Anthony Toto, both before and after he became Serjeant Painter in 1543, was responsible for a good deal of this work, both in the actual execution of it and in the drawing of designs for subordinates to complete. It seems perfectly feasible that Cawarden should have felt that some of these canvases were too good to be scrapped after they had fulfilled their purpose; and so the panels, quite possibly painted or designed by Toto, could have gone to Cawarden's executor.

In the Lumley Chapel in Cheam, the tomb of Jane Fitzalan, Lady Lumley, has relief alabaster panels showing Jane and her children, kneeling in rooms which are said to represent Nonsuch interiors. This may well be so, for through an open doorway can be seen an obelisk very similar to one which graced the Privy Garden at Nonsuch; but the carvings show no details of interior decoration or furnishings.

Other reputed relics of the interior of Nonsuch include two herms which now form the jambs of a bedroom fireplace at Pitt Place in Epsom, and part of a wooden staircase, panels and several wooden door-surrounds at Thames Ditton. The Pitt Place relics have a possible link with the Palace, which was demolished during the Keepership of the 1st Earl of Berkeley, who is believed to have rebuilt Durdans in Epsom with salvaged material from Nonsuch. When this was destroyed, the then owner is said to have used salvaged material in the building of Pitt Place. The Thames Ditton staircase and panels reached their present home twenty-five years ago from a summer-house in Cheam, and the door-surrounds from an old house in Norfolk; but it is quite impossible to say whether there is any foundation for the tradition that they originally came from Nonsuch.

Nearly all these reputed survivals of Nonsuch, then, still need further evidence before they can be accepted as valid. Some, or indeed all of them, may be authentic; but at present they lack proof, and it would be misleading to introduce them as factual into a documented account of the Palace.

Two other features of the Inner Court building remain to be considered. The cistern in the south-west tower (27) has been mentioned earlier. From it pipes ran to all parts of the Palace and to the fountains. At the conduit head, half a mile to the south, the spring water mentioned in the 1537 View and Survey of Cuddington fed ten wells of varying depth. In 1622 these were lined with bricks and enclosed in a vault lined with moss, and an adjacent cistern was repaired. An unsuccessful attempt was made in 1960 to locate the supply pipes at their point of entry into the south-west tower.

It was at this corner of the building, at the back of the south-west tower (32), that the king had access to the Privy Garden, and there was presumably a similar exit from the queen's side behind the south-east tower. Another doorway, not mentioned in any of the records, is shown in the Speed engraving, at the western side of the central bay; and he also faintly suggests similar doors at the foot of each of the towers near their junction with the main front wall. Speed's garden frontage—and our knowledge of the appearance of the ground floor of the south front depends entirely on him—includes one feature about which many different theories have been put forward. Between the central bay and the left-hand tower a large platform juts out from the wall and is supported on five pillars. This was for a long time thought to be a stage. It was then suggested that it might have been a mounting-platform for the royal coach, the incongruity of having a coach and horses driving through the Privy Garden and up to the ornate show-frontage being explained away by the need to have a more convenient mounting-place than the Outer Gatehouse. In 1959 the stand on top of the platform, tiny though it is in the engraving, was confidently identified as a *nef*, a stand for wine, in the shape of a sailing ship.

There is now sufficient evidence to discount all these theories and to state that the platform and the apparatus above it was a table-fountain, possibly used as a drinking fountain. In the Lumley Inventories there is a picture of a black marble table standing on four round legs of similar marble, the legs having moulded bases and capitals of white marble. Under the table, in the centre, just as in Speed's engraving, is what appears to be a fifth leg, in grey marble, and this continues above the table top as a column of black marble. This supports a shallow bowl, above which sit three parrots (the popinjays of the Lumley arms) with water streaming from their beaks into the bowl. Above the parrots is a tapering column of marble ending in a ball surmounted by a sharp point. This Lumley picture, although the fountain it represents might have been in any of the Lumley houses, has so much in common with Speed's platform that little further evidence is needed to connect the two. Positive proof that the fountain was in fact at Nonsuch is, however, provided by three items in the Nonsuch repair accounts. Between 1607 and 1609 masons were employed in taking down the "peramides" and bowl 'where the popin-jays stand in the garden'—the word "peramides" already having been used as a singular, to describe a tapering column. In 1616 William Cure, mason, was engaged to take down and set up again 'a table and fountain in the garden, called the Birds fountain'. He worked and polished two pedestals of "Raunce" and drilled two holes through them for the lead pipes, and worked and polished three small rounds of touch-stone and two bases and capitals of white marble for the pillars under the table. For the top of the "peramid" he made a ball and pike. These extensive replacements seem to have kept the fountain functioning satisfactorily until 1634, when £2 6s. 8d. was paid for 'two brazen parrots cast carved and gilt for a fountain table in the garden'.

Watson, Platter and the Parliamentary surveyors, having exhausted the wonders of the building, turned their attention to the estate surrounding the Palace; and again Watson's superlatives and rhetoric added colour to the more prosaic descriptions of the others.

6

The Nonsuch Estate

THE Nonsuch gardens, comprising the Kitchen Garden, the Privy Garden, the Wilderness and orchard, the Grove of Diana and the plot on which the Banqueting House stood, covered some 16 acres, lying mainly to the west of the Palace, towards Ewell; an indication of their layout is given on page 117. The Kitchen Garden lay to the east of the Palace, outside the east wall of the kitchen building. By the time Danckerts painted his picture of Nonsuch, some time after 1660, this garden had become so overgrown with trees that there can have been little clear space left for the growing of vegetables and herbs. Although it was enclosed within the 14 ft. brick wall which also encompassed the Privy Garden, it would almost certainly be walled off from the royal garden as Speed shows. The Privy Garden lay on the three exposed sides of the Inner Court, and was surrounded by a wall faced in brick, with chalk foundations. This is the wall which runs across the southern frontage of the building in the Hoefnagel view, in which the coping-stones can be seen. Watson tells us that the wall stretched for 500 paces. The foundations of the wall opposite the south front of the Palace were exposed during the 1959 excavation, and during 1960 further trenches were cut along the line of the wall towards the west, locating the point at which it turned at right-angles. In the following year it was established that the foundations of the south-east corner of the wall lay under the road surface of the avenue leading towards the Cheam gate.

Between the Privy Garden wall and the south front of the Palace was a distance of 201 ft. This distance has to be borne in mind in looking at the only existing view of the layout of the garden, that by Speed; for he shows only a fraction (possibly not more than 50 ft.) of the real depth of the garden. However, he does make an attempt to indicate the layout of some of the beds and the disposition of some of the garden ornaments. Garden layout in the grand manner was one of the manifestations of the Renaissance in Italy, many of the greatest artists applying their talents to this wider canvas. Inevitably, at Nonsuch, many Italian features were embodied in the gardens: alleys, some with the branches interlaced overhead, arbours, statues, topiary, aviaries and fountains of varying degrees of ingenuity.

Speed shows the 'knots', typical of the Tudor garden, consisting of patterns made with dwarf hedges of box and other plants; but the patterns are unlikely to have been as simple as Speed would have us believe, for they gradually developed into the most complicated designs. Watson saw them as 'plants and shrubs mingled in intricate circles as though by the needle of Semiramis'. After describing the knots in the beds before the south frontage, Watson tells us that among them 'deer, hares, rabbits and dogs gave chase with unhindered feet and effortlessly passed over the green'. Thomas Platter makes it quite clear that the garden plants were in no danger from these creatures, for they themselves were covered with plants, although they looked, from a distance, like real animals. From this we must assume that they were made of stone and overgrown with some kind of creeper; topiary is unlikely in view of the smallness of most of the subjects. Forty years after Speed drew them the knots were described by the Parliamentary surveyors as 'quarters and rounds set about with thorn hedges'. Surrounding this open space immediately in front of the Palace were walks and covered alleys, seats painted green, blue and russet, loftier plants and trees and twelve arbours, each with its own flower-bed. The arbours were made of wood, and they were painted, some white and some in colour. They must have been constructed with typical Nonsuch magnificence; when, in 1623, Bartholomew Rogers took them down and overhauled them, he mended 'parts of them, viz. pedestals, bases, balusters, mouldings, crown pieces, pendants, rails, seats, columns and all the other decayed works'. On another occasion there is a reference to the lead roof of one of the arbours.

On the eastern side of the Privy Garden the same layout of knots and walks was continued, but on the west, or king's side, was a maze. Here, says Watson, 'you will enter a tortuous path and fall into the hazardous wiles of the labyrinth, whence even with the aid of Theseus' thread you will scarce be able to extricate yourself'.

Flower gardening was of the simplest sort until the time of Elizabeth; in fact, some of the colour in early Tudor gardens was obtained, not by plants but by patches of coloured gravel or brick-dust filling in the spaces in the knot patterns. The first plantings in the Nonsuch gardens, then, would have been even less varied than those which Anthony Watson later saw. We have no list of them, but at the same time the Hampton Court gardens were being furnished with apple and pear trees at 6*d.* each and small cherry trees at 6*d.* a hundred; with yew, cypress, juniper and bay at 2*d.* each and holly at 3*d.*; with roses at 4*d.* a hundred; with gilliver-slips and mint, and Sweet Williams, violets, primroses and strawberries at 3*d.* a bushel.

Henry VIII is said to have sent his gardener, a French priest named Woolf, travelling on the Continent for the express purpose of acquiring a better knowledge of his work. He introduced apricots, from Italy, in 1524. George W. Johnson, in his *History of English gardening*, made it appear that it was at Nonsuch that Woolf first planted 'various salad and pot-herbs, varieties of the apricot, musk melons, the Kentish cherry, etc.', but in doing so he misquoted his authority. R. Gough, in the first volume of *British topography*, had merely said that these and other plants and trees came in during the time of Henry VIII: currants from the Levant, pippins from Holland, figs, and pale gooseberries from Flanders. Melons, cucumbers and other 'more expensive' garden products were reintroduced, their cultivation having lapsed during the Wars of the Roses. Until Henry's time most dessert apples were imported, but he sent his fruiterer, Robert Harris, to fetch 'out of France a great store of grafts, especially pippins, before which there were no pippins in England'. Some of these may well have reached the Nonsuch gardens, where in later years apple trees abounded. The apple *Nonpareil*, said to have been introduced from France by a Jesuit in the time of Mary Tudor or Elizabeth, may not have had any connection with the *nonpareil* of palaces; however, to the apple-sellers in Covent Garden in Restoration times it was 'a Nonsuch'. Two hundred pear trees came to Henry VIII from France, sent by M. de Sens; they came via Rye, three horses making three journeys to bring them to London. Most, if not all, of them went to Nonsuch, and the king commanded Guillaume de Dieppe to be at the Palace when they were planted.

By Watson's time the garden stock at Nonsuch, augmented by Arundel and Lumley, had matured until the plants and shrubs 'filled the whole front of the royal court with a fragrant sweetness'. The fragrance emanated from white violets, yellow and purple hyacinths,

cherries, plums and mulberries; sweet-smelling savory and 'thyme that
gives honey of exceptional flavour'; ferns; pears and apples; rosemary,
hyssop, figs and 'the rose, sometimes exceeding pale, sometimes
blushing deeply'. The list is still very short, but, if there were other
flowers, and they were recent introductions, Watson may have been
covering his ignorance of their names when he ended by saying 'I am
aiming at brevity to avoid boring you. If I were to recount every item,
my discourse would grow too long.'

John Parkinson, in a chapter on 'The ordering of the gardens of
pleasure' in his *Paradisi in Sole Paradisus Terrestris*, published in 1629,
calls a cultivated type of campion (*lychnis Chalcedonica*) the 'Bristow
or Nonesuch flower'. Single varieties were bright red-orange, white,
'blush colour', or pale red fading to white, but the Orange Nonesuch
had double flowers and was rare. These cultivated campions had been
'sent us from beyond the seas'. The great None Such daffodil, imported
from France, owed nothing to the Palace, for it came in as *Narcisse
Nompareille*.

By 1650 the Privy Garden was in a neglected condition; but the
surveyors reported that "with a litle labor" it might "answeare the
expectatyon of a very hansome garden plot". They found two yew
trees, a juniper and "six trees called Lelack trees which trees beare noe
fruit but onely a very pleasant flower". The surprising extent to which
the planting of fruit trees had been carried, in this pleasance where we
should today expect to find flower-beds, roses, shrubs, hedges and
ornamental trees, is noted by them without comment: 'There are in
the said privy garden one hundred and forty fruit trees.'

The permanent ornaments of the Privy Garden comprised
columns and fountains of varied shape, size and design. Near the south-
east tower a column can be seen in Speed's engraving. As portrayed
by him, the animal on top of the column looks very much like a circus
lion, but according to Anthony Watson 'where the lights of the
Queen's side open out . . . a snorting white horse prances among the
flower beds'. In the middle of the south frontage is a fountain, which
Watson's description and a picture in the Lumley Inventories in-
disputably identify as one of Lumley's additions. It stood, says
Watson, on a mound, and was set inside two circles of grass, one above
the other, each of which was reached by a rise of three steps. On the
top of this mound 'is set a shining column which carries a high statue
of a snow-white nymph, perhaps Venus, from whose tender breasts

flow jets of water into the ivory-coloured marble, and from there the water falls through narrow pipes into a marble basin'. In Speed's picture the lady has her back to the observer, but in the Lumley Inventories she is seen as she would have appeared from the Palace windows. From the fluted marble bowl over which she stands the water cascades through the mouths of two grotesque masks. The bowl is supported on a tapering column set on a square base, the near face of which consists of a carved panel showing a creature which is half horse and half fish. This stands in the centre of an octagonal marble bath, below which is a massive, sloping-sided base of black marble. On the outside, each angle of the octagon is decorated with a scrolled herm—a human head and shoulders on a tapering carved and enscrolled base. On the face of the nearest side of the bath the Lumley arms are carved within a beribboned cartouche. Speed's tiny sketch of the fountain does less than justice to it: the nymph is waving her arms and has her feet wide apart; he shows a waisted column supporting the bowl, and makes the two grass circles and the octagonal bath look like a three-stepped base of stone.

Round the nymph fountain were the six lilac trees, and in line with it, to right and left, were two other mounds. Watson mentions them, but gives no hint that there was anything on them; an unlikely omission, if the columns shown by Speed were in fact standing when Watson was writing. The 1650 Survey describes them as 'two marble pyramids or pinnacles called the Falcon Perches', but it is possible to identify them with pictures in the Lumley Inventories of two marble columns of which Speed's could be considered to be a rough-and-ready likeness. At the top of each of these columns is a ball, on which is perched, not a falcon, but the Lumley popinjay.

At the extreme left-hand edge of Speed's engraving, beyond the south-west tower, a small part of another garden ornament can be seen. This was a high, tapering column or obelisk, described by the Parliamentary surveyors as 'one pyramid or spired pinnacle of marble, set upon a basis of marble grounded upon a rise of free stone'. Near it they saw 'one large marble wash bowl or basin, over which stands a marble pelican, fed with a pipe of lead to convey water into the same'. Again, these two features are not mentioned by Anthony Watson, yet they can be clearly identified in the inventories, the base of the pyramid showing the Lumley arms.

Possibly because these embellishments by Lumley were quite new

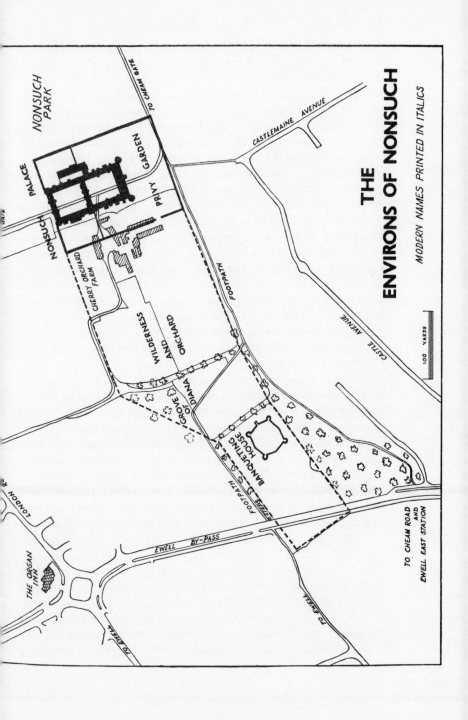

THE
ENVIRONS OF NONSUCH

MODERN NAMES PRINTED IN ITALICS

100 YARDS

NONSUCH PARK

TO CHEAM GATE

NONSUCH PALACE

PRIVY GARDEN

CHERRY ORCHARD FARM

WILDERNESS AND ORCHARD

GROVE OF DIANA

FOOTPATH

CASTLEMAINE AVENUE

CASTLE AVENUE

BANQUETING HOUSE

FOOTPATH

THE ORGAN INN

LONDON RD

EWELL BY-PASS

TO EWELL

TO CHEAM ROAD
AND
EWELL EAST STATION

when Elizabeth acquired the Palace in 1592, no repairs to them of any kind are recorded during her reign. Between 1607 and 1609, however, new stone steps had to be provided for the 'prancing horse' column, and the pyramid had to be set upright, repaired and supplied with new stone steps. On many occasions the "plomber" had to mend or "soder" the broken pipes supplying the fountains. The 'Arbour Court' is mentioned in one list of plumbing repairs; this is the only time the name appears, and it must presumably mean the Privy Garden.

The positions of the gates in the Privy Garden wall are nowhere very closely defined. Watson writes of a gate opposite the queen's side, between south and east. This implies that it was in the southern side of the wall, the side seen in the Hoefnagel view, but was towards the eastern end of that wall. Hoefnagel's engraving of the Palace was adapted and reproduced in 1608 in Antonius Albicius' *Principum Christianorum Stemmata*. The Privy Garden wall is extended, in this adaptation, in an easterly direction; and there is a gate shown in the place indicated by Watson. This position fits in very well with the contours of the land today. The modern roadway, after crossing the Palace site, makes a quarter-circle turn in the direction of Cheam. Watson's gate would be beyond this turn, a short distance along the Cheam arm of the avenue, and on the left-hand edge of the roadway. From here, if we imagine Watson coming through the gate and walking back towards the turn in the road, we can see, as he did, 'an easy ascent on to a small rise'; and we can still see a few of the successors to his 'ancient oaks, stately elms, walnuts and ashes arranged in oblique lines, and planted in perfect order, raising their leafy heads to the sky'. This 'easy ascent', and the footpath to which it leads, on or near the line of the mediaeval Portway, may be the path described in 1610 as 'the high walk'; there were 17 yds. of green-painted posts and rails going up the slope to the walk, two seats round trees, three other seats with a gate between two of them, and two gates at the end of the walk.

There may have been another gate in this south wall of the Privy Garden, towards the west, matching Watson's gate. In Hoefnagel's view the royal coach appears to be making for the south-west corner of the garden, where two outbuildings stand. These two buildings present a problem. Hoefnagel is our only authority for their existence in 1568, Watson does not mention them, they are outside the area covered by Speed's engraving and they cannot be identified with any of the buildings included in the Parliamentary Survey. Remembering

Watson's information that the passage-way through the west wing of the Outward Court led to the stables, it seems possible that these two buildings were privy stables and may even have housed a coach. An entrance gate in the Privy Garden wall would then have been necessary. However, several other possible explanations of the purpose of these two buildings could be put forward; certainly they would have ruined the appearance of this part of the Privy Garden, and it may well be that if they were stables they had been re-sited before Watson wrote.

In the west wall of the Privy Garden, beyond the maze, was a gateway leading to the less formal gardens. Through this, Watson went on his imaginary journey round the estate; Thomas Platter came through it in the opposite direction, having begun his tour of inspection at the point farthest from the Palace, in the west. There is no information about the position of this gateway, but it was probably level with the south frontage of the Palace, for Watson warns his visitor, on the way out of the garden, to avoid veering to the right and becoming lost in the maze.

A new gate was installed by Elizabeth in 1600; this, and the repairing of broken stone steps, being the only structural work carried out in the gardens during her eleven years as owner of Nonsuch. The new gate was doubtless made to match the others, although they may well have been larger. It was set in a Caen stone surround 6 ft. 6 in. high and 3 ft. 6 in. wide: a very small aperture in relation to the massive 14 ft. wall in which it stood.

The first glimpse beyond the west wall of the Privy Garden is through the eyes of the 1650 surveyors. Here, they said, there had been a wilderness growing, separated from the Little Park by a hedge, and with an old orchard on the north; but the trees in the Wilderness had been cut down within the past three months. The old orchard and the kitchen garden together contained seventy-two fruit trees and a fair lime tree. The walled gardens and the Wilderness and orchard were estimated to cover 10 acres.

The Wilderness, typical of Tudor and Stuart gardens, was in no sense a wild place, but a piece of landscape gardening in the grand manner, in which any apparent wildness of nature had been carefully contrived by the gardener's art. In some 'wildernesses' the hand of the gardener seems to have been so evident in the finished result that the whole area was no more than a formal garden, with trees instead of flowers and shrubs. At Wimbledon, for example, we read of young trees 'cut and formed into several ovals, squares and angles', with a lime tree or an elm in the centre of each oval and in the angles of the other figures. The eighteen alleys between these shaped clumps of trees were gravelled.

Watson elaborates this theme of the unsuitability of the name by quoting a number of examples to show the delight taken by 'the ancients' in calling things by names which conjure up entirely opposite meanings. Just as we have *bella* for ugly wars and *lucus* for a dark wood, the Nonsuch Wilderness might be called *desertum*, because it was *not* deserted by monarchs, great men, people of any kind, birds or four-footed creatures. He continues in similar vein for many hundreds of words, and it is not easy to pick out the hard facts from details which may be factual but may equally well owe their inclusion to Watson's classical education and fertile imagination.

If, for example, you take the right-hand path of the three which appear to radiate from the gate in the Privy Garden wall, you may chance to see woodland gods and fauns sitting on flower-decked seats, perhaps talking about Pan. Watson cannot guess why the flute-players are gathered together in the corners of the Wilderness, unless it be to drown the noise of the woodland animals: the terrifying roar of the lions, the savage grunt of the boar. A bear falls, killed by a shot from a gun; and a deer, struck by a forester's spear. Here are the Indian ass, the mute crocodile, the poisonous snake, the panther, the hunger-mad wolf. Tigers rend their prey, and dogs fill the whole place with baying. But he assures us that we need not despair, for the animals have grown tame through frequent association with men 'and scarce retaliate even when attacked'.

It is indeed difficult to know what factual basis there may have been for this kind of descriptive writing. Without further evidence, it is impossible to tell whether there were statues of gods or fauns, or whether there were wild animals, carved, alive, or in process of being killed. In an Italian garden of the period, in a warmer climate, a menagerie would have been perfectly normal; but without warmed winter quarters some of the creatures on Watson's list would have been distinctly uncomfortable for part of the year.

However, even if the evidence for the existence of a menagerie is doubtful, his description of the contents of an aviary may be accepted; for he himself has earlier referred to a 'wire-fenced enclosure crowded with pheasants and partridges from across the sea'. To these he adds 'pelicans, pouring out blood from their torn breasts to revive the dead bodies of their offspring', as well as peacocks and guinea-fowl. Also in the Wilderness, and presumably outside the aviary, are nightingales, larks, blackbirds, thrushes, robins, finches, turtle-doves, wood-pigeons and a dozen more, pleasing to eye or ear or palate.

In describing the flora of the Wilderness, Watson tells of 'leafy woods glorying in shady spots'. The three pathways were cut through these trees and were, presumably, Paul Hentzner's 'walks so embrowned with trees'. The trees owed their beauty to 'the care of skilful hands'. The countless young apple trees had already reached maturity, and there were blackberries and strawberries. The rest he gathers up into 'a sort of little nosegay', a six-line 'poem' doing little more than list the large trees—oak, walnut, ash, elm, sycamore, maple and plane; the fruits—pear, Syrian fig, plum, vine and 'Persian fruit'; the evergreens—yew, juniper, box, olive; and roses, periwinkle, hazel, honeysuckle, briars, thorns, dog-roses and ferns.

The trimmed trees at the end of the south walk, the 'canopies', offer perpetual moist shade beneath the circular spread of branches. The large plane-tree canopy in the northern part of the Wilderness 'receives a richer honour than any other tree'. Elsewhere, along one of the two outer, grassy paths through the Wilderness, Thomas Platter tells us how the trunks of the trees bordering the path had been used as the posts for a high board fence to form alleys like enclosed tennis courts, where ball games could be played.

Tracing a way through the Wilderness by one of the three paths, which may be assumed to have converged again at the western end, with Watson going from east to west and Thomas Platter going in the opposite direction, it can be deduced from the sequence of their accounts that one of the most important features of the 'wild' gardens, the Grove of Diana, lay just to the west of the Wilderness. This fits in with a local tradition that the Temple of Diana stood in a deep dell which can still be seen in the plantation to the west of Cherry Orchard Farm. Part of this area is today taken up by a paddock, known in 1802 as Diana's Meadow. The corner of the paddock nearest to Cherry Orchard falls sharply to form part of a large natural hollow. In the lowest part of the paddock is a small area kept moist by water seeping through the ground, although the general lowering of the water-table has robbed it of any claim to be called a spring. The rest of the natural hollow is covered by a plantation, in which there are several pits made by the digging of clay for the Nonsuch Pottery, which was established 100 yds. away some time after the demolition of the Palace. Into this present-day landscape the description of the Grove may be fitted, not with full certainty that this is exactly the right place but at least in the knowledge that it is the most likely.

Watson's journey has brought him along a woodland walk to an oak tree near 'the piper', presumably a statue of Pan, at the entrance to the Grove of Diana, a copse and glade with topiary arches, walls and shaded sandy walks. There is a natural spring in the Vale of Gargaphy (an actual feature of the landscape, it seems, because it is given a marginal heading in English, and not merely Watson's imagination), and near it the rock-well. Watson gives the impression that this was a fountain in the form of rocks round a well, with flowers and fruit growing among the rocks and a spray of water rising and falling. Platter, however, thought that natural water sprang from a rock into a basin. The repair accounts leave us in no doubt when we read of "mending with soder and newe pipe the pipes which serve to Diana", "mending the pipes where they were broken in Dianes Maze", and "the fountayne of Diana".

Round the fountain stood the statues which gave the grove its name—Diana and her nymphs (two of them, according to Platter) painted in flesh-colour, Actaeon transformed into a stag, and his three hounds. There were wooden steps near the fountain, and post-and-rail fencing was erected somewhere in the grove, possibly round the dell containing the fountain. Past the fountain Watson's path led to "a statelye bower for Diana", a woodland palace; for Platter, this was 'a small vaulted temple'; for the clerks responsible for making out the repair bills, 'the Banqueting House in the walks below the fountain of Diana'; and in modern parlance, a pinnacled, timber-framed, square summerhouse. On an arch, presumably over the entrance, was an eagle; a pelican stood on one pinnacle, and a phoenix on the other; and there were Latin inscriptions both inside and outside. The stately bower was showing signs of decay by 1610, when it had to be 'reared' and 'made up'. By 1622 workmen were busy 'taking down a little square Banqueting House by Diana's fountain, which was decayed; new framing and setting up another in the same place'.

Nearby, but apparently not built until 1610, was the equivalent of a bandstand, "a little room for the musicons" or "the standing for the music". This was of wood, painted russet colour. Elsewhere in the 'orchard', Watson says (but he is using the word in its older sense, to mean a wood containing all kinds of trees), stood a handsome pyramid with heads disgorging streams of water. To Platter this was 'a pointed tower spirting out water', and it was this fountain which, according to Hentzner, contained concealed pipes, which spirted water on all who came within reach. This is the only hint that the Nonsuch gardens contained any of the water hazards which beset the unwary visitor to many a garden planned in the Italian manner. The Nonsuch booby trap was probably operated by the weight of the visitor on a stone in the paving round the fountain. As such, it was probably an open secret, and in any case it would not have been difficult to get out of range as soon as the jets started. It was, in fact, a very modest piece of practical joking, compared with some of the ingenious devices we read of, such as jets of water soaking anyone who sat on a particular seat, or pouring down on those who climbed the only steps out of a garden.

Beyond the Grove of Diana, on a hill, and approached from the Palace by the middle sandy path through the Wilderness, stood the Banqueting House. Anthony Watson does little more than mention the building, and Thomas Platter seems not to have seen it through the trees as he entered the Grove of Diana from the London Road side. Very little was known about the building until the site was excavated in 1960; the discoveries made then, added to the description given in the 1650 Survey and details gleaned from the repair accounts, give us a fairly complete picture of what was one of the earliest permanent banqueting houses built in this country.

Temporary banqueting houses, put up for some specific occasion, were part of the pageantry of the Tudor sovereigns. In 1551, "againste the Marshall Seynt Androes comynge", a house measuring 57 ft. by 21 ft. was erected in Hyde Park, and another, 40 ft. long, in Marylebone Park. These were timber-framed, but the frames were almost certainly canvas-covered; tailors were engaged to sew the roofs, and basket-makers worked on the windows. The houses were decorated with boughs, flags and ivy, and the floors were strewn with rushes. Despite their temporary nature, brick-built cooking ranges were installed. Three years later Sir Thomas Cawarden, Keeper of Nonsuch and Master of the Revels, because he had "good experience heretofore in lyk things", was ordered to superintend the erection of even less permanent structures at Oatlands, consisting of 'certain banqueting houses of boughs and other devices of pleasure'. Elizabeth's arrangements for "thentertaynment" of the French Ambassador in 1572 included the building of a canvas-covered banqueting house in Whitehall, decked with birch and ivy, flowers, pendants and arms painted and gilded; "the Floore thereof being all strewed with Roze leaves pickt and sweetned with sweete waters". One of the most ambitious of these pavilions was that put up at Westminster in 1581 for the visit of 'certain Ambassadors out of France'. This is described by John Stow in his *Chronicles* as having thirty 40 ft. masts round a perimeter of 332 ft., the spaces being filled with canvas and the outside painted to resemble rusticated stone. There were 292 window-lights, and inside were ten tiers of staging. The canvas ceiling was painted with clouds, stars, sun and sunbeams; and hung with ivy, holly, bay, rue, pomegranates, oranges and other fruit, and flowers, spangled with gold.

The Banqueting House, then, was primarily a place of entertainment, the entertainment including eating; but the kind of meals which today would be called banquets were rarely, if ever, eaten in a banqueting house. The colossal meals which our forbears ate when they were really feeding filled foreign visitors with amazement. They required great kitchens and an army of servants, and the Banqueting House was not designed or intended for this kind of meal. The Tudor and Stuart banquet was more in the nature of dessert: light refreshments to be consumed whilst an entertainment was in progress. Purchases for the 1572 banquets included 8 lb. of sugar for marzipan (marchpane) at 9s., 8½ lb. of almonds at 1s. a pound, three dozen fine cakes for 7s. 6d., gold leaves to gild the marzipan, fruits, marmalade, cloves, saffron, cinnamon, ginger, eggs, pressed quinces and 'fruits counterfeit bought of Brayne th'apothecary'.

After all the expense and effort involved in putting up these temporary banqueting houses—the unusually large one described by Stow took 375 people twenty-four days and nights to build, and cost £1,745—their dismantling must surely have made the whole idea of this type of entertainment seem a wasteful way of doing the honours. However, the separation of the 'banquet' from the buildings associated with the ordinary business of living had come to stay, and, where circumstances permitted it, permanent buildings began to be erected solely for the purpose of entertainment and light refreshment. These permanent banqueting houses, of all shapes and sizes, appeared on large estates in various parts of the country. Many of them consisted of a single large room, ranging in pattern from the octagonal building, 21 ft. in diameter, planned by Henry Hawthorne for Windsor Castle in 1577 or 1578, to the 'round in the middle of four angles' seen by the Parliamentary surveyors at Wimbledon in 1650. An echo of the Nonsuch Banqueting House comes from Cornwall. Sir Arthur Champernowne, who died in 1578, drew up a plan for Richard Carew of Antony which involved making an artificial island in the middle of a salt-water fish-storage pond (the 'fishful pond') and erecting a banqueting house on the island. The shape of the artificial island— square with a round at each corner—was, as we shall see, very similar to the shape of the mound on which the Nonsuch Banqueting House stood.

Five acres of the land in Ewell parish which Henry had absorbed into the Little Park were enclosed to form a rectangle, at the east end of which was the highest ground in the neighbourhood. On this hill, between the years 1538 and 1546, the Banqueting House was erected. Owing to an error in the 7th Report of the Historical Manuscripts Commission, writers on Nonsuch have, since the publication of that report, been claiming that the first documentary evidence for the existence of the Banqueting House is dated 1547. The document referred to is an Inventory of the Wardrobe at Nonsuch, and the Banqueting House is, in fact, nowhere mentioned in it. The first true record comes in 1550, when Sir Thomas Cawarden had the Keepership of the Banqueting House added to his other duties at Nonsuch. However, the meagreness of the expenditure on the whole of the Nonsuch estate between the death of Henry in January, 1547, and Arundel's acquisition of the Palace in 1556 makes it quite definite that the building was erected before Henry died.

Some of the workmen from the Palace, then, masons and carpenters, bricklayers and chalk-diggers, sawyers, plasterers, brick-makers, lime burners and labourers, set to work on this hill overlooking the village of Ewell. They dug deeply into the top of the hill to lay stout foundations of chalk blocks to form a rectangle, the inner sides of which were faced with brick. These walls were continued for some 4 ft. above soil level, and were then topped with a wall of brick which was probably about 5 ft. high. Hundreds of tons of imported earth were then tipped round the walls which had been built, raising an artificial mound some 3 ft. to 4 ft. above the natural soil level; and the rectangular structure became the cellars of the Banqueting House. To retain the outer edges of the artificial mound, a wall of chalk faced with brick was constructed, in the shape of a rectangle with an obtuse angle in the middle of each side and with projecting three-quarter circles at each corner. The area between the cellars and this retaining wall, after being levelled off, will undoubtedly have been paved, in flags or cobbles or both. It is possible that spaces would have been left here and there for plants; but the platform was, fundamentally, a 50 ft. promenade all round the building, and it would have been quite adequate for outdoor musical and dramatic entertainments, and for refreshments, when the heat of summer made the Banqueting House itself unbearable. Access to the Banqueting House from the Palace was through a painted wooden gate and then by means of steps which existed on at least three of the four sides of the mound, on the north and south, and on the east side where the ramp is today. Writing in 1913 or thereabouts, Sir Alfred Clapham stated that the remains of these eastern steps were still visible, and he included them in his plan of the wall surrounding the mound. He drew them, not as a single flight of steps on the line of the present ramp, but as two flights, on either side of the ramp and at right-angles to it, with one side of each flight butted against the retaining wall of the mound. Willis reported that these steps could be seen in 1930. The visitor ascending either of these flights would have reached a landing, from which he would have turned at right-angles to step on to the mound. This arrangement agrees with the documentary evidence. The outer edges of the flights of steps would obviously need some sort of handrail; and we do in fact find that when another "payre of staires" was made in 1622, on the south side of the mound, they were furnished with "rayles and ballesters". At the same time repairs were carried out to another pair, already existing, on the north side. Possibly over the eastern or northern steps stood the 'great arch' of painted wood. It would seem appropriate for the retaining wall to have been surmounted by a balustrading, but there is no mention of such an embellishment, or indeed of the walls themselves, beyond their 'making up [i.e., repairing] and coping'.

In each corner of the mound the excavators discovered square, brick-lined sumps for collecting surface-water from the surrounding paving. From the sumps, the water ran into brick-walled, slate-roofed channels with glazed tile floors, and so out through the retaining wall.

BANQUETING HOUSE EXCAVATION PLAN, 1960

Courtesy of Nonsuch Palace Excavation Committee

PERIOD I
PERIOD I (CONJECTURAL)
PERIOD IA
PERIOD II
18TH & 19TH CENT.
TRENCHES

Scale of Metres

Scale of Feet

These arrangements appeared to have been made shortly after the building was erected, when experience had shown that the mound became waterlogged in bad weather. Their construction could not have been long delayed, for the slabs forming the bottoms of the sumps were pieces of Purbeck marble tombstones, plundered from Merton Priory or Cuddington Church, and still showing the recesses, and in some cases the fixing pins, where monumental brasses had been.

The building itself, measuring 44 ft. by 38 ft., stood in the middle of the paved area, the brick walls of the cellars rising above the paving to give a semi-basement type of cellar. These walls had simply been demolished to the level of the pavement when the building was pulled down, so that the excavation revealed the complete cellars, with their plastered walls rising to about two-thirds of their original height.

As originally built, the cellars consisted of two rooms. The larger of these, a rectangle running from east to west, measured 44 ft. by 20 ft. The main entrance was at the east end, where a flight of stone steps in the centre of the 20 ft. wall ran down to the brick-paved floor. In the opposite wall was another flight of steps. At some time during the life of the building, and certainly before the Parliamentary surveyors inspected it, an adaptation was carried out, dividing the cellar into two unequal parts by means of a brick wall. A large fireplace was installed in the recess for the entrance steps at the western end, and the brick fire-back completely blocked off this entrance. Just outside the recess a tunnel-mouthed oven with oval interior was built, entirely of bricks (Plate 15 (a)). The oven was heated by building a fire inside it and drawing out the fire before putting in whatever was to be cooked. The excavation revealed the burnt brickwork of the fire-back, flagstones and ashes where the hearth had been and ashes in the oven. The cellar had originally been a wine-cellar, and this use probably continued in the eastern part after the adaptation; holes in the cellar walls showed where the supports for racks had been. The brick floors seen during the excavation were not original, the cellars having been 'new paved with bricks' in 1628. About half of these bricks remained in position, but elsewhere all that was left was the thick mortar bedding on which the bricks had been set.

The other cellar, also running the whole length of the building, was shallower than the main cellar, and a narrow flight of steps, some of stone and some of brick, ran down from it to the floor of the cooking part of the main cellar, 3 ft. below. These steps had been put in as part of the adaptation, two of the treads being cut in the brickwork of the wall between the shallow cellar and the main cellar; the treads were found to be in a remarkably good state of preservation. In the middle part of the wall through which these steps ran, the brickwork had been increased in thickness, probably as a foundation for fireplaces in the rooms above. Behind this thicker part of the wall, jutting into the shallow cellar, was a typical garderobe pit. The arrangement already noticed on the Palace site, where chimneys and garderobes were often found together, was thus repeated at the Banqueting House. There appeared to have been no entrance to this secondary cellar from outside the building.

Above the cellars, and with its ground floor some 4 ft. or 5 ft. above pavement level, stood the two-storey Banqueting House. It was a timbered building, but no traces of stucco work were found to indicate that the plaster filling the spaces between the timber framing was anything other than ordinary plain plaster. Some resemblance to the decorative splendour of the Palace may, however, have been seen in the covering of the main timbers. In the 1650 Survey they are said to be 'covered with lead'; but it seems more likely that the material was slate, and in fact two pieces of carved slate were found during the excavation. At first-floor level a balcony jutted out at each corner, and from these the 'prospect' or view over the countryside could be enjoyed. In the tiled roof was a lantern or skylight, covered with lead. The parapet consisted of painted wooden lattice, posts and rails, and it was presumably on this that the King's Beasts 'about the Banqueting House' were affixed.

The entrance to the ground floor was at the east end. On the evidence of the excavation, the Director concluded that there must have been a landing over the entrance to the cellars and about 5 ft. above ground level. This was approached by means of an external flight of steps, quarter-round in plan, for which the brick foundations and an internal support were found. The visitor would ascend these steps and turn left on the landing to enter the main door, set in the middle of the short wall of the principal room of the building. This room, standing, it is presumed, over the entire area of the deep cellars, and therefore 44 ft. long by 20 ft. wide, was described in the 1650 Survey as a 'large hall wainscoted'. The surveyors found three other rooms on the ground floor and five on the first floor. The rooms were mostly wainscoted and matted, and there were windows 'quite round the whole house'. Just as the three cellars which the surveyors saw were the result of an adaptation at some unknown date, it is highly probable that the rooms on one of the other floors differed from the original plan. In 1622 carpenters made a partition 12 ft. high and 21 ft. long, portals, doors and a closet 12 ft. high, 9 ft. long and 6 ft. wide. From the length of the partition we may perhaps infer that an adaptation was being carried out on the first floor; that this floor originally had the same arrangement of rooms as the ground floor, and that a large room over the hall was now being converted into two rooms to make the five which the surveyors saw.

Very few remains, either of the decorations of the building itself or of the articles used by the people who frequented it, were found during the excavation. Among the demolition rubble filling the cellars was a massive block of stone, with carved moulding and a Tudor rose and cherub. This was the corner-stone of a chimney-piece. The garderobe pit yielded a small, exquisitely carved stone lion, probably from the royal arms. These, and a gilt filigree dress-ornament, coins, window glass and lead, and fragments of domestic pottery and glass, were all that came to light.

Associated with the Banqueting House were two outhouses, described in 1650 as 'one little building containing a bakehouse and a room wherein is placed a fair well with a wheel for the winding up of water, and one other little house used for a wash-house'. In the repair accounts the bakehouse is called a kitchen; it had a tiled roof and both it and the 'well-house' had brick floors, but the material of which the walls were built is not known. Before the excavation all that was known of their position was the statement in the 1650 Survey that they were 'in Nonsuch Park opposite to the gate leading to the Banqueting House'. One of them was eventually found near the hedge on the north side of the site, about 100 ft. away from the artificial mound. This was believed to be the bakehouse. The well was not discovered, but a damaged brick-lined channel which was found may have carried spilt water from the well-house.

The positions of the other buildings in the Nonsuch estate are not known with certainty. The Survey next describes the under-house-keeper's house, containing a hall, kitchen, buttery, milk-house, parlour, cellar and six rooms 'above stairs'. The house had its own garden and orchard. It was a timbered building with a tiled roof, and stood 'near adjoining to Nonsuch House on the east side thereof'. Surface finds near a clump of trees (formerly a small spinney) less than 100 yds. from the east wall of the Palace, coupled with eye-witness stories of a plough sinking into a large hole in the ground near here some sixty years ago, make it fairly definite that this is the site of the house and its outbuildings. Less certainly, it may be identified with a building described, from 1610 to 1620, as 'Lord Carew's lodging'. The lodging was obviously not in the Palace itself, for he had a cellar and larder built for him, nineteen 'lights of windows' in his larder painted, the larder walls and ceiling plastered and a new staircase erected, with a 'pair' of stairs, two landings, three doors and three clerestories of two lights each. At the same time twenty-two balusters were supplied for his 'Lodging and offices'. He had his own barn. A chimney in Lord "Carie's" kitchen was taken down and rebuilt 'stronger and higher' in 1618, because it 'annoyed the Queen's lodgings and other adjoining by smoking'. His name disappeared from the records after 1620, although Lady Carew still had lodgings in the Palace until 1622.

Adjacent to the under-housekeeper's house was a well-house. In it was 'a fair well of a great depth, a large cistern of lead and a wheel for winding up the water, with two large and strong buckets well bound with iron'. This may have been the well-house built in 1629, containing a well dug in the same year by Robert Michell. However, although this was 9 ft. in diameter, it was only 5 fathoms deep, so that it could hardly merit the description 'of a great depth'. Also adjoining the under-housekeeper's house was a small timber building with a tiled roof, the Saucery House. Its four rooms were occupied by the Yeomen of the Sauces.

A larger house, timbered and with a tiled roof, stood in the Park 'a pretty distance remote from Nonsuch House'. This was the Keeper's Lodge (for the Keeper of the Park, not of the Palace), and the premises comprised a hall, parlour, kitchen, buttery, larder, scullery, milk-house, bolting house, deer house, coal house and ten upstairs rooms. The outbuildings were a stable, a barn of three bays, a hay house and a thatched barn of five bays. There was also a 'very well planted' garden, and two little yards. The surveyors did not mention the well; an old well was stripped of its materials and filled in in 1621, and a new well was dug in a different place. The hall appears to have been built on mediaeval lines as a large, high, communal living and eating place for the whole household; but changing custom eventually caused it, like many similar structures, to lose its mediaeval function along with some of its loftiness. Twenty-five years before the Parliament men saw it, a new floor was built over the upper part of the hall, doors were installed, and gable-ends, a staircase and windows were put in.

'A pretty distance remote' from the Palace gives us a wide choice in attempting to site the Keeper's Lodge. With continuity of occupation of a site providing a possible starting point, we may consider Nonsuch Court, which stood, until recently, to the south-west of the Palace site and had an ancient well; Warren Farm, to the south-east; and the nineteenth-century Mansion House to the east. Even though the evidence is not very substantial, there is some justification for envisaging the Lodge as standing on the Mansion House site. It is near one of the main approaches to the Palace, from the Cheam gate; it has a garden wall of chequered flint and stone, and other walls in the outbuildings, which must go back at least to Tudor times; and it is connected to the supposed site of the Palace stables and to the London Road gate beyond by a raised 'ride' clearly visible in the turf.

Not mentioned by the Parliamentary surveyors but sufficiently near the gardens and Wilderness for Thomas Platter to have seen it during his short visit, was a 'standing'. This was a roofed but open-fronted shelter, the precursor of the modern grandstand and sports pavilion, from which the royal party could watch hunting in progress. More of these structures stood in the Great Park. In a survey of the Great Park made about the year 1558, one is described as "a faire stonding well buildid with ij storys couerid with tile and parte with leade". There were at this time three other standings in the Great Park, at least one of which was used as a 'hide' from which to shoot at the deer; and in a survey of September, 1650, one of the landmarks mentioned is the 'prince his standing'.

The principal house in the Great Park was the Keeper's House, which came to be known as Worcester House during and after its occupation by the Earl of Worcester as Keeper of the Great Park. It stood on the highest ground in the Park, where today the Royal Avenue, the Avenue and Delta Road meet. The surveyors in April, 1650, found it 'one entire pile of very good brick building, four storeys high, covered in tile, well built and ordered'. The first storey appears to have been a basement; it contained a kitchen, separate beer- and wine-cellars, pantry, dry larder, wet larder, dairy, wash-house and passage. On the ground floor the wainscoted hall had a tiled floor and a small dais of wood; the parlour and the withdrawing room were wainscoted and had wooden floors. Also on this floor were a great chamber, wainscoted, two other chambers, two closets and two rooms for servants. A large and fair dining room was on the first floor, which also contained four bedchambers, a withdrawing room and two closets. The six garrets on the second floor were 'all boarded and well-lighted'. On the north-east of the house was 'a very handsome garden plot' enclosed by a 10 ft. brick wall, and in front of the house a Green Court also 'severed from the said park by a brick wall of ten foot high'. From the Green Court ten steps led up to the hall door, and in line with this door, beyond the Green Court, a 'race' between two rows of well-growing trees set in a straight line extended 'it self a measured half mile in length'. This was 'a special ornament both to the house and park'. The Kitchen Garden was walled round and the back court railed; in a yard stood a coach-house, a pigeon-house and some sheds for poultry, 'all very useful and necessary'.

Near Worcester House was a Keeper's Lodge, a timbered house of two storeys and a cellar. On the ground floor was a hall and a parlour, with a kitchen, buttery, milk-house and wash-house. There were seven rooms on the first floor. The outbuildings comprised a tiled barn and a thatched barn of five bays each and a tiled shed. The premises stood in their own grounds: 'one garden, one orchard well planted, a Green Court and two yards'.

Although the Palace and the estate which surrounded it can now be seen in much sharper detail than would have been possible before the excavation, several problems connected with the building are still unsolved. Where, for example, was the famous Lumley Library housed? Where was the Chapel? Were there really, as the repair accounts seem to indicate, two pairs of sun-dials on the *north* faces of the five-storey towers? Should it be assumed that the Palace had no hall, because it is not mentioned in any of the available evidence? Problems similar to these, but which could be answered with reasonable probability, have been dealt with in the foregoing chapters; but it would be wrong to suggest that the 'reconstruction' of Nonsuch is complete, or can be completed unless further evidence is discovered.

7

The Early Life of the Palace

W<small>HEN</small> we come to consider the people of Nonsuch and try to envisage the pageantry and splendour which formed the background to their lives in the Palace, it is all too easy to allow imagination to take control. In our desire to recapture some of the glamour and romance of bygone days, we are apt to build up a picture of a life such as was never lived, in Nonsuch or any other palace. This picture is brilliantly coloured and has a distinguished cast giving a continuous performance. We people the apartments and courtyards, gardens and parks, with kings and queens, noblemen, officers of the Court, distinguished foreign visitors and a hierarchy of servants with old-world titles; but we forget that, at Nonsuch, such an assembly was comparatively rare, and that for by far the greater part of its life the Palace slumbered quietly in the Surrey countryside, with a housekeeper and a small staff as caretakers, and with a few rooms occupied by permanent residents as a mark of the favour of the royal owner.

Royal Nonsuch, then, was not in anything like continuous use by royalty, even when, during the period of Elizabeth's ownership, it was a favourite residence. It was only one of a large number of palaces and great houses which the Court might visit, in or out of rotation, on 'progresses' which were continuous except at Christmastime. Most of these stopping-places were reasonably near London, although the Court frequently travelled much farther afield. Around London, and with the Thames as a convenient highway, were more royal houses than even the most restless monarch could use if he were ever to stay in one place long enough to deal with affairs of state. The royal apartments in these houses were closed and sparsely furnished except when the Court was in residence; so that the progress arrangements must have involved a tremendous amount of planning and labour. A route would have to be worked out, so that the housekeepers would know when to prepare for their visitors; furniture would be carted in from one or more of the other palaces, whose 'wardrobe' or 'garde-robe stuff', including soft furnishings as well as tables, chairs, beds and the like, would be issued out on warrant and receipt to supplement the 'standing wardrobe' of the palace to be visited. Urgent repairs to the fabric of the building would be rushed through. Vast quantities of food and other necessities would be bought, the Clerk of the Market beating down the vendors in the neighbourhood of the Palace to well below the prevailing prices. Tents to accommodate those for whom there was no room in the Palace would be carted in and erected; this in itself was so much a part of Court life, and so large an undertaking, that it was made the responsibility of a Keeper of the King's Tents, Hales and Toyles; the Hales being temporary sheds for stables and the Toyles apparently a kind of hurdle for game-enclosures and barriers at tournaments. As soon as the Court arrived, the area for twelve miles around the Palace came under its jurisdiction, and tradesmen and others capable of useful service, such as carters, would not be able to call their goods or their time their own until they thankfully bent a loyal knee to the departing monarch. And it did not pay to grumble: many miles from Nonsuch, one John Rede of Ewelme was committed to Wallingford Castle on the 11th March, 1539, as a seditious tale-teller; he had dared to say, among other things, that the king had discharged all his workmen at Hampton Court, his parks and other places, because 'His Grace hath begun one other new work which shall be called None Suche'.

Evidence of the way in which the peripatetic life of the Court affected Nonsuch is most plentiful for the eleven years during which the Palace was owned by Elizabeth I. During its early life it appears to have been completely left out of the royal summer progresses except in 1545, although it seems strange that, after the enthusiasm which he put into the building of the Palace, Henry should then have virtually ignored its existence. It may be that documentary evidence of more frequent visits has been destroyed, or is hidden away in records which deal with other matters which have no apparent connection with Nonsuch; but the fact remains that, apart from this one occasion when the Court was in residence, one visit earlier in the same year, and one in the winter of his death, there is no proof that Henry ever used his magnificent and costly show-place, or that it fulfilled the hunting-lodge function which had been the main reason for its siting.

Not even during the building years, when any proud owner could be expected to want to watch the gradual fulfilment of his plans, is Henry recorded as having displayed any continuing interest in Nonsuch. John Godsalve, writing to Thomas Wriothesley on 13th April, 1539, said, 'This evening the King decided to go on Friday to Oteland and Nonsuche.' This projected visit may or may not have taken place, but in July of the same year Henry was at Oatlands, and during his stay there commissioned John Cradocke, for life, to buy mats throughout England and Wales for all the king's palaces within twenty miles of London. Even at this early date Nonsuch is included in the list of palaces requiring mats.

Catherine Parr paid a fleeting visit during September, 1544, when, with work on the exterior decorations still going on, the Palace was made ready for the queen's dining there. In the following year Henry himself paid two visits. In May, probably expecting to find the Inner Court out of the workmen's hands, he was indignant at finding that the supervisor of the plaster-workers, Giles Gering, had not made the progress expected of him. Giles 'brabbled much to us of his working', but Henry, on information received, accused him of not having been at Nonsuch 'past twice syne Christmas last' to oversee the workmen under his charge, although he had drawn his wages as if he had been there every day. Giles retorted with many "bragges" that the members of the Council knew why he had been away, that they had been content to allow him to draw his wages and that he was quite ready to expose the great and notable faults of the king's officers who were accusing him, faults of which the Council were already aware. Henry wrote a letter, which is reproduced in Appendix II, to "our right trustie and right welbeloued the Lordes and others of our privy counsull" on 21st May, 1545, asking them to explain matters, because he did "not a litle marvaill (in cace these his wordes ar true) that ye haue not made vs privey therto all this while". He wanted to get the matter settled immediately, so that he could charge Gering and others who had offended; and summed Gering up as 'a fellow that glorieth much in himself and his doings'. However, the storm must have blown over, for "Giles Geringe the moldemaker at Nonesuche" was granted an annuity of twenty pounds sterling on 21st September of the same year.

Henry was back at Nonsuch in July, 1545, and, for the first time, it can be said with confidence that it was a full-scale visit with all the bustle and activity of the royal progress. He arrived on the 4th July, and the Council met at Nonsuch on the 5th and 7th; but on the 7th the king moved on to Horsley. Tents were carted to Nonsuch, 'at the king's majesty's being there', by one John Briges, yeoman. He was paid 4s. for the twelve-mile journey, presumably from Westminster. During his stay, short though it was, the king found time to indulge his love of hunting—but possibly only as a spectator. He sat on yard-long cushions of purple velvet in a 'standing' in the Park to watch the hunting, whilst some bystander with a covetous eye watched the cushions: two of them were "stolen awaie" and were never recovered by the Keeper of the Wardrobe.

The furnishing of the Palace for Henry's visit must in itself have been a major operation. We have, unfortunately, no list of the contents of the Wardrobe dated 1545, but an undated Inventory, compiled under Letters Patent dated 14th September, 1547, covers many of the Palace Wardrobes as they were at the end of the reign of Henry VIII, and devotes eighteen folios to Nonsuch. The Inventory makes it appear that at this time the Palace was kept more fully furnished than might have been expected; but the items which take up the last five pages are known to have been added to the Nonsuch Wardrobe after the death of Henry. Many of the items in the main part of the list must, however, have been at Nonsuch at the time of the king's visit in July, 1545, and we may use the Inventory to indicate the kind of surroundings in which the royal household lived. Two other lists dated 1547 will help to fill in some of the details.

Hangings (tapestries, bed-curtains and 'window-pieces') were in many colours and materials: crimson velvet, 'verders' or French tapestry with prominent foliage, and embroidered flowers and fruits in colour, yellow and white satin embroidered with 'Antique' motifs and the seven works of Mercy, and tapestries 'of divers histories'. There were carpets of silk and gold lined with buckram, carpets of tapestry with the king's arms, the Garter and the 'King's word', carpets of verders, of silk, of dornyx (silk, worsted, woollen or partly woollen fabric from the Flemish town of Doornik or Tournai), carpets of satin 'embroidered with sundry of the king's beasts, antique heads, grapes and birds, fringed round about with a fringe of red silk and lined with red buckram', carpets painted, carpets plain with self-coloured embroidery, with rows of gold and silk of divers colours; but also, among those added in 1547, 'two-and-twenty old carpets of sundry sorts of frame work, sore worn and the most of them moth eaten all ready'.

The four-poster beds in the state apartments were very large in comparison with modern beds; in fact, with the curtains drawn, they formed a room within a room, giving a degree of privacy and seclusion which it would otherwise have been difficult to obtain amid the bustling life of a small palace. The top, or ceiler, and the drape at the head of the bed, known as a tester, were richly ornamented. In addition to the ceiler forming a 'roof' for the four-poster, its sides would hang down as a deep fringe. For this reason none of the Nonsuch beds of which we have details quite equals the gargantuan dimensions of one of the ceiler-tester 'sets' described. This set comprised a ceiler measuring 14 ft. 3 in. by 12 ft., of dark crimson velvet, with one half double valanced and the other half single, and embroidered with flowers of gold, the crowned head of a woman and wings. The tester of the same material had two pictures embroidered between three trees; its height was 9 ft. 9 in. and its width 13 ft. 6 in. Other ceilers and testers, some of them for much smaller beds, were of white Turkey silk, of purple silk embroidered with dolphins, of blue and crimson satin, of striped red and russet velvet. Valances, curtains and counterpanes were of similar materials; the counterpanes included one embroidered with a picture of two horses, and others were of white sarcenet embroidered with popinjays, of velvet lined with black buckram and of quilted yellow silk lined with green linen.

The "apparrell" of the "beddesteddes" included bolsters and pillows of fustian filled with down, fustian quilts filled with wool, and sheets. The four pallets or mattresses specifically mentioned were made of new tick filled with feathers and measured nearly 8 ft. each way, and their full-length feather bolsters were over 27 in. wide. The bedsteads themselves were gilded and painted, one of them being of walnut hatched with gold and light blue. The smallest of the four principal beds measured 7 ft. 6 in. each way. The largest was not far short of the dimensions of the Great Bed of Ware, which measures 10 ft. 9 in. square; at Nonsuch the king's own bed was: 'One bedstead gilt with gold and silver and painted with light blue, being in length 9 ft. and in breadth 8 ft. 7½ in., the ceiler, tester, six small valances and bases made of panels of crimson gold tissue, purple velvet and crimson velvet embroidered with the king's arms and badges crowned; with a bed, a bolster and two pillows of fustian filled with down; four quilts of linen filled with wool; a counterpane, 10 ft. wide and 13 ft. 6 in. long, made of panels of russet and yellow silk, quilted, lozenged with cord of Venice gold, bordered with embroidery of white cloth of silver, fringed with Venice gold and silver and lined with white fustian.'

There is mention of only one mirror, 'a fair glass of Steel set in walnutry carved and part gilt'. Decorated tables included one in black and white representing a king and justices, with the legend *Audite illos et quod iustum est iudicate.* Another showed Christ and the three kings, in alabaster, and a third was 'of wood burned with a picture of Our Lady with angels'. Indoor recreation was provided for by a pair of playing tables made of white bone and brass, 'wrought with white and green work' and with thirty men in them; a chess-board of cloth of gold and cloth of silver decorated with roses and pomegranates, 'having 30 chessmen of horseback and foot'; another chess-board was of 'marble glase' and had thirty-two men.

Chairs were of white cloth of silver and crimson velvet fringed with white and crimson silk, of purple velvet fringed with purple silk, of cloth of gold "reyzid" (raised, with a nap) with crimson velvet, of black velvet with flowers of cloth of silver and crimson velvet. To preserve the chairs during their long periods of idleness there were '18 cases for the said chairs great and small, of new buckram of sundry colours'. There were stools in great variety: folding stools, square stools and footstools, covered with velvet. Cushions were everywhere, of green and purple velvet, cloth of gold, purple tinsel, silk and damask. Two were made of crimson silk decorated with gold lions; one, of needlework on a purple ground, had 'King Henry's letters and hawthorns'. In addition to two small altars for the private closets, there were vestments and eight altar fronts for the chapel. One altar front was of green velvet, embroidered with fleurs-de-lis, our Lord in the sepulchre and figures on horseback; this was 2¾ yds. long and a yard deep. Two of the other frontals were of cloth of gold and black velvet embroidered with eagles and flowers, and of embroidered black velvet with a panel of cloth of silver. One of the vestments was of cloth of gold and mulberry velvet, "with all th'apparell to the same".

These, then, were the kind of trappings among which Henry moved at Nonsuch in 1545. We know that these furnishings were kept in the Palace from 1547; they are all authentic contents of the Standing Wardrobe at Nonsuch, although it is unfortunate that we do not know exactly when they were taken there. As to the kind of life the king lived during his brief visits, we are on far less certain ground. All that could be done, in the complete absence of any information except that already mentioned, would be to work out the general pattern of a day's routine for the king and his household, based on information unconnected with Nonsuch. Much of this has, however, recently been covered in *The Royal Residences of Great Britain*, in which Neville Williams describes the functions of all the officers of the household under their two heads: the Lord Chamberlain supervising all those, including noblemen, who personally waited on the king, and the Lord Steward being responsible for everything connected with the provision and preparation of food. It may therefore be better to take only one example of the extreme care that was taken to safeguard the person of the king in the daily routine of a palace; the ceremonial and the precautions which it describes could be matched in several other aspects of the administration of the household, particularly those concerned with the serving of food.

Following the instructions laid down in 1526 in Wolsey's *Ordinances of Eltham*, the Gentlemen and Grooms of the Privy Chamber get up at six. They light the fire, clean and sweep the room and then fetch the king's doublet, hose and shoes. Later they dress him in a reverent, discreet and sober manner. When it is time to make the king's bed, a Groom of the Bedchamber or a page goes to summon four Yeomen of the Wardrobe, who bring the bedclothes; he also summons four Yeomen of the Bedchamber and a Gentleman Usher. Four yeomen go to one side of the bed and four to the other, the groom stands at the foot of the bed with a torch, and the Gentleman Usher stands to one side giving the orders. First, one of the yeomen prods the straw (presumably a palliasse) with his dagger, and then the featherbed is put on top of the straw. A yeoman tumbles all over it to test it for hidden weapons, after which (if he has survived) it is considered safe to put on the blankets and sheets. These are laid by the eight yeomen, and their orders require them to lay them so carefully that all parts touch the bed at the same instant. The bedclothes are then tucked in and the pillows smoothed. Where each yeoman's hands have touched a pillow he is required to make the sign of the cross upon it and to kiss the place; he will thus get the first taste of any poison he may have been careless enough to leave there for the king. Now that the bed is made, it will be watched over by a page or groom until the king is ready to retire for the night.

Henry visited Nonsuch once more, in December, 1546, a month before his death. Whilst he was there he signed a number of documents. The King's Apothecary spent 1s. 4d. on 'perfumes for Nonsuch' on 13th December. A week later the king wrote from the Palace to the Council of Scotland. On 28th January, 1547, he died.

With or without the king, however, life went on at Nonsuch. Work on the building had continued from 1538 until at least 1545, the parklands and gardens had to be maintained, the deer tended, the Park Pale kept in repair and the Palace itself kept in a state of reason-able readiness for a sudden outburst of activity. From the outset, then, these various aspects of the maintenance of the Nonsuch estate required a responsible supervisor; and he in turn appointed subor-dinates to do the actual work, paying them out of the fees which he received as an officer of the Crown, but not leaving himself out of pocket.

Sir Ralph Sadler or Sadleir, knighted in 1542, a Gentleman of the Privy Chamber, was appointed as the first custodian of the Nonsuch estate a month before building began. His appointment was confirmed by Letters Patent dated 3rd January, 1541, but it was back-dated to the Feast of the Annunciation of the Blessed Virgin Mary (25th March) in the 29th year of Henry's reign (1537–8). On paper, at least, he had a wide range of responsibilities. He was Steward of the king's manors of Nonsuch, Ewell, East Cheam, West Cheam, Sutton, Banstead and Walton-on-the-Hill, and for this office his fee was £5 a year. As Bailiff of the same manors he received a further £5. For acting as Keeper of 'the site and capital messuage of our manor of Nonesuche' he received 2d. a day, as Keeper of the Park 4d., as Keeper of the Wardrobe 6d. and as Keeper of the Gardens and Orchards 4d. The fees were taken out of the manorial revenues due to the Crown, and were payable in equal half-yearly instalments. The fact that these fees were being paid from such an early date in the history of the Palace may tempt us to think that the building must have gone up more quickly than has hitherto been suggested, for it may seem rather out of character for Henry to pay for services which simply could not be performed. However, sinecures were by no means uncommon, and in any case a closer look at the terms of the appointment will clear up most of the difficulties. Sadler is to take custody of the site, as well as the building, not yet begun, which is to stand on the site; and exactly the same phraseology is used when his successor takes over in 1543. So that the expression 'capital messuage' meant, so far as Sadler was concerned, 'the palace to be built or now in course of construction'. From the date of his appointment, the Keepership of the Park, gardens and orchards entailed actual responsibility; for one of the earliest tasks of the Palace workmen was to enclose the Parks so that they could be stocked with deer, and some farm and garden crops continued to be grown after the Codingtons had left.

The only serious problem remaining concerns the highest fee of all, that of £9 2s. 6d. a year for the custody of the Wardrobe. Henry may have allowed this office to continue as a sinecure for several years. If this is not the explanation, it must be concluded that there was a considerable amount of royal household furniture at Nonsuch from a very early date. If this is accepted, we must go on to envisage furniture in the Cuddington manor house ready for the king's use during the early years, and in parts of the Palace itself well before our earliest documented royal visit, in 1544. If this is so, then it may be that Henry was at Nonsuch at various times during these early years to watch the progress of the building and to hunt; but we have no other evidence to support this inference.

Sadler, engaged on affairs of state which eventually took him to live in Edinburgh in 1542, may never have been to Nonsuch; certainly he would not have been able at any time to give to his various offices the daily attention which a daily wage might suggest. Instead, his deputies carried out the different functions for which he was drawing wages and he paid them out of his own pocket. For the year ended 29th September, 1542, the gross income from the manors of Nonsuch, Banstead and Walton was £94 14s. 10½d. Of this, the king received £40 3s. 6d. The rest went to Sadler, after his steward, John Skynner, had deducted £6 1s. 8d. to pay the two park-keepers, William Tanner and Simon Cavell; £4 as his own fee; £1 for the under-steward at Banstead and Walton; and 8s. 8d. as his expenses at the time of keeping the lawdays and courts at Banstead and Walton. The steward paid over the Keepership fees to Sadler, but was not, except in the case of the two park-keepers, responsible for paying the deputies who did Sadler's work for him.

Sadler's term of office ended on 29th September, 1543, and his successor, Thomas Cawarden, was appointed on the same terms by Letters Patent dated 2nd March, 1544, his expenses since the previous September being made good. Cawarden, knighted at the siege of

Boulogne in 1544, was, like his predecessor in office, one of the Gentlemen of the Privy Chamber. He was an ardent supporter of the re-
formed religion, high in favour with Henry VIII, and continued to
hold office, albeit precariously, under Mary Tudor. By Letters Patent
dated 11th March, 1545, he was appointed, with effect from the previous
March, to the important office of Master of the Revels at Court—the
office *Magistrum iocorum revelorum et mascorum nostrorum.* The Master
of the Revels was originally called the Serjeant of the Revels, but
Cawarden 'misliked' to be termed a serjeant, as he was 'of the King's
Privy Chamber', and so he became the first Master. He was also Keeper
of the Tents, Hales and Toyles. In 1548 he was Sheriff of Surrey, and
first Knight of the Shire in 1553, 1554 and 1558.

Although he lived at Blechingley, and had many other estates and
duties, Cawarden seems to have had a great deal more regard for
Nonsuch than had its royal owners, at least after the death of Henry.
In fact, so firmly entrenched had he become by 1556 that he was only
ousted from his keepership after a pitched battle. After his death a
great mass of documents, including unique records of his official
transactions, went to Loseley. Many of those relating to the Revels
have been sold, but a large collection of Loseley Manuscripts is de-
posited in the Guildford Muniment Room. From this source, and from
the printed transcriptions of Kempe and Feuillerat, many details of
Cawarden's life and work, at Nonsuch and elsewhere, are known.

His position as Master of the Revels was an onerous one, for which
he received a daily wage of 4s. From this source alone his income was
seven times that of a master craftsman. He had to maintain a large
theatrical wardrobe and a collection of stage properties for use at
Court entertainments—masques, interludes and the continuous revelry
arranged by the 'Lord of Misrule' for the twelve days of Christmas.
Demands were made on him at short notice, and he frequently had to
commission new properties, costumes and scenery. Toto, Modena
and many others worked to supply these needs, and a great amount of
canvas, timber, papier-mâché and costly clothing material was used.
His work brought him into contact with writers of masques and interludes, including Nicholas Udall and Thomas Heywood. The scale of
these entertainments in the cradle-days of modern English drama, and
the valuable nature of the properties under Cawarden's charge, is
illustrated by the payments for some of the clothes worn by the Lord
of Misrule during the Christmas festivities in 1552. One of three robes

made for him contained 9 yds. of white bawkdyn, a rich brocade, at 16s. a yard, embroidered with knots of cloth of gold costing £9 6s. 8d., and with fur, red feathers and a cape. His coat of flat silver with leaves of gold and coloured silk cost £27 10s. The Christmas revels during that and the previous year cost £717 10s. 9d.

It was Cawarden who paid the tailors and carpenters who made and maintained the tents which made the royal progresses possible. It was he who paid for the carriage of tents to Nonsuch in 1545. The temporary banqueting houses at Horsley and Oatlands, in Hyde Park and Marylebone Park, were erected under his supervision. With so many calls on his time, he can have had little enough to spare even for his estate at Blechingley; at Nonsuch, his servants deputized for him: Thomas Bothe as Keeper of the Palace and also in charge of the Wardrobe, Robert Foster, later replaced by Roger Marshall owing to 'notable offences and misdemeanours', as Keeper of the Little Park. There was also a 'pale walker', and Tanner and Cavell, formerly servants of Sir Ralph Sadler, were still living in the Great Park in 1558.

After the death of Henry VIII, Cawarden's duties at Nonsuch, apart from routine maintenance, were chiefly concerned with the issue and receipt of furnishings and with the control of deer-hunting. In September, 1547, the wardrobe was augmented by two deliveries from the 'lodging' which Edward VI had occupied in his father's palace of Westminster. Some of this material had been bought by Henry from the Duchess of Suffolk. In the same month Cawarden received various items 'parcel of the late Duke of Norfolk's stuff attainted'. These are the last recorded 'accessions', but records survive of a number of loans from the wardrobe during the ensuing years. Thus, on 11th November, 1547, Cawarden received a warrant to deliver certain furnishings to the Auditor of the Lord Protector. Somerset signed a warrant dated 24th August, 1549, to the "Keper" of the king's standing wardrobe at Nonsuch "to requier you that imediately upon the sight hereof ye delyver or cause to be delivered" to the Earl of Arundel, by way of loan, in such sort as the same might be redelivered, thirty pieces of "Verdors" with broad blooms and six carpets of verdors. In the first year of Mary's reign, by warrant dated 9th April, Sir John Gage notified Cawarden of the 'Queen's majesty's pleasure' that he would deliver to David Vincent, Keeper of the Wardrobe at Hampton Court, such material as Cawarden should think meet and convenient for the service of Her Majesty at Hampton Court 'against the coming of the

Prince of Spain'. In February of the same year Cawarden, and all other
Keepers of Wardrobes, had been summoned to Westminster to give
an account of the items in their charge.

Meanwhile Cawarden had enlarged his interest in the Nonsuch
estate. By Patent dated 12th March, 1550, he had been made Keeper of
"the Banketyng House within the Park there" but he received no
additional fee for this new responsibility: "the fee of the bankating
house and the litle parke of Nonesuche" for the year ended Michaelmas,
1555, was £6 1s. 8d., or 4d. a day. On 19th November, 1547, he had
acquired a twenty-one year lease on a house and 158½ acres in the
common fields outside the Park Pale. Edward VI visited Nonsuch in
1550, the Privy Council meeting there four times between the 10th
and 15th September; and in the following July Cawarden received
£156 9s. 2½d. for repairs to the building.

With the return to the old religion under Mary, Cawarden was
soon forced to realize that his best days were over. He continued in
office, and full use was made of his knowledge and experience; but his
wings were clipped in no uncertain fashion during the first year of the
new reign when news of Mary's intention to marry Philip led to in-
surrections in various parts of the country. On 26th January, 1554,
Cawarden was ordered to arm himself, his servants and his tenants at
Blechingley, and to be ready to move at an hour's notice against the
rebel force, raised by Sir Thomas Wyatt in Kent, which was sweeping
round to attack London by way of Kingston. Three days later Lord
William Howard of Effingham, Lord High Admiral of England,
knowing Cawarden's religious convictions and being informed of the
feudal scale on which he had been able to equip his contingent out of a
suspiciously well-stocked armoury, decided that these preparations
were more likely to be for the aid of the rebels than for the support
of the queen. He therefore ordered the Sheriff of Surrey, Sir Thomas
Saunder, to seize Cawarden's arms and weapons. No fewer than
seventeen cartloads of arms were taken, William Saunder of Ewell
helping the Sheriff to impound enough cannon, smaller weapons and
armour to equip a small army. Although Cawarden managed to clear
himself on this, the first of five indictments during Mary's reign, only
four cartloads of arms were returned to him.

However, life at Nonsuch continued on its uneventful course, in a
quiet backwater with the Palace of little more interest or use to Edward
and Mary than a furniture repository. At about the same time as

Cawarden was being disarmed, he received from his steward, Alen Byrd, the accounts for Nonsuch and the neighbouring manors for the year ended 31st December, 1553. Thomas Bothe had been paid £10 for acting as Keeper of the Palace, Simon Cavell £3 10s. for the old park (the Great Park) and Robert Foster the same for the new park. After all deductions, Cawarden received £43 11s. 6d.

During Mary's reign the Nonsuch deer were sent as gifts to many different people: thirty-one warrants to the Keeper to deliver venison survive in the Loseley collection at Guildford, and there are others in other collections. Some of the warrants have the signature—MARY THE QUENE—impressed by a wooden stamp. Arundel and Sir Robert Rochester wrote from Hampton Court on 27th August, 1553, ordering two bucks to be sent for the queen's use to 'Hampton Court or else where her highness shall then lie' on the 29th. 'Our right entirely beloved cousin the Lord Cardinal Poole, Legate *a Latere*' was to be given a buck out of the Great Park in July, 1555, 'permitting our said cousin to hunt for the same deer, as it so like him'. The warrant is indorsed 'This to be brought to Lambeth Tuesday, being the third of September'.

Antoine de Noailles, French Ambassador from 1553 to 1556, was given permission in February, 1556, to kill two does in the Great Park, the Keeper being notified by the queen's warrant of 5th February. Next day the Council wrote to their "loving Frende Sir Thomas Cawarden" informing him that the French Ambassador "for the better recreacion of himself and his wief, hath desired to visit the Quenes majesties howse of Nonesuche, the gardens, parks and other commodities about the same". The queen, they said, had addressed a warrant for their pastime of hunting, and her pleasure now was that Cawarden would show them the house.

The visitors came, and doubtless enjoyed their recreation and pastime until 'it happened by mischance of certain greyhounds untimely slipped' two deer were killed in addition to the two authorized in the warrant. This was a serious matter for the park-keepers. The ambassador had a certificate drawn up to exonerate them, in which he begged 'that no displeasure should accrue to the park-keepers of the parks at Nonsuch'. He signed and sealed the document at Nonsuch on the 15th February, 1556.

Other recipients of Nonsuch venison included "oure trustie and wel beloved the maior and his bretheren of our Citie of London", the

Lady Kempe, the Marquis of Winchester (by virtue of his office of High Treasurer) and the Wardens of the Company of Grocers for their feast on 18th July, 1556, this last being received by "Thomas Piket, grocer, dwellinge at the signe of the Cocke in Wood Street".

The blow which deprived Cawarden of most of his Nonsuch fees and perquisites fell five months after this order had been executed. Mary, we are told, having no use for the Palace building, was contemplating its demolition. Instead, it and the Little Park, as well as the reversion of Cawarden's lease on the house and $158\frac{1}{2}$ acres outside the Park, were 'sold' to Henry Fitzalan, 12th Earl of Arundel. The sale was more in the nature of an exchange, the cash payment being only £485 13s. 4d. and the main part of the transaction being Arundel's surrender to the Crown of the manors of Stowbardolf, Cantlowe, Strumpshaugh and Scroteby, in Norfolk. The Great Park was not included, and Cawarden continued to act as its keeper on behalf of the queen. The Letters Patent recording Arundel's acquisition of the Palace were dated 23rd November, 1556. The new owner was to have the income from the estate as from 29th September, free of all deductions except the fees granted to Cawarden for the custody of Nonsuch House and Park.

Sir Thomas was under house arrest during the summer of 1556, and imprisoned in the Fleet from May until at least July, 1557, being under close confinement for a month for his obstinacy in not acknowledging his offence. It was thus inevitable that he should be out of touch with what was happening at Nonsuch, where Arundel was behaving as if his Letters Patent had cancelled Cawarden's life-tenure of the Keeperships of the Palace, Wardrobe, Banqueting House, Little Park, gardens and orchards. Cawarden had had some warning that changes were on the way, for the Palace was almost stripped of its furniture; and although the furnishings did not reach their new custodians until 17th and 18th November, 1556, they must have taken some little time to sort out, pack and cart. In the receipts given by the new keepers, Henry Plessington at Richmond Palace and Ralph Rowlandson at the Tower, many of the items described in earlier pages can be recognized. The Richmond list included "two Playing tables, two Chesse bourds with 60 men in them, two Tables with pictures, one fyer fork and peire of tonges". A few soft-furnishing items were left behind and were not disposed of until eighteen months later.

One of the most interesting of the Nonsuch documents at Guild-ford contains Sir Thomas Cawarden's account of his dealings with the Earl of Arundel during this time of change of ownership. The document itself is undated, but, in a later hand, it has been endorsed "*c.* 1557". It illustrates the determined way in which Cawarden clung to his Nonsuch interests after Arundel had acquired the Palace, so that in the end his servants had to be turned out by force. To Cawarden it was the justifiable complaint of a man deprived of his rights by the high-handed actions of Arundel and his son-in-law, John, Lord Lumley. There is no indication of the name of the person to whom the complaint was made, or that the moving rhetorical question with which he ended was ever answered. He records that Arundel (some consider-able time before the date of the Letters Patent under which he acquired the Palace) had the queen's permission to stay at Nonsuch for a time. The earl asked Cawarden to prepare the house for him, and to let him have hay for "horsemeat". He also said he wanted to keep two or three gelding at Nonsuch: in fact he kept there, free of cost, between twenty and thirty, as well as cattle and sheep to provide meat for his household; and his friends also grazed their horses there. Arundel then sent for Cawarden and told him that he proposed to buy the house and Little Park, and asked Sir Thomas what he should pay him for his interests. Cawarden replied that he would be very loth to sell his living, but that if Arundel would help him to acquire the Great Park, and the queen would allow her debt to him to be treated as part of the purchase money, Arundel need pay him no compensation. He was particularly anxious to be able to find a place for his men, who would be turned out of their jobs and homes if the Palace and Little Park were sold; if he could transfer them to the Great Park he would be able to have his 'revengement' on 'mine enemy William Tanner the keeper there' by turning him out.

This discussion led to no definite conclusion, and the two met again in London at Hallowtide, 1556. Arundel asked for pasture for a few sheep; he sent 200 ewes, of which 100, with their lambs, stayed in the Park until May, 1557. They were replaced by 260 others, which remained there until August. Discussions on Cawarden's purchase of the Great Park continued all this time, but no satisfactory arrangements could be found for the placing of his men. He scarcely seems to have realized that in the meantime Arundel had completed his purchase of the Palace and Little Park, and had a perfect right to do many of the things of which Cawarden was complaining. Whilst the discussions were in progress, he relates, Lord Lumley several times stayed at Nonsuch at Cawarden's expense. During these visits Lumley, with the help of William Saunder, of Ewell, "slyly sought to exclude my servauntes in the same park dwellinge". On Midsummer Eve Lumley and Saunder had put Lumley's man into the Banqueting House, taking the keys from Cawarden's deputy, Thomas Bothe, and warning Bothe to prepare to leave his house. The same evening they had returned, and accused Richard Butler, the 'pale walker', of stealing lead. Butler "before them bothe and others prouid himself a treue man", yet they turned him out of his lodge and ordered him to keep out of the grounds.

On 5th August William Saunder reinstated the dismissed keeper of the Little Park, Robert Foster, and put one of Arundel's men into the Keeper's Lodge with him, telling them to stay in possession of the Lodge for the use of Arundel. Lumley's servant announced that Arundel's pleasure was that neither Cawarden's new park-keeper, Roger Marshall, nor the pale-walker, should again enter the grounds; at the same time he ordered Thomas Bothe to give up the keys of the Palace, to clear any things of his out of it, and that "he shold come no more within the gates therof".

By the end of August there was no shadow of doubt as to Arundel's intention of moving in at an early date. In his name, Lumley ordered the Park to be cleared of cattle, and at the same time had the following letter delivered to Thomas Bothe:

'You shall perceive that my lord my father [i.e., father-in-law] had thought that, upon my declaration unto you that His Lordship was minded to occupy your house, for that the same was needful if he should lie at Nonsuch, that you had sought to have placed yourself in some other house. And now, perceiving the contrary, hath willed me to show unto you his pleasure, that you with speed depart out of your house, to the end the same may be ready at his commandment at his coming thither, which he intendeth very shortly. His pleasure is that you depart within these three weeks at the furthest.

'Farewell. From Arundel Place, the 30th of August, 1557.

Your friend,
Lumley.'

Robert Foster, the dismissed park-keeper, succeeded in stirring up so much trouble over the apples and walnuts growing in the Park that the rival parties came to blows, and he and his wife were directly responsible for tricking Arundel's men into attacking and wounding two of Cawarden's servants and two innocent bystanders. The wives of Cawarden's servants began to gather apples and crabs in the Little Park, as they had done for many years. Arundel's and Lumley's men and Foster forbade them, in Arundel's name, and both parties agreed not to meddle with the fruit until Arundel's wishes in the matter were known. The very next day "my lordes Folkes and Fosters wif gathred them hooly and Fosters boy carried them to Kingston and thear sold them at the markett".

Having been cheated out of even a share in the apples, Cawarden's servants—Thomas Bothe, William Dethick and Roger Marshall—and "one Barthilmewe Hillard the Borowshed of Cheiham", with their children, began beating and gathering walnuts in the Little Park. Arundel's men and Foster "diswarned" them, but, after the apple incident, Cawarden's people refused to take any warning from them, or from William Saunder, who was sent for and came with a number of servants to keep the peace. Eventually Saunder persuaded both parties to leave the nuts alone to enable him to get in touch with Arundel. William Dethick reported matters to Cawarden, who took strong exception to this interference with his servants and sent Dethick back to Nonsuch to tell them to gather the nuts. Bothe and Dethick decided to let Saunder and Arundel's men know Cawarden's instructions, and so they walked towards Ewell, "thei bothe in their Jerkins, hauing no weapon but only their daggers and eache of them a rydynge rodde in their handes". At the inn in Ewell they found William Saintalbons and six other men of Arundel's at dinner. Bothe told them that Cawarden had said that the walnuts were to be picked; Saintalbons replied that Arundel had said that they were to be left alone, and the six men were there to see that he was obeyed. They agreed that neither side should touch the nuts until Arundel and Cawarden had conferred together.

Meanwhile, back in the Little Park, events had been moving rather too quickly, and this compromise between Bothe and Saintalbons came too late to avert disaster. Dethick's manservant and Barthilmewe Hillard began gathering walnuts, Barthilmewe having been hired to beat because "he was a good beater of walnuttes". Roger Marshall and Butler had intended to go with them, but as they passed the park-keeper's lodge they noticed that the door was open "and no cristian creater therein". Knowing that Cawarden was dissatisfied with them for allowing Arundel's men to put Foster back in the lodge after his dismissal, Marshall and Butler went in and "put forth a table, a table trestle, a forme, Cubboard and a kettle of Robert Fosters" and shut themselves in. Foster's wife arrived and tried to get in, and then went hot-foot to Ewell to tell Saunder and Saintalbons that she was "pulled out of her hous".

Arundel's men made Bothe and Dethick go with them from Ewell, up past the Banqueting House where Dethick left them to get his horse ready to ride to Cawarden. The rest went on until they came to the lodge, where Arundel's party drew their swords "and with great noys and violens ran at the said doar with their Fete". They then fetched a battering ram and broke the door down. As it fell, Foster and his wife, standing by, suddenly cried out: "Thei come. thei come. thei come." My Lord's men looked round and saw four men running towards them from the direction of the walnut tree. In a calmer moment they might have realized that this apparent attack from the rear was not an armed intervention, but merely four harmless people running to see what the noise was about. The runners were John Goldsmythe, a very sick man, in a long gown, with a kerchief and hat on his head, a staff of his own and one that had belonged to his father; Dethick's man with a hazel pole with which he had been beating down walnuts; another Marshall, Thomas, with a pikestaff, returning from hare-hunting on the Downs; and Barthilmewe Hillard, empty-handed.

Against this menace, spurred on by cries of "Down with them. Down with them" from Foster and his wife, four or more of Arundel's men, with drawn swords, prepared to sell their lives dearly. They rushed at the intruders, and the sick man, although he picked up a cowl staff and tried to defend himself against three attackers, was struck in the shoulder and gave up. Dethick's man, fending off two assailants, was unprepared for Foster creeping up behind him and felling him with a blow in the neck; as he went down he was wounded in the arm and hand. Marshall, with his pikestaff, gave a good account of himself against three and then four of Arundel's men. He struck one of them on the forehead with the pike of his staff; another, after many blows had been exchanged, closed with him, but Thomas "bore him over and staggered withall". Eventually he went down with a great blow on the head from a sword, and as he lay face downwards two or three more struck him and one gave him two great dagger-wounds in the head.

Hillard, the "Boroweshed", called to them to keep the peace, saying that he was the queen's officer. He took no part in the fighting, but "euer kept the peas". His attempts to assert his authority merely incensed Arundel's men, who ran fiercely after him "crieng to him awey villayne, away villaine. or elles we will keyyll ye. away." Little wonder that when people living near came and besought him to stay and keep the peace he "durst not".

Turning back now to the real business of the day, Arundel's men again approached the Keeper's Lodge, with their swords ready. Thomas Bothe, whose son had found a staff and given it to him, barred their way, and besought Saintalbons, as he was a gentleman, to order his men to put up their weapons, and not to run upon the two who were within the lodge and destroy them. Probably feeling that he had already done more than enough to uphold the honour of Arundel, Saintalbons agreed to call off his men, and there was no more bloodshed. Cawarden later questioned his servants, separately and together, but could find no reason to doubt their version of what had happened. The fight had not been provoked by them, for they were not prepared for fighting; if they had been armed they would have given a good account of themselves.

He goes on to say that he had never had any recompense from Arundel for the loss of his rights at Nonsuch, except an offer through Mr. Pelham which was worse than nothing. It was being said that his Patent for the Keepership was forfeited after the affray, and people were being told that he was an unreasonable man and would come to no order. Yet in spite of saying that the Patent was void, Arundel had offered that their lawyers should discuss the matter and had said that he would be good to Cawarden, but for his stubbornness. Far from these things being true, Cawarden himself had never heard that his Patent was not valid. Why then should Lord Lumley and Mr. Saunder first shoulder him from the keeping of the Banqueting House, then from the Mansion House, thirdly from the Paler's Lodge, fourthly from the garden rooms, fifthly from the Park-keeper's Lodge, sixthly from the Housekeeper's Lodge and seventhly to the pit brink, excluding all his servants by force of arms, and then driving out all the cattle from his herbage and taking away all his pannage?

Despite his complaints, Cawarden was left with only the Keepership of the Great Park, where his servants Bothe, Tanner and Cavell were living when the Park was surveyed about the year 1558. By this time the deer in the Great Park, which had numbered 560 in the first year of Mary's reign, had been reduced to 250. It may be that the remnants of the Nonsuch wardrobe material were transferred to the Keeper's Lodge in the Great Park when Arundel took possession of the Palace, for the last dated issue was made by Thomas Bothe on the 1st May, 1558.

The last link between Cawarden and Nonsuch is a letter dated 18th July, 1558; but this time the connection is between Cawarden as Master of the Revels and an apparently reluctant visitor to the Palace. In the letter, a bridegroom asks for the loan of a masque, which probably includes the text as well as the properties, to relieve the gloom of his wedding day at Nonsuch. Sir Thomas Copley, Member of Parliament for Gatton at the age of nineteen, writes in his twenty-fourth year to Sir Thomas Cawarden:

'Right Worshipful, after my duty remembered (as from one whom your courtesy and friendship hath emboldened at every need to presume on the same) these may be to require you (if conveniently you may) otherwise I will not require it, that it might please you secretly to lend me the use of one of your masques, for one night against this my marriage, which (in ill hour to me) is like to be solemnised on Sunday next at Nonsuch. Where my hope is I shall see you, and so I do most heartily require you I may do.'

It is most unlikely that his hope of seeing Cawarden was fulfilled, for by this time Arundel and Lumley were firmly established in the Palace, and a new chapter in the history of Nonsuch had begun.

8

Arundel and Lumley

HENRY FITZALAN, 12th Earl of Arundel, was born about the
year 1511. Henry VIII was his godfather, and his biographer tells us
that not only was he the 'first and eldest Earl', but also exceeded all
others of his time 'in his calling and in true nobility; he feared God,
did good to many, and was not the harmer of any'. The biographer
was writing for the benefit of Arundel's surviving kinsfolk; a more
dispassionate account of the career of the noble earl would have
tempered the description of the undoubted virtues of the man by
recalling the treasonable intrigues in which he was involved and the
tangle of financial troubles which he handed down to his heir. On
balance, however, such an account would probably have summed him
up as being one of the leading figures of his day, no worse for guile and
double-dealing than many of his contemporaries and a good deal better
than most of them.

At about the age of fourteen his father put him into the king's
service, apparently in spite of Wolsey's desire to put him into his own
livery. Thereafter he was in continuous attendance on the king and was
in great favour. In 1540, at twenty-nine, he was made Lord Deputy of
Calais in place of Viscount Lisle, at a substantially increased fee. On
the death of his father in January, 1544, Henry Fitzalan, hitherto Lord
Maltravers, became 12th Earl of Arundel. He returned to England,
and was elected K.G. in April, 1544. In the July of that year he
preceded the king to Boulogne as Lord Marshal of the Field. An
engraving of the siege of Boulogne, in the possession of the Society
of Antiquaries, shows one segment of the army of 30,000 under
Arundel's command, with the king himself directing the artillery. So
many engines of war are crowded into this one part of the front that
the town ought to have been reduced to a heap of rubble in a day or so.
In fact, it was not until the 11th September that he was able to lead

his troops through the breach made by the artillery. Returning to England he was made Lord Chamberlain, an office which he retained until 1550. In that year his enemies brought against him a number of unsubstantiated charges, as a result of which he was ordered to keep to his house and pay a fine of £12,000. He was quickly released and two-thirds of the fine remitted; but in 1552 he was accused of complicity with the Duke of Somerset, who had been committed to the Tower on charges of felony and treason. Arundel was confined to the Tower for a year, and, although he asserted his innocence, eventually bought his freedom by signing a confession and agreeing to pay a fine of 6,000 marks in six annual instalments.

Just before the death of Edward VI, in July, 1553, Arundel's fine was cancelled; he rejoined the Council and pretended to join in the scheme for settling the succession on Lady Jane Grey. Instead, he warned Mary of Northumberland's plans to trap her, and she accepted his advice to keep out of the way for a time. For ten days Arundel kept up his counterfeit support of Northumberland, but on the 19th July, after addressing the leading citizens of London, he and his followers pledged themselves to support Mary, and she was proclaimed queen. Arundel himself apprehended Northumberland, who was executed.

More than restored to favour, for Mary undoubtedly owed her accession and possibly her life to him, Catholic Arundel was made Lord Steward of the Household, and at Mary's coronation he was appointed High Constable, a position which he had held when Edward VI was crowned. It was he who met Philip of Spain at Southampton in July, 1554, on his way to Winchester for his marriage to Mary on 25th July. During the next few years he undertook two peace-making missions abroad. In 1555 he was elected High Steward of Oxford. In the following year, the year in which he acquired Nonsuch, his eldest son, Henry, Lord Maltravers, died. During the heat of the troubles over Cawarden's Keepership of Nonsuch, Arundel lost his daughter Mary, who, still in her teens, died of puerperal fever seven weeks after the birth of a son, Philip, through whom the Earldom of Arundel later passed to the Howards of Norfolk.

Two months later, on 21st October, 1557, Arundel's second wife died. Very soon after the death of his first wife, who had borne him three children, he had married Mary, daughter of Sir John Arundell. From 1551 until her death the second Countess had appeared at many public functions, close to the royal party; now it was her turn to be the centre of well-nigh royal obsequies. Four days after her death a 'goodly hearse' or bier was set up in St. Clement's Church without Temple Bar, and on the 26th October a great procession conducted the coffin to the church. First came the Bishop of London, with St. Paul's choir, and the clergy of London. Then came the coffin, with four heralds in their coats-of-arms, each carrying a banner. The chief mourners were the Countess of Worcester and Lady Lumley, Lord North and Sir Anthony Selenger. After them came 100 'mourners of men', and as many ladies and gentlemen all in black. These were followed by a great many poor women in black, twenty-four poor men in black bearing torches and many of the Countess's servants in black carrying torches. On 28th October the Bishop of London sang Requiem Mass, and the Abbot of Westminster 'preached her a goodly sermon'. After the Mass the Countess was buried, her chief officers standing round with white staffs in their hands, and the heralds in their coats-of-arms. The account of the funeral ends: 'And, after to my Lord's place for dinner, for there was a great dinner.'

Arundel thus came to Nonsuch at a time of great personal sorrow, when his eminent position and enjoyment of royal favour must have seemed of little worth compared with what he had lost. Little wonder, then, that he should cling to his only remaining child, lavishing both wealth and affection on her, and depending more and more upon her and her husband. Jane Fitzalan, born about 1537, was married at a very early age to John, Lord Lumley. The date of the marriage is not known, but a translation by Lumley of Erasmus' *Instructions to a Christian Prince*, in the British Museum, is signed 'Your lordship's obedient son, J. Lumley, 1550'. As Lumley's own father was executed in 1538, he can only mean 'son-in-law'. Jane had received the classical education usual for girls in her station, and a number of her Greek and Latin exercises and translations are preserved in the Royal Library at the British Museum. Jane's brother Henry had matriculated at Queen's College, Cambridge, in May, 1549, with John Lumley, who, at the age of thirteen or fourteen, had successfully petitioned for the reinstate-ment of the Lumley barony, which had been extinguished by the attainder of his father; but the new barony was limited to his male heirs. Both boys left Cambridge before receiving degrees. Two days before the coronation of Mary in 1553, Lumley was created a Knight of the Bath, and my lord and lady, an old married couple of about nineteen and sixteen, were present at the coronation. Jane was one of the six principal ladies who sat in the third chariot of state, dressed in crimson velvet, with the horses' trappings of the same material. Lumley attended Philip of Spain on his marriage in the following July. As we have seen, it was Lumley who acted for Arundel in ousting Cawarden from Nonsuch, and the Lumleys spent more of their time at the Palace than at any of the other Lumley residences, Jane, her father's 'nurse and dear beloved child', being mistress of the household until her death in 1577.

In August, 1557, Lumley had ordered Cawarden's Deputy-Keeper to leave Nonsuch within three weeks, implying that Arundel was about to move in. It is not until the following year, however, that we have our first evidence of his being there, from a letter written at Nonsuch on the 12th May. Cawarden was still actively interested in the Great Park; the Malden Court Rolls for 1558 record that Thomas and Roger Marshall and other tenants of Sir Thomas Cawarden had stopped up the two gates of Nonsuch Park, through which the people of Malden used, of long time, to pass and repass with their cattle. On 28th June the Earl of Rutland tipped the yeomen and grooms of the stable to the tune of 6s. 8d. at the end of a three-day visit to Arundel at Nonsuch. Later in the year Arundel attended a peace conference between England, France and Spain at the Abbey of Cercamp; but before even the preliminaries were completed news came of Queen Mary's death and he returned home.

Arundel had given up his position as Lord Steward of the Household shortly before Mary died. On Elizabeth's accession, although she probably mistrusted him, she was unwilling to risk the opposition of so influential a man. His popularity, indeed, was not confined to those who shared his religious beliefs, for he had acquired a reputation for settling disputes by level-headed reasoning where others would have resorted to force. However, the insecurity of the relationship between Elizabeth and Arundel is shown by its very extremes, for it ran the whole gamut from courtship to imprisonment. She began by restoring him to all his offices, including that of Lord Steward. At her coronation he was appointed High Constable for the day before, and High Steward for the day itself. Before the end of the year their names were being coupled together. The Spanish Ambassador, Gomez Suarez de Figueroa, Count de Feria, who had come to this country with Philip, wrote to the King of Spain on 29th December, 1558:

'The Earl of Arundel has been going about in high glee for some time and is very smart. He has given jewels worth 2,000 crowns to the women who surround the Queen, and his son-in-law Lord Lumley has been very confidential with her. I was rather disturbed at this for a time, as an Italian merchant, from whom he has borrowed large sums of money, told others here that he had heard that he [Arundel] was to marry the Queen; but I did not lose hope as the Earl is a flighty man of small ability.'

Arundel was elected Chancellor of the University of Oxford in January, 1559, and Lumley replaced him as High Steward there. Arundel had held his position as Chancellor for only a few months when he resigned, probably on religious grounds; Lumley was still in office at the time of his death fifty years later.

The summer of 1559 brought great activity to Nonsuch, the new owner doubtless rushing through many of his plans for the completion and embellishment of the Palace and gardens in time for a magnificent house-warming party. The guest of honour was Elizabeth herself, who was including Nonsuch in her summer progress. This summer the progress began on 17th July at Dartford. Next she was entertained at Cobham Hall before moving on to Eltham and thence to Nonsuch and Hampton Court. The visit to Arundel at Nonsuch is undoubtedly one of the most colourful events in the whole history of the Palace, with the twice-widowed statesman, at the age of forty-eight, entertaining the queen, not yet twenty-six, in so extravagant a manner that it became the talk of the town. Henry Machyn, of the parish of Trinity the Little by Queenhithe, who described himself as a citizen and merchant tailor of London, but whose chief occupation seems to have been that of funeral furnisher, recorded in his diary the account which is familiar to all students of Nonsuch. The version which follows is modernized, partly because his spelling is so archaic and partly because missing parts of his damaged manuscript always have to be filled in from a later and inaccurate version.

On Saturday, 5th August, Elizabeth travelled from Eltham to "Nonshyche", my lord of Arundel's, and there Her Grace had great feasting and banquets every night. On the Sunday evening Arundel provided the most costly entertainment ever seen. After supper (probably eaten in the Palace) there was a banquet of the kind described in Chapter 6: this would almost certainly have taken place at the

Banqueting House. A masque was performed and drums, flutes and 'all the music that could be' kept the festivities going until midnight; as for the food, the like of it had never been seen or even heard of. On the Monday Elizabeth watched coursing in the Park from one of the 'standings'. After a great supper, the choirboys of St. Paul's acted a play, with their master, Sebastian Westcott, one Philips and "Mr. Haywode". This was followed by a great banquet, the food being served on rich gilt dishes, and drums and flutes provided music. According to our later author, Strype, filling in a gap in Machyn's manuscript, the party broke up at three in the morning. Before the queen left Nonsuch for Hampton Court on the 10th August, Arundel presented her with a cupboard of plate.

If Arundel's hospitality and gifts had had an ulterior motive, and he really was expecting Elizabeth to succumb to such flattering attention, he must soon have realized that he had thrown away a great deal of money, for the queen had no intention of being pushed into matrimony. Accordingly he decided to recoup some of his losses, making use of his position as Lord Steward to charge as much as possible of the cost of the "sopers" and "goodly bankets" to the expenses of the queen's household. He claimed not only for the food and drink consumed (the latter amounting to £154 18s. 8d.) but for wardrobe expenses, dishes, pots and stabling. The total cost was £951 14s. 5d., of which £356 worth came from the queen's own stores: some of the provisions had been carted from Hampton Court.

However, we must not make too much of the implications behind this apparently mercenary act of a supposedly disappointed man; to do so is probably to put a modern interpretation on a transaction which may well have seemed perfectly normal 400 years ago. Certainly there were no signs that Arundel was out of favour in 1560, for in September of that year he was granted the Great Park of Nonsuch in exchange for the manor of Coombe and other lands in East Greenwich, and a payment of £264 10s. Lumley had been appointed Keeper of the Great Park in place of Sir Thomas Cawarden, who had died on 20th August, 1559, and the terms of Arundel's grant required him to continue to pay Lumley the keeper's fee of 4d. a day. By 1561 Arundel's lavish spending had run him into difficulties: he owed £800 to a London upholsterer, £750 to a merchant tailor and £450 to a merchant. He was still regarded as a firm candidate for the queen's hand, sponsored by Parliament; although Elizabeth herself was at this time encouraging Robert Dudley, Earl of Leicester. In the following year Arundel quarrelled with this most promising of his many rivals, and by 1562 had taken the first step towards the tangle of intrigue which marred his later years.

The queen's illness in October, 1562, gave rise to a meeting at Arundel's house with the object of obtaining support for Lady Catherine Grey, sister of Lady Jane Grey, as Elizabeth's successor. Thomas, Duke of Norfolk, who had married Arundel's daughter Mary and had re-married in 1558, was present at the meeting. Other considerations apart, Arundel had a particular interest in supporting Lady Catherine, for there was afoot a proposal for the betrothal of her son with Norfolk's infant daughter. However, the meeting ended inconclusively, and Lady Catherine remained a prisoner in the Tower, to which she had been committed for secretly marrying Edward Seymour, Earl of Hertford. When news of the meeting reached Elizabeth she sent for Arundel, and their first major quarrel was the result. In 1564 he surrendered his office of Lord Steward, and did it so offensively that he was ordered to keep to his house for a time, but he was released after a month.

A new Spanish Ambassador, Guzman de Silva, arrived in 1564, and in July, 1565, he visited Nonsuch. He wrote that the house was excellently embellished and fitted and had beautiful gardens. He found Arundel suffering from gout, so that Lumley showed him and another visitor, Sir Henry Sidney, over the house and gardens. Lumley seems to have made a good impression, for in November the ambassador wrote to the King of Spain: 'Lord Lumley is a very worthy gentleman, a good Catholic, and a devoted adherent to your Majesty, as indeed are all good people in the realm'. By this time Arundel had clearly abandoned hope of marrying Elizabeth, for in February, 1566, Don Guzman reported Lumley as saying that his father-in-law wanted to know whether the King of Spain wished the Archduke's aspirations in this direction to be helped on, because, if so, Arundel 'as your servant could not avoid doing so and serving your Majesty in this as he would in all things'. Because of his gout, Arundel proposed to travel to Italy to take the baths, and the queen had given her consent; but many people thought that when the time came Elizabeth's permission would be withdrawn.

In the end, however, he did make the journey, but so serious did he believe his trouble to be that before he left he made over all his

9. THE WINE-CELLAR

A view from east to west, with the east wall of the Inner Gatehouse at the far end

10. THE KITCHEN FOUNDATIONS

Courtesy of Nonsuch Palace Excavation Committee

(a) View from the south. The main kitchen block lies to the right of the cobbled courtyard

(b) The well

(c) Main sewer and side-drain

11. INNER COURT DETAILS

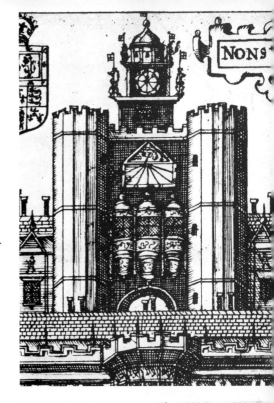

(a) South front of the Inner Gatehouse, from Speed's engraving

(b) South-west tower, from Hoefnagel's drawing

12. INNER COURT FOUNDATIONS

(a) South-east tower base

Courtesy of Nonsuch Palace Excavation Committee

(b) Inner Gatehouse, seen from the Outward Court

Courtesy of Nonsuch Palace Excavation Committee

(c) South-west tower base. Less damaged than the south-east tower. Doorways and tiled flooring can be seen

Courtesy of D. Cousins

13. NONSUCH PLASTER

Fragments of the plaster-stucco decorative panels which filled the spaces between the main timbers of the outside walls of the Inner Court

Courtesy of Nonsuch Palace Excavation Committee

(a) Cherub. Overall height 8½ in.

(b) Ram's head. Length 10½ in.

(c) Lettering. Height of letters 2½ in.

(d) Swag of fruit and flowers. Overall height 9⅛ in.

14. NONSUCH SLATE

Fragments of the carved slate panels which covered many of the main timbers of the outside walls of the Inner Court

Courtesy of Nonsuch Palace Excavation Committee

(a) Trophy. Overall height 13½ in.

(b) Instruction for fixing—
Troisiesme pillier

(c) Guilloche. Overall length 7½ in.

(d) A modern sculptor's demonstration carving slate, for comparison with an angel's wing fro Nonsuch. Overall length of Nonsuch fragment 8½ i

(a) Western entrance to cellar blocked up by fireplace; brick fire-back, stone hearth. On the right, a brick-built oven

15. THE BANQUETING HOUSE

Courtesy of Nonsuch Palace Excavation Committee

(b) General view from the east end. Cellar steps in foreground

(a) Henry Fitzalan, 12th Earl of Arundel

(b) George Berkeley, 1st Earl of Berke

16. PEOPLE OF NONSUCH

(c) and (d) Barbara Villiers, Countess of Castlemaine, Duchess of Cleveland,
Baroness Nonsuch in her prime and in later life

possessions to Lumley. He reached Padua and stayed for a year, during which time his gout was cured. Writing home on 1st March, 1567, the Spanish Ambassador said that Elizabeth had summoned the Earl of Arundel, and Lumley had told him that Arundel would be home within two months. Lumley was certain that the queen would show his father-in-law great favour. There is no hint of this summons in a letter sent to Arundel by Elizabeth on 16th March, 1567, nor any suggestion that their relations had ever been strained; but, after reading her good wishes for his health, the sheer effrontery of the later part of the letter and its bantering tone must have angered him considerably. The queen's visit to which the letter refers lasted from 21st to 27th January, 1567.

Only a verbatim transcription can do justice to this letter, although a few words have had to be omitted where the original is damaged. It reads:

"By the Queene.

Right trusty and right welbelouid Cosin we greete you well (*inserted*—And give you our harty thanks for such things as you haue sent vs. we wold haue written vnto you before this tyme, if we might haue had certen knowledge where our lettres might haue found you) where by your lettres and otherwise we perceiue you ar determined to retourne shortly . . . we are very glad both therof, and also that you haue receyvid such commoditie in this your journey to the recovery of your health, as we heere. Wisshing it to be so well confirmid in yow, as upon your retourne, you may enioy the contynuaunce therof heere at home in your wone natif contrey, as we well hope you shall, and wish it also to be.

"In the meane tyme, we haue in the later ende of this winter seeking to take the ayre for a small tyme in Surrey, visited your house at Nonesuche. Where we had dyvers wayes very good contentation. And did so well ayre every parte of your house, as at your comming we thinke you shall fynde it seasonable for you. And so we wishe yow to fynde it.

"Yeven vnder our Signet at our Pallais of Westminster the xvjth day of March 1566 [i.e., 1567] In the ixth yere of our Reign."

Arundel's return to England gave rise to a tremendous demonstration of the popular esteem in which he was held. At Canterbury he was met by an escort of over 600 horsemen, and the column had grown to 2,000 by the time he reached London. Here he was met by officers of the queen's household, and the Earls of Huntingdon, Sussex, Warwick and Leicester and many others; and the bells of the city pealed a welcome. Among the presents he brought for Elizabeth, he is said to have given her her first pair of silk stockings, bought on his way through Genoa. Even if they were not her first they will have been acceptable, for once she had worn silk 'she never wore cloth hose any more'.

By May, 1569, with Spanish support, Arundel's scheme for the marriage of Mary, Queen of Scots, and the Duke of Norfolk was afoot. The plan included the deposition of Elizabeth and the restoration of the Catholic religion. Norfolk and Arundel told the new Spanish Ambassador, Gueran de Spes, that the business was costing a great deal of money; they were deeply in debt, and begged him to let them have money. They were told that they would receive payment when they had achieved something. Lumley reiterated the request, saying that he, Arundel and Norfolk would bind themselves to repay an advance. In June, 1569, 6,000 crowns were sent by the Duke of Alva. By the end of September Elizabeth, now aware of the plot, had detained Arundel, Lumley and Pembroke at Windsor and had summoned Norfolk to present himself for interrogation along with the others. Although the prisoners insisted that the proposed marriage was the wish of the whole Council, Norfolk was sent to the Tower on 11th October. The Spanish Ambassador kept his king informed in a series of letters, all of which arrived together; the king was alarmed lest one of the four prisoners, closely pressed, should reveal the purpose behind the marriage, but Don Gueran assured him that they had been extremely cautious in the answers they gave during their interrogation. Arundel, his period of imprisonment prolonged by the rising in the north, was at first confined to Arundel House in the Strand; he was later removed to Eton and finally to Nonsuch. In April, 1570, Sir Francis Englefield wrote 'Arundel remains still at Nonsuch and Lumley in Mr. Hampden's house by Staines'.

As he was now unable to attend to his affairs, Arundel's debts mounted, and his imprisonment brought on a renewed attack of gout. However, through the influence of Leicester, he was set at liberty and restored to the Council in 1570. Lumley was also released, and the two immediately resumed their underground activities. Norfolk, having

made full submission to Elizabeth, was released towards the end of the
year and joined them. Through Roberto Ridolfi, a Florentine merchant, a correspondence, in cypher, had been kept up between the
Queen of Scots, the King of Spain and the Pope, and Norfolk, Arundel
and Lumley. In May, 1571, a servant carrying letters in cypher, one of
them to Lumley, was captured, and tortured in the Tower until he
confessed, although he cannot have had much information to give, for
it was not until 7th September that the Duke of Norfolk was arrested
and taken to the Tower. On the 28th Lumley joined him there, and
Arundel was ordered to remain under arrest at Nonsuch. Norfolk was
executed on 2nd June, 1572. Arundel was released in December, and
Lumley in April, 1573.

The rest of Arundel's days were spent in comparative seclusion.
Although Nonsuch was at times his prison, he seems to have had a
deep-rooted affection for it and to have lived there for much of his
time. Just before his arrest in 1571 he dated from Nonsuch a letter to
the Keeper of the Great Park, ordering him to deliver to the Archbishop of Canterbury, on request, as many deer as he might want,
'winter and summer yearly', and if the Archbishop should wish to
come and hunt them the keeper was to give him the same service as
he would give to Arundel himself. Despite Arundel's recent release
from imprisonment, the Queen was at Nonsuch in July, 1573, and
the Council met there on 3rd October, 1575. The Court was there
again on 19th August, 1579, only a few months before the death of
Arundel.

Jane, wife of John, Lord Lumley, died on 9th March, 1577. She had
borne three children, Charles, Thomas and Mary, but they had died in
infancy. The monument in the Lumley Chapel of St. Dunstan, in
Cheam, mentioned in Chapter 5, commemorates Lady Jane and her
children; but the designs for the Lumley monuments were not prepared
until 1590, and the bodies are not interred in the massive table tomb to
which the 'Nonsuch' panels are affixed.

Before taking leave of Arundel there are two aspects of his life at
Nonsuch which merit our attention; two things which he handed on
to Lumley, and which to a large extent shaped Lumley's later life;
these were his library and his debts. Arundel, not a particularly learned
man, and with a rooted dislike of foreign languages, had acquired the
library of Cranmer when it was confiscated on his arrest in 1553.
Many of these books, bearing the signature *Thomas Cantuarien'*, still

survive. Arundel's own books included works on military tactics and history, as well as Latin and Greek classics and music, probably bought for his children. Lumley's books were added to these two collections to form the beginning of the Nonsuch library; but the most important factor in its development was the introduction into the Nonsuch household of Humphrey Lloyd, a young man, a Master of Arts, whom Arundel brought back with him from Oxford after his brief spell as Chancellor in 1559. Nominally physician to the household, Lloyd became literally one of the family, for he married Lumley's sister Barbara, and their son Splandian inherited the manors of Ewell and Cheam.

Humphrey Lloyd, a native of Denbigh, is not known to have done anything to justify his appointment as a physician. His interests were antiquarian, and he found in Lumley a kindred spirit. Together they worked to build up a library remarkable for its size and comprehensiveness in a private house at this time. Lloyd is said to have been the one who did the actual work of searching out and collecting. He, Arundel and Lumley were members of the Elizabethan Society of Antiquaries. After Lloyd's death in 1568 Lumley continued to collect books, particularly in the spheres of history and the sciences. The whole library became his on the death of Arundel, and when Anthony Watson described it about the year 1590 he confessed that he was extravagant in his love for its choice selection of so many books. The section on Jurisprudence included 'the most complete foundations of every kind of law, treatises, glossaries, decretals, decrees, and precisely written formulas of common law and statutes'. If you were ill, there were doctors in the library to cure you, or musicians to soothe. Theology comprised a 'great and glorious array'; there were many translations of the Bible, the utterances of all the fathers, homilies, discourses and meditations. The histories had been collected from the best of the Greek and Roman writers, and recalled the vicissitudes of empires, the fashions of the ages, the first beginnings of the earth and of city life and the constitutions and administration of kingdoms and states.

The contents of the library were listed in more sober fashion in 1596 by a member of Watson's household, Anthony Alcock, who made a catalogue in the form of a shelf-list under seven main headings, with an author index. This catalogue has not survived, but a fair copy of it made in 1609 by 'Mr. Holcock' (i.e., Alcock), with corrections by

Dennis Flemynge, is at Trinity College, Cambridge, and the main part of this 1609 version was reprinted in 1956. The catalogue shows that there were about 2,800 volumes in the library, divided under the headings: Theology, History, Arts and Philosophy, Medicine, Cosmography and Geography, Law, Music. The Nonsuch library was eventually "dysparsed sundery ways", to quote Lumley's own words; but the story of that dispersal belongs to a later chapter. My purpose here has been to describe the growth and maturity of an outstanding private library, which, even by the time of Arundel's death, had become "righte worthye of remembrance".

A far less acceptable legacy from Lumley's father-in-law was the heavy burden of debt which had been growing for many years. We have noted, on the one hand, instances of Arundel's lavish spending— the 2,000 crowns for Elizabeth's ladies; the cupboard of plate given to the queen in 1559; the purchase, furnishing and completion of Nonsuch; and his year's holiday abroad. And, on the other, long periods during which his affairs were neglected, either through absence or imprisonment. As early as 1555 Lumley was helping to ease Arundel's financial difficulties, and the tradesmen's debts of 1561, which have already been described, were met by Lumley's letting of various lands to Sir Thomas Pallmer for eight years. In May, 1567, Lumley borrowed £1,300 on Arundel's behalf from Alderman Jackman and Alderman Lambert, and a further £600 in July, the security being various manors which had belonged to Arundel. After Lambert's death in 1568 the loan was repaid and immediately renewed. The new expiry date came and went, Jackman agreed to an extension, and a few days later he too died. Soon afterwards, in September, 1569, "the saide Erle and lorde Lumley were comytted to close and safe kepinge, so as none could have accesse to them for conference touchinge their affares". By the time they were released from custody Jackman's executors had moved in and taken possession of the pledged lands.

Even in the quieter days towards the end of his life, when there were no extraordinary financial calls on him, Arundel failed to make ends meet. His expenditure in 1574 was £79 18s. 11¼d. greater than his income of £3,819 0s. 3¼d. In 1577 the debit balance was only £17 14s. 7½d.; but on his death, on 24th February, 1580, his affairs were in such a sorry state that Lumley, his executor and residuary legatee, had to petition the queen for forbearance concerning money due to her until such time as he had been able to pay the funeral expenses and satisfy other creditors.

By this time the whole of the Arundel estate amounted to only £1,900 a year. The earldom of Arundel passed to Philip Howard, Earl of Surrey, son of Thomas Howard, 4th Duke of Norfolk. With it went lands valued at £700 a year. A total of £11,000 was owed to the queen, and £13,000 to others; and Lumley estimated that the funeral, "which ought to be honorably donne", would cost £1,000. On a note of justifiable self-pity, he added that he had never had any other advancement or preferment in his marriage than this, and that he had in fact had to help Arundel by disposing of lands of his own which had been worth £600 a year 'of old rent' and would by this time have been worth twice that amount. Even if he did no more than meet the debt to the queen, spread over thirteen years, he would be left with only £400 a year to live on. He asked the queen to forgo the next half-yearly instalments, both of the income from the Earl of Surrey's lands (which Elizabeth was to have for three years) and also of the repayment of the £11,000. He further petitioned her to consider the deferment of these repayments until the other debts due to her subjects were satisfied.

This debt to the Crown had its origins in 1526, when the City of Florence undertook to pay Henry VIII, over a period of twenty-five years, the sum of £11,250 owed to the king by a number of Florentine merchants. The original reason for the merchants' debt was unknown by 1574. In 1545 the City of Florence took on responsibility for another debt owed to the king by one Antonio Giudotto and his father-in-law. This debt was for 60,000 ducats; Henry paid the city fathers nearly 12,700 ducats for them to take over the debt, and they then became bound to pay the 60,000 ducats over thirty years. This was equivalent to £15,000, bringing the total debt to £26,250.

By the date of Elizabeth's accession, £13,900 had been repaid. The balance was "estalled" to Lumley in 1563, and he was to pay £771 17s. 6d. a year from the Feast of All Saints, 1564, until the whole was paid. For what consideration he and Arundel took on this burden is not clear; the debt, he says later, 'was such as Lodge and divers others refused to compound for and offered to the Florentines and divers others, yet none would take it. My lord and I did take it, being in a manner a desperate debt' but the rate of repayment was 'a great and too great a payment considering this hard recovery on coming by that

which is thereof to be had and recovered'. The difficulty of recovering
from the Florentines must have been obvious when the debt was taken
over, for they were well in arrears with their annual payments by the
end of Mary's reign, and paid nothing during the six years following
Elizabeth's accession. Nine years later Lumley was already more than
£5,600 in arrears with his annual payments, the total outstanding at
that date being £10,245. As security for the payment of the debt,
Arundel and Lumley had handed over to the Lord Treasurer and others
lands valued at £800 a year, but Lumley was to continue to have the
use of the lands until such time as he defaulted on his annual repayments. This arrangement was already proving more than irksome by
1570, when Arundel and Lumley jointly petitioned the queen for some
easement of the conditions. Arundel asked that part of the debt might
be remitted (and he would then forgo a promised gift by the queen of
land worth 100 marks a year). He also asked that the lands earmarked
as securities might be changed; he wanted to sell some of them to pay
his debts, and, even if he were allowed to sell them, he could not expect
a fair price for them whilst they were encumbered, so that he would
be forced to sell other lands which he would prefer to keep. In addition,
he was anxious to settle his estate on his posterity, and, as things stood,
he was powerless to do so until the Florentine debt was fully repaid.

Apart from the folly of taking over the debt in the first place,
Arundel and Lumley had only their own participation in intrigue to
blame for a substantial part of the ensuing financial loss. In 1570
Lumley had surrendered to Ridolfi the 'instrument of debt' for 60,000
ducats as well as Elizabeth's assignment of the debt; Ridolfi was to
hold them as security for Lumley's debt to him of £1,825. The
Ridolfi conspiracy was exposed a year later, Lumley was imprisoned
and Ridolfi was left in possession of the documents. Lumley was never
able to recover the instrument, Ridolfi reaped whatever payments the
Florentines made and Lumley had to keep up his payments to the
Crown.

Successive pleas for leniency did not fall on deaf ears, and at the
time of his death Arundel was in debt to the Crown by an amount
actually greater than the 1574 total of the Florentine debt. Lumley's
petition of 1580 was equally successful, for the £11,000 was still outstanding eleven years later, and this factor determined the whole of the
later history of Nonsuch.

Despite this background of continuous financial worry, Lumley, having lost his wife, children and father-in-law, seems to have been able to evolve a satisfying mode of life with his books, his interest in all the sciences, his antiquarian researches and a second wife. He married Elizabeth, daughter of John, Lord D'Arcy of Chiche, in 1582, and settled the Nonsuch estate on her; this settlement had to be changed later when the queen acquired the Palace, the manor of Stansted in Sussex being substituted for Nonsuch. In 1582 the queen granted a licence to Lumley and Dr. Richard Caldwell to make over to the 'College or Commonalty of the Faculty of Medicine of London' (the Royal College of Physicians) an annuity of £40 to provide, in the terms of the grant itself, "an excellent Reader that shall reade openlye in the house of the Colledge of the Phisicons in London . . . all the whole course of the Arte and science of Surgery for ever". The selected Reader was to travel in France, Germany and Italy for two years to hear other surgeons read and to observe their practices, and the readings were to begin in the Easter term of 1584.

To this period, too, may belong the fairly considerable additions to the garden ornaments of Nonsuch which we have already noticed; for Lumley was by no means allowed to live the quiet life which he would doubtless have preferred, but had to keep the house and gardens at Nonsuch in a state of readiness for the frequent visits of Elizabeth and her Court. Even in the first summer, a few months after Arundel's death, the Court moved in and spent at least a month there; the Lords of the Council were at Nonsuch on 29th May, 7th June and 5th July. On the 22nd June, and again on 8th July, Sir Francis Walsingham, Secretary of State, wrote to Sir Henry Sydney or Sidney, Lord President of Wales, 'from the Court at Nonsuch'. Next year's visit took place towards the end of the summer; the queen was hunting there on 1st September, and William Cecil, Baron Burghley, the Lord High Treasurer, recorded in his diary that his duties had taken him to the Court at Nonsuch on 21st and 30th September; on his second visit the Lord Chamberlain was also there. In 1582, the year of Lumley's second marriage, the queen wrote letters from Nonsuch on 17th July and 9th August; but in the following year there is no record of a royal visit. During this time the quiet, scholarly Lumley seems to have taken on a new lease of life, to judge from the heavy jocularity of a letter he wrote to Sir William More of Loseley on 30th August, 1583.

Sir William was to attend a conference at Leatherhead, but Lumley suggested that the meeting might be held at Nonsuch, 'or else after your conference to come to me to bed'. If they would come to Nonsuch he would be 'most glad of it, not for any other respect than to have yourselves to be refreshed by the sight of your best dogs outrun by my slothful deer. And in so doing (if otherwise the same be no displeasure to yourselves) I shall think myself right greatly beholden unto you for your so good company.'

By 25th July, 1584, he was again entertaining the queen, and yet again in October, and the Council met at Nonsuch on 3rd August. An important conference took place at the Palace in August, 1585. Lord Howard of Effingham, previously Lord Chamberlain, who became Lord High Admiral in 1585, arrived on or before 2nd August. From the 10th to the 20th the Delegates of the States General took part in discussions which led to the signing and sealing by Elizabeth of a provisional assistance treaty, whereby England was bound to support a United Netherlands. The English 'deputies' were Howard, Lord Hunsdon, Sir Francis Knollys, Sir Christopher Hatton and Sir Francis Walsingham, Burghley and Leicester. Part of a letter written at Nonsuch during these negotiations, and signed by the first five of these deputies, survives. It is apparently addressed to Burghley as Lord Treasurer, the missing part referring to an earlier warrant for defraying the expenses of the forces to be employed beyond the seas. It goes on to authorize the sending of £6,000 to Richard Huddlestone, who, on 2nd August, had been appointed Treasurer to Her Majesty's Forces in the Low Countries. The letter is dated 11th August, 1585.

Throughout August and September the Court was at Nonsuch, possibly with short visits to neighbouring palaces, and on 3rd October the queen met the Commissioners of the Hansa Cities there and offered them certain privileges. In this and the following year attempts were made to enlist Lumley's help in further secret moves on behalf of Mary, Queen of Scots; but he was one of the commissioners for her trial in October, 1586.

The queen was at Nonsuch again in May and July, 1587. It is unfortunate that the account of her next visit, often quoted, is 'in fact a fiction'. According to the *English Mercurie*, No. 50, for 23rd July, 1588, Elizabeth reviewed in Nonsuch Park 'last week' the troops of horse which had been raised by members of the Council and the nobility against the threat of Spanish invasion. The troops were ready to take the field at an hour's warning, and the queen expressed the highest satisfaction at their gallant appearance. The *Mercurie* is, however, the invention of Philip Yorke, M.P. for Reigate from 1741 to 1745 and later 2nd Earl of Hardwicke, and was written and printed in 1744 as a piece of scholarly entertainment for his family and friends. Copies discovered by people who did not know their origin were accepted as genuine for a time; but paper, type and surviving letters all confirm that they were fabrications.

In 1589 the Lords of the Council were at Nonsuch on 16th July; Elizabeth signed two warrants there on 10th August. On 2nd August, 1591, Robert Cecil was admitted into the queen's Council at Nonsuch.

His major preoccupation with Nonsuch did not lead Lumley to neglect his other estates; nor did he forget that his roots were elsewhere. Over half of his income came from land in Sussex, and a quarter from Durham, where he held Harte in Hartlepool, purchased in 1586 for £5,350, as well as the castle and domain of Lumley. He spent a great deal of time in collecting and recording information illustrating the history of the Lumleys, tracing his ancestors back to Liulph, who moved to Durham shortly after the Norman Conquest. Liulph's grandson adopted as his surname the name of the place where the family lived, and became the first 'de Lumley'. A mile from their original home, during the later years of the fourteenth century, the Lumleys built their castle. An account of the castle, and records illustrating the family history, collected under the direction of John, Lord Lumley, are contained in the Red Velvet Book, in the archives of the Earl of Scarbrough.

The book begins with the description of Lumley Castle. This is followed by three deeds in Latin, and a copy of a Latin inscription for the walls of the castle, tracing the descent of the family from Liulph. The same 'family tree' appears in Watson's description of Nonsuch, in the church at Chester-le-Street, and on the Lumley monument in the Lumley Chapel at Cheam. Next comes a description of the Lumley arms, originally six silver popinjays, or parrots, on a red field, with a silver pelican as a crest, but later changed to a red fess between three green parrots on a white field. Then is given the descent of the royal family from Adam, followed by the arms of all the family connections of the earlier Lumleys. The main value of the book to the study of Nonsuch rests in its later pages, which consist of an inventory of the contents of all Lord Lumley's houses in the year 1590, with a few later additions and deletions. The inventory was compiled from separate books listing the contents of each house and signed by the "severall wardropers", but unfortunately John Lambton, Steward of Household to Lumley, was too efficient and amalgamated all the books into one. As a result, there is no separate list of the contents of Nonsuch, but only one comprehensive list covering the contents of all the houses: the pictures "sorted together for the memorye of your Lordships house" and the furnishings listed as "A summarye of certayne stuffe within your Lordships houses the 22 May Anno 1590".

In examining the inventory, then, allowance must be made for the fact that many of the articles were at other Lumley residences, notably at the town house on Tower Hill, at Stansted in Sussex and at Lumley Castle. A great deal of it must, however, relate to Nonsuch, and there is definite evidence to support this assertion. The first nineteen pages of the inventory contain the drawings of 'furniture' mentioned in Chapters 5 and 6. Three of these coloured pictures show the designs prepared for Lumley for the tombs of himself and his two wives. Of the remaining items, seven can be identified with complete certainty as belonging to Nonsuch. In the lists which follow these pictures over 250 paintings are described; they include portraits of Lumley's family and ancestors, royal portraits, people with whom Arundel's public life had brought him into contact; religious, mythological and historical subjects; full-length portraits, pictures "of a smaller scantlinge"; works by Holbein, Gerlach Flicke, Steven van der Meulen, Segar (Sir William, Garter King-at-Arms, or his brother Francis), Durer, Hubbert, Hans Eworth, Jaques Pindar, Antonio Moro, Frans Flores, Cornelius Van Cleef, Schorel, Vincent of Macklen, 'Cleave Haunce' and Hilliard, although in the vast majority of cases the artists are not named. There was "a great booke of pictures doone by Haunce Holbyn" for Edward VI, containing portraits of certain lords and ladies, gentlemen and women of the time of Henry VIII. The pictures were valued at the very modest figure of £623. Included in this total were 'a special picture of Christ cast in mould by Raphael, brought into England from Rome by Cardinal Poole', 'The Passion of Christ cut in black stone' and a picture, in folds, of the Passion, 'very ancient and notable'.

Following the lists of pictures comes the summary of the "stuffe" in his Lordship's houses. This was estimated to be worth £5,380, and included 57 'suits' of hangings of arras, silk and tapestry; 121 carpets (including 15 carpets of velvet for tables and windows); over 200 bed-coverings of various kinds, 4 gilt bedsteads, 23 of walnut and 40 of wainscot, 75 pallet beds, 95 livery beds, 32 wool beds; 231 chairs, stools and forms in leather, marquetry, wainscot and needlework; 89 tables, of which 14 were marble; cupboards; bed-linen, blankets and 109 cushions, of cloth of gold, velvet and silk. The musical instruments merit listing in the original spelling of the inventory. There were "Great standyng wynd Instruments with stoppes, 8; Vyrgynalles paires, 5; Rygalles paires, 2; Jryshe harpes, 2; Lutes, 8; Howboyes, 10; Bumbardes, 3; Crumpe hornes, 4; Recorders, 15; Vyolens, 13; Vyoles, 41; Sagbuttes, 4; Cornettes, 12". The armour is separately valued at £480 17s. 8d.; the value of the plate and silver vessels has not been written in.

The reason for the making of such an inventory at this particular time is not far to seek. The debt to the Crown, the Florentine debt, was still unpaid, and Lumley was anxiously casting round for some means of repaying it which would not unduly lower his standard of living. As a first step, he would want to take stock of his resources. Many discussions must have taken place in 1590 and 1591 between him and the queen's officers, and in August, 1591, he entertained Elizabeth at Stansted; although it seems likely that by that time the discussions had already led to agreement on the device whereby Elizabeth took Nonsuch in payment of the debt but Lumley continued to live there. This proposition, put forward by Lumley, is contained in a document described as being "of about the date 1601", but which can be no later than 1591. It is 'A note of remembrance for the Lord Lumley his debt to the Queen for which he offereth his house at Nonsuch'. If the queen would be pleased to take his house at Nonsuch, he said, she would be paid in an instant, the memory of her father would be continued, she would acquire for herself a place to withdraw to, and, whilst living there, would save nearly a thousand marks a month. With regard to Lumley's land about the Palace, he would leave it to the queen to take it or leave it on any reasonable terms. If he had to continue paying back his debt at the rate of £600 a year out of his poor living, it would take nineteen years to clear it. He and his wife would be left in great distress and the house would be forced utterly to decay; the burden of the debt would rest wholly upon him although it had come to him from 'another man from whom I had reason to have expected a better fortune'. He had thought fit to make this suggestion partly because it was his duty to pay what was due to the queen, and partly because of his wish to be able to maintain himself, in his later years, at a reasonable standard, so that he would be able to serve the queen. The mass of the debt, being the Florentines' debt, "was made by us from a doubtfull debt".

Two other documents, also undated but certainly belonging to 1591, provide glimpses of the negotiations in progress; they are reproduced in Appendix II. Lord Burghley, in a 'Memorandum of matters to be communicated to the Queen's Majesty' evaluated the Palace at £200 a year, the Little Park at £112, the Great Park at £160, the Meadows at £60 and a close outside the Park at £2, giving a total annual value of £534. These were to be assured to the queen, with a re-grant of the lands to Lumley without rent during the queen's reign. Lumley was to receive, in exchange, other lands worth £500 a year, but he was to pay the £500 to the queen during the rest of her reign. Burghley pointed out that, if Lumley were to die before the queen, the arrangement would not be quite as beneficial to her as it appeared: the £500 income from the 'exchange' lands would go to Lumley's heirs; the queen would have to pay someone to act as Keeper of the Little Park and Palace, and would only receive £222 in rents on the Great Park and Meadows.

Mr. Justice Popham, Attorney-General, who in the following year was nominated Lord Chief Justice and was knighted, also watched the interests of the queen during the negotiations. A memorandum by him suggested that the documents which were to commit the queen to her side of the bargain should remain in the hands of the Lord Treasurer until Lumley had completed the legal formalities on his part. On the queen's side the lands being exchanged for Nonsuch were to be leased to the Lord Treasurer and Mr. Fortescue, with a grant of the reversion of those lands to Lumley. Lumley's assurance of Nonsuch to the queen had to be enrolled and the fine thereon acknowledged, and he had to enter into bonds for the performance of the covenants he was entering into.

The formalities were completed on 21st January, 1592, by a 'final concord'. Lumley and Elizabeth his wife remitted and quitclaimed to the queen the capital messuage of Nonsuch, two gardens, one orchard, 350 acres of land, 104 acres of meadow, 900 acres of pasture and 250 acres of woods, with appurtenances in Nonsuch and Cuddington. Lumley became Keeper in his own house; even though the original proposals were modified, and he was required to take out a lease on the Great Park, the rent was excused after a few years, and he could scarcely have wished for an easier escape from the crushing burden of debt. In fact, in many ways he can hardly have noticed the change, for he continued to enjoy the use of the Parks and gardens, and to occupy a substantial part of the Palace. Many of the items which featured in the 1590 inventory, including most of the pictures, will have been removed from the royal apartments at this time, but he retained his library and sufficient household equipment to enable him to live there very comfortably for another seventeen years; and he was no longer responsible for capital expenditure on the building, which, after fifty years, was beginning to give trouble. On the whole it may be concluded that the transaction was eminently satisfactory to both parties, Elizabeth acquiring, and Lumley only theoretically losing, a home to which each of them was particularly attached.

9

Under Three Queens

THE new owner of Nonsuch lost no time in taking up both her responsibilities and her privileges. By 31st March, 1592, £6 9s. 5d. had been spent on the building, but actually more work than this had been done, although it was paid for during the ensuing financial year. The first thing to be done was to take precautions 'against the rage of fire, if any such chance should happen'. To this end, iron hooks, chains, ladders, ropes, poles and leather buckets were provided. Elizabeth spent part of this first summer in her new home; she was in residence on 10th August and on 2nd October, and the Privy Council met there on 6th and 7th August.

Various internal adaptations were carried out during the following year, consisting mainly of the partitioning of rooms to provide more suitable accommodation for various officers of the Court and the Squires of the Body. At the same time new presses were made to house the queen's robes. The queen was to go to Nonsuch on 17th May, and the Court was in residence on 22nd and 26th May and 8th June, Privy Council meetings being held on 31st May and 17th June. The Privy Chamber and the approach to it were recarpeted with 'fine mats', whilst other parts of the royal apartments were supplied with ordinary mats, in 1594–5. Elizabeth was at the Palace unusually late in 1594. She left Greenwich for Nonsuch on 1st October, and was visited by Burghley on the 14th; she wrote two letters 'at our Manor of Nonsuch' on 25th October.

For "her Majesties progress" in the summer of 1595, no fewer than four Bottle Houses were constructed. The largest of these measured 21 ft. by 11 ft. The others were for the Lady Warwick, the Lord Treasurer and Sir Robert Cecil. A new house "for the confectionarye" was put up during the same year. Although Lumley continued in residence, and it has always been assumed that his duties as Keeper made him a kind of caretaker-tenant, there was by this time a housekeeper, one Thomas Ditton, who received an additional payment for opening and shutting doors for the workmen. Hans Jakob Breunings von Buchenbach, visiting England in 1595, saw "Richmondt, Nanschitz, Hanticourt, Otlandt und Windtsor".

The Lords of the Council sent letters from the Palace on 6th and 16th September, 1595, the Court being there at least from the 26th August to 27th September and from 2nd to 19th October. No work seems to have been done between April, 1596, and the end of September, 1597, but the 'Progress charges' amounted to over £32. On 24th September, 1596, the Court was to go 'this day week' to Nonsuch, and two days later the queen was to travel 'on Friday to Mitcham and so to Nonsuch'. The Court and Privy Council were there on 4th and 10th October, the Court still being in residence on the 12th. Paul Hentzner's visit took place in 1598. During that year a new loft in the stable yard, of lath-and-plaster construction, and with gables and dormers, was erected; and the Court was in residence from 17th September to 3rd October. By the next summer, 1599, preparations were already going forward for the building of the new stables described in Chapter 4. In addition, there were 'many decayed places' to be mended in time for the queen's arrival early in August, when she came with the usual appendage of 300 carts of bag and baggage. She came by way of Wimbledon, where she was entertained by Burghley, and the Kingston churchwardens had to pay for mending the roads ready for her journey from Wimbledon to Nonsuch. On the 4th she was reported to be in very good health and a-hunting in Nonsuch Park. On the 14th she was not expected to move on unless the Spaniards landed, but by the 18th she had been away and 'returned here yesternight'. The French Ambassador was brought to see 'all the singularities of the gardens, which pleased him infinitely'. The queen left for Hampton Court towards the end of the month, apparently on the 28th; she was still in 'very good health' and 'liked well of Nonsuch air'. Rowland Whyte, writing to Sir Robert Sydney from the Palace on 8th September, 1599, informed him that the queen was back at Nonsuch, "which of all other places she likes the best", and on the 15th Her Majesty was well and still at Nonsuch.

Sunday, 23rd September, 1599, was the day chosen by Thomas Platter and his party to drive down from London by coach to see Nonsuch; when he later wrote his Travels he mistakenly recorded the date as the 26th. He brought with him a letter of introduction from the Mayor of Dover, to 'my lord Cobham, Governor of the Cinque Ports in England', asking him to allow Platter and his party to see the royal palaces and anything else they wished. They found Cobham at his lodging in the Outward Court, where the Lord High Admiral (Howard of Effingham) and other officials had their quarters. After reading the letter, Cobham summoned a guide to show the visitors over the Palace, but they were unable to go into many of the apartments as they were occupied, the residents having stayed indoors to await morning service. On reaching the Presence Chamber, they were placed well to the fore to await the arrival of the queen. Between noon and one o'clock men with white staffs came in from one of the inner chambers; these were followed by a number of 'lords of high standing', and then, alone, the queen.

Elizabeth, says Platter, 'although she was already 74' (she was in fact sixty-six), was very straight and erect, and very youthful still in her appearance, seeming no more than twenty years of age. She was most splendidly attired, in a gown of pure white satin embroidered with gold, with a whole bird of paradise as a panache, set forward on her head and studded with jewels. She wore a necklace of large pearls, and had costly rings over her elegant gloves. Her bearing was dignified and regal.

With the queen comfortably settled on her cushions, the proceedings began. A 'splendidly arrayed' lady-in-waiting came in and stood by the queen, and her secretary stood on her right; the gentlemen with the white staffs and several other knights ranged themselves on her left. She read for a time from some books which had been handed to her by a knight on bended knee. Then a preacher in a white surplice (Platter says elsewhere that it was the Archbishop of Canterbury in his robes) stood on the floor facing the queen and preached a sermon. Two bishops, in black satin cassocks, stood beside him, helping with the responses at the beginning and end 'just as in the Roman church'. However, partly because it was hot and getting late, and there were so many people in the Presence Chamber, Elizabeth was not long in deciding that she had heard enough. She summoned one of the knights, and, as he knelt before her, told him to sign to the preacher to bring his discourse to an end. After the service she withdrew, accompanied by the lady-in-waiting and the gentlemen. The noblemen attached to the Court were very grand, dressed mainly in the French manner except that they wore short cloaks or, occasionally, Spanish capes, and their hats were not as broad as the French. Their numerous retainers, mainly tall handsome fellows, did not wear cloaks, but tabards, folded back, in their master's colour and with his distinctive crest on their sleeves.

Platter was invited to wait in the Presence Chamber to see the ceremony of serving the queen's luncheon: the full ritual being gone through even though the queen had withdrawn to the private apartments. Guards, in red tabards with the royal arms embroidered in gold on their backs, carried in two trestle tables and put them down to form one long table near where Elizabeth had been sitting. Then two more guards, each carrying a mace, came in; they bowed as they entered the room, again in the middle of the floor, and again in front of the table. After laying the table, these two guards withdrew, to be replaced by another pair who, bowing, put plates and other things on the table, and yet two more who added carving knives, bread and salt. The preliminaries ended with the arrival of three gentlemen, two of whom had maces, and a charming lady-in-waiting who bowed three times; these four stood in front of the table to await the arrival of the food.

The meal was carried in by guardsmen, their red tabards folded back. They came in in single file, each carrying one covered dish of food. Platter felt that there must have been about forty of them, all very tall, fine, strong men, the like of whom he had never seen in all his life. Each put his dish on the table, one of the gentlemen removed the cover and the lady-in-waiting carved a large piece off the food on the dish. This piece was given to the guard; he was supposed to eat it to show that he had not poisoned it, but most of them either tasted a mere morsel of it or carried it out again untouched. With the carving finished two of the guards brought in wine and beer; this was poured out and tasted. With the meal served with as much ceremony as if the queen herself had been there, the various dishes were offered to her in her private apartments. She took whatever she fancied, and the dishes were taken out again for the use of the lords of the household. Two further relays were brought in, served and removed with similar ceremony. The light collation (it was, after all, only luncheon, and a very hot day) included 'some very large joints of beef, and all kinds of game, pasties and tarts'. This was followed by dessert, and then the musicians, with trumpets and shawms, played for a time in the Presence Chamber. Not until they had finished were the tables cleared away, and the attendants withdrew, bowing themselves out. Leaving this impressive pageantry in quest of his own luncheon, a certain terseness enters Platter's style, almost as though he feels that something better might have been done for him. 'We went to a tent before the Palace,' he writes, 'and took our luncheon there.'

After lunch Thomas Platter and his party toured the gardens, and when they came back they found that the gentlemen of the Court had eaten in the meantime. As Thomas needed a passport, Cobham directed him to the Lord Admiral. Several petitioners were already kneeling in front of him; when it came to Platter's turn he made his request in French. The Admiral instructed his secretary to write an open letter to all those in charge of royal residences, asking them to allow the visitors to see not only the larger rooms of the palaces under their care but also the small royal closets and their treasures. The authority of the Admiral was needed because there had recently been an attempt to poison Elizabeth by means of poison smeared on the arms of her chair, and she was now refusing access to her apartments anywhere without the approval of the Admiral.

With the letter safely in his hands, and the secretary given 'a small token' for his pains, Thomas and his party entered their coach and set off for Kingston, which they reached safely in the evening.

Five days later, on 28th September, 1599, occurred the event which has kept alive the name of Nonsuch through all the years of neglect; for on this day the Palace was the setting for one of the dramas of national history. Robert Devereux, 2nd Earl of Essex, Lieutenant and Governor General of Ireland, favourite of Elizabeth and Master of the Horse, had been ordered to stay in Ireland and proceed against the rebel Hugh O'Neill, Earl of Tyrone. They met on 7th September, but Essex, instead of carrying out his instructions, arranged a truce. Elizabeth wrote rejecting his action, and on 24th September Essex set out for London with a large company which included the Earls of Southampton and Rutland, Sir John Harington, knights, captains and gentlemen of the army. Essex came post-haste, with half-formed ideas of a *coup d'état*, which dwindled as he and his company neared London. Most of his followers dispersed in London, but with six of them he rode to Nonsuch early on 28th September. On the way from Lambeth they were overtaken by Lord Grey of Wilton, who was riding to Nonsuch to see Cecil. One of Essex's party rode up to Grey and asked him to let Essex ride ahead, so that he could be the first to bring news of his return. Grey refused, and, ignoring the threats of the tired travellers, hurried off to warn Cecil, but not the queen, of the approaching cavalcade.

Alighting at the 'Court Gate' (presumably at the bottom of the steps before the Inner Court gatehouse), Essex hastened through the Presence Chamber and the Privy Chamber, and, muddy and unkempt after his long journey, burst into the queen's bedroom at ten o'clock in the morning. Although Elizabeth appeared to take the intrusion in good part, the incident still further reduced the prestige of the erstwhile favourite; for he surprised her whilst she was dressing, with her face unpainted and without her wig. Accustomed as she was to flattery and courtly manners, and to being seen with her personal charms enhanced by artifice and adornment, she must have been very angry indeed at being placed at such a disadvantage. After a short conversation she sent him away to wash and change whilst she arrayed herself for battle, in some such style as that described by Platter, or by Paul Hentzner when he saw her at another palace: 'pearls with rich drops in her ears, false red hair, a small crown on her head, her bosom uncovered, her dress white silk, bordered with pearls the size of beans, a collar of gold and jewels'. At twelve o'clock, when Essex had made himself presentable, he again went up to see the queen; he stayed for half an hour, and as yet all appeared to be well, Elizabeth treating him most graciously. Within the next hour or two Cecil apprised the queen of the treasonable plans with which Essex had left Ireland, confirming her worst suspicions, some of which had been implanted, also at Nonsuch, by Francis Bacon, formerly a close friend and adviser of Essex but shortly to be one of the chief speakers for the prosecution at his trial. After dinner Essex had another interview with the queen; he found her in a very different mood; she called him in question for returning from Ireland, and particularly for leaving his post when things were in such a hazardous state. She ordered him to explain himself to four members of the Council, whom she had appointed to examine him. Elizabeth was by no means satisfied by their failure to come to any conclusion, and at eleven o'clock sent a message ordering Essex to keep to his chamber. On the next day the full Council met in secret session. During his examination Essex was kept standing for five hours; but afterwards it took the Council only fifteen minutes to reach a decision. They reported to the queen, who said she would need time to consider the answers Essex had given. Essex remained confined to his room, and the Court divided into two factions. Rowland Whyte, as the spectator to whom we owe much of our detailed knowledge of the affair, appears to have watched every move with the keenest interest: 'It is a world to be here,' he wrote, 'and see the humours of the place.' On 2nd October Essex was committed to the custody of the Lord Keeper at York House and remained in captivity for nearly a year. Released in August, 1600, he immediately began the plotting which led to his trial and execution in February, 1601.

Sir John Harington, godson of Elizabeth, knighted by Essex during the Irish expedition, had come to Nonsuch with him, and tried to appease the queen's anger. His reception was so remarkably lacking in cordiality that he was still recalling it in his letters seven years later. He went into the queen's chamber, to be greeted by: 'What, did the fool bring you too? Go back to your business.' She walked quickly to and fro in wrath, and, when he knelt before her, caught his girdle. 'By God's son I am no queen,' she swore. 'That man is above me.' These words 'did sore hurt' Harington, but his share in the folly of Essex was forgotten in a day or two, and he was bidden to go home. He wrote: 'I did not stay to be bidden twice; if all the Irish rebels had been at my heels I should not have made better speed, for I did now flee from one whom I both loved and feared too.'

The heavy wear and tear caused by the prolonged activity at Nonsuch in 1599 had to be made good during the following year. The mats, even the fine mats provided for the Privy Chamber five years earlier, had suffered badly and those in many of the rooms had to be replaced; in the queen's bedchamber the mats had to be mended and pieced together. The abnormal use of the kitchens had revealed a number of flaws there, and extensive repairs had to be carried out on the ovens. In this year, 1600, after two changes of plan, the queen arrived on 8th August, via Tooting and Beddington, intending to move on to Oatlands. She was out riding and hunting every day, having suddenly decided, on the day of her arrival, to stay until the following week. Even then she was only away for a day or two, returning on 16th August. Four days later the Ambassador of Barbary was received in audience; he was given a princely welcome, additional furniture and hangings being brought in from Hampton Court. There was a full Court of lords and ladies, and a strong guard, the guardsmen in their rich coats and the pensioners with their axes. After a rest in the Council Chamber he was taken through the apartments on the king's side, entering the gallery at its western end. The queen was enthroned at the far end of the gallery in great state, and gave audience there. Elizabeth liked "this ayre soe well" that, by 24th August, she seemed determined to stay longer than she had originally planned, and was still there on 26th.

The Palace Locksmith was provided with a new timber-framed house, on two floors, in 1601. This was a place for him to work in, but it probably included living accommodation. It may have been out in the Park near the stables, along with a new 'house to hang ladders in and four Bottle houses under the same'. Although Elizabeth is said to have spent a part of each summer at Nonsuch towards the end of her life, and was certainly there in 1602, no progress charges are recorded after 1st October, 1600. On 15th September, 1602, a proclamation was issued prohibiting the hunting of game within six miles of the Palace. The Earl of Worcester speaks of country dancing in the Privy Chamber on 19th September in the same year, before the queen's majesty, who was exceedingly pleased therewith. Philip Julius, Duke of Stettin-Pomerania, touring England in 1602, called at "Nonschitz" on 27th September. He thought the house and gardens beautiful, and mentioned the stuccoes or plaster-stone set in highly gilded reglats of stone (i.e., slate), the gardens after the English fashion and the Grove of Diana containing a representation in stone of the *fabula Actaeonis*.

The reign of Elizabeth was undoubtedly the golden age of the life of Nonsuch. There is a tradition that she was out hunting from Nonsuch one day when some important dispatches were brought to her, and that she went into the nearest house to hold a Council meeting. The house, at the corner of Malden Road, Cheam, and Park Lane, acquired the name of the Council House, and later of White-hall. Willis quotes a story to the effect that Elizabeth was returning to Nonsuch from Banstead Downs during the last year of her life when she saw the sun reflected in the Palace windows, and thought that the place was on fire. She was so put out when she discovered her mistake that she moved to Richmond. She died there from the effects of a cold on 24th March, 1603.

The Lumleys continued to live at Nonsuch, not, apparently, taking any part in the life of the Court. Lumley himself frequently stayed at his house on Tower Hill, but many of his letters were written from Nonsuch, where he seems to have managed the estate, and his adjacent manors of Ewell and East and West Cheam, as a benevolent

country squire. In 1596 he wrote from Tower Hill on 6th November
to Mr. Julius Caesar, Judge of the High Court of the Admiralty,
through whom a petition from the inhabitants of Malden was being
presented to the queen. The petition related to the repair of the parish
church, and Lumley asked Caesar to help them in any way possible.
Lumley's spelling, at all times archaic in comparison with that of most
of his contemporaries, became worse as he grew older; but his wife,
Elizabeth D'Arcy, ran him a close second. From Nonsuch on 9th
September, 1600, she wrote to Caesar, now Master of the Requests,
addressing him as "Good Mr. docter Secar", and endorsing her letter
"To my assured good frend Mr. Doctor Seasar Master of the Reques".
The "reques" which she put forward was made on behalf of one of her
Nonsuch servants, married to a bad woman who had kept him in the
toils of the law for so long that she had ruined him. Lady Lumley
asked Caesar to help the servant, and she would be "behowlding" to
him. She ended by assuring him of her "afecsinat" well-wishing to
Caesar and his good wife.

Lumley's second marriage was childless, and he accordingly
decided to settle most of his estate on his young cousin, Richard
Lumley, born in 1589. In 1595 he made provision for Richard's
education by leasing the manor of Lumley to two trustees, who were
to use £50 of each year's profits towards the "better mayntenance" of
the boy during his minority and nonage, paying for his education and
bringing up. At about this time Lumley must often have been in
Durham, working more of his family pride out of his system. One
manifestation of this was the erection, in the parish church of Chester-
le-Street, of 'two and twenty monuments or thereabouts'. To ensure
that they would not be defaced, destroyed or taken away, and that the
parish clerk would 'sweep and rub the said monuments and keep the
same fair and beautiful', he made over, on 30th April, 1597, an annuity
of forty shillings to be paid out of the profits of the manor of Lumley.

At Nonsuch, although his accommodation in the Palace was free
of charge, Lumley paid a rent of £222 a year for the Great Park. On
15th November, 1599, he wrote to Cecil, "Chefe Secretory" to the
queen, asking him to try to persuade the Lord Treasurer to agree to
the deferment of payment for the time being. The result was the
remission of the rent for the remainder of Lumley's twenty-one-year
lease. The Great Park was not to any considerable extent under
cultivation at this time, but two years later Lumley sub-let half of it to

one Ferdinando Malyn at a rent of £130 a year. Malyn's ground, when he took it over, was rough, full of bushes and roots, without hedges and without houses. He spent £300 on building houses and clearing the ground, and later claimed that he was harvesting 1,400 quarters of grain.

Inside the house, Lumley continued to improve his library. He had promised his "very loveinge Freendes the Vicechauncellor the Non-Regentes and Regentes in the University of Cambridge", in 1587, to present some of his books to the University library. He intended to compare their catalogue with his books, and if he had duplicates of any which they lacked he would send them, with 'some certain number of other books'. He asked them to be patient if it took him a long time to select the books. During the eleven years which elapsed between the promise and its fulfilment, the library was catalogued at least once (in 1596) and possibly twice, for the preamble to the Inventory described in the preceding chapter ends with the words ". . . howseholde stuffe and Regester of Bookes. Anno 1590". This is perhaps slender evidence for the existence of a catalogue of 1590; but Lumley demonstrated, in his book stock, his propensity for discarding old editions in favour of new, and it is just possible that he did the same with his catalogues: for when we turn to the place, in this 1590 Inventory, where the Register of Books should be, there is merely a note, written by Lumley himself probably ten years later, referring to Alcock's catalogue of 1596. However this may be, eighty-nine volumes went to Cambridge in 1598, and thirty-four to the Bodleian in the following year. He also gave away many to his personal friends. After this weeding-out, Lumley appears to have added very few books to his library.

The new reign brought a number of changes. Lumley had now repaid his debt to the Crown, and could no longer be treated as an unpaid caretaker. He continued to live at Nonsuch, and the Crown paid for repairs to his 'lodging'—mending the slates and leads and providing him with a new range and 'boiling pan'. But he was now paid a fee of £26 13s. 4d. a year for his services as Keeper of the Palace and Little Park, as well as running an expense account. For the quarter ended Lady Day, 1606, he received his fee of £6 13s. 4d. and £21 10s. 10d. which he had paid to gardeners, weeders and others; in the quarter immediately prior to his death in 1609 the total payment amounted to £46 5s. 8d. His lease of the Great Park continued, but only until 1605.

James I, in the year of his accession, called on Lumley (presumably without due warning) at Lumley Castle. Lumley was not there to welcome him, and so the Bishop of Durham showed the king round, lecturing him at great length on the subject to which Lumley had devoted so much research: his long and noble pedigree. In the end the king could stand no more. He stopped the Bishop, still in full spate, with "Oh, mon, gang na further. I maun digest the knowledge I ha' this day gained, for I didna' ken Adam's ither nam was Lumley." By Patent dated 19th September, in the first year of James I, Nonsuch was settled on the queen, Anne of Denmark, a woman with a mind and life of her own, and with expensive tastes which kept her in debt. She could see Nonsuch proving to be a liability rather than an asset unless the hold of Lumley could be loosened. Sir Thomas Chaloner wrote to Lord Sydney: 'The queen cannot conveniently keep house at Nonsuch without she could procure the Great Park, of which Lord Lumley has a lease, and some of his lordship's adjoining lands; without these parcels the fair house at Nonsuch will be nothing pleasing to the queen, if she lie at her own charge, for she hath nothing here but the bare park.' Lumley surrendered his interest in the Great Park in 1605, and on the 25th September of that year he was granted an annuity in compensation.

Nonsuch now belonged to the queen, but records of her visiting the Palace are few, whereas the king and the two princes, Henry and Charles, were frequently there during the early years of the reign. Devoted as he was to hawking and hunting the hare, the country round Nonsuch must have been very much to the liking of James I. Just when affairs of state were most pressing, and his presence in London most needed, he would escape into the country, leaving many of the attributes of kingship behind him. Decorum and ceremony were abandoned, and he was careless of language, morals and sobriety. To increase the number of refuges available to him, he spent a great deal of money on the royal residences, insisting that they must always be ready to receive him. Although he eventually concentrated mainly on Royston, Theobalds and Newmarket, he spent, during his reign, nearly £5,600 on Nonsuch.

The king's first visit took place in 1603, when Philip Gawdy mentioned in a letter to his brother that the king had gone to Nonsuch and Oatlands to take the air for three or four days. He was there on 14th August, 1603, and the two princes were taken there from Oatlands on 26th August. In September, 1604, Prince Henry and the Lord Admiral, Lord Howard of Effingham, were in residence, and the new pattern of life in the Palace was beginning to take shape. The prince apparently took over the rooms in the east wing, for we read now of 'the King's side and the Prince his side' and of the 'doing of sundry needful reparations against the Prince coming'. Sir Thomas Chaloner, envoy to Scotland under Elizabeth, who had accompanied James I on his accession to the English throne, was made governor to Prince Henry in 1603. By 1604 both he and the Lord Admiral had been allocated 'lodgings' in the Palace.

Prince Henry Frederick was the eldest son of James, born on 19th February, 1594. He matriculated at Magdalen College, Oxford, in 1605, was created Prince of Wales in 1610 with celebrations almost worthy of a coronation, and died of typhoid fever on 6th November, 1612. His passing was more lamented by the common people than by his parents; James left the sick-room at St. James's, heard the news of the prince's death with 'great insensibility' at Theobalds, and very soon afterwards prohibited the wearing of mourning in his presence. The sickly Prince Charles, who, at the age of five, although he was unable to stand or to speak, had been created Duke of York and had always been favoured above his brother, became heir apparent.

However, Prince Henry spent many happy days at Nonsuch during his early teens. It is said that he had boxes kept at his three houses at St. James's, Richmond and Nonsuch, and made anyone who swore in his hearing put money into them. The money was given to the poor. He was at Nonsuch for most of August, 1605. His father had been there for a week in May, possibly to make arrangements for the suite of rooms which was being made ready for Prince Charles, with separate kitchen, buttery and saucery, and lodgings for his tutor. Repairs were carried out during the year on Prince Henry's kitchen, which had its own cistern. The under-housekeeper, John Gittins, was paid for opening and shutting the gates and doors, presumably to admit the workmen. For several years the east wing was referred to indiscriminately as the Queen's Side or the Prince's Side, and the west wing as the King's Side or the Duke's Side. By 1606 further lodgings had been allocated: to the Lord Chamberlain, the Earl of Nottingham, the Lord Treasurer, the Earl of Essex, the Earl of Oxford and Sir John Harington. Many repairs were carried out between October, 1605, and

September, 1606, particularly roof repairs and the repair and replacement of matting, in readiness for the visit of the Court in August.

Having bought out Lumley's interest in the Great Park, the king
decided to impark it again. On 28th May, 1605, a grant was made to
Lord Lumley to preserve game and waterfowl within five miles of
Nonsuch, with the assistance of William Richbell, Keeper of the game
there. The proposal to impark brought a protest from Ferdinando
Malyn, Lumley's tenant, who pointed out to the Earl of Salisbury that
because he had spent so much time and money in bringing his half of
the Park into tillage, Lumley had been given a higher compensation
than he would otherwise have had; whereas Malyn himself was likely
to be turned out "on the suddaine" without any recompense for what
he had done to improve the land. Whether he received compensation
or not, the imparking went forward, and Edward Somerset, 4th Earl
of Worcester, was appointed Keeper by Patent of the fourth year of
James I. The Nonsuch estate was enlarged in 1606–7 by the absorption
of adjoining lands beyond the northern boundary, including Rutherwick copse and various fields to the north of the Hogsmill river. Some
of these lands were acquired by purchase at twenty years' value, and
others by exchange. Although the newly imparked and enlarged
Parks of Nonsuch covered only a fraction of the area of Henry VIII's
original hunting estate, based on Hampton Court, James and his family
could be assured of a good day's sport within their confines and on the
Downs to the south. Prince Henry was never happier than when he
was in the saddle, but, we are told, his pleasure in hunting came from
riding and not from the hunt itself. In September, 1606, work which
ultimately cost £1,076 and continued until January, 1609, began on
the re-paling of the enlarged Great Park, 'for his highness's pleasure
and disport in hunting', the provision of two new cart-bridges across
the river, new gates, new boats for the ponds and the repairing and
enlarging of the two lodges. The work included the felling of a hollow
elm and using it as a channel for a ditch at the Park gate 'next Kingston'.
The new Park was six miles in circumference.

Whilst work was going forward on the repair and enlargement of
the great lodge, it was at times referred to as the 'new' lodge; but only
about £33 out of the £1,076 seems to have been devoted to this
building. There was, however, in May, 1607, a payment to the Earl of
Worcester of £600, part of 'a more sum', to be laid out by him on the
new building of a lodge in the Great Park of Nonsuch. The lodge thus

acquired the name of Worcester House, not merely because Worcester held the office of Keeper but because the house was rebuilt for him. It appears to have been completed during 1609.

Lord Lumley's health was now failing. His last surviving letter from Nonsuch was written for him, only the signature being in his own hand. It was addressed to Robert Cecil, created Earl of Salisbury in 1605, and was dated 28th June, 1608. In the letter Lumley pleaded the cause of his servant, George Smith, a recusant, who, more than a dozen years earlier, had been allowed to compound, so that Lumley had had much help and comfort from his service. Now there were rumours of new troubles approaching Smith for the same cause; and this, at a time when Lumley needed him most, with his last day approaching. If Smith were to be imprisoned, Lumley would not find anyone to give him the same love and good dealing. He was responsible for many weighty matters of law on Lumley's behalf, besides having to support an extremely old mother and a houseful of small children. Below the shaky signature "Lumley" was written 'good my Lord bear with the lameness of mine arm and nakedness of my sight'.

In December the bewildered old man was being harried for payment of a debt which he had already settled once, as a result of a complicated legal quibble connected with the attainder of Ridolfi in 1572. It is not surprising that at one point the statement on the case contains the words 'the Lord Lumley remembereth not'. He died on 11th April, 1609, and was buried by night at Cheam in a wooden coffin covered with brass-studded red leather, a lead coffin inside that and a further wooden coffin containing the body. With him died the Lumley barony of the second creation, for it was limited to his heirs male.

The Lumley library, pruned slightly by the gifts its owner had made, now became the property of Prince Henry. The terms under which the books became his are not known, but it seems likely that they were a gift. A new catalogue was made, and this simplified the task of weeding out books which were already in the prince's own library at St. James's Palace. Legal and medical books were also discarded before the library was moved from Nonsuch. The Lumley books were ultimately merged with the Old Royal Library to form the Royal Library, now housed in the British Museum; but Lumley's own gifts and the subsequent discarding of unwanted duplicates have led to a wide dispersal of books with the familiar 'Lumley' inscription.

The Venetian Ambassador was shown over the Palace— 'the most beautiful of all those owned by His Majesty'—by Prince Henry on 11th July, 1607, and a week later Prince Charles travelled to Nonsuch. The ambassador of the Duke of Lorraine, with nine people in train, included the Palace in a fourteen-day progress in July or August in the same year.

Many repairs to the stonework of the Palace walls, paving and fountains were carried out between October, 1607, and March, 1609. Timbers, including some of those in the corner towers, were replaced, lead repaired, the accommodation for the princes' hunting horses improved, including the making of a rack, a manger and two partitions for the Duke of York's "nagge". The Duke and Princess Elizabeth, later Queen of Bohemia, visited the Palace in August, 1609. Their mother, Queen Anne, delighted in the many pleasures of a royal progress. This may have been the reason behind an unusually heavy repair bill, in 1610, much of it for painting, for repairs to the Banqueting House, and building a stand for musicians in the Grove of Diana, during the period preceding her visit in September. She stayed for ten days before moving on to Hampton Court. Prince Henry had been at Nonsuch a few weeks earlier. He was visited on 31st August, 1610, by Phineas Pett, shipbuilder, who, since presenting the prince with a model of a warship in 1607, had received many marks of favour. The prince, who was out hunting, promised to send Phineas a buck; all that had been killed on that day had already been given away.

This is the last recorded visit of the prince, or indeed of any member of the royal family, until James was at Nonsuch in June, 1622; except that in 1612 a payment was made for keeping the gates 'at the Queen's being at Nonsuch'. In that year, the year of Prince Henry's death, the Agents of Savoy travelled down to Nonsuch in two coaches. The hire of the coaches and four horses for two days cost them £4. Lacking royal visitors, the Palace was by no means allowed to go to rack and ruin. Every year repairs or maintenance of some kind were carried out; one year only £24 was spent on the buildings, but on several occasions the expenditure was over £200. John Ernst, Duke of Saxe-Weimar, visited Nonsuch in the autumn of 1613, and observed the Inner Court, the plasterwork and pictures; the gardens, fountains, the grove and grotto of Diana, the statues representing Actaeon's Metamorphosis. He copied the various verses and mottoes about the place, and noted some of the pictures—portraits of English kings, gentlemen and their wives, the mother of Philip II of Spain, Bathory King of Poland, and the Treasurer Cecil. He was particularly impressed by a carved bust which was said to be an exact image of Christ. It is of interest to note that the named pictures were amongst those which belonged to Lord Lumley in 1590, and that the other pictures, even though they are described in general terms, could well have been amongst those listed in detail in the Lumley Inventory of 1590; and the 'carved bust' might conceivably be the Raphael 'special picture of Christ cast in mould'. It has been assumed that Lumley moved most of his pictures from Nonsuch when he surrendered the Palace to the queen; but this evidence, written four years after Lumley's death, seems to indicate that at least a number of them were left, and either sold to the Crown, or not considered worth removing, by his widow.

The queen died in 1619. In the following year, on 16th May, James Hay, Viscount Doncaster, Master of the Wardrobe to James I, was granted the Keepership of Nonsuch House, gardens and Park. On the 10th February, 1621, it was reported that the Spanish Ambassador was so unpopular that he intended to spend Shrove Tuesday at Nonsuch to avoid the fury of the people of London. His flight appears in a somewhat different light when we read that the king had shown him extraordinary honour by assigning the fine royal palace of Nonsuch to him as a summer residence. The Court was at Nonsuch on 30th June, 1622, and John Williams, Bishop of Lincoln, wrote to the Earl of Middlesex from Nonsuch on 12th August, 1623. By a warrant dated 2nd June, 1624, a Mr. Barrett was to take forty brace of partridges a year from the bushlands of Sussex to stock the fields of Nonsuch.

In the previous year James had named Nonsuch as one of the palaces to be settled on the Infanta Maria as part of her jointure, but Charles had come back in October from a long visit to Spain during which religious differences had compelled him to abandon his suit of the princess. In 1624 he was betrothed to Princess Henrietta Maria of France. Married by proxy, like her predecessor Anne of Denmark, Henrietta Maria came to England almost equally unenamoured of her husband, and, like Anne, became mistress of Nonsuch.

Charles I came to the throne on 27th March, 1625. His proxy marriage took place in May, and his queen came to England in June. At the end of July she visited the Palace which was to form part of her jointure; the Court was there on 20th August and the king was at Nonsuch on 3rd November, when he conferred a number of knight-

hoods. During this year extensive adaptations were carried out at the
Keeper's Lodge, and throughout the reign of Charles, although the
Palace features but little in national history, and the recorded visits of
the king and queen are few, the building was adequately maintained.
The annual expenditure on repairs and maintenance of the Palace,
gardens and outbuildings was usually higher than it had been under
James I, and in the first sixteen years of Charles' reign the total spent
was £4,616.

Charles and Henrietta Maria set out for Nonsuch on 14th August,
1626; the Venetian Ambassador was received on 30th August, and a
letter from Charles was dated at Nonsuch on 5th September. In that
year two new sun-dials were installed on the inner faces of the five-
storey turrets, John Marre, "Dyaller", being responsible for 'striking
out the lines and placing the gnomons', although the Serjeant Painter,
John De Creetes, did the actual painting. The grant of Nonsuch to
Henrietta Maria took place in March of the following year, and the
effects were soon apparent. Between October, 1627, and September,
1628, work was done on the lodgings of the maids-of-honour, and the
queen, naturally dissatisfied with the austerity of the chapel, ordered the
installation of a great new folding altar; John Hooke, turner, being
paid for "turneinge of 4 greate feete for Thalter in the Queenes
Chappell". There appears to have been an outbreak of fire during this
or the previous year, for workmen were engaged on taking down
divers pieces of timber that were burnt and putting up new pieces in
their place.

The king was at Nonsuch in June and July, 1629, a year in which
four or five times the usual amount was spent on maintenance work—
repairing the Inner Court, replacing the gallery wainscoting, digging
a new well and carrying out a number of other repairs. For the next
eleven years Charles governed without Parliament; during this time
he apparently visited Nonsuch only three times—in July, 1630, and
August, 1632, on both of which occasions he conferred knighthoods;
and in September, 1634, when he was visited by Archbishop Laud and
the queen gave audience to the Savoy Ambassador. A stage, 'with
steps of ascent on either side thereof', was erected in the queen's Privy
Chamber in 1632, and her billiard table was repaired. The inhabitants
of Ewell and Cheam claimed, on 24th January, 1634, freedom from the
duty of providing 'land carriage' on demand, owing to the service they
were required to do at the king's house of Nonsuch. During the king's

visit this year, his groom-saddler, William Butcher, was drowned in Nonsuch Park, and his wife Elizabeth petitioned the Council for compensation.

On the 1st July, 1636, Henrietta Maria granted the Keepership of the house, gardens and Little Park jointly to Sir Algernon Percy, 10th Earl of Northumberland, and Sir Henry Rich, 1st Earl of Holland, one of the queen's favourites. Fears of the plague in 1636 and 1637 caused orders to be issued forbidding people from London to come near the Palace, the great concourse of pedlars, tradesmen and others at Ewell fair being regarded as a particular source of danger; but these fears did not prevent the carrying out of normal maintenance work. They may, however, have played a small part in the building up of considerable arrears in the payment of moneys due from the Crown. Thomas Powell, under-housekeeper (who still occupied the under-housekeeper's lodge at the time of the 1650 Parliamentary Survey), and the gardener, John Rogers, were paid £347 6s. 10d. on 16th May, 1638, for their fees and expenditure on the house and garden during the past six years. Arrears of pension amounting to £1,800, and the reimbursement of £1,600 laid out on the Park, garden and walks at Nonsuch, were claimed in a petition submitted by George Hooker on 10th November, 1638. In 1639, the year of Charles' invasion of Scotland, which was halted by lack of funds, £208 was spent on a new pair of gates for Nonsuch. Next year the Scots marched south; the queen went to Nonsuch on 3rd August 'to stay some months, away from the noise of London'. An undated account for repairs amounting to £324 probably relates to this year.

The stirring events of the Civil War affected Nonsuch but little. Accounts for maintenance work are missing for two or three years, and work may in fact have been interrupted, but if so it was resumed in the latter part of 1644. In November, 1642, a labourer was hedging late one Saturday night when he saw about 200 Cavaliers on horseback arrive at Worcester House. He left his work and watched, through the Park gate, the dispersal of the Cavaliers into 'all the lodges in both the Lord Worcester's Parks'. There was great merriment, and lights in all the rooms of the houses. The labourer hurried off to Kingston to warn the commander of the Parliamentary forces, but he was not very well received. The Cavaliers entered Kingston, 'with ringing of bells for joy', on 13th November.

Henrietta Maria, militantly helping the Royalist cause on the

Continent and at home, was impeached by Parliament in May, 1643. She fled to France in 1644. There she pawned her jewels, and continued to do all she could to secure help for Charles. By 1648 she was virtually destitute, and entered a Carmelite nunnery.

From June, 1644, the accounts for repairs and maintenance continue until March, 1648, and they cover many of the normal items, such as repairs to stonework and roofs. We may, perhaps, read in them a story of neglect or even of wilful damage: in 1645 gutters had to be replaced because the old lead had been 'stolen away'; in the next year windows in the king's and queen's privy lodgings were 'new glazed', the wells at the conduit-head had to be re-opened by digging and the water 'brought home' from the conduit-head to the house. However, these things may have had nothing to do with the Civil War; certainly two of the tasks paid for in the year ended 31st March, 1647, were perfectly normal: the clearing of snow from gutters and hopper-heads, and the cleansing of the brick drains, by a boy creeping through them, for two shillings.

Charles surrendered to the Scots in May, 1646; he was taken over by Parliament in January, 1647. On 14th August he was taken to Oatlands, and on 24th to Hampton Court. Although he 'escaped' to the Isle of Wight in November, he remained in custody there. In the following July the Cavaliers began a number of risings, and Parliament alerted its forces against the possibility of attempts to occupy the royal palaces near London. Nonsuch itself was not attacked, but a fierce and bloody skirmish took place outside the pale of the Little Park, about 200 yds. from the Banqueting House. Thomas Herbert, Groom of the Chamber to Charles I during his captivity, and created a baronet in 1660, described the affair in his *Memoirs of the two last years of the reign of Charles I*. At the beginning of July the Earl of Holland, with the Duke of Buckingham, Lord Francis Villiers, the Earl of Peterborough and several others, gathered a considerable party of horse and foot, marched into Surrey, and drew up near Kingston-upon-Thames. They expected to be joined by other officers and private soldiers who had served the king, but few came to reinforce them. They marched towards Reigate, but before they could reach it were engaged by Colonel Rich's Regiment of Horse; after a skirmish, they were forced to retreat towards Kingston. In 'a pass between Ewell and Nonsuch Park', which is believed to be the footpath which is today known as Ox Lane, the fight was joined with great fierceness and valour. Many of the gentlemen on both sides were killed, including Lord Francis Villiers, who, according to report, after fighting with great courage, was offered quarter but refused to accept it. The remnants of the Cavalier force retreated towards Kingston.

The Parliamentary forces issued, from Nonsuch, *A Letter of a Great Victory* obtained by Sir Miles Livesey on Friday, 7th July, 1648. It put the Royalist force at about 700 horse, of whom 400 escaped through Kingston towards Harrow. Apart from the twenty-three Royalists killed, it claimed 200, including the Earl of Holland, wounded, and 100 taken prisoner, with nine boats full of pistols and saddles and 300 'arms', besides 'good store of pillage'. Livesey's losses were put at only three killed and twenty wounded. Six of the dead are said to have been buried in Cheam churchyard.

Although the Palace stood for another thirty-three years, the execution of Charles I on 30th January, 1649, marks, to all intents and purposes, the end of Royal Nonsuch. Never again would it see the Court in residence, or provide a meeting-place for the Lords of the Council. Stripped of its treasures, leased, pledged as security, sold, restored to the Crown, used for offices, given away and finally pulled down, the building of which parts lingered on into the reign of James II had lost its purpose and its meaning and had become the mere ghost of a past splendour, a physical expression of a way of life which could never return.

10

Decline

THE date on which the Parliamentary forces took control of Nonsuch is not known, but that they were there before the execution of Charles I is shown by the dispatch describing the 'great victory' of 7th July, 1648. The Palace was leased to Algernon Sidney at a rent of £150 a year whilst arrangements were being made to dispose of it and other possessions of the royal family. On 22nd September, 1649, the contents of the Palace were examined so that the items which were worth selling could be listed. There was so little at Nonsuch in comparison with other palaces that it seems quite possible that most of the articles of value had been removed for safe keeping, unless we are to believe that a good deal of looting had gone on before the new order was established. Thirty-one pictures were sold to various buyers for £282, twenty-four back-stools of wood, covered and gilt, brought £18 and a marble-inlaid table £20. Nothing else was sold; the pictures alone at Oatlands realized £733, at Wimbledon £1,079 and at Somerset House, Whitehall and St. James's over £10,000. In the same year the trees—oak, ash and elm—which were fit for shipbuilding for the Navy were marked ready for felling, and a list of them was furnished to the Trustees for the sale of the late king's lands on 21st December. As a result of a later survey, the Commissioners of the Navy were informed on 29th April, 1650, that the number of trees available to them would be considerably fewer than had originally been marked. This may have been partly due to the recommendation of the surveyors of the house and Parks to the effect that trees near the Palace should not be cut down. The number of oak trees to be felled was reduced from 835 to 521, of elm from 613 to 428 and ash from 314 to 136. The felling went on through the summer, and sawpits were dug and trackways made to facilitate the handling of the timber. John Turner, 'tenant of

Nonsuch Park', was awarded £15 compensation in September for damage suffered as a result of this activity.

At the beginning of April, 1650, the Parliamentary Survey, which provides so much of our information about Nonsuch, was compiled. The materials, after allowing for demolition expenses, were valued at £7,020, the annual value of the Little Park was set at £402 12s., the 180 deer were estimated to be worth £240, the 2,462 trees not marked for the Navy £407 10s. and the underwood £50. The Survey was sent to the Surveyor General on 6th April. On the same day he received a similar Survey of the Great Park, where Worcester House and the other buildings were given a net demolition value of £1,820; eight red deer were worth £20 and 300 fallow deer £400. All the trees except 1,819, which were 'good for little save the fire', had been marked for the Navy. Those which remained were worth only £280 2s., but the various groves and coppices contained young wood worth £1,084 18s. The annual value of the land in the Great Park was put at £550. The surveyors added a memorandum to the effect that Charles Kirke, son of George Kirke, claimed to hold for life, by Letters Patent of Henrietta Maria dated 1639, the office of Keeper of the Great Park, with the keeping and benefit of all the lodges and houses, and the right to appoint and dismiss the under-keepers. He also claimed to be entitled to a fee of two shillings a day, £15 a year for cutting hay for the deer, a fat buck and doe in season and the herbage and pannage of the Park. The surveyors had not seen any grant on which the claim was based, but they had collected verbal evidence which they transmitted to the trustees and humbly left the matter 'to their further judgements'. These judgements were, in fact, exercised with exemplary fairness: George Kirke, Gentleman of the Robes to Charles I, had been informed upon as a papist on 31st October, 1645, and his estates had been seized and sequestered. Yet when the Great Park was ultimately sold, Kirke's son Charles was compensated for his loss of the Keepership; better treatment than the two of them received later, at the hands of Charles II, after a brief restoration of their rights.

A buyer was found for the Palace and Little Park only a week after the Surveyor General finished perusing the Survey. A Particular of Sale, based on the Survey, was prepared on 11th April, and on the 15th the premises were jointly contracted for by George Smythson, John Saunderson, Thomas Lilburne, William Bradford, George Watkinson and Francis Wilkinson. The method of fixing the price to be paid completely ignored any 'use' value of the Palace and other buildings. The purchasers were simply asked to pay the demolition value of the materials, the value of the deer and trees and sixteen times the annual value of the parkland. This gave a total of £14,158 12s., of which the first 'moiety' was to be paid within eight weeks and the balance within six months. When the second payment was completed they would be given a lease for ninety-nine years. The estate was assigned to Robert Lilburne's regiment during the Scottish campaign of 1651–2, as security for the men's pay. On 28th June, 1653, two of the purchasers, Thomas Lilburne and Francis Wilkinson, wrote to Captain Adam Baynes about the price they should charge when selling Nonsuch, but confessed that they could not remember the place very clearly. Baynes, a trafficker in land, was acting on behalf of Major-General John Lambert; the agents for the owners said that they would be glad if Lambert would have Nonsuch, and hoped it would "prove a good pennyworth". They were prepared to accept something less than £9,500 (presumably as the net price of the house itself), but had refused an offer of £9,000 and had also refused to sell the house, the land and the woods separately. At a Council meeting held on 17th May, 1654, William Sydenham, Commissioner of the Treasury, John Jones, Cromwell's brother-in-law, and Walter Strickland were instructed to negotiate with the purchasers of Nonsuch House and Park, with a view to settling them on Cromwell in exchange for other state lands. This proposal was not, however, put into effect, for on 31st October, 1654, the Palace and Little Park were conveyed to John Lambert of "Wimbleton", Major-General of all the forces in England and Scotland, for £14,800, which gave Lilburne's soldiers only 12s. in every pound due to them.

The sale of the Great Park in 1650 was complicated by the interest of Charles Kirke in the Keepership, and of the Rector of Long Ditton, some of whose glebe and tithe lands had been incorporated in the Park. The Crown had been paying the rector £6 17s. 9½d. a year on account of these lands. To compensate Charles Kirke for his losses through the impending sale of the Park, the Great Park Meadow was granted to him subject to the right of the purchaser of the Park to any wood growing in the meadow. £770 was to be deducted from the total purchase price as the new owner of the Park would not have the use of the meadow; this sum was calculated as being equivalent to seven times the annual value of the meadow. The

new owner would, however, have to take over the annual payments
to the rector, and to cover this condition of sale a deduction
equivalent to sixteen of these annual payments was made. The net
result was a total price of £11,591 8s. 8d., which, like the price of the
Palace and Little Park, was based on demolition rather than use values
plus sixteen times the annual value of the land.

These details were settled at high speed. The Survey of the Great
Park was sent to the Surveyor General on 6th April. On the 10th the
Particular of Sale was 'made forth examined and signed' and by the
12th April a purchaser had been found. Yet, although he contracted to
buy the Great Park on that date, it was not until two years later, on
12th May, 1652, that the Trustees were authorized to draw up and seal
the conveyance of the premises, to Colonel Thomas Pride, 'purger'
of Parliament, regicide and veteran of Naseby, Dunbar and Worcester.
Pride is said to have done well for himself as Contractor for Victualling
the Navy, and he appears to have spent a fair amount of his time on his
new country estate. He was High Sheriff of Surrey in 1655, knighted in
1656 and selected to serve in the Upper House in 1657. He died at
Worcester House in 1658. His widow appears to have carried on his
work of despoiling the Park, felling the timber and converting the land
to agricultural use; but the Restoration came in time to save some of
the deer.

There is a dearth of information for the years during which
Lambert owned the Palace. One of Cromwell's most distinguished
soldiers, Lambert had been in service since the beginning of the Civil
War and commanded the army of the north in 1647; after playing a
leading part in the victories at Dunbar in 1650 and Worcester in 1651,
he was appointed Deputy-Lieutenant of Ireland in 1652. In the following year, as a member of the Army Council of Officers, he was to a
large extent responsible for the position of Protector being offered to
Cromwell. Thereafter he was a member of Cromwell's Council of
State, and in 1655 was made Major-General in charge of the northern
counties. The vehemence of his opposition to Cromwell's proposed
assumption of the title of King led to his dismissal and he retired to
private life, and to his favourite hobby of tending the rare plants in the
fine gardens at Wimbledon House. During this period he would have
had leisure to enjoy the amenities of Nonsuch, but no records of his
use of the Palace or Park have survived. On the death of Cromwell on
3rd September, 1658, Lambert was restored to favour under Richard

Cromwell. After a year of uncertainty, with Richard's Parliament unable to control the Army, plans for a Royalist rising were discovered, and Lambert staged his own version of 'Pride's Purge', occupying Palaçe Yard and excluding Members of Parliament by force. He formed a Committee of Safety and exercised, for a short time, almost as absolute a power as had Oliver Cromwell. Three months after his rise he had been supplanted by Monk, who ordered the Commons to issue writs for the summoning of a 'free' Parliament. London went wild with joy at the news, and the restoration of the monarchy could now be openly discussed. On the 1st May, 1660, the necessary measures were passed by Parliament, and the king, who had been living with a meagre Court at Brussels, was proclaimed on the 8th May. He landed at Dover on the 25th May, the frigate *Nonsuch*, with 34 guns and a crew of 120, being one of the 30 escort ships. She had been built at Deptford in 1646 by Peter Pett, and may well have owed her name to the friendship between Phineas Pett and Prince Henry which began in 1607.

The restoration of Henrietta Maria's jointure lands was agreed by the House of Commons on 23rd June, and Nonsuch Palace and both Parks were in her hands soon after that date. In December, 1660, she granted the Keepership of the house, gardens and park to George, Lord Berkeley, during the life of his lordship and afterwards to Sir Charles Berkeley and Sir Maurice Berkeley during the life of Charles, son of Sir Charles Berkeley, if the queen should live so long. Berkeley had already held the office since 5th September, having bought it for £1,100 from the elderly Countess Carlisle just before her death. Under the new grant the Keeper's fees were to be continued at the old rate of £13 6s. 8d. for the custody of the Palace, £6 13s. 4d. for the garden and walks and the same for the Little Park. The grant was confirmed by Charles II, by Letters Patent dated 11th December, 1660. In addition to his fees, payable quarterly, Berkeley was to be reimbursed for necessary expenditure on keeping clean and airing the house, keeping and weeding the courts and yards, keeping and weeding the gardens, maintaining arbours and enclosures, repairing the Park Pale and providing hay and other winter food for the deer. The confirmation, however, was more important in the future story of Nonsuch than the original grant; for it provided that the Keepership of Berkeley, Sir Maurice and Sir Charles, should continue after the decease of "our said deare Mother", Henrietta Maria. At the same time

Richard Edes was appointed Gamekeeper, at a fee of 12*d.* a day and an annual livery allowance of 26*s.* 8*d.* By Letters Patent of 19th November, 1660, Edes had been appointed to the office of Falconer 'to attend the king in his recreation of hunting', at a pension of £44 a year.

Berkeley had not long been in office when he discovered that the expenses at Nonsuch (for which he could claim and, eventually, receive reimbursement from the Crown) included the paying of taxes. In his own interests, for he might wait a long time to get his money back, he wrote to the Treasury to complain that the Commissioners for Surrey had imposed taxes on the house and Park. It was pointed out that 'until these last usurpations' the estate had never been taxed, and that it was tantamount to asking the king to pay taxes to himself. It was accordingly ordered on 13th March, 1661, that the taxes should be suspended, and that 'the precedent of these last ill times, when his Majesty's lands were in private men's hands', should not be made use of.

The fees for the Keeper and Gamekeeper for 1662 were covered by warrants dormant, and this method of noting that the fees were due, without actually paying them, seems to have continued until Lord Berkeley had to dig his heels in. By 1667 the arrears had reached sizeable proportions. He submitted a claim to the Treasury early in November, but only succeeded in starting an enquiry into the reasons why the king should be asked to meet these charges on houses and lands which belonged to the queen mother. Berkeley called at the Treasury on 2nd and 5th December, but it was not until the following April that he received nine years' fees; the accidental overpayment of eightpence was poor compensation for the trouble he had been put to in collecting his dues.

In return for surrendering his Letters Patent as one of His Majesty's principal Secretaries of State, and for a rent of £100 a year, the Great Park and Worcester House were leased on 8th July, 1663, to Sir Robert Long, Chancellor of the Exchequer from 1660 to 1667, and Auditor of the Exchequer from 1662. Long had been Secretary to Charles II in exile. He was concerned, whilst the lease was being negotiated, about the possibility that the Park might at some future time be taken back by the Crown. It was, by 1663, 'utterly disparked' and the land ploughed, so that, he said, it would cost more than it was worth to impark it again. He therefore asked that an order should be issued for disparking it in law as it was already disparked in fact. The result was that a declaration was issued on 29th June, 1663, for the

disparking and disfranchising of the Great Park and the discharge of
the keepers and other servants there. The lease gave all the deer to Sir
Robert to dispose of, incorporated the disparking and disfranchising
order, dismissed Charles Kirke and George Kirke from their Keepership and ordered them to depart from their lodges.

The Little Park, however, was still being maintained as a deer park.
One of Berkeley's duties was to provide hay for the deer, and in
February, 1663, he was reimbursed £74 1s. 1d. under this heading. In
that year, on 25th July, Samuel Pepys rode to Epsom; finding the town
full, he had to spend the night at Ashtead. Returning to Epsom the
following day he called at Durdans, but Lord Berkeley and his family
were staying in London. Pepys walked in the courtyard and on the
bowling green, where, he says, he had seen so much mirth in his time.
Elsewhere he speaks of 'Durdans, where I have been very merry when
I was a little boy'. Epsom was again full of visitors, most of them
citizens of London, and Pepys marvelled that they had ever had it in
their heads or their purses to go down to Epsom. Riding back towards
London, through Ewell and a mile beyond Nonsuch, his "little dogg
fell a-running after a flock of sheep feeding on the common" until he
was out of sight. The dog, anxious to find his master, raced back
towards Nonsuch and Pepys followed after, "being by many told of
his going that way and the haste he made". Passing through Ewell,
he lost track of the dog on the outskirts of Epsom. He rode back to
Nonsuch and then decided to put up for the night in Ewell, employing
people to look for the dog. After ordering supper he walked out
through Nonsuch Park to the house, which he examined from the
outside, and looked through the great gates into 'a noble court'. But
its splendour belonged to the past, for he commented that he believed
it to have been a very noble house, and a delicate park around it. On
the day of his visit a doe was killed, to be taken to the Court. Whether
the Palace was in fact being lived in at this time is not clear. Its owner,
Henrietta Maria, is not known to have visited it after the Restoration,
and she finally left the country on 29th June, 1665; yet the possibility
of a visit was not ruled out: a proposal, of about 1664, for a bridge over
the Thames between Westminster and Lambeth was supported by the
suggestion that it would be convenient for the king and the two
queens to use when travelling to Greenwich, Nonsuch and Hampton
Court. The only recorded royal visitor was Charles II himself. Lord
Berkeley, writing from Durdans on 15th September, 1664, to the

Countess Dowager of Devonshire, told her that he had been busy preparing for the reception of the king, who had killed a stag at Nonsuch and had then honoured him by dining at 'my house', by which he presumably meant Durdans.

Repair works directly charged to the Office of Works were resumed, after a gap of some fifteen years, in 1663. In September 36,000 Cornish slates were bought and carried to Nonsuch by land and water, to be put in store ready for the repair of the roof. In addition to this expenditure under the hands of the officers of the Works, Lord Berkeley received a warrant, on 1st March, 1665, for £1,000 for repairs to the fences. This was the year of the Great Plague, a disaster which gave considerable impetus to the work of restoring Nonsuch to full serviceability. On 26th July a royal proclamation was issued for removing the Receipt of the Exchequer, together with the Tally Office, to the King's Honour of Nonsuch, 'by reason of the great and dangerous increase of the plague in and about the City of Westminster'. The Exchequer was to be opened at Nonsuch on 15th August. On 7th August the Lord Treasurer, the Earl of Southampton, issued instructions to the Chamberlain and Auditor of the Exchequer, the Clerk of the Pells and the Tally Cutter, regarding the removal of the various items under their charge.

Meanwhile the officers of the Works had been busy organizing the "sundry Workes repairacions and alteracions" necessary for erecting and fitting out various offices at Nonsuch. A great deal of leeway in ordinary maintenance work had to be made up. There were upwards of 150 leaks in the lead of the roof, and in some places the internal walls were green with mould. In places, floor joists had rotted because the roofs were damaged and the rain had come through; wainscoting had also suffered in this way. Solid, 'plastered' floors had sunk—in the guard chamber, gallery and kitchen. Many ceilings needed repair, including that in the chapel. Over 1,300 ft. of window lead were repaired or replaced, 227 ft. of new glass put in and 4,500 small panes or 'quarrels' were stopped. Lead was repaired or replaced on the roof, and the cisterns and pipes unstopped and made good; and a great quantity of rubbish was swept up and carried out of the house. These repairs, and the adaptations, continued right through August and into September, and cost £455, of which £88 was spent on timber of various kinds and £8 on laths. Much of the work consisted of erecting lath-and-plaster partitions, benches, shelves, tables and screens. A chest was made for the tallies, and a bench for cutting them on. In the back yard—presumably the yard outside the north front of the kitchens—a Court of Guard was erected, and in it were placed two beds, 17 ft. long and 2 ft. high, for the soldiers. A pulpit and benches were provided in the chapel. Only 36s. was spent on bricks as against £10 10s. for lime, 49s. for sand and 42s. 6d. for hair. Glass and glaziers' labour accounted for over £38. However, the temporary, utilitarian nature of the work is revealed by the smallest item in the accounts, that for 2s. spent on size and colours.

A proclamation for continuing the Exchequer at Nonsuch was issued on 26th September, 1665. By November the Lord Treasurer appears to have reached a state of exasperation over the dislocation in the work of his department caused by its dispersal. He promulgated rules for the attendance of Officers of the Receipt. From Easter to Michaelmas they were to attend from 8 a.m. until noon, and from Michaelmas to Easter from nine until noon. They were not to be absent without leave for more than a week. They were to attend to their duties in person, and not to 'remit all to their clerks as of late hath been done'. Although it would not be possible for these orders to be carried out completely during the abode at Nonsuch, they were to be punctually performed when it should please God to bless them with a return to Westminster.

Samuel Pepys, appointed Surveyor General of the Victualling Office in 1665, was a frequent visitor on business, which he pursued with zeal and efficiency, but still leaving himself time to indulge some of his other interests. He first became aware of the proposed move to Nonsuch on 11th August. The day before, with the week's total plague deaths announced as over 3,000, he had made his will: 'the town growing so unhealthy, that a man cannot depend upon living two days'. The sight of the bustle at the Exchequer seems to have further unnerved him, for he went home to set his house, 'and all things, in the best order I can, lest it should please God to take me away, or force me to leave my house'. On the 21st September he was up before six, and set out for Nonsuch by coach. He had £100 with him to pay in at the Exchequer, and rode in some fear of being robbed. Two of the officers he went to see were still in bed, as they had to do a turn on watch every night. Nothing at all had been done about the business which had occasioned his visit; making no allowance for the prevailing distress and upheaval, he confesses that this 'vexed' him. However, making the best of a bad job, he took a walk round with the one member of the particular department who was on his feet. He walked up and down the house and Park, and once again was struck not only by its magnificence but by its decline. "A fine place it hath heretofore been," he writes, "and a fine prospect about the house." He then describes the house, and says "I walked into the ruined garden". In the garden he found "a plain little girle, to sing very finely by the eare only, but a fine way of singing, and if I come ever to lacke a girle again I shall think of getting her". He dined in Ewell with some of the Exchequer men, and set off for home at about four o'clock, "in fear for the money" he had with him.

On a borrowed horse, Pepys set out from Greenwich early in the morning on 29th September, 1665, and, riding hard, had "a very fine journey and a fine day", and so reached Nonsuch by eight o'clock. This was "chappell-time", so he went to chapel, and afterwards called at various offices about his tallies. He found that these had been got ready for him, but incorrectly, "strung for sums not to my purpose". He had much ado to persuade the "dull fellows", especially Mr. Warder, Master of the Pells, to put matters right. Eventually he succeeded, walked to Ewell where he "did spend a peece upon them, having a whole house full, and much mirth by a sister of the mistresse of the house", had "much pleasant discourse" and, after dinner, mounted his horse and reached Greenwich before nightfall. With winter approaching, the great inconvenience of having the Exchequer so far from London became ever more apparent. On 20th November Pepys was up before daybreak, and with two men for company rode on horseback through very bad roads and worse weather to Nonsuch. There he collected his tallies and made up a party to go to Ewell, "and there dined very well, and I saw my Besse, a very well-favoured country lass there, and after being very merry and spent a piece" he took horse and travelled back to London, by a different and much better road, but still in heavy rain and high wind. After this experience he decided to travel in comfort for his next visit, eight days later. Again he was up before dawn, and was picked up by a hackney coach drawn by four horses. Just over London Bridge he remembered an urgent letter, so he borrowed a candle from some paviours who were working there, took out his portable writing equipment and wrote his letter before resuming the journey. The roads were again very bad, but his mission was successfully accomplished and he went on to dinner with Sir Robert Long at Worcester House. Here there were a couple of ladies, kinswomen of Sir Robert, "not handsome, but rich", with whom Pepys was "mighty merry".

By this time, however, the cold weather had substantially reduced the death-roll due to the plague. The Lord Treasurer was becoming increasingly anxious to get things back to normal. On the 19th December he wrote 'until his Majesty thinks fit to remand the Exchequer to Westminster again, which we hope may safely be done speedily'. Early in January he was with the Court at Oxford, and knew that the move was imminent. He wrote on 5th January to Sir Robert Long at Nonsuch to say that the royal proclamation for the return to Westminster would be sealed the following day, and would then have to be printed and distributed. The appointed day was to be 20th January, but he suggested that some of the officers should go back before that date, so that business could be conducted in both places, 'for Sir George Downing complains much that the delay between Westminster and Nonsuch retards all'. The proclamation was duly issued on 6th January, 1666. Although he makes no mention of the presence of the Exchequer, the Palace was thus still being used for offices when John Evelyn visited it on 3rd January; and the Mr. Packer whom he visited was in fact an officer of the Exchequer.

As they thankfully scraped the Nonsuch mud off their garments, and set about unpacking their belongings in the familiar surroundings at Westminster, the officers of the Exchequer had no inkling that within nine months they would be hastily throwing things into boxes ready for a return to Nonsuch. The Fire of London broke out at one o'clock in the morning on Sunday, 2nd September, 1666. By Tuesday the fire had become so widespread that a royal warrant was issued for removing the Exchequer to Nonsuch, by river and road. The warrant ordered all mayors, bailiffs and others to help, at their peril. Pepys, busy everywhere, sending his own goods and treasure to a place of safety, trying to organize the pulling down of houses to check the spread of the fire, lending a helping hand where he could, was so weary and footsore by Tuesday evening that he could hardly stand. Yet somehow he managed to record his experiences and the heartbreaking sights he saw during these terrible days. On Thursday, the 6th, covered with dirt from head to foot, he made his way to Westminster, hoping to get a change of clothing; but he found no place where he could buy a shirt or even a pair of gloves. He found Westminster Hall full of goods from houses destroyed or threatened by fire. The contents of the offices in Westminster had been removed, and the Exchequer money put into vessels to be taken to Nonsuch.

Soldiers had been called out to guard the treasure on the Monday following the outbreak of fire and they stayed on guard until the Friday, by which time it is to be assumed that the move to Nonsuch had been completed. Some of the guards were sent out to 'press' boats into service, boats which would otherwise have been in commission all round the clock for evacuating the goods of private citizens. Seven barges were obtained, and the records and treasure, tied in boxes, were loaded into them by porters and labourers. "Beere fire and candle" were provided for those who guarded the treasure. The total cost of the move was £105 14s. 4d.

Lord Berkeley, unperturbed by these two temporary incursions of officialdom, was making himself so much at home in his 'lodgings' at Nonsuch now that the owner was abroad that he almost regarded the place as his own. In June, 1667, he was taken to task by the Treasury for pulling down a lodge in the Park. When he was interviewed on the matter he agreed that he had pulled it down without orders, his reason being that it was so old and decayed. A Captain Cooke, acting for Berkeley, had sold the materials; orders were given for the sale to stop and the materials to be reclaimed. The 'lodge' thus unceremoniously pulled to pieces and surreptitiously sold was, in fact, the Banqueting House. Three and a half years before Barbara Villiers appeared on the scene at Nonsuch, Berkeley had committed an act of vandalism for which she has always been blamed. The materials had been taken to a barn in Ewell, and carpenters in the employ of the Works had to take planks off the barn so that the instructions of the Treasury could be carried out. Ninety-one cartloads of material were seized: lead, timber, wainscot, bricks, stone, tiles, glass, fifteen window frames and some old iron. Rooms in the Palace, including the 'Great Kitchen', were prepared and made secure as storerooms for the spoils. Some of the lead was taken direct to Hampton Court. The total value of the materials was £121 6s. 7½d.

The official probe into Berkeley's actions did not stop there. He was found to have put a farmer tenant, William Bullen, into a house in the Park which was supposed to be for the use of the officers of the Works. Captain Cooke was ordered to send Bullen to the Treasury for examination. He appeared on 3rd July, and it was decided that Lord

Berkeley himself should be examined. Berkeley's interview ended inconclusively, the two parties being asked to set down their claims to the title of the lodge; but he turned the tables very effectively by demanding the arrears of Keepership fees due to him. No more was heard of Bullen's tenancy, but the Keeper's fees were eventually paid, and, for a time, kept up to date.

Extensive repair works were carried out between June, 1667, and May, 1668. Much of the expenditure was on sheet lead and "soder", which together accounted for £88. This was used for roofing, guttering and water-supply pipes. Plumbers were not, however, the most numerous among the various categories of workmen employed; the main wage-bill was for bricklayers and slaters. The bricklayers were engaged on repairing the heads of chimneys over the king's privy lodgings, and the slaters worked on the roof of the Inner Court building. In May, 1669, stocks were laid in for a major onslaught on the roof: 50,000 blue slates 'of the smaller sort' and 17,000 'of the largest sort' were bought and piled up ready for use. Between June, 1669, and May, 1670, 42,000 more slates were bought, as well as tiles and tile pins. The tiles were used over the kitchens and the Porter's Lodge, labour costing £16 15s. For the main roofs the slater was paid £100 12s. 6d. The plumbers were again busy with their "soder"; this year no new lead was bought, but they had to 'cast old lead into new'. The total cost of the year's work was £507 3s. 7d., the heaviest expenditure for many years, and highly significant at this fateful date in the life of the Palace: for it demonstrates that, however much the building had deteriorated since the days of Elizabeth and the early Stuarts, it was still sufficiently sound in 1670 to be worth re-roofing; its rapid decline in subsequent years can only have been due to neglect after it had passed out of royal ownership.

Henrietta Maria died in 1669. Before December of that year Berkeley had expressed to the Treasury his concern about the future of the Palace and Little Park. It was decided that nothing needed to be done at the moment, but that when the Park was granted to 'any person' it was to be done in such a way that no charge should fall to be met by the king. Whatever discussions had been going on behind the scenes is not revealed, but in July, 1670, a draft was prepared of a grant to Barbara, Countess of Castlemaine, only daughter and heir of the late Viscount Grandison, in consideration of *his* eminent services, of the dignities of Baroness of Nonsuch, Countess of Southampton and Duchess of Cleveland, with reversion to her eldest son Charles, to be called Earl of Southampton, and his heirs male, and after them (because the paternity of Henry, later Duke of Grafton, had not yet been acknowledged by the king) to George, her 'second' son, and his heirs male. Her sons and daughters were to have the precedence of children of a duke, and she was to have a pension of £20 as Countess and £40 as Duchess. The grant was sealed on Friday, 29th July. Mr. Henry Brounker called in at the Treasury on 22nd July, 1670, and after his visit a warrant was issued for the taking of a 'particular' or inventory of all the king's possessions at Nonsuch. The repairs which had been completed by mid-summer apparently did not go far enough for Brounker: he was at the Treasury again on 14th November, and a further £1,000 for the repair of Nonsuch was allocated. On 9th December, 1670, a warrant was issued to the Attorney General to prepare a grant to George, Viscount Grandison, and Henry Brounker, of the Palace, the Little Park of 671 acres stored with deer, and in the custody of Berkeley and others, and the Great Park containing 1,030 acres in lease to Sir Robert Long. The property was to be held at an annual rent of 10s. The grant was completed on 18th January, 1671, and gave the grantees the franchise of 'freebord' and 'ringwalk' outside the pales of both parks, made them the recipients of the £100 a year rent which Sir Robert Long was paying for the Great Park and gave them liberty to dispark and impark. Brounker and Grandison were thus, on paper, the new owners of Nonsuch; in fact, they had received the grant, not on their own behalf, but as trustees for the new Baroness of Nonsuch and her sons.

The story of Barbara Villiers, of her wanton life, her extravagances, her hold over Charles II even in the sphere of government, has been told many times; in fact, the first 'Life' of her was published within a month of her going to her uneasy rest in 1709. The daughter of William Villiers, 2nd Viscount Grandison, who was fatally wounded in the Royalist cause in 1642, she was twenty-eight when she was created Baroness Nonsuch. For some years she had been drawing a very handsome income. In 1668 she was granted £4,700 a year out of the Post Office revenues, but, quite apart from her extravagant spending, her gambling kept her constantly in need of money. She is said to have won £15,000 one night and lost £25,000 another. The grant of Nonsuch came shortly after the arrival at Court of Louise de Keroualle, and it has been suggested that Barbara had exacted Nonsuch as part of the price of her appeasement after a bitter quarrel with Charles, whose wandering eye had come to rest too often on this beautiful maid-of-honour to his sister Henrietta. However this may be, Barbara certainly received enormous money gifts from the king at this time, including £10,000 a year from the Imposition on Wine, and the same on the Excise of Beer and Ale; and it was said that she scrutinized all promotions, both spiritual and temporal. Although Charles' interest in her was waning she was still, with her dark auburn hair and deep blue eyes, strikingly beautiful. Even after another ten years of 'pleasure unrestrained, unfaltering—unless through lack of cash—and unrepentant', Bishop Burnet wrote of her 'I never heard any commend her but for her beauty, which was very extraordinary and has been now of long continuance'.

Of just what benefit the gift of Nonsuch was to Barbara Villiers it is difficult to say. As far as is at present known, she never lived there or even visited the place. The income from Sir Robert Long's rent on the Great Park was a mere drop in the ocean, and, even if she had got rid of the deer in the Little Park and let it out to farmers, the income would scarcely have been sufficient to cover even the most essential annual repair work on the Palace itself. It may be that she let the building, but there is no evidence of anyone living there until 1681, and even then the information is tantalizingly slight. It is not until 1682 that Barbara and her trustees reappear in the surviving records of Nonsuch, and then they come, not to enjoy the beauties of the Palace and Park but to convert them into ready money.

Meanwhile Sir Robert Long had taken steps to strengthen his hold on the Great Park. An undated petition from him, probably written during the early summer of 1670, recalls how the Park was totally destroyed during the late troubles, the wood being cut down, the pales taken away and the soil all converted to tillage. Since being granted the lease in 1663, he said, he had bought out the Keeper and spent over £2,500 on repairs to Worcester House and the other buildings. His present lease was for two lives, and he asked that it might be extended to three. On 25th August, 1670, a Treasury Warrant authorized the Attorney General to add a third life to Long's lease, and the new grant, for ninety-nine years, was made on 29th September. Sir Robert was to pay £400 and was to plant twenty or more young, straight, thriving trees of oak, ash or elm each year upon some convenient part or parts of the premises.

Lord Berkeley found himself faced, in 1671, with a set of circumstances very similar to those which had confronted Sir Thomas Cawarden in 1556. The Palace and Little Park had passed from the Crown to private ownership, and he held his Keepership from the Crown. As with Cawarden, this situation eventually led to blows; but, partly through the apparent indifference of the new owner and partly owing to her relations with the king, the continuance of Berkeley's Patent was unchallenged, and he enjoyed his fees and perquisites in comparative peace, until 1682. Barbara Villiers lived in Paris from 1677 to 1684, paying occasional visits to this country. On one of these visits, in July, 1679, Charles gave the Commissioners of the Treasury warning to look to themselves, because she had come over to have a 'bout' with them about money, having lost £20,000 and jewelry in one night's gambling. She was in England again in June, 1682, and it was now the turn of Berkeley (created Viscount Dursley and Earl of Berkeley on 11th September, 1679) to 'look to himself'. She and her trustees, Grandison and Brounker, accused Berkeley of killing great quantities of deer, felling trees and ploughing up land which had not been ploughed in living memory. To get rid of him once and for all as Keeper, she decided to destroy the things over which he exercised Keepership—her palace and her park. He would then have no right to enter the premises.

She accordingly entered into an agreement with one Fryth or Frith, a builder, whereby he was to have the materials of the Palace for £1,700, this figure to include all the buildings in the Park except the lodges and the two houses at the Park gates. A warrant of Charles II, dated 31st July, 1682, authorized the trustees to sell the materials of the Palace as the Duchess directed because it was in such a bad state of repair. She then told Berkeley of her intention to have the Palace pulled down and to dispark the Park. Berkeley persuaded her to agree to transfer the sale of the materials to him, and he promised to pay an extra £100 so that she could compensate Fryth for his trouble in negotiating the original agreement. The agreement between Barbara Villiers, Brounker, Grandison and the Earl of Berkeley (acting through his agent, William Smith of the Middle Temple) was signed on 29th August, 1682. By it, the 'first or lower court and all the buildings on every side of that court, and the cellars' were leased to Berkeley for sixty years if Barbara Villiers should live so long, and for two years thereafter. The lease included the right of access through the Park gate 'towards Epsom'.

The Outward Court was thus intended to be left standing until Barbara's death, after which, presumably, Berkeley or his heirs would have two years in which to pull it down. The lease cost Berkeley only 15s., shared between the three lessors; and it included a two-year lease on the remainder of the Palace and courts, the stables, coach-houses and gardens, during which time, in return for a payment of £1,800, he could help himself to the materials. He had liberty of access for carts to take away the materials of the Inner Court, the garden walls, fountains, figures and pavements, the cisterns and the pipes.

Demolition was probably begun before the end of 1682, for in June, 1683, it was described as 'begun and continuing'. On 14th June Barbara and her trustees lodged a complaint, addressed to the Lord Keeper of the Great Seal, to the effect that Berkeley was pulling down or threatening to pull down buildings not included in the agreement. With the support of his relatives, and William Smith, Theophila Cooke and others, he was claiming to have right and title to the soil of the Park, the trees, deer and all the lodges, houses, barns and other buildings, and they were denying the right of Grandison and Brounker to take possession of the lodges. Berkeley replied, in December, that he had been pulling down only what he was entitled to. He asserted that he did not claim absolute ownership of the Park, but insisted that his Letters Patent as Keeper gave him the right to deny access to the lodges and other buildings, which were at the disposal of the Keeper. He regarded the complaint against him as the first step in ousting him from the office of Keeper. The Duchess, he said, obviously realized that the Keepership was valuable, because she had once offered him an alternative office worth £1,000 a year; but he had had to buy the Keepership in 1660, and he was entitled to compensation if he was going to lose any of his rights.

The argument over the Park went on until 1687. As regards the Palace itself, with the Inner Court, or most of it, pulled down and probably carted to Durdans, at least one member of Berkeley's family continued to live at Nonsuch, either in the Outward Court or in one of the lodges, until 1686. This was his daughter-in-law, Elizabeth, Viscountess Dursley, whose husband became the 2nd Earl of Berkeley in 1698. A letter of 24th October, 1682, refers to her return to Nonsuch, and she wrote from Nonsuch on 12th May, 1686. Robert Coke (who was probably the Captain Cooke of the Banqueting House incident), grandson of Lord Chief Justice Sir Edward Coke, and the nephew of Berkeley's only sister, died at Nonsuch in June, 1681. Robert's widow, Theophila, was mentioned in the complaint lodged by Barbara Villiers in 1683.

During the years of dispute between Barbara Villiers and Berkeley, he was also in trouble with the Exchequer. His Keepership fees were usually very much in arrears, and business was conducted in so leisurely a manner that his warrant for £1,000 for the repair of the Little Park pale, approved in 1665, was still a subject of dispute in 1685. The money had not actually been paid to Berkeley in 1665, although payment had been authorized. It was warranted again on 15th April, 1667, and again on 14th December, 1670. This time the £1,000 seems to have been paid. When (or whether) the money was laid out by him for its intended purpose is not known; but it was probably all spent during the 'sixties in repairing the neglect which the fences had suffered during the interregnum. Normally he would have been required to account for every penny of the money, being 'charged' with it until he could be discharged by the submission of a statement of account supported by vouchers and full particulars. Possibly because the expenditure had been spread over many years, he failed to do so. His application to the king to be 'acquitted and released' of the charge was granted on 23rd March, 1679; the release was to be as final as if he had rendered a proper account and obtained a 'quietus' thereon. Charles II may have been content to accept Berkeley's word that the money had been used for its proper purpose, but the watchdogs at the Exchequer were not prepared to let matters rest. A month after the death of the king, Henry Guy, Secretary to the Treasury, wrote to Berkeley demanding an account, with the vouchers thereof, of the £1,000 'imprested' to him for the repair of Nonsuch Park. The demand was repeated, this time by Laurence Hyde, Earl of Rochester, the Lord High Treasurer, on 15th March, 1686.

As on a previous occasion when he felt that he was being hectored, the earl seems to have retaliated by lodging a complaint himself; a complaint not directly connected with the point at issue, but so much more serious that it was almost certain to sidetrack the Treasury officials. His petition has not survived, but the chain of events makes its purport clear: that the owners of Nonsuch were disparking the Little Park as they had threatened in 1682, and that they had no legal right to do so. Henry Guy referred Berkeley's petition to Barbara on 31st October, 1685, asking her to let the Earl of Rochester know if she had any objection to it. The objections came in so promptly that a fortnight later Guy was passing them on to Berkeley for his comments. He was equally prompt, and on 28th November Henry Guy joined battle in support of Berkeley's petition and against Brounker, Grandison and Barbara Villiers.

Permission to dispark had been given in the original grant of Nonsuch to Henry Brounker and Viscount Grandison in 1671. No action had been taken, but an undated document signed by Charles II informed Brounker that the Duchess of Cleveland had satisfied the king that it was to the advantage of both herself and her heirs that Nonsuch should be 'suddenly disparked'. In this way all suits and contests between her and Berkeley would be avoided. The duchess proposed to let the land out at a rent. Charles instructed Brounker, according to the power given to him in the grant, to lease Nonsuch to her for a term not exceeding twenty-one years, to enable her to proceed on these lines. This was written on 25th August, and the year must have been 1684, for it is addressed to 'my lord Brounker' and Henry did not succeed his brother William as Viscount Brounker until that year. The disparking, or at least the preparations for it, must have been begun early in the following year. As a result of the Earl of Berkeley's complaint, the disparkers were ordered to stop; the peremptory tone of the official correspondence shows very clearly that Barbara Villiers no longer commanded the enforced respect which had been hers whilst Charles was alive.

Henry Guy's letter of 28th November, 1685, to Viscount Brounker, informed him that the late king's permission for disparking Nonsuch had been later countermanded by Lord Godolphin's signification of the king's pleasure to the contrary. He asked to be informed whether the disparking was or was not continuing, and what had been done in the matter since the countermand had been given. On the 1st December a letter in the same terms was sent to Viscount Grandison. Grandison sent in a report to the Lord Treasurer on 7th December; but, because he had neither addressed it nor signed it, Guy sent it straight back to him telling him to send his lordship such an account of Nonsuch Park as he (Grandison) would sign. Without waiting for a reply, the Lord Treasurer wrote on the following day to both Brounker and Grandison. He asserted that one of them had given directions for disparking Nonsuch without the consent and approbation of the other. He ordered them to stop until the king's pleasure should be known.

A year later Berkeley again reported that the Duchess of Cleveland was attempting to dispark, despite the fact that the Lord Treasurer had notified the two trustees of the king's decision that Nonsuch should not be disparked. Accordingly, on 5th April, 1687, the Lords of the Treasury wrote to Brounker and Grandison, requiring them, in the king's name, not to dispark or to fell trees until both they and Berkeley had been heard at the Treasury Board. Barbara now took the law into her own hands. She enlisted the help of her second son by Charles II, Henry, 1st Duke of Grafton, a distinguished sailor and soldier, and sent him down to Nonsuch to carry out the disparking by force. The clash with Berkeley, defending law, order and the Berkeley interests, resulted in the indictment of Grafton before two justices at the 'King's Head' in Epsom on 16th May, 1687. Berkeley accused Grafton and other malefactors of illegally forcing an entry to Nonsuch Park with swords, sticks, hammers, axes and other arms on 10th May, thus disturbing the king's peace. Berkeley actually claimed to have had 'peaceful and lawful possession and seisin' of the Park, containing 400 acres, until his 'free tenement' was invaded, he was expelled and had since been kept out by force of arms. The case of Rex v. the Duke of Grafton was heard in the Court of King's Bench in Trinity Term, 1687, when Grafton replied by charging Berkeley's men with inflicting bodily harm upon him so that he despaired of his life, and Barbara claimed that they had insulted her by forcibly excluding her from the Park. Grafton must have been well served by his legal advisers, for in the Michaelmas Term they lodged an exception to the indictment on the grounds that it was incorrectly worded. The Court upheld the exception, the indictment was quashed and the defendant was awarded costs. News that this loophole had been found must have leaked out very shortly after the first hearing, for on the 16th June, three days after the end of the Trinity law sittings in 1687, the Duke of Beaufort wrote to the duchess: 'The Duke of Grafton has had the better of Lord Berkeley in the business of the riot at Nonsuch.'

Why the decision was not challenged, at least to the extent of meeting Barbara Villiers' next move by a fresh and correctly worded indictment, remains a mystery. The Earl of Berkeley had put up a good fight over the years to preserve his rights at Nonsuch, yet he seems to have accepted defeat; his twelve and a half years' arrears of fees had been paid in May, 1687, and he allowed himself to be paid off on 25th March, 1688, with the year's fee due up to that date. If Berkeley's sudden abandonment of the struggle is difficult to understand, the dropping of the case by the Lords of the Treasury is even more so. Their authority had been deliberately flouted, and their statement of the king's wishes had been ignored; but, once the Duke of Grafton had been cleared of the charge against him, they too lost interest in what happened to Nonsuch.

Barbara Villiers had already satisfied herself that the Crown had no right to interfere with the conduct of her affairs at Nonsuch. On 13th April, with Grandison, Brounker, the Duke of Grafton and the Duke of Northumberland (her youngest son by Charles II), she had conveyed the remainder of the Palace and both Parks to Richard Topham and Michael Bebington. The purpose for which the conveyance was made was set out in an indenture of release which has not survived; but it is clear that it was intended to ensure the succession of her son, Henry, Duke of Grafton, Topham and Bebington being merely trustees. A deed of the same date, preserved at the Old Cottage in Cheam, contains the undertaking of the parties to levy a fine in the Court of Common Pleas during Trinity Term, 1687. This was duly carried into effect, so that, whilst the Duke of Grafton was being charged with illegal entry into Nonsuch in one court, he was being accepted as one of the people who had a right to dispose of Nonsuch in another.

With this legal activity in 1687 the documented story of the Palace building ends. It was not, as has so often been stated, demolished soon after Barbara Villiers aquired it, although it was only by a legal fiction that it continued to be described in documents as a 'Capital Messuage or Mansion House' until 1731. By some means Berkeley's sixty-year lease on the Outward Court must have been terminated, and demolition of whatever he had left standing must have begun quite soon after Barbara had assured herself that the Crown and the Keeper could not interfere; any later references to the building describe only the ruins.

The reasons for the demolition of Nonsuch can only be surmised. Many suggestions have been put forward over the years, some of them manifestly impossible, such as the legend that it was knocked down by the Parliamentary forces during the Civil War. Fears that the Crown might take back the property, Barbara Villiers' need of money to pay her gambling debts, the possibility that the timber-framed Inner Court building, particularly behind the decorative slate panels, was full of dry-rot, have all been considered as explanations; yet it may be that, to Barbara, it was simply an obvious, commonsense thing to do. The Parks, let out to farmers, would be a source of income; the Palace was a building for which she had no conceivable use, a building which, even in its best days, had cost a good deal of money to maintain. It was hers to do as she liked with, and what she liked was to exchange an annual maintenance bill (or an asset deteriorating through neglect) for ready money. No thoughts of its past glory, or of the opprobrium of later generations, are likely to have entered her shrewd and calculating mind. And so, with her anger against Berkeley spurring her on, she reached her decision to demolish the Palace, and by a strange trick of circumstance it was Berkeley himself who was responsible for carrying at least the first part of her decision into effect. Between them they inflicted what was "probably the heaviest loss which English architecture has suffered since the Dissolution of the Monasteries".

11

Later Owners

Barbara villiers' gambling increased as her charms faded. She was constantly in debt, and her state pension was not always paid as regularly as she would have liked. In 1692 she was compelled to sell Cleaveland House. In 1697, saying that she had had to borrow £10,000, she appealed to the Lords of the Treasury for the payment of the arrears of her pension. The pension from the Post Office funds continued to be paid by Queen Anne. On 25th November, 1705, Barbara was tricked into a bigamous marriage with Beau Fielding. Her sons appear to have protected her from the worst consequences of this blunder, which was decidedly out of character for the shrewd, worldly-wise widow of sixty-three. When she had finally disentangled herself from Fielding, she went to live at Chiswick, where she died on 9th October, 1709.

The son who was to have inherited the Nonsuch estate, Henry Fitzroy, Duke of Grafton, died in 1690 as a result of wounds received during the siege of Cork. On 6th June, 1693, Barbara mortgaged the estate to Joseph Fells. New trustees, James Mundy of the Inner Temple and Cardell Goodman of St. Martin in the Fields, were appointed in 1694. Fells assigned his interest in Nonsuch to five of his creditors in June, 1699, and a Chancery decree was issued in December, 1704, for the paying-off of the mortgage. Henry Fitzroy's son, Charles, 2nd Duke of Grafton, was granted the Nonsuch property three months before Barbara Villiers' death, to hold it in trust for her during her life. Charles Fitzroy was known as the greatest courtier of his time. He was a keen huntsman, and may well have regretted the fact that his legacy from his grandmother was not a hunting estate round a stately home, but a number of farms with a rubble-heap on one of them. His portrait, by Kneller, one of a series commissioned by Jacob Tonson

217

of the members of the Kit Cat Club, is in the National Portrait Gallery.
Grafton was Lord Lieutenant of Ireland from 1720 to 1725.

He mortgaged Nonsuch to the Duke of Marlborough in 1711, and
it was again mortgaged, in 1728, to Thomas Gibson and John Jacob,
of London, as security for £10,000. Three years later an Act of
Parliament was passed for the sale of the Grafton estates in Surrey and
elsewhere, and the final disintegration of the Nonsuch estate began in
that year, when the Great Park and the Little Park were sold to separate
purchasers and were never afterwards reunited. The Great Park,
known by then as Worcester Park, was sold in 1731 by the Duke of
Grafton to his former steward, John Walter, whose son and heir, Sir
George Walter, was one of the three trustees who had been nominated
in the Act for the sale of the duke's estates. In 1750 the Park was sold
in Chancery, to William Taylor, who had established the Malden
Powder Mills on the banks of the Hogsmill in 1720. On 2nd January,
1742, according to the *Gentleman's Magazine*, "about 1 in the morning
the Powder Mill of Maiden was blown up with the Magazine, containing
40 Barrels of Gunpowder. Great Damage was done to the Houses, the
windows of the Church at 400 yards distance were entirely Shattered.
The Explosion was heard in London, and 12 miles round the Place,
and the whole Country was alarmed, but as no satisfactory Account
could then be given of the matter it was generally supposed to be an
Earthquake." William Taylor is said to have pulled down the remains
of the original Worcester House, and his son William erected a new
mansion, Worcester Park House, at the bottom of the hill to the south-
west, in 1797. In the early years of the nineteenth century there were
twelve gunpowder mills on the banks of the Hogsmill. Two of Taylor's
mills, on lease to Messrs. Curtis and Hardy, blew up in 1854. The
danger to people using the nearby road led to a demand for the closing
of the mills, but they continued in operation until the last of them
caught fire and exploded within living memory. The name of their
founder survived until recent years in Taylor's Shrubbery, a coppice
in Kingston Road, Ewell, on either side of Salisbury Road.

Among the separate farms into which the Great Park was divided
after the destruction of Nonsuch were Bowling Green Farm or Stone's
Farm, from which Stoneleigh takes its name; Sparrow Farm (the
Sparrowfield of 1650); Coldharbour Farm, in the vicinity of Stoneleigh
West Schools; and Worcester Park Farm, whose ancient farmhouse
stood at the Royal Avenue end of Delta Road and appears to have

been the Keeper's Lodge described in the 1650 Survey, left standing when the old Worcester House was demolished by William Taylor. In this farmhouse, in 1851, Holman Hunt and Millais worked. The ancient brick wall of the garden is seen in Millais' picture, *The Huguenot*, and he found in the nearby Hogsmill River the perfect setting for *Ophelia in the Stream*. The scene can no longer be identified: a mile and a half upstream, near the Meadow Walk railway bridge on the outskirts of Ewell, stood a willow known locally as 'the Ophelia tree'; but there appears to be a stronger case for another willow, a short distance from Worcester Park Farm, on the stretch of the river which runs parallel with Worcester Park Road. Great walkers though they were, it is unlikely that Millais would have wanted to spend time in making the daily journey to Ewell, where he had friends and where Holman Hunt's uncle lived, at either of which homes they would have been welcome guests. The weed-choked door in Holman Hunt's *The Light of the World* was inspired by the sight, by lantern light, of the door of a disused hut belonging to Taylor's powder mills. The artist describes the "glorious avenue of elms" in front of the farmhouse (the Royal Avenue), "the dragging pulsation of the powder mill down in the vale below" as he worked on his picture all through the autumn nights, and how, as winter came on, "people skated in the valley two hundred feet below".

In 1859 the railway came. The part of the former Great Park round Worcester Park Farm was bought by the Landed Estates Company in 1865; this land was merged with other areas outside the Cuddington parish boundary, and the development of the modern Worcester Park began. By 1867 the name of Worcester Park Farm had been given to a farm off Central Road, Worcester Park. On 13th January of that year the Iron Church (locally known as the Tin Church) was opened, the priest-in-charge, the Rev. Thomas Smith, being appointed by the Landed Estates Company. In later years priests from London conducted the services, but in 1878 the Vicar of Malden provided two services a day. By 1890, although the church now had a priest-in-charge, the fabric of the building was in a bad state. A quarrel with the Vicar of Malden led Charles Smith, a wealthy furrier, to transfer his allegiance to Cuddington, and he bore the greater part of the cost of the permanent church of St. Mary the Virgin, which was consecrated in 1895.

A new mansion, Worcester Court (which, until 1959, housed a

private school), was built in 1873 on the site of the original Worcester House. Some years later workmen who were demolishing one of the ancient barns came across a large store of mead, so potent that it quickly brought the day's labours to an end. Worcester Court and the church marked the western limit of the new development in Victorian times; they were reached, from the station, by the Avenue. Here, at No. 41, H. G. Wells lived in 1896–7, and in *Ann Veronica* he describes Worcester Park ("Morningside Park") as "a suburb that had not, altogether, as people say, come off". Like Roman Gaul, it was divided into three parts: the Avenue, with its "consciously elegant" curve running from the station to "an undeveloped wilderness of agriculture" (a wilderness which a later generation of residents fought hard, and with some success, to preserve); the Pavement, the group of shops near the station; and beyond the railway arch "a congestion of workmen's dwellings". Along the main road which ran under the arch was "a sort of fourth estate" of small villas "with meretricious gables and very brassy window blinds". Although his heroine can take walks in open country, towards "Caddington" and the Downs, she is not wildly enthusiastic about her surroundings in Morningside Park. " 'Ye gods!' she said at last. '*What* a place! Stuffy isn't the word for it.' " Her walk to the Downs, across fields and along a "pretty overhung lane", would today involve passing through some miles of suburban streets, for during the decade prior to the Second World War most of the remaining areas of Nonsuch Great Park, comprising Coldharbour, Stoneleigh and Sparrow Farm, were built on.

The Little Park of Nonsuch was sold in 1731 to Joseph Thompson. The plan of the estate made in the same year, now in the British Museum (page 233), shows the early stages of the laying out of the gardens which surround the present Nonsuch Mansion House. The house built by Joseph Thompson survives to this day, incorporated in the Mansion as the kitchen wing, and some of the outbuildings erected for him form part of the premises occupied by the Park Superintendent. Thompson's house was, after his death on 14th October, 1743, occupied by his nephew, the Rev. Joseph Whately. Thompson, a Dissenter, left Nonsuch to Whately on condition that he took Holy Orders. Joseph's elder brother Thomas lived at Nonsuch, and it was probably he who was responsible for bringing the gardens up to the pitch of perfection which made them famous throughout the nineteenth century. Thomas's book *Observations on modern gardening, illustrated by descriptions* was published in 1770. It ran into several editions, and was translated into French. It was widely praised as "the grand fundamental, and standard work on English gardening". Manning and Bray record that Thomas Whately of Nonsuch Park died on 3rd March, 1765, at the age of eighty, and was buried at Malden; this was the father of Thomas the gardener. The younger Thomas was a Member of Parliament, Secretary to the Treasury in 1764–5, and became Under-Secretary of State under Lord North in June, 1771. In January, 1772, he became Keeper of His Majesty's private roads and Guide to his Royal Person in all his progresses, but died that year.

The development of the estate under the Whatelys is illustrated by two maps. On Rocque's map of Surrey (*c.* 1762) the avenue, which, on Joseph Thompson's survey map of 1731 stopped short of the Palace site, is shown as a continuous road linking the two entrance gates; but, after crossing the Palace site, it turns at a sharp angle towards the Cheam gate, instead of making a wide curve as at present. Immediately inside the London Road gate, to the left, is a small building which also appeared on the 1731 map, and which may be one of the 'houses at the gates' surviving after the demolition of the Palace. At about the northern edge of the former bowling green a road turns off the avenue at right-angles, to a cluster of buildings mainly to the north of the present Cherry Orchard Farm. The Whatelys' house, small in comparison with the Cherry Orchard group, is lettered "Nonsuch Farm". A road leads from it directly to the south, across Cheam Road to Banstead Downs. James Edwards, on his map of 1790 more fully described on page 232, shows the avenue still turning at a sharp angle, but by this time it is lined with trees. The small building inside the London Road gate is still there, and there are two buildings on the present Mansion House site and three outbuildings across the drive. Joseph Whately, Vicar of Widford, Hertfordshire, from 1768 to 1790, and Prebendary of Bristol from 1793 until his death in 1797, directed in his will that the Nonsuch estate should be sold.

The estate was bought in 1799 by Samuel Farmer, M.P. for Huntingdon, of Crabwall, Cheshire, which he inherited from his brother William Gamul Farmer. The Farmers owned the manor of Lagham in Godstone, and, with Nonsuch, their Surrey estates covered over 2,000 acres. For the erection of the Mansion House during the years 1802 to 1806 Samuel commissioned Jeffry Wyatt, the architect who was knighted in 1828 for his work in transforming Windsor

Castle, at a cost of £700,000, from a virtual ruin into a stately and noble building recapturing the romance of mediaeval times. Wyatt changed his name to Wyatville, to distinguish himself from the other architects of the same name, when the first stone of the new buildings at Windsor was laid. A wag of the time, possibly having seen some of his less felicitous work (and 'felicity' is the last epithet which anyone could apply to the stucco-Gothic exterior and chilling, tomb-like interior of the Nonsuch Mansion House) wrote:

> "Let George, whose restlessness leaves nothing quiet,
> Change if he will the good old name of Wyatt;
> But let us hope that their united skill
> Will not make Windsor Castle—Wyatville."

Samuel Farmer died at Nonsuch on 18th May, 1838, at the age of ninety-one. His son, William Meeke Farmer, had died in 1836, so that the estate passed to Samuel's grandson, William Francis Gamul Farmer. Born in 1812, William Francis Gamul married Matilda Wilkinson, who presented him with seven sons and four daughters. He enlarged the house in 1845. He was a Justice of the Peace, and High Sheriff of Surrey in 1849. He died in 1860, his widow surviving him by twenty-nine years. The fountain at the Cheam gate of Nonsuch Park was erected to his memory by his children in 1895. By 1860 the gardens laid out 130 years before by Joseph Thompson and developed by the Whateleys had become famous. A wistaria on the garden wall was 120 ft. long; two cedars of immense size, a Scotch fir 12 ft. in girth, and what was perhaps the finest plane tree in England, are mentioned in Swete's *Handbook of Epsom*, and he tells us that the Nonsuch orchids were justly celebrated throughout the land and had won prize after prize.

In 1860 the estate passed to Captain William Robert Gamul Farmer, to whose wife Charlotte, a life-long supporter of temperance who died on 18th December, 1906, the fountain at the London Road gate is dedicated. The Ordnance Survey of 1866–7 shows "Redgate Lodge" on the right of the London Road entrance and "Bellgate Lodge" at the left of the entrance from Cheam. The gardens round the Mansion House contain several outbuildings, and to the south of the dell is a greenhouse of greater length than the Mansion itself. The avenue makes a wide curve in turning from the London Road gate in the direction of Cheam. The Cherry Orchard is fully planted with fruit trees, and the present farmhouse is shown with its entrance road from the avenue.

The present Park Superintendent inherited from his predecessor a worn and mutilated Visitors' Book from Captain Farmer's time in which the entries begin in 1864 and end in 1893. Most of the pages are devoted to house parties for Derby Week, but the Epsom Spring Meeting was also made the occasion for parties in the later years, as well as the Epsom Ball in May from 1884 to 1887 and in November, 1889. Most of the faded sepia photographs which illustrated the book have been torn out; the few which remain are so delightful that the loss of the others is doubly regrettable. Owing to mourning, there was no Derby party in 1865, 1869 and 1889, and in 1872 the party was only a family one owing to further building. Among the recurring names are Sir Thomas and Lady Gresley, the Hon. Percy and Mrs. Wyndham, the Hon. Somerset and Mrs. Calthorpe, Lord and Lady Rosslyn, Lord and Lady Drogheda, Lord Lonsdale, Lord and Lady Westbury and Lord and Lady Arthur Wellelsey. The last few pages consist of actual signatures, whereas the earlier pages are lists of names. On the penultimate page, almost having the last word as did her namesake 200 years earlier, there stands out in a bold and underlined diagonal the name Adelaide Villiers.

Mr. F. R. Fielder, now living in Epsom, recalls his years of service at Edwardian Nonsuch under Captain Farmer. The domestic staff included a butler, two footmen, a housekeeper, a lady's maid and seven other maids. The head gardener had a staff of eight, and the large out-door staff included a head cowman and a poultry farmer. The head coachman and grooms completed the establishment. The house was lit by gas, the nearest electricity being at Sutton. Street lighting ended at the Cheam cross-roads and began again at Windmill Lane at the boundary between the parishes of Ewell and Epsom, for various influential people in Ewell still regarded lamp-posts as a modern intrusion and successfully vetoed their installation.

In his footman's livery of buff coat and red plush breeches, white stockings and patent-leather shoes, Mr. Fielder accompanied Captain Farmer, High Sheriff of Surrey, to the Assizes at Kingston and Guildford. On the Guildford run horses were changed at Leatherhead, ready for the long pull up Hawks Hill, and were changed again on the return journey. As soon as they were seen in the distance by the major-domo at Guildford, he gave a deft flick of the toe to send the red carpet rolling across the pavement, and, as the C-spring carriage came to a halt through the concerted efforts of the coachman on the reins and the footman on the brake, three trumpeters blew a fanfare which sent a chill through the hearts of the inmates of the cells. For their visits to the shops in Sutton and Croydon with the ladies, a more sober style was considered to be sufficient; on these occasions the coachman and footman were clad in buff coats and top-hats with cockades. During the London season the family moved to their large house in Wilton Crescent.

The house at Nonsuch was full of life at its most gracious: a constant stream of visitors taking tea on the lawn, dances, music and dinner by candlelight. Tables and sideboard were lit by several four-branched silver candlesticks with red shades, and in winter a great log fire added its flickering light. Later, the butler stood in the hall handing out silver candlesticks to light the way to bed. Sir Arthur Glyn often came over from Ewell to pay his respects to Captain and Mrs. Farmer and their daughter Alice, who later married Colonel Colborne; and Major-General Robert Baden-Powell, as he was then, was a frequent visitor. Conversation during and after dinner would dwell on the past glories of Nonsuch Palace, and Captain Farmer's death in 1910 occurred whilst he was planning to excavate the site of the Palace.

Captain Farmer was succeeded by his daughter, Alice Matilda Mary, the wife of Colonel the Hon. Francis Colborne. Colonel Colborne had a distinguished military career in Afghanistan, the Sudan, the Boer War and the First World War. He was a Justice of the Peace and a Deputy Lieutenant; he died in 1924. His widow was the last private owner to reside at Nonsuch. Writing in about 1925, Charles J. Marshall noted that Mrs. Colborne kept up the tradition of the Nonsuch lilacs, as every known kind of lilac was then growing in the Mansion House gardens. The Queen of Spain, visiting Nonsuch some years earlier, had been interested in the copies of portraits of Henry VIII, Catherine of Aragon, Anne Boleyn and Mary Tudor which were hanging in the house. Although the copies were probably made during the eighteenth century, the Queen was certain that she recognized a jewel worn by Mary Tudor as one of the Spanish crown jewels. Queen Mary and Princess Mary paid a visit in 1918, and Princess Beatrice was a frequent guest.

Mrs. Colborne died on 13th May, 1936, and the property was placed in trust for the great grand-daughter of William Francis Gamul

Farmer, Miss Pamela Mary Farmer, who married Mr. Frederick Anthony Vivian Parker on 20th January, 1937. Two months later, at her home at Alverstoke, Gosport, she received a telegram from an uncle saying that he wished to speak to her urgently. She telephoned him from a nearby shop, and was told that a picture which was being auctioned by Messrs. Lofts and Warner with the rest of Mrs. Colborne's effects seemed likely to sell for between £4,000 and £5,000. Mrs. Parker had never seen the picture, which had been for many years in a disused room. It was considered to be worthless, and when the rain was found to be coming in through the ceiling of the room it was not thought necessary to remove the picture to a place of safety. In the catalogue of the sale it was described as "A portrait of a man in black coat with white ruffles". After a week-end of expert examination and consultation, it was attributed to Frans Hals, and this was confirmed after it had been bought by Mr. Arthur de Casseres, the art dealer. Bidding began at 500 guineas and ended at 12,100 guineas. The discovery created something of a sensation, and it was played up in the national Press to such an extent that one photographer in all seriousness took pictures of the nail on which the painting had been hanging. The Dutch Government later bought the painting, and it now hangs in the People's Museum at Haarlem.

In 1937 the London and Surrey County Councils, and the Sutton and Cheam and Epsom and Ewell Corporations, combined to provide £118,000 for the purchase of 263 acres of the Little Park, including the Mansion and the site of the Palace. The Epsom and Ewell Council already owned Cherry Orchard Farm, which they purchased in 1935. The Park was opened to the public on 29th September, 1937, by the Chairman of London County Council, as part of the ceremonies marking Epsom and Ewell's Charter Day. A good deal of friendly rivalry exists between the elected representatives of the two Boroughs as to who took the first steps towards safeguarding the Park from the speculative builders, and this rivalry extends to a number of local organizations. It is, however, indisputable that the present Nonsuch Society was formed for this express purpose, as the Nonsuch Park Preservation Society. The Park is now managed by the Nonsuch Park Joint Management Committee, consisting of representatives of the Borough Councils of Epsom and Ewell and Sutton and Cheam. As the years go by, good management requires the severing of some links with the past in the interests of the present and the future. Occasionally an elderly, rotten and dangerous tree in Park or garden has to be felled, and the lodges at the entrance gates, damp and decayed beyond further use, have been demolished, that at the Cheam gate in 1938 and at London Road in 1955. But the Committee has planted many more trees than it has removed during the years of public ownership. In the winter of 1953–4 a commemorative Coronation Avenue of oaks was planted between the Mansion House and the Park entrance opposite Sparrow Farm Road, contributions towards the cost being received from a number of local societies. On 10th January, 1959, the Management Committee invited the Freemen of the two Boroughs, and former members and officers of the Committee, to the ceremonial unveiling of a public clock erected on the Mansion House to commemorate the twenty-first anniversary of the opening of the Park to the public. The ceremony was performed by the Rt. Hon. J. Chuter Ede and Sir Sydney Marshall, Charter Mayors of Epsom and Ewell and Sutton and Cheam.

The present members of the Farmer family have retained their interest in Nonsuch and its locality. Generations of their ancestors lie in Cheam churchyard, where their graves are carefully tended; in the church is a tablet to the memory of two who lost their lives in the First World War, and in the churchyard the family memorial has recently been moved to a better position. The great grand-daughter of William Francis Gamul Farmer, Pamela Mary, now Mrs. Thompson, has in her possession the four Tudor portraits which the Queen of Spain admired, as well as a portrait of Samuel Farmer, and three of his embroidered waistcoats. In 1959 she presented to the Nonsuch Park Joint Management Committee a large portrait in oils of William Francis Gamul Farmer. In the same year, by arrangement with Captain Farmer's niece, Mrs. Olive Fenwick, his portrait was presented to the Committee by his nephew, the Rev. A. F. G. Farmer, sometime Vicar of Yattendon in Berkshire. The two portraits now hang in the Mansion House.

Whereabouts Unknown

Nᴏᴛ the least remarkable aspect of the history of Nonsuch was the speed and thoroughness with which it fell into oblivion. Now that the events of 1682 and 1683 are known, there is little doubt of the truth of the tradition that Berkeley rebuilt Durdans with materials from the Palace. Durdans has since been twice rebuilt, but during the winter of 1959 Martin Biddle and I saw, in the walls of the oldest part of the cellars, re-used stones, with carved mouldings, similar to those which were carted from Merton Priory for use at Nonsuch. The use of Nonsuch materials at Durdans is mentioned by John Aubrey. John Toland, writing in 1711 on the attractions of Epsom as a place for taking the waters, goes much further than Aubrey. "Even the houses of the very townsmen are every where mighty neat, built most of 'em after the newest manner, and extremely convenient, being purposely contrived for the entertainment of strangers, and therefore beautified by the owners to the utmost of their ability, to which the ruins of Nonsuch Palace have contributed not a little."

Earlier attempts to establish the date of demolition of the Palace have relied upon three main sources of information; but the first of these now appears to have given too early a date for the complete demolition which it seems to imply, and the other two appear to prolong the life of the Inner Court for at least two years after Berkeley is known to have bought the materials and carted many of them away. A new translation of Camden's *Britannia*, with additions, was published in 1695. The Surrey additions were contributed by John Evelyn. Of Nonsuch 'so much magnified by our author for its curious structure' he said 'now there's nothing of all this to be seen, scarce one stone being left upon another'. A number of later writers copied his phraseology, as well as the quite inexplicable mistake with which his note ended: although he had visited the Palace in 1666, he said in 1695 that the havoc there was due to the late Civil Wars. Rawlinson's paraphrase of Evelyn, printed in the second volume of Aubrey's *Surrey* and including the error, is corrected in the Appendix by a note supplied by the Rev. Robert Lumley Lloyd, lord of the manors of Cheam and Ewell with Cuddington. "Nonsuch," he says, "was all standing at the Death of King Charles II." A note written by Peter Le Neve, Norroy King-at-Arms, in a copy of Aubrey's *Surrey*, some time after 1704, read: "In the time of King Charles the 2d, given to Barbara dutchess of Cleveland, who sold it. Part of the house was standing in King James the 2d's time or there about, and seen by me P. le Neve, Norroy. It was done with plaister work made of rye dough, in imagry, very costly; had 2 courts, the innermost was the finest." The words "part of" before "the house" were inserted as an afterthought, and this, coupled with his mention of the Inner Court decoration, seems to indicate that demolition was not very far advanced when he saw the Palace, and that he must have been there in 1682 or early in 1683; unless, of course, he paid two visits, one before and one after demolition began.

A sketch in the Ashmolean Museum, initialled "I.T." and dated 23rd September, 1702, shows a panorama towards London from Epsom Downs. Worcester House is indicated, as well as the ruins of Nonsuch. The ruins are, however, appreciably more substantial than Evelyn would have us believe they had been seven years earlier. The sketch is very small, but at least one wing of the building, and a tower, are still standing. John Toland later looked across the intervening valley from the same vantage point, "the most eminent part of the Downs. Within a mile and a half is the place, and only the place, where that other splendid Palace of Nonsuch lately stood: a fit subject of reflection for those, who are inclined to moralise on the frailty, uncertainty, and vicissitude of all things". In a footnote he adds: "A great part of it stood in my own time, and I have spoken with those that saw it entire"; he was born in 1670. By 1736, according to Salmon's *Antiquities of Surrey*, the story of the demolition of the Palace had become decidedly garbled: "the Levellers of Fourty One laid the House even with the ground" but "The delightful scite of Codington invited new Possessors to build after the Restoration. Nonsuch was once more in splendor, and Worcester Park."

From all these accounts, inaccurate though some of them obviously are in points of detail, a reasonably clear picture of the progress of the demolition of the Palace emerges. Beginning in 1682 or 1683, the internal fittings, panelling, doors and other woodwork would be stripped out of the Inner Court. The twenty-year-old slates on the roof may have been worth selling, although a large dump of broken slates was found during the excavation; but the stripping of the roof would add to the valuable haul of lead from the battlements and the water-pipes, and to make this more convenient to carry away Berkeley had a special smelting furnace constructed in the kitchens. Evelyn, commenting on the Nonsuch stuccoes in 1697 in *An account of architects and architecture*, said he had heard that they had been "translated, and most ornamently plac'd by the late most Honourable Earl of Berkeley, at his delicious villa, Durdens". The excavation showed, however, that only some of the plaster panels could have been 'translated' to Durdans, for many of them were destroyed; and also that much of the carved slate was broken up. Statues, fountains and flagstones from the Inner courtyard and gardens would almost certainly have gone by August, 1684, when Berkeley's two-year demolition lease expired, as well as stone and sound timber from the walls. In the absence of evidence, we may assume that Berkeley washed his hands of Nonsuch after the disputes of 1687, and that the demolition of the Outward Court, on the authority and for the benefit of Barbara Villiers, began soon afterwards. But eventually the work of demolition slowed down, if the sketch of 1702 is to be relied upon, and it may be that once the more valuable parts of the building had been disposed of, and the demand for building stone in the neighbourhood had been met, Barbara Villiers was no longer interested in the trickle of income which would have come in during the later years. She may therefore have abandoned the remains, knowing that the local residents would help themselves to stone, bricks and hard-core once she removed her workmen. Apart from the ordinary evidence of destruction revealed during the excavation, reminders of the demolition workers were found in fragments of stoneware wine bottles, two of which had borne dates later than 1700. A small sketch of 1731, which has been thought to represent a corner of the Palace still standing and of considerable height, is discussed on p. 232.

The last person to describe the ruins of the Palace was Richard Pococke, who was successively Bishop of Meath and of Ossory. On the 28th November, 1754, he set out from Guildford and travelled to Nonsuch. He outlined its history in his travel diary, saying that it was much damaged during the Civil Wars, and that the Earl of Berkeley had built Durdans with the materials. There was at Nonsuch, he said, "only a farm house". In 1757 he came again, entering the Park by the Cheam gate. This time he noted the later history of the estate: the sale of the Little Park by the Duke of Grafton "near thirty years ago", and of Worcester Park "which Lord Leicester bought of the Duke of Grafton for Sir George Walton, who was steward to them both, and it has since been sold in several parcels". On this visit he examined the foundations of the Palace "which appear to have been built round a court. I saw signs of the foundations of towers to the north, which I suppose to be those represented in Speed's maps of Surrey; the grand front seems to have been to the south, as there represented, and there are ruins of offices for twenty acres to the south; they said also that there was an avenue to the east, and there are remains of a large canal. The way to go to it is to keep on in the road to Epsom till one comes within half a mile of Ewell and then one furlong further to the left out of the road there is a farm house built close to it."

Either Joseph Whateley or his gardening brother Thomas decided to remove this eyesore from sight, as a disfigurement of the landscape which they were tending and beautifying. In 1798, a year after Joseph's death, William Gilpin's *Observations on the Western parts of England relative chiefly to Picturesque Beauty* were published. Describing Nonsuch, he says that the "very vestiges" of the Palace and gardens "cannot be now traced; except here and there, in the form of a canal, or a terrace". He suggested that the demolition was due to the prudent foresight of the Duchess of Cleveland, who, "fearing a resumption" of the Palace by Charles II, pulled it to pieces and sold the materials. He felt that the actual siting of the Palace had little merit, and that it ought to have been built on the Banqueting House site. There it would have commanded a view over country which he condescendingly describes as "in some parts pleasing". Joseph Thompson's house, where the Mansion House now stands, was, at the time of Gilpin's visit, still occupied by Joseph Whateley. He said it was "a house, now modernised, which is said to have been formerly the habitation of Queen Elizabeth's Maids of Honour". In the garden was a large chalk-pit, which Thomas Whateley had planted and "formed into a pleasing little sequestered scene".

Gilpin was the last writer for a hundred years to give an accurate description of the position of the Palace. "The body of the edifice," he wrote, "formerly stood in a field, across the road, opposite to a little farm, now known by the name of the Cherry-garden." The Whateleys had levelled off such of the walls as still stood above ground level, the cellar and pits caused by the digging-up of foundations during demolition were filled in with rubble, and a thin covering of loam was spread over the site; and this must have been done after Richard Pococke's visit in 1757, and before 1797. Joseph Whateley, who died in that year, was alive when Gilpin came to Nonsuch; and by then the levelling-off had settled and the site had presumably been covered with turf, so that not a vestige of the foundations could be traced. The tree-lined roadway which was laid through the centre of the site by the Whateleys completed the erasure of Nonsuch from the map of Surrey.

The nineteenth-century visitor to the Park, whether he came out of casual interest or in search of material for a book, had only the most nebulous of recorded information against which to check the reports of local residents, handed down by word of mouth from forbears who had seen the Palace or the final stages of its demolition. The hints given by Pococke and Gilpin, placing the site opposite Cherry Orchard Farm, seem to have been passed over. The whole area, formerly occupied by the Palace, its garden walls, the Under-housekeeper's house, the stables and Cuddington, and the extensive sewage system of the Palace, produced during farming operations such a crop of brickwork and stone, and so many sudden descents of the plough into holes which all became Palace cellars, that local tradition eventually became completely unreliable as a means of fixing the site of the main building. The sewage vaults became secret passages (one of them from Hampton Court) and the Palace and Mansion House sites were linked, we were told in 1959, by an underground passage large enough to accommodate a carriage and pair. Other underground channels, unlined, whose purpose was probably to provide an escape for the 'earth-bourne' when it welled up every few years, became a part of the network of secret ways essential to an imaginary life of intrigues and clandestine meetings in Ewell and Cheam. Confused by what he heard from the local people, the Victorian visitor might still have read his Pococke and Gilpin without feeling any confidence, as he stood in the Park opposite Cherry Orchard Farm, that he was actually on the site of the Palace; for only half of the site would be visible, to the east of the roadway, and it would be discernible only as two shallow terraces in the gently rising field. Without any other evidence, these terraces, if they were noticed at all, might have been anything; in fact, by about 1900, when Captain

Farmer and his guests were discussing Nonsuch over the port, the terraces had become ramparts where, in the tall grass, Henry VIII's archers hid to repel attacks on his royal person by marauding parties of Frenchmen. Even if he had noticed the terraces, the visitor might still have been reluctant to accept them as marking the approximate levels of the two courtyards of the Palace; for as Gilpin suggested, the proximity of the steep bank to the south makes the position an unusual one for the siting of a pleasure palace.

Still very uncertain of the authenticity of what he had heard and seen, the visitor might have gone away to search among contemporary maps and plans for an accurate indication of the site of the Palace. After lengthy research he would have found only three maps which gave even an approximate position; and on two of these the scale was so small that their value was corroborative rather than intrinsic. John Ogilby, in his *Britannia*, published in 1675, marked Nonsuch on his route-map of the road from London to Arundel. It was shown in its correct position, at the end of the avenue leading from the London Road gate of the Park. Ogilby's work was revised by John Owen as *Britannia depicta, or, Ogilby Improv'd*, and, even as late as 1724, when the fourth edition was published, Nonsuch was still included. In 1731, when the survey map of Nonsuch Park was drawn for Joseph Thompson, no indication of any building was shown in 'Nonsuch Field', to the east of the avenue. The avenue itself lay well to the west of the present avenue, and in later years became an approach road to Cherry Orchard Farm. On the west of the avenue in the 1731 map, the field enclosing the present Cherry Orchard Farm buildings was lettered "The Vineyard", and here, near but well to the west of the Palace site, was a faint rectangular sketch; but the sketch probably represented the new farm building, and was not a drawing of the fairly considerable remains of one of the towers of the Palace, as has been suggested. The most useful map—still very inadequate, but helpful so far as it went—appeared in 1790. It was drawn by James Edwards for his *Companion from London to Brighthelmston*, and covered the country between Tooting and Ewell. Its value from the point of view of Nonsuch was threefold: it showed the modern avenue leading through the Park from the London Road gate to the Cheam Road gate, it marked the "Site of Nonsuch Pallace" near the point at which the avenue turned in the direction of Cheam, and it indicated the position of the Whateleys' house some distance away from the Palace site.

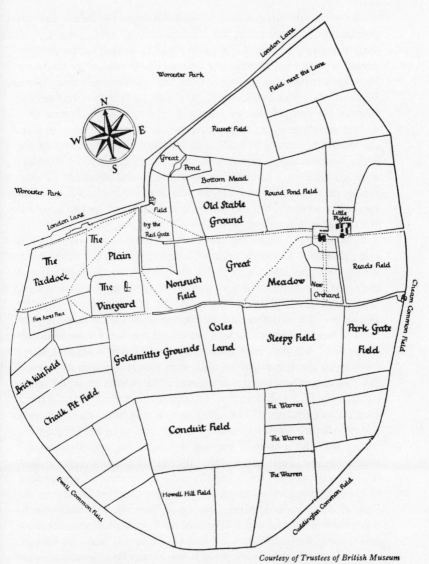

Worcester Park

London Lane

Field next the Lane

Russet Field

Great Pond

Bottom Mead

Round Pond Field

Worcester Park

London Lane

Field by the Red Gate

Old Stable Ground

Little Pightle

The Plain

The Paddock

The Vineyard

Nonsuch Field

Great Meadow

New Orchard

Reads Field

Cheam Common Field

Five Acres Piece

Coles Land

Sleepy Field

Park Gate Field

Brick kiln Field

Goldsmiths Grounds

Chalk Pit Field

Conduit Field

The Warren

The Warren

The Warren

Ewell Common Field

Howell Hill Field

Cuddington Common Field

SURVEY MAP OF THE LITTLE PARK, 1731
(Adapted from *A Survey of Nonsuch Park, the seat of Joseph Thompson*)

So slight was this evidence on the position of the Palace that it is perhaps not surprising that, for a century after Gilpin, writers, even local historians, avoided the issue. What is surprising is that the only person to write with confidence and accuracy on the matter was a romantic novelist, the daughter of the Rev. Sir George Lewen Glyn, Vicar and Rector of Ewell. Anna Lydia Glyn had shocked the family at Rectory House by daring to write a novel entitled *Fifty Pounds for a Wife*. Possibly as an act of penance, and certainly as a labour of love, she turned her attention to Nonsuch Palace, studying many of the printed sources and the actual landscape in the Park, in order to obtain a background for a romantic story of life in and around the Palace during the reign of Charles I. In the preface to her book, *A Pearl of the Realm*, she wrote: "I think I may venture to claim for my tale historical and topographical accuracy, having done my best to subordinate fiction to facts, so far as I have been able to ascertain the truth." Her fiction is now, after sixty-five years, as much a period-piece as the Palace itself; through her pages the people of Nonsuch, Ewell and the Manor House at Ewell Court lived and loved, parted and reunited, fought and died, through the troubled time of the Civil War. Her facts, however, as far as the building is concerned, are remarkably good. In places she allowed her imagination to lead her a little too far; for example, her frontispiece was an imaginative redrawing of the Hoefnagel scene, from inside the Privy Garden wall, with a large entrance archway in the central bay between the two towers. She was in no doubt about the true site of the Palace: "the terrace yet exists that raised the Inner Court above the outer". She added that, within living memory, there had been, in the Cherry Orchard, "an open cesspool and innumerable stones and tiles". Starting on this evidence, she used Manning and Bray's version of the 1650 Survey for her description of the Palace. The Survey was decidedly vague in its description of the relative positions of the various rooms in the Palace, but Miss Glyn sketched them all in with a bold hand, interrupting her narrative from time to time to quote from Leland, Evelyn and the Survey. Although her work was fiction, and although a number of her details were not correct, much of what she had to say about Nonsuch was far more reliable than the descriptions given by many later writers.

Anna Glyn's description of the site and orientation of Nonsuch seems to have had no effect in putting the Palace back on the map. Most writers continued to avoid mentioning the site. Clapham and

Godfrey suggested that the Palace had lain on the axis of the avenue leading to the London Road gate, and that the remains of a wall they had seen were "in all probability" remains of the Privy Garden wall; although they do not seem to have deduced anything from the contours of the ground, they did go so far as to say that the building "lay rather to the north" of the Privy Garden wall. One writer in the 'thirties placed the building across the avenue from Cheam, with the Hoefnagel frontage facing the Cheam gate of the Park; another was clearly of the opinion that the modern Mansion House occupied the site of the Palace. It was left to Cloudesley S. Willis, Ewell's local historian, to point the way which led ultimately to the very rapid rediscovery of the building in 1959.

Cloudesley Willis, concerned, during the decade after the First World War, with the threat of the spread of Greater London to the mediaeval and Georgian village of Ewell and its neighbourhood, decided to compile a local history before all the familiar landmarks disappeared. His book was published in 1931, and had a chapter devoted to Cuddington and Nonsuch. The importance of his work in paving the way for the excavation is strikingly illustrated by comparing the 1931 information on the siting of Nonsuch with the new details, the results of his personal observation, in the second edition of 1948. In 1931 the village of Cuddington was "somewhere hereabouts" (where the footpath from Ewell meets the angle of the avenue in the Park). The Outward Court "began about half way down the avenue" from the London Road gate; the Inner Court was "beyond it, so that there was only a short space of garden" between the Inner Court and the high footpath to Ewell. This description was based on the Fitz-william painting. Willis made no mention of the terracing visible in the field, or of the first rise in the road surface at the entrance to the Outer Gatehouse; but later, describing, with the help of the 1650 Survey, the layout of the Palace, he noted that "the rise in the ground can still be seen" where the eight steps led up to the Inner Gatehouse. He described the visible remains of the Privy Garden wall, extended the Kitchen Garden northwards as far as Diana's Dyke and put the Palace stables on the site of the Mansion House. For the Grove of Diana he favoured the site indicated in Chapter 6, basing his opinion on local tradition.

Before the second edition of his book was published, Willis had seen two deep trenches cut through the site of the Palace for sewers; had seen the north-east corner of the foundations, a great brick drain of the kitchen and what he took to be the east wall of the Inner Court, when anti-glider trenches were being dug during the early days of the war; and had noted various Tudor brickmaking sites and the constructional details of the brick sewer near the London Road gate of the Park. Unfortunately he did not, so far as is known, plot on a large-scale Ordnance map any of the things he saw; and his verbal descriptions, no doubt perfectly clear and lucid when he wrote them, were decidedly difficult to follow by anyone who had not seen, with him, the things he described. The result was that although information on the siting of parts of the Palace was available in print in 1948, it failed to 'register' except with the few people who had seen the same evidence, or who, with Willis's book in hand, had gone to the Park to sort out his information on the spot. This information, then, was not recorded on a large-scale map, although he showed the approximate position of the Palace, with Cuddington Church in the Inner Court, on a 4-in.-to-one-mile sketch map of Epsom, Ewell and Cuddington; the information was recorded in difficult phraseology; and it enabled only one axis to be fixed, and that for only part of its length, with any degree of accuracy.

It was, however, very largely on this information, supplemented by the courtyard dimensions from the 1650 Survey, that the pre-excavation reconstructed plan of the Palace was prepared in 1958. Some of the difficulties and uncertainties met with in interpreting Willis's information are indicated by italics in the following extracts from his book. Willis noted that the 1933 sewer trench "revealed the north-west front of the Palace which lay right and left across the avenue. Two feet south of the fence of Cherry Orchard Farm, that turns to meet the avenue, was a mass of chalk masonry 14ft. long (*presumably along the trench?*) and 8 ft. deep with brick on top; 14 ft. to the south was a similar block 12 ft. long and 10 ft. deep with some Reigate stone. These were the foundations of the Outward Gatehouse (*through the front and rear faces, or through the corner turrets?*). At a distance of 115 ft. south, the depth of the Outward Court (*this dimension was in fact 135 ft.*), were two chalk piers 14 ft. apart and about 8 ft. deep, the foundations of the Gatehouse of the Inner Court. (*How thick were these piers?*) At Cherry Orchard Farm Gate, just beyond the Outward Court, the sewer trench cut through a flint and rubble wall (*how thick?*) and 30 ft. south of this another. At this point (*but the landmark, the Farm gate, is some distance from the sewer-trench, and is approached by a diagonal path*) there were human remains with sometimes a rough Reigate stone slab laid on them. It seems clear that here were the north and south walls of Cuddington Church. And the Inner Court of the Palace lay over the burials. The trench revealed nothing of the south-east front of the Palace.

"In December, 1945, a deep sewer trench was dug in the road from the avenue to Cherry Orchard Farm. Near the avenue (*how near?*) more of the flint foundations of the church and human burials were disclosed. Further west (*how far?*) were two masses of deep chalk masonry laid in hard white lime mortar. Beyond were a deep block of brickwork and a brick culvert of about 18 in. internal diameter. The foundations ran out at the farmhouse."

The description of the anti-glider trenches gave no measurements; they were simply "in the angle of the avenue," and they showed "the extent of the buildings on that side". They led Willis to conclude that "the Inner Court stood so near the wall of the Privy Garden that there was only a depth of about fifty yards between the wall and the south-east front of the Palace". The actual distance revealed by the excavation was 201 ft.

A note by Miss M. Maitland Howard on pottery and other material found in a layer of kitchen refuse cut through by the anti-glider trenches appeared in 1946, in Volume 49 of the *Surrey Archaeological Collections*. This gave references on the 6 in. Ordnance map to an area of about 100 sq. ft. in which the refuse was found.

Although the difficulties to be overcome in transferring to the drawing-board Willis's verbal account of his observations have been pointed out, the importance of his record cannot be over-stressed. It left sufficient to be deduced or conjectured to make the filling-in of the gaps an interesting exercise, although it was not realized early in 1958 that the deduction and conjecture would so soon be put to the test. The major uncertainty was concerned with the east-west axis of the building. Willis did not record the distance between the roadway of the avenue and the north-east corner of the building which he said he had seen out in the field in the anti-glider trench. He could not know, nor, in the absence of that measurement, was it possible to deduce, whether the roadway ran centrally through the site. On the north-south axis the lack of some of the detailed measurements made it difficult to arrive at a reasonable conjectural position for the south frontage of the Inner Court. However, the work of preparing both a site plan, in relation to the modern roadway, and a building plan was pressed forward, and when we had our bluff called by the excavations in 1959 we were found to have cut the 370 ft. north-south dimension of the Palace by about 30 ft. and to have misjudged the size and position of the Kitchen Court. The site plan had shown the modern roadway running straight through the central axis of the Palace instead of placing it about 7 ft. to the west of centre and at a slight incline, and had also placed Cuddington Church a few feet to the north of its actual position.

One final piece of pre-excavation evidence must be mentioned. Too late for his information to affect any of the research which preceded the excavation, and when the reconstructed plan had already been sent to the printer, I received a visit from Mr. W. J. Pickering, of Epsom, a retired County Divisional Planning Officer. In the course of his duties he had, in 1933, inspected the sewer trench which ran through the Palace site. This led him to spend a week-end in the trench, in company with Mr. F. H. Wiltshire, a former Clerk to the Banstead Urban District Council. They investigated and noted all they could see, and supervised the preparation of a specially marked copy of the contract drawing and of a sectional drawing of the trench. Mr. Pickering described the blocks of masonry they had seen, the pottery fragments, gravestones and skeletons; at the northern end the trench had cut into the very corners of what they assumed to be two cellars, some distance apart, and lying at an angle to the avenue. With so little time and no shoring-up equipment they had not been able to investigate these cellars at all fully; but they had led them to conclude that the Palace building had lain at a considerable angle to the avenue. It was apparent from this description that they had in fact seen, not the corners of cellars but the angles of the two octagonal turrets on the western side of the Outer Gatehouse, and this was confirmed during the excavation. But the most significant fact which emerged was that an accurate and detailed drawing had been prepared and that steps had been taken to ensure its preservation following the abolition of the Epsom Rural District Council. On 11th May, 1959, it was located. It provided the perfect counterpart to Willis's verbal description, recording, to the inch, the position of everything he described and more; and it gave a more definite starting point from which to take measurements: not 'the fence of Cherry Orchard Farm', but the dead-centre of a manhole cover. Seven weeks later these measurements were put to good use in marking out the first trenches in the open field on the eastern side of the avenue.

13

The Excavation

"THE archaeologist is apt to think that monastic houses and feudal castles are alone worthy of his attention; but the recovery of the ground plan of Nonsuch would be an achievement of even greater architectural value, while its wealth of historic associations places it far above them all in sentimental interest." When Sir Alfred Clapham wrote these words, it is very doubtful whether he, an architect, had any real hope that archaeologists would feel much enthusiasm for the task he suggested. The recovery of the ground plan of Nonsuch would be a tremendous undertaking in terms of sheer physical labour. It would absorb funds which many archaeologists might think could be put to better use and, as he himself admitted, the Palace had not been built sufficiently long ago to give it a respectable antiquity bringing it within the usual sphere of archaeological, as distinct from antiquarian, investigation. Even when, over forty years later, the excavation of Nonsuch began to be seriously considered, it was realized that the project could only be carried out if there could be a fusing together of the interests and the enthusiasm of architectural historians and archaeologists, and if sufficient general interest could be aroused to enlist the support of people who, whilst perhaps not fully appreciating the more technical aspects of the work, would be attracted to it as an adventure in re-creating the past. For though the excavation would be a skilled operation, requiring expert supervision at every point, a large volunteer labour-force, skilled and unskilled, would be required. In addition, the general public, whilst not able to take an active part in the work, might, if their interest were stimulated, contribute towards the heavy cost. Moreover, the educational opportunities of the project, both for volunteer excavators and for visitors, would, if properly used, attract further support.

The first welding together of the skills of architect and archaeologist for the purpose of rediscovering Nonsuch took place in 1930. Captain A. W. G. Lowther, a well-known member of the Surrey Archaeological Society and for many years its Secretary, trenched the centre of the Banqueting House site in that year. He cut his main trench across the middle of the cellar, and branched out from this trench into the area of the shallow cellar. He drew a plan recording his findings, and after the excavation had been filled in, a concrete surround was laid down to indicate the position of the cellars. This was done partly in the interests of future visitors and partly in the hope of preventing the planting of trees within the area, for the roots of existing trees were causing damage to the foundations. This excavation, limited to the Banqueting House and limited in scope, was obviously exploratory rather than exhaustive. It gave an indication of what lay beneath the soil, without in any way claiming to have cleared up all the problems of the architecture and life of the Banqueting House. No report was published, and even Cloudesley Willis, assiduous as he was in collecting and recording information, noticed it only by saying that the three cellars "were unearthed last year".

A further twenty-eight years were to elapse before the various interests came together again, and in sufficient strength to bring the full-scale excavation of both Palace and Banqueting House within the realms of possibility. Martin Biddle, then an archaeological consultant to the Ministry of Works, with considerable experience on several excavation sites in this country and in the Middle East, had some years previously directed the excavation of the Manor of The More, near Rickmansworth. The More, one of Henry VIII's progress houses, had a history going back to the thirteenth century. A long series of superimposed houses presented a difficult problem of archaeological interpretation, but it was the Tudor house which led his thoughts on to the study of Tudor palaces in general and, in particular, to the enigma of Nonsuch. In 1955 he decided that Nonsuch must be excavated when the opportunity could be found. He gave a lecture on The More to the Royal Archaeological Institute in January, 1957, and during the discussion which followed Sir John Summerson mentioned the importance of Nonsuch, and expressed his hope that Martin Biddle would one day undertake its excavation. These two, the architectural historian and the archaeologist, formed the nucleus of the team for which Nonsuch had been waiting. By many discussions and voluminous correspondence

(a) Painted glass, showing part of the
motto DIEU ET MON DROIT. Height of
letters 1¾ in.

(b) A goblet. Height 6½ in.

17. GLASS FROM NONSUCH

Courtesy of Nonsuch Palace Excavation Committee

(c) Fragments, mainly handles, little more than an inch long, in
plain, coloured and white glass

(a) Tin-glazed delft jug. Height 4¾ in.

(b) Bellarmine jug. Height 5½ in.

18. POTTERY
FROM NONSUCH

*Courtesy of Nonsuch Palace
Excavation Committee*

(c) Delft bowl. Height 3½ in.

(d) Delft platter. Diameter 13 in.

19. COARSE POTTERY

Courtesy of P. H. Witkowska

Selected from the many similar articles, complete, damaged or
fragmentary, found during the excavation

(a) The North Front

20. NONSUCH MANSION HOUSE, *c.* 1845
Engraved for Brayley's *History of Surrey*

(b) London Road gate on Derby Day

21. AERIAL VIEW OF THE EXCAVATIONS

View from the east, mid-September, 1959. Cherry Orchard Farm beyond the trees. Compare with the map showing the Environs of Nonsuch, and with the Plan of the Excavations

(a) Director's office

22. EXCAVATION BACKROOMS

Courtesy of D. C. Haiselden

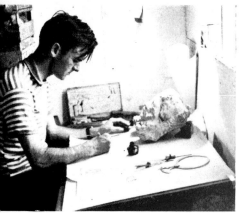

(b) Drawing office

(c) Indexing stone

23. VISITORS

Courtesy of D. C. Haiselden

(a) End of conducted tour

(b) Some of the 26,000 visitors to the 'museum'

(c) Last-day crowds

(a) Towards the end of the first week of the excavation. Outward Court Gatehouse. Cellar trench in middle distance

Courtesy of D. C. Haiselden

24. FROM BEGINNING TO END

(b) One of the rubble heaps in September, 1959

Courtesy of D. C. Haiselden

(c) Filling-in. Mid-October, 1959

Courtesy of Southern News Pictures

the way was gradually prepared by Martin Biddle for what was to be the largest operation of its kind ever undertaken in a single year in this country.

His first approach to the Ministry of Works for provisional approval and support for an excavation, as a contribution to the *History of the King's Works*, met with sufficient encouragement for the project to be further discussed, still in a purely tentative way. Contact was next established with people in the neighbourhood likely to be interested, including Captain Lowther and Mr. Philip Shearman, of Ewell, Honorary Secretary of the Nonsuch Society and Honorary Local Secretary of the Surrey Archaeological Society. The Nonsuch Society, in 1954, had sought and obtained permission to carry out an excavation on the Palace site, but had taken no further action.

By January, 1959, official support had been received from the Ministry of Works, with the promise of financial backing up to a definite limit; and a committee was being formed to deal with the organization of the excavation and the raising of supplementary funds from voluntary sources. The request by the Ministry to the local authorities for permission to carry out the excavation was made on 28th January. The starting date proposed was 6th July, and it was anticipated that the work would take about twelve weeks. Approval was given by the Nonsuch Park Joint Management Committee, and the way was clear for translating tentative proposals into positive action.

The Nonsuch Palace Excavation Committee met for the first time on 19th March, 1959, at Lambeth Bridge House. Sir John Summerson agreed to serve as Chairman, and Martin Biddle, who was to be the Director of the excavation, was elected Secretary. The Ministry of Works was represented by Mr. A. J. Taylor and Mr. J. G. Hurst, of the Ancient Monuments Inspectorate. The other members were Mr. Howard Colvin, editor of the *History of the King's Works*, Mr. C. G. Cobbett, Borough Engineer of Epsom and Ewell and Surveyor to the Nonsuch Park Joint Management Committee, Mr. R. P. Brownjohn, Mr. Philip Shearman and myself. Without noticeable competition I was elected to the office of Honorary Treasurer. Many matters of policy and practice were discussed, and after the meeting the arrangements for 6th July went rapidly forward, details being left in the hands of the Chairman, the Secretary and Director of the excavation and the Treasurer.

The enrolment of an adequate labour-force was one of the most urgent matters to be dealt with. Of prime importance was the appointment of an Assistant Director of the excavation, to help with general administration, to take charge of work on the finds and to be responsible for taking over full control in the absence of the Director. Responsible to the Director himself would be the Site Supervisors, skilled and experienced, working under his direct control yet capable of developing particular parts of the site allocated to them along lines laid down by him. These had to be people known to possess that extra sense of responsibility which would ensure that the Director was called upon for advice and instructions when, and not after, they were needed. The remainder of the work would be carried out partly by paid labour and partly by volunteers, but experienced volunteers would be especially valuable. The size of the overall labour-force would be governed by the number of Site Supervisors available. Realizing that summer-holiday arrangements are usually made many months ahead, the Director had prudently obtained a number of offers of help before the Committee meeting. During the next few weeks he sent a duplicated leaflet and enrolment form to all colleges, schools and technical institutes round London, and to each of the hundred branches of the W.E.A. in the London area. News of the forthcoming excavation and of the need for volunteers was released to the local and national Press on 23rd April. Recruitment exceeded expectations, and, because so many of the offers of help came from people living within reasonable daily travelling distance, it was possible to enrol considerably more than had originally been planned.

For those who came from farther afield, and were prepared to stay for at least two weeks, the Committee approved the offer of a small daily subsistence allowance and assistance towards the cost of fares. Living accommodation had to be found, and eventually, through the good offices of the Town Clerk of Epsom and Ewell, the Civil Defence Club at Bluegates, a few hundred yards from the site, offered a part of its premises for use as dormitories and kitchen for the duration of the excavation. The Town Hall made useful preliminary contacts for us in our search for beds and mattresses, which eventually came from Surrey County Council stores at Esher and Guildford, and for a caterer. Insulated food containers were borrowed from the County's School Meals Service, and tea-urns from the Epsom Municipal Baths. At the last minute pillows were borrowed from a number of private residents in Ewell, and pillows and more beds from the County Council's Educational Research Centre at Glyn House, Ewell. The rooms at Bluegates were arranged, swept and garnished by local voluntary labour on 4th and 5th July; a stock of kitchen equipment and breakfast food was bought; and arrangements were made for the caterer to deliver each day sandwich lunches on the site and a hot evening meal at Bluegates.

Preparations for the more technical aspects of the operation were going forward at the same time. Much of the financial support provided by the Ministry was given "in kind", a substantial item being the services of six paid labourers for the whole twelve weeks. In addition, they sent huts, wheelbarrows and heavy tools, great quantities of storage boxes and bags for finds, and part of the stationery used on the site. The services of the Ministry of Works did not, of course, stop there. The whole project was an official excavation under the auspices of the Ancient Monuments Inspectorate of the Ministry and the Excavation Committee, and the whole range of Ministry experts, such as laboratory specialists, was therefore available if required. Moreover, the ability of the Ministry to get things done, adequately and at high speed, was of the utmost assistance to the day-to-day work on the site. Supplies were rushed down at short notice, and the department maintained the fullest possible liaison, by telephone and by frequent personal visits. Often in their spare time, and often in anticipation of an emergency call, officers of the department would appear on the site with a fresh stock of some article or other likely to be needed. And although, at the end of the excavation, the filling-in of the site was arranged locally, the heavy expenditure was met by the Ministry.

All the arrangements with the Ministry were made by the Director himself. Locally, Epsom's Borough Engineer agreed to provide fencing for the site and to have it erected by Corporation labour. His sign-writer also prepared the various painted notice-boards which were needed. The Borough Treasurer made all the necessary arrangements for the Excavation Committee to take out third-party insurance with the Corporation's insurers, and his Deputy agreed to act as auditor of the Committee's accounts. As the weeks went by, both before and during the excavation, we appreciated more and more the tremendous value of the ready and enthusiastic help which we received from both the members and the officers of the two Borough Councils of Epsom and Sutton, and of the Park Management Committee and

Park Superintendent. Because of their interest, a great deal of equipment was obtained on loan, and many problems which might have
involved months of discussion were settled more or less on the
spot.

Throughout the weeks of preparation we had been spending money
on behalf of the Excavation Committee, money not reimbursable by
the Ministry. On my election as Honorary Treasurer at the March
committee meeting, I learned that a donation of £200 had been
promised by the Marc Fitch fund subject to the submission of a statement of accounts, and that it was hoped that the British Academy
might be willing to make a contribution. It was agreed that an appeal
for donations should be incorporated in the news release to be given to
the Press. This produced a fairly encouraging response, but it was soon
apparent that something more would have to be done if we were to
reach our rock-bottom minimum estimated requirement of £400. By
this time I had prepared a 'pictorial guide' to the excavations and sent
it to the printer, but I was so uncertain what the public response might
be that I decided to finance it myself, prepared to face a possible loss, or,
if it succeeded, to hand over the profits to the Committee as a donation.
The 1,000 copies I planned to have printed seemed, as I travelled about
canvassing advertisements, getting my drafts approved by the ad-
vertisers and visiting the printer in the cold, wet days of late April,
hopelessly over-optimistic. At this stage, then, and for many weeks
afterwards, I discounted the Guide as a possible source of income.

An appeal addressed to each of the Residents' Associations in the
northern part of Epsom and Ewell brought very useful contributions
from most of them, and gifts, some of them quite substantial, continued
to trickle in from private individuals. At the end of June, however, our
credit balance stood at only £230, and our only certain sources of
future income were the British Academy and a collecting-box which
was to be put on the site. First sales of the Guide, which had arrived
from the printer on 10th June, had varied considerably among the
twenty-five or so local shops which had agreed to take a supply on sale
or return. However, the overall picture was sufficiently encouraging
to tempt me into sinking the whole of the profit I hoped to reap on the
first (and most costly) thousand on a reprint of the same size. If the
gamble came off the basic financial requirements of the excavation
would be met.

In late June and early July the quickening of interest in the neighbourhood could almost be felt. I conducted various organized groups round the site, but it was the arrival of the advance party which gave us our first real glimpse of the reaction of the general public to the excavation. On Friday, 3rd July, a survey party consisting of the Director and Colonel and Mrs. Haslam drove into the Park in a Land Rover bristling with equipment, and from the moment when they began work until the filling-in was completed at the end of October, visitors flocked to the site from far and near. The rural charm of the setting, the long spells of fine weather and the accessibility of the site all combined to bring over 60,000 visitors during the twelve weeks from 6th July to 28th September. To their interest and their generosity much of the success of the excavation was due; for they placed funds at the disposal of the Committee far in excess of anything we had envisaged, enabling a great deal more work to be carried out than had originally been planned, and leaving a balance of funds for the subsequent work on the finds and the recording of results.

This happy state of affairs could not be foreseen early in July, however, and the early stages of the work on the site went forward as planned. During the first week-end the whole area was marked out as a grid by driving in pegs at intervals of 25 ft. each way, two huts were erected and the fencing of the site began. On the Sunday a survey was carried out by proton-magnetometer, but the existence of electric railways half a mile away on either side of the site invalidated the results. The first trenches opened on the following morning were in the open field of the Park, in a line parallel with the avenue; they were placed opposite the positions at which the 1933 sewer trench had revealed foundation walls on the other side of the avenue. Volunteers and Ministry workmen set to with a will, and by mid-morning they had exposed the top of the foundations of the outer and inner walls of the north front of the Outward Court, immediately to the east of the gatehouse. By the evening the cellar wall by the Inner Court was visible, near the Inner Gatehouse. Throughout the day representatives of the Press and radio came and went, and thereafter the excavation featured in newspapers and magazines at home and abroad, and in sound and television broadcasts.

By the end of the second day the east wall of the Outer Gatehouse and the cobbles of the courtyard had been uncovered. Loose rubble had been removed from the narrow trench over what proved to be the cellar, and a wall in the south front (for which no pre-excavation

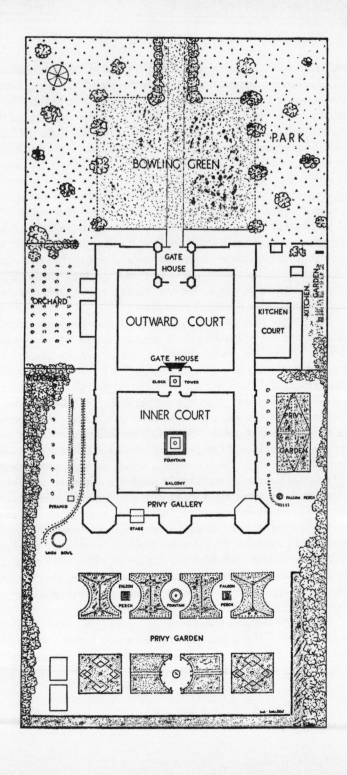

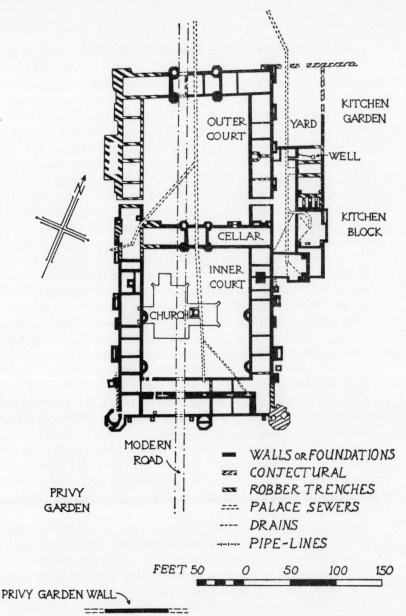

KITCHEN
GARDEN

OUTER
COURT

YARD

WELL

KITCHEN
BLOCK

CELLAR

INNER
COURT

CHURCH

N

MODERN
ROAD

PRIVY
GARDEN

WALLS or FOUNDATIONS
CONJECTURAL
ROBBER TRENCHES
PALACE SEWERS
DRAINS
PIPE-LINES

FEET 50   0   50   100   150

PRIVY GARDEN WALL

R.B., M.F., M.B.
Courtesy of Nonsuch Palace Excavation Committee

EXCAVATION PLAN OF NONSUCH, 1959
(Opposite: Reconstructed plan, drawn in 1958
by J. M. I. Griffiths, on similar scale)

measurement existed) had been exposed. This was at first thought to be the main south-front wall seen in the Hoefnagel and Speed views, and it was not until 17th July that the true front wall was discovered farther to the south. With the work thus well begun, volunteers and visitors came in increasing numbers. The visitors at first caused some embarrassment, for the fencing was still incomplete and they were able to wander where they wished. It was planned to admit visitors only in conducted parties at intervals during the day, and they were to be shown round by students working on the excavation. During this first week, however, there were no means of marshalling visitors for this purpose. The majority, who came because they were interested in seeing what was afoot and in finding out what it was all about, were welcome, even though they caused many interruptions of the work; but there was a small minority of the younger element who came only to make trouble. Visitors, welcome and unwelcome, were particularly numerous in the evening, and it was apparent by the end of the third day that the single volunteer guard we had on duty in the evening was being overwhelmed in his triple capacity as policeman, Guide salesman and public-relations officer. From then onwards, evening 'staffing' was increased; from a small beginning, with another volunteer and myself, the practice of explaining the excavation to parties of evening visitors grew until, with the fencing completed, the trenches roped off, and the increasing crowds needing to be conducted round, we were able to establish a considerable panel of guide-lecturers. In addition to serving in the evenings, these guides were able to relieve the excavators of any need to break off their work and attend to visitors at week-ends, and for much of the time on weekdays. At times the number of visitors reached 3,000 a day; as many as eight conducted parties would be on the site at the same time, with a long queue awaiting admission.

The security problem took longer to solve. The presence of the guides took care of the site until dusk, but after they had left there were a few incidents such as stone-throwing and trampling in the trenches by groups of youths. For some weeks members of the Bluegates team slept on the site as a security guard, until the Nonsuch Park Joint Management Committee generously provided a nightwatchman. The first occupant of the post arrived, and left, on 25th July. He was replaced on the 31st, and the new watchman remained until after the official closing date. In addition, the police, once they had been in-

formed that an unnecessary strain was being put on the organization
by these unwelcome visitors, could not have been more helpful and
co-operative. Patrols by car or motor-cycle would look in from time
to time, and the appearance of a police-dog at irregular intervals had a
remarkably sobering effect.

With arrangements for receiving visitors more adequately organized, it was apparent even by the second week that the guide-lecturers
would have little time to do more than explain the nature of the building of which the foundations were gradually emerging, and that any
attempt to fill in historical details would make the tour too long. There
seemed to be quite an interest in the historical background, however,
and to cater for this without affecting the conducted tours I suggested
that the Epsom and Ewell Library's collection of Nonsuch material
should be exhibited. The Town Clerk and Mr. Brownjohn arranged
for the loan of a sectional aluminium hut normally used by the
Corporation as a transportable polling station, and the "museum"
opened its doors on Saturday, 18th July. Its inception was due more
to a desire to make interesting material available to the public than in
the expectation of raising any considerable amount of money; an
admission charge of 6d. was made, partly in the hope that we should
more than cover the inevitable expenses on insurance and labour
for erecting and dismantling the hut and partly to keep out undesirable
visitors. In the event, the display, augmented from time to time by a
selection of recent finds, was seen by more than 26,000 people, and,
after expenses had been met, added over £600 to the excavation
funds.

The second thousand copies of the Guide, except for the supplies
in the hands of shopkeepers, sold out on 15th July, nine days after the
start of the excavation. The printer had been paid, and, with August
Bank Holiday ahead, I decided to plough the profit back by ordering a
reprint of 3,000. This order had been given twice more when, the day
before the end of the excavation, the last of 11,300 copies was sold. In
addition, to bridge the occasional gaps whilst new deliveries were
awaited, off-prints of the reconstructed plan were made, and some 2,000
copies were sold. However, through meeting the printer's bills out of
the proceeds, it was not until more than half-way through the excavation that I was able to make any substantial contribution to the funds
from this source; but since then the Guide income of £840 has been the
principal factor in financing the greatly expanded work of the final

weeks of the excavation and the subsequent work, still continuing, on the thousands of finds.

To many archaeologists used to seeing excavation projects hampered, dragged out over a period of years and curtailed in scope, through financial stringency, this amazing generosity of the Nonsuch visitors may seem to have removed all financial hazards from the path of those responsible for the excavation. This view would not have been shared by those who had the day-to-day task of balancing commitments against income. When it became apparent that the original target would be substantially exceeded, discussions began on the most beneficial way in which the additional income could be used. No hasty decision could be reached, for at any time the golden summer weather might change, and a few sharp showers had shown all too clearly that a spell of bad weather, by keeping visitors away, would cut off our income without reducing our expenditure. However, the Director was determined to make the fullest possible use of the unique opportunity presented to him, unique in the sense that such a set of circumstances could never again be expected to arise: an adequate organization on the site, and a reasonable assurance of adequate funds, to permit a full excavation of the whole site of the Palace instead of limiting the operation to the more accessible eastern half and a few trenches under the trees on the west. To achieve this, on land covered with trees and undergrowth, and with time running out, additional paid labour would be needed. The volunteers, of whom no fewer than 500 must have worked on the site for varying periods, with daily attendances averaging eighty, included many who could handle pick and shovel or wheelbarrow with good effect. But for this new all-out drive a guaranteed daily supply of 'navvy' labour would be needed, to clear the way for the lighter and more delicate work of the experts and their teams of volunteers.

The week beginning 10th August marked the turning point in the excavation. At that date the credit balance stood at £315. By the end of the week it had been decided not only to engage our own paid labourers but to pay an outside firm to clear away the undergrowth from the plantation and to scrape off by machine the top few inches of matted roots which would have considerably delayed the work of trenching. The Committee thus became an official employer of labour, and I had perforce to learn the intricacies of P.A.Y.E. and National Insurance; the weekly 'pay parade', when I disbursed the modest

subsistence allowances to the volunteers living at Bluegates, was
suddenly transformed into a complicated exercise involving as much
as £170 a week.

Even with this expansion of the paid labour-force decided upon and
implemented, a constant watch had to be kept on expenditure and
income, both actual and prospective. Each week fresh estimates were
drawn up for the remaining weeks, and we were prepared to retract at
short notice if the weather turned against us. On the other hand,
excessive caution would have meant a lower output of work, and it
would have been too late, on 29th September, to regret that we had not
made the fullest possible use of the funds available. We aimed, therefore, to keep expenditure about a week behind actual or prospective
income: by 21st August the balance was down to £8, to be restored the
following day by the first £200 of *Guide* money. The lowest ebb, to
£5, was reached on 11th September, but work ended with a balance of
£225, although there were many bills to come in.

In the earlier weeks the volunteers and Ministry workmen had
located and cleared at least the upper parts of the foundations of most
of the eastern part of the Palace, and had in places excavated in considerable depth. The south-east tower, an important target in the early
stages as a guide to the extent of the building, had proved elusive, and
was not in fact found until the eleventh day, farther to the south than
had been anticipated. The first of the thousands of fragments of plaster
stucco were discovered in a soakaway outside the south frontage on
18th July; and the two finest pieces of Merton stone, the carved and
gilded boss and the gargoyle, were found on 31st July.

The position of the north and south walls of Cuddington Church
was known, on the other side of the avenue, from the 1933 trench
drawing. Corresponding positions were marked out in the open field.
Trenches dug here, although they revealed burials, showed no signs
of the church itself, and it was realized that the trenches were too far
to the east. Extending the trenches back towards the avenue produced
results on 25th July, when a part of the east end of the building came to
light. It was eventually found that the whole of the chancel lay in the
field, the nave being under the roadway and beyond it to the west.

At an early date it was realized that a full examination of the
foundations of the two gatehouses would be impossible unless the
ancient elms which stood over each of them could be removed. Permission to do so could not be lightly given, and many discussions took

place between 20th July, when the question was first mooted, and 4th August, when the Director was authorized to make his own arrangements for them to be felled. They were taken down by a firm of 'tree specialists' on 11th August, and, to the relief of all who had been concerned in the discussion on their fate, were found to be rotten inside. When the trunks had been carted away, and the remainder burnt, the same firm stayed on to prepare the western half of the site. After the undergrowth and dead trees had been cleared, a bulldozer started work, on 14th August, on scraping off the top two or three inches of roots, ivy, brambles and leaf mould. The work was carried out with such skill and precision that not the slightest damage was done to the foundations, which were in some parts only a few inches below the surface. Some marking pegs had been put in position on 13th August, and this work was continued as each part was cleared by the bulldozer. Digging began in earnest on 17th August, with only six weeks to go before the closing date.

With all obstructions cleared, and the new 'navvies' (mainly muscular students) on duty, work now went forward at a tremendous rate, and not only in the newly opened area on the west. It had been decided to clear the great wine-cellar of its hundreds of tons of rubble, and, under the burning sun and usually stripped to the waist, the labourers filled barrow after barrow and trundled them up steep ramps, out of the cellar and away to the growing mountains at the side of the site. They worked from 8 a.m. to 6.30 p.m., and one pair achieved distinction by filling and emptying 125 barrow-loads in a day. They also prepared the way for the volunteers by removing tree-roots and rubble from the gatehouses, and by opening up further squares in the kitchen area. Some of the volunteers still worked alongside the paid labourers, apparently preferring the heavy work; but the greater part of the voluntary labour was now expended on work with brush and trowel.

From the outset, the Director had based all his detailed planning of the day-to-day work on two fundamental principles. On the assumption that all excavation involves destruction, since the process of obtaining archaeological evidence often involves the destruction of that evidence itself, he had insisted upon the perfect recording of every stage of every part of the excavation. The primary records were the many site notebooks compiled by the Site Supervisors. Surveying went on continuously, much of it being carried out by Mr. Brownjohn in his spare time, and many detailed plans of individual features being made by Colonel Haslam. In addition, the camera had an important part to play. From the bottom of trenches to the top of a high, wheeled ladder, the excavation was photographed over 400 times for the official record. The second principle was that, if the vast undertaking was to be completed in time to permit the site to be fully recorded, it could only be done by means of a perfect organization and strict discipline during working hours for both paid labourers and volunteers.

On the western side, a flint wall of a Cuddington building was found in the central area on 18th August. The walls of the nave of the church were exposed on the 25th, and this part of the site, clearly visible from the roadway, became a centre of interest as it was developed over the ensuing weeks. Part of the perimeter of the octagonal base of the south-west tower was recognizable by 28th August. From these beginnings, the progress during the final four weeks was remarkable. On Sunday, 30th August, I recorded the current state of the excavation on a copy of the reconstructed plan. By that date, on the west, the walls of the nave of the church had been extended back from the roadway, but had not yet reached the west wall. Very short lengths of the outside and inside walls of the west wing, both of the Inner and of the Outward Court, had been located, the latter as "robber trenches". The inside south-west corner of the Inner Court was visible, as well as a small part of the foundation of the adjacent tower. In the cellar area short lengths of the two walls could be seen and, at the west end, brick drains had been found. A glance at the completed excavation plans, both of the Palace and of Cuddington Church, will indicate the achievements of the next four weeks.

The eastern part of the site continued to develop. The well in the kitchens was discovered on 30th August, and its excavation aroused so much interest that visitors were kept on the move only with great difficulty. The emptying of the wine-cellar was completed on 2nd September and it was then subjected to patient cleaning with brush and trowel ready for photography. During the process the drainage gulleys and soakaway were exposed. In the centre of the site the edge of the metalled roadway of the avenue covered the two western turrets of the Inner Gatehouse. To enable the plan to be completed, and the garde-robe in the north-western turret to be emptied, permission was obtained to close the avenue to vehicular traffic for a few days from 15th September. The chief remaining feature of interest which had so far not been discovered was the Inner Court fountain. The brick base for the cistern below the fountain was found on 17th September, in the chancel of the church, three-quarters hidden by the roots of a sycamore tree.

The question of the future of the site had, from the outset, been very much in the minds of all those who were concerned with the excavation, and it was a question asked by many of the visitors. The decision as to whether the foundations, or any parts of them, were to be left exposed rested with the Nonsuch Park Joint Management Committee. Before their special meeting on 23rd September the matter had been very thoroughly discussed both locally and with representatives of the Ministry, and the Director and Mr. Taylor were invited to attend the meeting of the Committee. However disappointing, both to the general public and to many of those who had put in so much work on the excavation, the decision to fill in the whole site may have been, there can be no doubt that the decision was the right one. The foundations were composed largely of chalk, which is a perfectly sound material so long as it is kept dry and protected from frost; exposed to the rigours of winter, only very costly treatment, renewable every few years, would have preserved it. Although the mortar in the foundations was in places rock-hard, in others it was crumbling, so that large areas of the footings would literally have had to be taken to pieces and rebuilt. Even the bricks, so fresh and colourful after a shower, were soft and would have shared the fate of the chalk under sudden frost.

Once this decision had been reached, the end came all too quickly. The final Saturday and Sunday brought record crowds of visitors. The car park and the adjacent meadow were filled with cars, and, with large conducted parties literally on each other's heels all round the site, a three-deep queue stretched at times 100 yds. outside the entrance gate. Many of the visitors, after having had to wait for admission, decided at the end of their tour not to join the queue outside the exhibition hut; but even then over 1,000 people saw the exhibition on the Sunday. For the excavators, many last-minute details had to be attended to. Amongst these was the implementation of a decision of the Excavation Committee, which had met at Glyn House on 10th September. The Committee had agreed that if the Park Management Committee should decide that the site was to be filled in, it would be permissible and prudent, before the bulldozers arrived, to remove any interesting and accessible pieces of Merton Priory stone and treat them as finds. This was carried out during the final week-end, and in the process, on the Sunday, a fine carved head was discovered.

After the interest and excitement of the preceding three months came the sudden realization that nothing now remained except to clear away as quickly as possible. The last items of equipment had gone by Thursday, 1st October, and filling in, by means of a Muledozer, Traxcavator and lorry, began on the following Monday. By the 15th October half of the foundations were hidden, and by the end of the month the 6,000 tons of excavated earth and rubble had been tipped and pushed back and the site had been levelled off.

Early in October, before the machines arrived to fill in the excavation, I visited the deserted foundations for the last time, looking back over the full days of our 'none such' summer, remembering the vast amount of devoted work which had brought to light the impressive scene around me, and the pleasure and interest which the excavation had given to so many thousands of people. Every brick and stone, every turn in the foundation walls, was a familiar friend, after so many hours spent in explaining the site to so many people. It seemed impossible that Palace and church were so soon to be hidden again, and hidden, probably, after so thorough an investigation, for all time. However, no regrets or sentiment of mine could put off the inevitable, and I forced myself to think of the people who, in years to come, would walk over the site looking for signs of the Palace. The excavation plan would be their chief guide, but, unless they went to the Park armed with a measuring tape, they would still have difficulty in relating the plan to the ground they were walking over. Thinking of the day when there would be only turf and trees to see, I paced out two measurements which, I felt, although they would scarcely satisfy a surveyor, would serve for most purposes until the trees were felled or until the site was marked out.

The slight rises in the road surface are still, as they were before the excavation, the first signs to be looked for. At the rise nearer the London Road gate, there is a gap in the trees on the Cherry Orchard side of the avenue. Starting at the middle of the trunk of the last tree before the gap, eight paces towards the rise places the visitor opposite the middle of the north-west turret of the Outer Gatehouse, which lies to his right about five feet beyond the edge of the road. He is, in fact, standing over the foundations of the front wall of the gatehouse shown in the Fitzwilliam painting. The entrance archway is on his left, just off the road. Near the second rise in the road surface there is a gap in the line of large trees on the left of the avenue, and in this gap are the foundations of the Inner Gatehouse; but here my measuring tree has already been felled. For the more technically minded, who are prepared to take more accurate measurements, the best starting point is a man-hole cover, on the grass verge on the Cherry Orchard side of the avenue, identifiable by its proximity to the first rise in the roadway. From the centre of this cover, in a line parallel with the avenue, there is a distance of 55 ft. 7 in. to the centre line of the north-west turret of the Outer Gatehouse.

During the winter of 1959–60 the cleaning, piecing together, photographing and drawing of the finds went on in preparation for the official report on the excavations, but we were already looking ahead to the project which was planned for 1960.

The Excavation Committee, at its September meeting, had decided to seek permission to excavate the site of the Nonsuch Banqueting House during the summer of 1960. It was agreed that on this occasion no financial help should be sought from the Ministry of Works, but that the excavation should be paid for entirely from voluntary sources. It was thus solely under the aegis of the Excavation Committee, and, except that no paid labour was engaged, the arrangements closely fol-lowed those which had proved so successful in 1959. Many of the local volunteers, 'diggers', guides, museum attendants and receptionists, had decided to keep in being the friendly team which had been built up during the 1959 excavations, and had formed themselves into the Nonsuch and Ewell Antiquarian Society. For the Banqueting House excavation, this body, augmented by other volunteers, and with experienced Site Supervisors, carried out the whole of the work under the direction of Martin Biddle. Quite apart from their participation in the actual excavation, they erected the 1,000 ft. of fencing delivered on loan by the Corporation, put up a hut and a large marquee, painted and erected notice-boards and installed electric lighting. They sold Guides (published, this time, officially by the Committee), manned the aluminium polling station which was now making its second appear-ance as a temporary museum, dealt with finds as they accumulated, conducted 16,000 visitors round the site during the four weeks covered by the excavation and provided a 'security patrol' until midnight each night.

Once again the Excavation Committee received the fullest possible co-operation from the Epsom and Ewell Corporation, in one of whose 'open spaces' the site lies. Fencing, museum hut, marquee, tools and surveying equipment were made available on loan; other tools were lent by the Ministry of Works and by building contractors, and one contractor delivered a wooden hut which he generously placed at our disposal for the duration of the dig. On a different plane, however, co-operation was conspicuously lacking: the weather, which had contributed so much to the success of the previous year's excavation, was decidedly unhelpful between 11th July and 7th August, 1960. Heavy showers were frequent, and there were days of continuous downpour. However, the work went forward with scarcely a hitch, and achieved its primary objective, which was to establish the ground plan of the Banqueting House. A secondary aim, to locate the two outhouses associated with the building, was partially fulfilled, in that foundations believed to be those of the bakehouse were found towards the end of the excavation.

Whilst work on the Banqueting House was in progress, a few trenches were dug on the Palace site to supplement the information obtained in 1959. The south-western corner of the Privy Garden wall was located, and a minor correction to the church plan made. Search in the neighbourhood of the south-west tower failed to reveal the entry-point of the water-supply pipes, and a further wall of Cuddington barn, which it had been hoped to find, was not discovered.

Financially, the 1960 excavation was completely self-supporting. There were many small incidental expenses, but the heaviest item was for the transport of the many articles borrowed from many different places. With only four weeks during which the site was open to visitors, sales of the Guide could not rival the figures for 1959. However, over 4,000 copies were sold, to make a contribution of over £200 to the funds. The exhibition hut, which on one day was visited by 1,169 people, added a further £200. We were thus able to meet all expenses and still afford to engage a local contractor to fill in the excavation by machine. In less than four days the 500 tons of rubble were pushed back into the trenches, leaving only the final levelling and cleaning of the surface to be done by volunteers.

With the foundations of the Palace and the Banqueting House, after they had been fully recorded in minute detail, buried again beneath a protective covering of earth, the search for Nonsuch was at an end. By

the spring of 1961 both sites were green again, and it was already
difficult to visualize them as they had so recently been, swarming with
busy workers and visitors.

The Long Ditch excavation occupied a fortnight in the summer of
1961, but from 1960 onwards work by volunteers on the finds, and on
the transcribing of documents, was continuous until 1963, when the
finds were transferred to the London Museum.

In the Park itself, the scene has changed. A new groundsman's
lodge was erected in 1969 in what was formerly a corner of the Privy
Garden of the Palace, close to the re-buried foundations of the South-
east tower. The local historical and amenity societies objected strongly
to the proposal to build the lodge in such a position, but the Park
Management Committee, faced with the problem of a number of
unpleasant incidents occurring in the park, felt that no alternative
position would give such effective control of the area. Possibly as a
result of the discussions on the siting of the lodge, a Preservation
Order was placed on the site of the Palace early in 1970.

Eleven years after the main excavation, the site of the Palace is
still not marked out, and the visitor still has to look for the manhole
cover mentioned on page 256, and for the rises in the road surface of
the avenue; but funds have been made available by the Park Management Committee for the plan to be laid out on the ground during
1970–71.

APPENDIX I

The Building of Nonsuch

An analysis of the Building Accounts for the period
22nd April to 14th September, 1538
(Public Record Office E101/477/12)

The accounts are divided into five main sections, each covering a pay period.
In this analysis the various pay periods have been indicated by figures in
parentheses, in accordance with the following table:

(1)   22nd April to 20th May
(2)   20th May to 15th June
(3)   17th June to 13th July
(4)   15th July to 10th August
(5)   12th August to 14th September.

In preparing the analysis, the Accounts were first transcribed in full. They
contain a vast amount of interesting detail, which could only be fully
exploited by printing the full transcription; but it was felt that for the present
purpose the repetition of long lists of names and other recurring items might
be found rather wearisome. Instead, the analysis gives, in modern spelling,
every item included in the 'Emptions' or purchases during the first five
periods, and a summary of the numbers and types of workmen employed on
selected dates.

The analysis begins with details of the labour force, and these are
followed by classified lists of the materials used, tools and utensils, and then
by a section containing every reference to demolition and construction work
in which actual parts of the buildings are mentioned. Wherever possible the
stated purpose for which an article was bought, or the material on which it
was to be used, has been the deciding factor in allocating a particular item to
a subject-heading; thus, the scuttles used at the lime kilns will be found under
Lime, and not under *Utensils*. This arrangement, intended to depict the
building operation 'in the round' for the benefit of the general reader, may
well prove to be an embarrassment to any who wish to use the analysis for

some specific purpose; but even they, with less labour than has gone into its compilation, will be able to abstract the information they require.

Both in transcription and in analysis a number of matters called for investigation and decision. I have identified with reasonable certainty all save three of the place-names, both in Surrey and over the border into Sussex, with the aid of *The Place-names of Surrey* (abbreviated to P.N.S.), *The Victoria County History of Surrey* (V.C.H.), the *Surrey Archaeological Collections* (S.A.C.), the publications of the Surrey Record Society and Manning and Bray's *History and Antiquities of Surrey* (M.B.). Using the modern form in the text, I have given the original spelling in italics as a footnote where it seemed likely to be of interest, and have used the same method for other unusual words which I have modernized. Similarly, in the text itself, words for which I have been unable to find a modern equivalent are printed in italics.

A word may perhaps be said about the abbreviations used in the Accounts, especially those used in connection with weights and measures. Roman numerals are used throughout, although, in a different but possibly contemporary hand, a few Arabic figures have been written in the margins of f. 21; and the Roman numerals are used in the familiar form:

$$m^l = 1,000, \ C = 100, \ l = 50, \ x = 10, \ v = 5, \ i \ (or \ j \ if \ it \ is \ the \ last \ digit) = 1.$$

Much use is made of dd (*dimidium*) to indicate $\frac{1}{2}$, and it always refers to the letter immediately to the left of it.[1] Four-score is always written iiij.$\overset{xx}{}$ Thus $m^l m^l$ dd Ciiijxvj$\overset{xx}{}$ dd gives 2,696$\frac{1}{2}$. The hundred symbol is used in several different ways. xx^c is the measure of a load of stone, which I have interpreted as 20 cwt. Firewood is bought by the C, which made two loads; in this case it must simply mean 100 large logs of agreed length, which were split up after delivery. A sawyer and his fellow were paid one shilling the C, which would be a day's wage for each of them and here the 'hundred' can scarcely have had its modern meaning of 120 deals, or boards, but may possibly mean 100 sq. ft. of surface area sawn. Other wood was carted by the load, and only in the case of squared timber are we told the size of a load: in this case 50p' (feet).[2] The sizes of nails were indicated in pence,[3] and they were

---

[1] Except where 'half a hundred' stands on its own, with no other figures before or after it, as dd C.

[2] *pedes*.

[3] 6*d*. nails, for example, were nails which, at the time when the system was introduced, had cost 6*d*. per hundred. When prices changed, the 6*d*. size nails no longer cost 6*d*. per hundred, but nails of that size continued to be sold as '6*d*. nails'. The system is still used in U.S.A.

bought by the thousand except for sprigs, which came by the bag, and rough nails, by the *Some*.[1] Tile pins were bought by the bushel or the quarter, which contained eight bushels. Ropes were bought by the lb., as was ironwork of all kinds, the cost of 1 lb. of iron depending upon the amount of work which had been put into it by the smith in making the particular article; the usual price was $1\frac{1}{2}d$. a lb., but where old iron was being reworked the smith received only $\frac{1}{2}d$. a lb.

Many of the pages have suffered damage. Several different hands appear in the accounts, and some pages are written in a hasty, slip-shod style very different from the neatness of most of the calligraphy. I found, however, nothing to suggest that these different hands indicated any marked difference in the date of writing. Scribal corrections are numerous, and there are a number of errors which the scribes did not notice. Spelling is inconsistent, even from line to line, and some of it is phonetic: the word 'iron', for example, being rendered in four different ways.

THE LABOUR FORCE AT NONSUCH. APRIL TO SEPTEMBER, 1538

Table showing the number of men at work on selected dates

	22nd April	29th April	20th May	17th June	15th July	12th August	13th September
Freemasons	–	6	20	26	44	47	47
Bricklayers[2] (later Rough Layers)	–	2	8	50	95	98	95
Plasterers	–	–	–	1	–	–	–
Chalk Diggers	–	–	7	11	9	10	12
Carpenters[2]	–	–	7	39	88	114	119
Sawyers[3]	–	–	11	23	27	30	30
Carters	–	–	4	13	7	12	14
Scaffolder	–	–	–	1	1	1	1
Hodmaker	–	–	–	–	1	1	1
Thatchers	–	–	–	–	–	–	2
Servitors	–	–	–	3	–	–	–
Clerks	2	2	2	3	4	4	4
Labourers	–	6	51	106	166	167	191

The Register of days worked
The days on which a man worked are indicated in the Accounts by a line of

---

[1] 12,000, from the French *somme*, a pack-horse load.
[2] Including apprentices.
[3] Number of names listed. No details given of actual days worked.

ciphers linking his name in the left-hand column with the amount paid to
him shown on the right of the page. The ciphers are in groups of six, Sundays
being omitted. A normal week's work thus appears as: oooooo. For any day
on which a man did not work the centre of the cipher is inked in. The
numerous public holidays on saints' days and the three-day holiday at
Whitsun are indicated by vertical lines in place of the ciphers; if a man was
paid for such a day a cipher was written above the vertical line. This symbol
may therefore indicate either 'holiday with pay' (when it applies to the whole
of the labour force) or 'paid for working on an unpaid public holiday'
(when it applies to selected groups of workers). These vertical lines,
currently written in with the line of ciphers, resemble the letter t, and a
group such as o●otot means 'present, absent, present, on holiday, present,
worked in lieu of holiday'. A small c (that is, one-half of a cipher) is written
over a cipher to indicate a half-day, of normal work if the cipher itself is
inked in, but of overtime if the cipher is open. There are a few instances of
ciphers being placed one above the other, presumably to indicate double
time such as working on a paid holiday; the extra pay in most such cases
is a little less than one-sixth of the weekly wage.

The system broke down in the case of the chief clerk, as he worked a
seven-day week after the first few weeks; he is paid 'by the space of 28 days'.

Days marked as Holidays in the Register
1st May. *St. Philip and St. James*
    All were paid.
3rd May. *Invention of the Holy Cross*
    All were paid, the masons being shown as working, and the Warden
    receiving 8d. and the Lodgemen 1/– in addition to the day's wage.
30th May. *Ascension Day*
    The masons, the Chief Warden of the carpenters and the clerks worked.
10th, 11th and 12th June. *Whit Monday to Wednesday*
    The Warden of the masons, the Chief Warden of the carpenters and the
    clerks worked.
20th June. *Corpus Christi*
    The masons, the Chief Warden of the carpenters, the chief clerk and
    3 labourers worked.
24th June. *St. John the Baptist*
    The masons, the Chief Warden of the carpenters, the chief clerk and
    2 labourers worked.
29th June. *St. Peter and St. Paul*
    All were paid, the masons receiving an extra half-day's pay on the eve.
25th July. *St. James the Apostle*
    All were paid, the masons receiving double pay for the day and an extra
    half-day's pay on the eve.

15th August. *Assumption of the Blessed Virgin Mary*
   The masons, the Chief Warden and Warden of the carpenters and the
   clerks worked.
24th August. *St. Bartholomew*
   As for 15th August.
14th September. *Exaltation of the Holy Cross*
   All were paid and presumably worked, as the day is not shown as being
   a holiday on the later pages.

Table of Wages

	Daily	Rated Weekly	10 hours' Overtime
Freemasons			
Warden		4/–, later 5/–	10*d.*
Setters		3/8	10*d.*
Lodgemen		3/4	10*d.*
Carpenters			
Chief Warden		5/–	10*d.*
Warden	9*d.*		10*d.*
Carpenters	6*d.*–8*d.*		6*d.*–8*d.*
Apprentices	4*d.*–6*d.*		4*d.*–6*d.*
Bricklayers (Rough Layers)			
Chief Warden[1]	10*d.*		10*d.*
Warden	8*d.*		10*d.*
Layers	6*d.*–7*d.*		6*d.*–7*d.*
Apprentices	4*d.*–6*d.*		5*d.*
Plasterer	7*d.*		
Chalk Diggers	6*d.*		
Carters	1*s.* 2*d.*		
Scaffolder	6*d.*		
Hodmaker	5*d.*		
Thatchers	6*d.*		
Servitors	5*d.*		
Labourers	4*d.*–5*d.*		4*d.*–5*d.*
Clerks			
Chief Clerk	8*d.*		
Clerks and Under Purveyor	6*d.*		

Impressment of Labour
   Arresting Workmen. (3) To John Maxborne for his costs and expenses
riding to Edenbridge, Lingfield, Blechingley, Dorking, Reigate and Horley

---

[1] Later designated Warden, and the Warden at 8*d.* becomes a Rough Layer at 7*d.*

with the king's commission to 'rest' and take up workmen; 13 days at 6*d*. a day over and besides his wages, for himself and his horse. To Thomas Forard, freemason, for riding in Gloucestershire, Wiltshire, Herefordshire and Worcestershire; 30 days at 8*d*. To Thomas Frelove, freemason, for riding in Northamptonshire and Bedfordshire; 10 days at 8*d*.

(5) To the masters and wardens of the carpenters in London in reward for their pains going from place to place in the City to arrest and take up workmen, 5/–.

Compensation to the pressed men, at 6*d*. for 20 miles. (2) To 3 freemasons, 6*d*. each. (3) To 4 freemasons, 6*d*. each; to one, 2/–. To 4 Rough Layers, 1/– each; to 22, 1/6; to 7, 2/–.

MATERIALS, TOOLS AND UTENSILS

Stone
Purchase. From Richard Aynscome of Reigate, Quarryman, at 3/6 a load delivered. (1) 22 loads, (2) 8 loads, (3) 14 loads, (4) 26 loads, (5) 26 loads.

Total 96 loads

Carriage
Luke[1] Stone. (5) Carriage by boat[2] from London to Ditton, 31 tons at 8*d*. a load.

Luke Stone and Caen Stone. (5) Carriage from Ditton to Cuddington, 35 loads at 8*d*. a load.

Merton Priory Stone. Carried at 8*d*. a load of 1 ton by carters from Wimbledon, Cheam, Merton, Tooting, Mitcham, Morden, Clapham, Sutton, Putney, Wandsworth, Malden and Cuddington. (1) 354 loads, (2) 1,029 loads, (3) 1,336 loads, (4) 529 loads, (5) 395 loads.

Total 3,643 loads

Hand-barrows to carry stone. (1) 3 at 4*d*. each, from Thomas Fenner of Cuddington.

Tiles
Plain[3] *tiles*. Purchase, at 4/10 a thousand, delivered, from Kingston, and 5/– from Streatham. (2) 19,000, (3) 89,000, (4) 80,000, (5) 71,000.
Ridge tiles. Purchase, at 4/10 a hundred, from Kingston. (2) 200.

Plaster
Plaster of Paris
Purchase (4) from John Fyner of St. Mary Overies, of 13 mounts[4] at 5/–

---

[1] Liége   [2] *batlage*.   [3] i.e. plane, flat.
[4] *mownts*, 30 cwt.

a mount of 1½ loads delivered at St. Catherine's Pool; and of 3 mounts from John Frank of Billingsgate, delivered at Tower Wharf, at the same price.

Carriage by boat of 17 loads from St. Catherine's to Kingston, by John Selbey of Weybridge, at 8d. a load; and of 7 loads from London to Kingston, by Hugh Hobbs of Staines (4).

Carriage from Kingston to Cuddington (5) of 23½ loads at 8d. a load, by carters from Kingston, Ham, Thames Ditton, Long Ditton, Tolworth and Surbiton.

Hair for plaster

Certain hair bought by great (3) 37/– by convention. Riding costs, to take the said hair, 2 days at 8d. a day in addition to wages. (5) A 'parcell' of hair bought by great, 20/–. Carriage from Reigate to Cuddington, 15 wain loads at 1/8 a load.

Lime and Bricks
Kilns

A damaged page of (1) relates to a payment to Thomas Carpenter of Cuddington for (? building) lime kilns. (3) Cartage of 5 loads of bricks from Hampton Court to Cuddington to make the lime kilns, at 8d. a load.

A bow of iron for the mouth of the lime kiln (1) 36 lbs., 4/6. Hoops of iron to set the lime kilns (2) 2, 28 lbs. each, 7/–. 2 to set before the mouth of the lime kiln, 42½ lbs. each, 10/7. 2 to set the kiln, 26½ lbs. each, 6/7. (3) 2 for the mouth of the lime kiln, 8/6. Mending a hoop, 2d. (5) Working 4 mouths of iron for the lime kilns, 176 lbs. at ½d. a lb.

Fires. (1) 2 axes for the lime burners, 1/– each, and 2 hatchets, 7d. each. (2) 2 axes to break wood for the lime kiln, 1/–. Wedges, steeled (1) to cleave wood at the kilns, 3 for 2/2. (2) 3 to break wood at the lime kiln, 2/4. 2 Fire forks (1) and 2 prongs, for the kilns, 3/6. (For Firewood, see separate section after *Timber*.)

Compensation for damage to crops. (4) For 1½ acres of rye and wheat where the lime kilns are, 16/– paid to Robert Hall of Ewell. For 2 acres of barley where the brick is made, 15/– to Richard Bray and George Codyngton. To the same, 10/– for 2 acres of tares, where the brickmakers do make bricks. For 1 acre of barley where the lime kilns are, destroyed by laying wood on it, 7/6 to Raynald Wilkyns of Ewell.

Bricks

Payment (5) to John Seborow, William Hudson and William Merten of Stoke D'Abernon[1] for digging, moulding, setting and burning 600,000 bricks, at 2/– a thousand standing in the kilns, the king finding wood.

---

[1] *Stook.*

Lime

Burning. Payments to John Paige[1] of Uxbridge for setting and burning kilns each containing 10 loads at 8/– a kiln delivered outside the kiln mouth, the king finding wood. By convention. (2) 8 kilns, (3) 23 kilns, (4) 22 kilns, (5) 36 kilns. (5) includes 'digging'.

Cartage of lime from the kilns to 'the place' by Thomas Whytfield of Ewell. (3) 100 loads at 4/8 for 25, (4) 21 kilns (i.e. 210 loads) at 1/10½ a kiln, (5) 150 loads at 5/4 for 25. By convention.

Purchase of lime. (2) 16 loads of 40 bushels bought from William Dean of Kingston at 6/– a load delivered.

Scuttles for the lime kilns. (1) A dozen at 2d. each.

Bushel measure for lime. (2) 8d; binding with iron, 1/–.

Timber

Selection

Riding Costs. (3) A carpenter, riding to Burstow[2] Wood, Sturtwood,[3] Leigh[4] Wood, Ewood,[5] South Wood,[6] Grovelands,[7] Epsom[8] Common, Bookham[9] Common, to mark and choose out timber for the king's works: 20 days at 8d. a day in addition to his wages.

(4) A carpenter, riding to South Wood, Leigh Wood, Burstow, East Tye[10] and Grovelands, to mark and choose out timber: 16 days at 8d. a day. John Maxborne, riding to Horley, Hounslow[11] and other places, both to mark out timber and to set out work for sawyers: 11 days at 6d. a day for himself and his horse. John Life, riding from wood to wood to look out timber: 12 days at 6d. a day for himself and his horse.

(5) A carpenter, riding to Horley, Burstow Wood, Leigh Wood and Bookham Common: 6 days at 6d. a day for himself and his horse over and besides his wages. John Maxborne, riding to Cobham Park, Bookham Common, Green Dean,[12] and *Borsam Cross*,[13] 17 days at 6d. a day for himself and his horse. John Life, riding to East Tye, Godstone, Burstow Wood and Rutherwick:[14] 6 days at 8d. a day for himself and his horse.

Felling, Hewing, Squaring and Handling

Malden. (2) Hewing and squaring 65 loads at 1/– a load.

Rusper[15] and Newdigate.[16] (3) Felling, hewing and squaring 21½ loads at

---

[1] *Paxe* in (2). [2] *Bristow.* Horley. [3] *Start wod.* Newdigate (P.N.S.).
[4] *Lee.* [5] Newdigate (P.N.S.) [6] Banstead (M.B.).
[7] *Grovelond.* Leigh (P.N.S.). [8] *Ebbesham.*
[9] *Bowcham.* [10] *Estey.* Merstham (S.A.C., XX).
[11] *Howslow.* [12] East Horsley (M.B.). [13] Not traced.
[14] A copse in Long Ditton parish, to the north of the stretch of the Hogsmill river parallel to Worcester Park Road.
[15] *Rowsper, Rosper.* [16] *Nudgate, Nidgat.*

1/2 a load. Sawing and breaking, 40 man-days at 6*d.* a day, and (4) 6 man-days.

Leigh Wood. (4) Felling, hewing and squaring by a carpenter of 27 loads in Leigh Wood of the king's own wood, at 1/2 a load. Sawyers, for sawing and breaking great timber to bring it to the load, 6 days at 6*d.* a day. (5) Cutting and slitting timber, sawyers working 15 days at 6*d.* a day. Felling, hewing and squaring 120 loads at 1/2 a load.

Rutherwick Wood. (5) Felling, 2 men working 20 days, 1 working 10 days, at 6*d.* each a day. Hewing and squaring 67 loads at 1/– a load.

South Wood. (5) Hewing and squaring 80 loads at 1/– a load.

Ewood. (5) Felling, hewing and squaring 1½ loads for 1/10.

Saw-pits. (3) Making saw-pits in Rusper and Newdigate, 2 labourers working 15 days at 5*d.* a day. (4) 2 pits in Leigh Wood and 2 in Newdigate, at 4*d.* each. (5) Making 8 saw-pits (? in Leigh Wood), 2/8.

Rollers.[1] (4) 7 rollers, in Leigh and Newdigate, made by a carpenter, at 2*d.* each.

Cutting of cross cuts[2] (5) in Leigh Wood, 2 sawyers, 2 days at 6*d.* each a day.

Ropes to load timber on the wains. (4) 2 in Leigh Wood, 1 in Burstow Wood, 2 in Rutherwick and 1 in South Wood: 145 lbs. at 1½*d.* a lb.

Square Timber. Purchase of (2) 113 loads of 50 ft., from Ifield,[3] Charlwood, Reigate, Merstham,[4] at 5/4 and 5/8 a load. (3) 37 loads from Ifield, Charlwood, Merstham and Kingston at 5/4 and 5/8. (4) 212 loads from Ewell, Alderstead,[5] Horley, Capel, Ifield, Charlwood, Kingston and Cobham, at 5/– to 5/8. (5) 164 loads at the same prices from the same places and from Leigh, Fetcham and London.

Board. Purchase of (1) 477 ft. of elm board from Cuddington at 1/8 a hundred feet. (2) 4,082 ft. of *'playnche'*[6] board from Capel and Leigh, (3) 5,359 ft., (4) 2,000 ft. and (5) 3,287 ft., all from Leigh, and 300 ft. from Chiltington, all at 1/11 a hundred feet delivered.

Laths ('*Hart Lathe*').[7] Purchase, by the load of 3,000. (1) 1 load from Kingston (price missing). (2) Nearly 9 loads and (3) 8½ loads, from Ifield and Leigh, at 9/4 a load. (5) 1 load from Capel at 9/4.

Wainscot. Carriage from Ditton to Cuddington, (5) 25 loads at 8*d.* a load, by carters from Chessington, Stoke D'Abernon, Epsom, Cobham, Bookham, Fetcham, Thames Ditton, Ditton, Ashtead and Banstead.

---

[1] For rolling logs to the saw-pits.
[2] *cross carvis.*   [3] *yfilde.*   [4] *Maistam.*   [5] Merstham.
[6] Planks, about 10 ft. long, 1 ft. 6 in. wide and 1½ in. thick.
[7] Laths made from the heart-wood of the tree.

Quarters.[1] (5) A load of single quarters, containing 100, from Kingston, 9/8.

Scaffolding. Poles. Purchase at 2/4 a load. (1) 36 loads from Capel and Dorking. (2) 4 loads, (3) 41 loads of alder poles to make scaffolds, and (5) 6 loads, all from Dorking.

Hurdles.[2] Purchase. (1) 12 dozen at 2/2 a dozen, and (2) 28 dozen at 2/4, from Chipstead. (3) 6 dozen, and (5) 4 dozen, at 2/4, from Leatherhead.

Fencing. Cartage of 'Pale Post, Shore and Rail'.

From Charlwood. (3) 174 loads, (4) 104 loads, and (5) 89 loads, at 2/2 a load, by carters from Leigh, Horley, Charlwood, Buckland, Betchworth and Reigate.

From Leigh. (3) 58 loads, and (4) 6 loads, at 1/10 a load, by carters from Leigh, Buckland, Horley and Betchworth.

From Holmwood. (3) 63 loads, (4) 59 loads, and (5) 15 loads, at 1/8 and 1/10 a load, by carters from Mickleham,[3] Headley and Dorking.

From Newdigate. (3) 18 loads, (4) 14 loads, and (5) 27 loads, at 2/2 a load, by carters from Betchworth, Newdigate, Buckland and Leigh.

From Langhurst[4] Wood to Mickleham Down, 9 miles at 2d. a mile, (5) 78 loads, by carters from Warnham, Horsham and Capel.

From Mickleham. (4) 5 loads, and (5) 226 loads, at 1/– a load, by carters from Mickleham, Headley and Dorking.

Unclassified Timber. (The first two groups are probably also fencing material).

From Hartswood.[5] (3) 41 loads at 1/10, (4) 8 loads, and (5) 7 loads, at 1/8, by carters from Reigate.

From East Tye. (4) 12 loads, and (5) 62 loads, at 1/8 a load, by carters from Nutfield, Blechingley, Merstham, Chipstead, Reigate and Banstead.

From Leigh Wood, at 2/2 a load of 50 ft. (1) 62 loads, 1 load being described as 'of the old hewing', (2) 60 loads, (3) 76 loads, (4) 71 loads, and (5) 70 loads, 38 of 'the timber of Thomas Greens and Richard Sparks' and 32 of 'the king's timber'. Carters from Leigh, Horley, Buckland, Betchworth, Reigate, Charlwood, Dorking and Capel.

From Rutherwick Wood. (4) 46 loads at 6d. a load, by carters from Long Ditton, Malden, Rutherwick and Kingston.

---

[1] The smaller vertical timbers of a timber-framed building; or the framework of panelling.
[2] For the platforms.   [3] *miclam.*
[4] Sussex, 3½ miles N. of Horsham.
[5] Buckland (P.N.S.).

The Great Pieces for the Towers

The Great Wain. (4) Making a new cart and all manner of necessaries belonging to the cart to carry the great pieces for the towers, 6/–. Making the iron-work for the cart, pins, clouts[1] and other necessaries, 3/3. (5) Clouts and nails for the king's great wheels, 3/10. Treadling and spoking, 4/–.

(5) A new axletree[2] for the wheels, 1/–. Carriage of the wheels from *Baychford*[3] to Nettlefold[4] for mending, 6*d.*

Carriage of the king's great wain (5) from Nettlefold to Buckland and Baychford on two occasions to take up the principal pieces for the towers, 1/2. Carriage of the whole wain from Baychford to Rusper Wood for loading, 8*d.*, and from Baychford to Leigh Wood for loading, 4*d.* Carriage of the wain from Leigh to Newdigate, 4*d.*

Carriage of 3 principal pieces of 80 ft. and 1 of 89 ft. in August and 1 of 80 ft. in September (4) by carters from Buckland, Betchworth and Horley, at 5/4 each piece for the journey from Leigh to Cuddington. From Manwood[5] to Cuddington, 1 of 80 ft. at 5/4, 1 of 55 ft. at 2/4, by carters from Betchworth and Buckland. From Newdigate to Cuddington, 2 of 80 ft., at 5/4 each, by carters from Betchworth and Leigh. (5) From Rusper to 'Nonnesuche', 7 of 80 ft., at 6/8 each, by carters from Newdigate, Buckland and Horsham.

Total, 1 of 89 ft., 14 of 80 ft., 1 of 55 ft.

Firewood[6]

Carriage from Kingswood at 1/6 the hundred, a hundred being 2 loads. (1) 27 loads, by carters from Epsom, Ewell, Chipstead and Cheam. (2) Turner's wood, 120 hundred, by carters from Banstead, Kingswood, Sutton, Epsom, Ewell, Chipstead and Cheam. Herne's wood, 4½ hundred, by carters from Banstead and Ewell. Kempsall, 28½ hundred, by Ewell, Epsom and Banstead carters. (3) Kempsall, the king's wood, 479 hundred; Herne's wood, 57 hundred, and (4) the king's wood, 151 hundred, by carters from Epsom, Ewell, Banstead, Walton, Chipstead and Kingswood.

Purchase. (4) 1,550 bought and delivered at the kilns for lime and brick burning, at 30/– a thousand, from Ewell. 6,500 delivered in the wood at 15/– a thousand, from John Herne of Tooting. 9,300 bought and delivered at the kilns at Nonsuch, from Thomas Carpenter of Cuddington, at 30/– a thousand. 12,000 delivered in the wood at 15/– a thousand, from Roger Turner of Kingston.

---

[1] Patches of iron.   [2] *extre.*   [3] not traced.   [4] Dorking (P.N.S.).
[5] *Manhod.* Leigh (V.C.H., III).   [6] *Talwod.*

Nails

Purchased from James Ketell, Ironmonger, of London

Sizes	Double 10d.	Single 10d.	6d.	5d.	4d.	3d.	2d.	Sprigs	Rough nails
Prices per thousand	10/–	5/–	3/4	2/4	2/–	1/6	10d.	10/– a bag	6/– a Some
(1)		1,000	1,000	1,000	1,000			1 bag	1 Some
(2)	1,000	1,500	8,000	7,000	9,000	8,000		1 bag	1 Some
(3)		2,500		2,000			5,000		2 Some
(4)	5,000	10,000	8,000	10,000	10,000			4 bags	2 Some
Totals	6,000	15,000	17,000	20,000	20,000	8,000	5,000	7 bags	6 Some

The 10d. and 5d. nails bought during period (3) are described as Flemish.

English nails purchased from Reynold Warde, Nailman, of Dudley.

Sizes	Double 10d.	Single 10d.	6d.	5d.	4d.	3d.	2d.	Rough nails	Lathe nails
Prices per thousand	11/4	5/8	3/6	2/10	2/4	1/8	10d.	10d.	10d.
(3)	4,000	4,000	13,000	12,000		3,500		35,000	
(5)	4,000	6,100		4,000	4,000		12,000		32,000
Totals	8,000	10,100	13,000	16,000	4,000	3,500	12,000	35,000	32,000

Tile pins[1], bought by the quarter (8 bushels) from John Dowset of Kingston, at 6d. a bushel. (1) A quarter, (2) 7 bushels, (3) A quarter and a half, (4) The same, and (5) 2 quarters and 5 bushels.

Garnishing nails (3) 500 for 4d. from James Ketell.

Tools

   Masons

Rubbers[2] for the masons to whet their tools on. (1) 1 at 3/4, (2) The same, (4) 1 at 4/–.

Trowels for the setters. (2) 4 at 4d. each, (3) 6 at 4d.

Setting hammers at 4d. each. (2) 2, and (3) 13.

---

[1] Usually small wooden pegs, driven through holes in the tiles, which hung by the pegs.

[2] Whet-stones.

Stone axes for the rough-layers. (2) 6 of 7 lbs. each, 7/2. (3) 13 of 8 lbs. each, 17/–.

Setting chisels. (4) Making 2, 1*d.* each, and working 2, ½*d.* each.

Beating[1] and sharpening of tools. (1) 2/– (no details). (4) Beating 1,200 masons' and rough-layers' axes, 3 for 1*d.*, and 2,600 small tools for the masons, 10 for 1*d.*

Chalk Diggers

Axes. (1) Stone axes steeled[2] to hew chalk, at 2*d.* a lb. Number and price missing.

Mattocks. (1) Steeling and mending 4 mattocks for the lime burners and chalk diggers, 4*d.* each. (2) Purchase of 2 mattocks steeled for the chalk diggers, 11 lbs. each, 3/8, and Steeling 4 mattocks for the chalk diggers, 4*d.* each. (3) 12 mattocks steeled for the chalk diggers, 19/–, and Steeling and mending mattocks for the chalk diggers, 5/1½. (4) Steeling and mending 11 mattocks for the chalk diggers and the foundation, 3/8. (5) Steeling and mending 27 mattocks and hammer heads for the chalk diggers and miners of the church, 3*d.* each.

Crowbars. (2) 2 crows of iron for the chalk diggers, 26 lbs. each, for 6/6.

Picker.[3] (3) A picker for the chalk diggers to fell down chalk, 12 lbs, 1/6.

Carpenters

Raising hooks for the carpenter. (4) Making 2, 1*d.* each.

Drift pins[4] for the carpenters. (5) 5, 3 lbs. each, for 7½*d.* Dressing two drift pins, 2*d.*

Hammer (5) to drive in the drift pins, 11 lbs. at 2*d.* a lb.

Other Tools and Equipment

Spades, Shod. (1) 6*d.* each (number missing).

Shovels. (1) 6*d.* each (number missing). (3) 5 iron-shod shovels at 5*d.* each, 4 bare shovels at 4*d.* (5) 6 shovels, 2*d.* each.

Marking iron. (5) To mark ladders and wheelbarrows, 2*d.*

Grindstones. (2) 2 5ft. stones at 5/– each, and 2 winches at 2/7 each.

Hooks to draw mortar. (2) 2 for 10½*d.*

Line (straight-edge). (2) 1 at 4*d.* (4) The same.

The Gin.[5] (4) Making 4 clasps, bolts and rings for the Gin, 10*d.*, and 4 clasps and staples for another Gin, 9*d.* (5) 4 hasps and 8 staples for the Gin, 4*d.*

---

[1] *Bateryng.*
[2] Steel was 'shut' or welded on to the edge of an iron tool.
[3] A large hand-chisel.
[4] Punches for driving nails below the surface of the wood.
[5] *Jen* (for hoisting heavy weights), consisting of a rope over a pulley, with a hook at the free end and an axle and winding wheel at the other.

Other Ironwork will be found under various specific headings. For example, the stay-bars for the windows of the Inner Court are listed under 'Demolition and Construction'.

Utensils

Scuttles (in addition to those used at the lime kilns). (2) 3 dozen at 1/4 a dozen. (3) 1 dozen, 3/–.

Scoops. (5) 6 at 2*d.* each.

Pails. (1) 4 at 4*d.* each. (2) 17 at 2*d.* each. (3) 42 at 2*d.*, to put water in for the masons and rough-layers to set their stone with. (5) 24 at 2*d.* each.

Baskets. (3) 2 dozen at 1/4 a dozen. (5) 5 dozen at the same price.

Wheelbarrows. (3) 20 carted from Hampton Court to Cuddington, 8*d.*

Cowls.[1] (2) 8, to carry water, at 1/– each. (4) 4 ears for the cowls, 1*d.* each.

Hoops for vessels at the mortar heaps. (2) 50 at 1*d.* each. (3) 18 at 1*d.* (4) 48 on tubs that hold water, 1*d.* each.

Miscellaneous Purchases

Glue. (2) 1 lb., 3*d.*

Wax. (2) 1 lb., $6\frac{1}{2}d.$, and Resin, 1 lb., $\frac{1}{2}d.$, to make cement[2] for the masons.

Bast Ropes at 8*d.* each. (1) 2 dozen, (3) 4 dozen, (4) 2 dozen, (5) 3 dozen. The first 2 dozen are described as being for making scaffolds.

DEMOLITION AND CONSTRUCTION

Merton Priory

(1) 13/4 paid to John Whytokers of Merton for uncovering (i.e. stripping the roof from) the body of the church at Merton Abbey.

Site Clearance

Trees. Damaged portion of (1) relates to a payment 'in prest'[3] to Thomas ... for hewing timber beside the (?Inner) Court. (2) Purchase of a cable[4] to pluck down trees, 87 lbs., 10/10.

Cuddington Church. (5) Steeling and mending 27 mattocks and hammer heads for the chalk diggers and miners[5] of the church, 3*d.* each; adding 8 lbs. to a bar of iron for the miners of the church, 4*d.*

Great Barn. (5) Uncovering of the great barn and setting the 'slattes' together. By convention, 12/–. 3 chisels for the carpenters to pluck down boards of the old barn, 2*d.* each.

---

[1] Tubs with two ears through which a cowl-staff was placed for carrying.

[2] *simon.* Wax and resin or pitch were used to make cement for places where mortar would be unsuitable owing to excessive dampness.

[3] An advance of money for work not yet completed.

[4] *gable.*   [5] *myners.*

Cuddington

Continued use of buildings and crops. (2) Payment to Richard Seward, tiler, for dry laying 49,000 plain tiles at 8*d.* a thousand. (3) To the same, 53,000 plain tiles on the old hall and other lodging, at the same price; and underpinning a barn, 60ft.×22ft., with flint, by convention, 16/8. Building a barn for the king's corn, William Girldler of Merton. By convention, 40/–. (4) Dry laying and lathing of the barn for the king's corn, 27,000 tiles at 9*d.* a thousand, John Whytakers of Merton. Making 3 pairs of hooks and hinges, 2 for 2 great barn doors and the other for a small door for a new barn to put in the king's hay, 41 lbs. of old iron at ½*d.* a lb.

Workshops

The Pay House and office. (1) 1 ream[1] of large paper, 8/–, and one ream of small, 3/–. Ink, 3*d.* 2 lbs. of penner's[2] dust and a dust-box, 9*d.* Red wax, 2*d.* 1 lb. of counters,[3] 8*d.* 2 hour-glasses, 4*d.* each. (3) A piece of silk a penny broad[4] for the Pay House board, 12 yards, 1/–. (4) A padlock for the chest in the Pay House, 3*d.* (5) Pack-thread,[5] 4 lbs., 1/8.

Masons' Lodge. (3) 6½ loads of straw to thatch the masons' lodge, at 2/– a load, from Cuddington. A key for the masons' lodge, 3*d.*

Carpenters' Shop. (5) 10 loads of straw to thatch a working house for the carpenters, at 2/– a load, from Banstead. 22 loads from Ewell, Chessington, Leatherhead, Epsom and Cuddington. 16 bundles of hazel rods for the thatcher, at 2*d.* a bundle of 100.

Water Supply

Well bucket. (2) 1/–. A chain and hooping of the bucket, 34 lbs. of iron, 5/9. A winch of iron for the well, 2/7. (4) Making wedges and gudgeons for the well, 7*d.*

Well ropes. (2) A small hempen rope for the well, 48 lbs., 6/–. (5) A hempen rope for the well, 56 lbs., 7/–.

The Inner Court

Doors. (3) 23 pairs of stone hooks for the doors of the Inner Court, 204 lbs., 25/6. Shutting[6] of 4 stone hooks, 4*d.*

Windows. (3) 30 iron stay-bars of 3 lights each and 91 standards for the same serving the nether lodgings in the Inner Court, 1,770 lbs., £9 8s. 9*d.*

---

[1] *realme.*   [2] *pynners.*   [3] *compters.*
[4] Silk ribbon to divide the board into compartments, for reckoning by means of counters.
[5] Probably for making lines for bricklayers and masons.
[6] Welding. Appears once as *shottyng* and twice as *shettyng*.

Six stay-bars of 1 light each, and six standards, for the spiral staircases[1] about the said Court, 72 lbs., 11/6. Cutting shorter of 8 standards for the windows, 4*d*. (4) 296 bars of iron for timber windows about the Inner Court, 2,000 lbs. at 1½*d*. a lb. Cutting, shutting, lengthening and new working 20 old bars for the stone windows, 2/4. (5) 264 bars of iron for bay windows of wood in the Inner Court, 2,158 lbs. at 1½*d*. Shutting and working 15 bars for 5 windows of the nether storey of the Inner Court, 78 lbs., 3/3.

Inner Gatehouse

Foundation. (5) Digging and casting a foundation for the Inner gate containing 23 ft. one way and 21 ft. another way, 6 ft. broad and 5 ft. deep. By convention, 10/–.

Kitchen

(5) Working a bar of iron for an oven mouth in the kitchen, 16 lbs., 8*d*.

Cellar

(5) Working a bar of iron for a step going into the cellar, 28 lbs., 1/2. Working two windows[2] for the cellar, 24 lbs., 1/–.

Chimneys

(3) A cramp of iron for a chimney, 2/–. (5) 3 parells[3] with the boards of chimneys at 8*d*. the parell.

Locks and Keys

(1) Two stock-lock keys, 4*d*. each, and (2) The Same. (3) A lock for the stocks, 6*d*. (4) A stock lock and staple, 9*d*. (2) Garnets[4] and staples for the stocks, 4/6. 2 staples, 2*d*.

LIST OF SUPPLIERS

Banstead
Richard Moyse.   Straw, £1
Billinghurst
John Penfold.   Pails, 4/–
Robert Wynson.   Pails, 6/–
Blechingley
Richard Chelmeley and Thomas Ward.   Hair, £1 17s. 0d.
Robert Whatman.   Ironwork for the great wain, 7/1

[1] *vices.*   [2] *lawnslet.*
[3] *perrellis*—parells, the frames of fireplaces, consisting of jambs and mantel.
[4] *garnettes.*

Capel
   John Palmer.   Planks, £1 8s. 6d.
                                         Scaffold Poles, 9/4
                                         Square Timber, £2 4s. 8d.

   Henry Peter.   Scaffold Poles, 4/8
   Robert Young.   Laths, 9/4

Charlwood
   John Saunder.   Square Timber, £5 19s. 10d.

Cheam
   William Marchall.   Straw, 4/—

Chessington
   Thomas Baule.   Straw, 8/—

Chiltington
   John Fynche.   Planks, 5/9

Chipstead
   Henry Cocok.   Hurdles, £5 5s. 4d.

Cobham
   Robert Adown.   Square Timber, 8/—

Cuddington
   Thomas Blak.   Straw, 13/—
   Thomas Carpenter.   Elm Board, 8/—
                                         Firewood, £13 19s. 0d.
                                       Straw, 8/—
   Thomas Fenner.   Hand Barrows, 1/—

Dorking
   John Auncell.   Scaffold Poles, £4 15s. 8d.
   Robert Broker.   ,,   4/8
   John Hether.   ,,   11/8
   William Hether.   ,,   7/—
   John Hoker.   ,,   9/4
   William Lukes.   ,,   4/8
   John Palmer.   ,,   7/—
   William Palmer.   ,,   9/4
   John Stapler.   ,,   £1 3s. 4d.
   Thomas a wode.   ,,   4/8

Dudley
   Rainolde Warde, Nailman.   Nails, £15 19s. 8d.

Epsom
   John Elliot.   Hazel Rods, 2/8
   John Olyuer.   Straw, 8/—

Ewell
   Richard Braye.   Square Timber, £15

Henry Chapman, Smith.	Tools and Ironworking, £6 6s. 1d.
	Line, 4d.
	Measure, 8d.
	Pails, 1/–
Simon Folcard.	Pails, 8d.
Richard Hewat.	Straw, 2/–
William Sandis.	Pails, 1/–
– Saunder.	Firewood, £2 5s. 9d.
Fetcham	
Thomas Rogers.	Square Timber, £1 3s. 10d.
Hampton Wick (The Wyke)	
John Agilders, Smith.	Supplying Stay-bars and Standards for windows, Chain, Locks and Keys and Tools, and Sharpening tools, £50 8s. 3½d.
Horley	
John Braye.	Square Timber, £7 1s. 1d.
Lawrens Bristow.	Square Timber, £11 17s. 0d.
Ifield	
William Hychcok.	Laths, £5 17s. 2d.
	Square Timber, £18 5s. 4d.
Kingston	
Thomas Baker, Ropemaker.	Ropes, 18/1½
William Dean.	Lime, £4 16s. 0d.
John Dowset.	Laths, 9/4
	Line, 4d.
	Pails, 4d.
	Shovels, 2/9
	Tile Pins, £1 7s. 6d.
Thomas Gollye.	Square Timber, £3 2s. 6d.
Henry Hartley.	Tiles, £34 0s. 8d.
Richard Isok.	Supply and hooping of vessels, 19/–
William Morer.	Pails, 1/10
	Props, 1/–
	Quarters, 9/8
	Spades and Shovels, 7d. and (?)
Richard Ramsey.	Tiles, £8 9s. 2d.
Richard Rundill.	Fireplaces, £1 4s. 0d.
Lawrens Thorley.	Square Timber, 10/10

Roger Turner. — Firewood (delivered in the wood), £9 0s. 0d.

Leatherhead
Thomas Sans. — Hurdles, 9/4
Thomas Till. — Straw, 14/–

Leigh
John Bristow. — Laths, £1 17s. 4d.
Planks, £20 13s. 8d.
Square Timber, £2 11s. 0d.

William Bristow. — Laths, 9/4

London
John Fyner of St. Mary Overies. — Plaster of Paris, £3 5s. 0d.
John Frank of Billingsgate. — Plaster of Paris, 15/–
James Ketell, Ironmonger. — Baskets, 9/4
Cable, 10/10
Counters, 8d.
Dust-box and Dust, 9d.
Glue, 3d.
Hour-glasses, 8d.
Ink, 3d.
Nails, £19 10s. 10d.
Pack Thread, 1/8
Paper, 11/–
Resin, ½d.
Ropes, £5 1s. 0d.
Scuttles, 5/8
Silk Ribbon, 1/–
Wax, 8½d.
Whetstones, 7/4

William Lewyn. — Grindstones, 10/–
John Quyney. — Square Timber, £7 18s. 2d.

Merstham (Alderstead)
Richard Best. — Square Timber, £40 7s. 10d.

Nutfield
John Clement. — Wheels for the great wain—Fitting treads and spokes and supplying new axle-tree, 5/–

Reigate
Richard Aynscome. — Stone, £16 16s. 0d.
John Skynner. — Square Timber, £13 3s. 0d.
John Smith. — Hair, £1.

Streatham
    William Bateman.   Tiles, £8. 10s 0d.
    Henry Hollond.   ,, £7 10s. 0d.
    Richard Rundell.   ,, £2 10s. 0d.
    William Rundell.   ,, £2 10s. 0d.
Tooting
    John Herne.   Firewood (delivered in the wood),
                              £4 13s. 9d.

Other Suppliers
    Sir Anthony Brown, Kt.   Square Timber, £12 19s. 6d.
    John Story.   Tile pins, 2/6
    Robert Wryghte.   Making the great wain, 6/–

SUMMARY OF EXPENDITURE

(Figures for first pay-period approximate owing to damage to manuscript)

22nd April to 20th May, 1538			£	s.	d.	£	s.	d.
Wages ...	...	...	21	6	0½			
Emptions	...	...	15	18	3			
Carriage	...	...	12	16	3			
						50	0	6½
20th May to 15th June								
Wages ...	...	...	86	2	7			
Emptions	...	...	70	8	10½			
Carriage	...	...	54	14	9½			
						211	6	3
17th June to 13th July								
Wages ...	...	...	196	11	11			
Overtime	...	...	10	1	4			
Emptions	...	...	111	10	8½			
Carriage	...	...	136	0	3			
						454	4	2½
15th July to 10th August								
Wages ...	...	...	301	13	9			
Overtime	...	...	22	2	4			
Emptions	...	...	162	10	6			
Carriage	...	...	65	0	7½			
						551	7	2½

12th August to 14th September			£	s.	d.	£	s.	d.
Wages ...	...	...	364	19	6			
Overtime	...	...	7	2	9			
Emptions	...	...	199	9	4			
Carriage	...	...	66	2	9½			
						637	14	4½

£1,904 12s. 7d.

Selected Documents, 1374–1650

CUDDINGTON INVENTORY
1374[1]

Inventory of all the goods of lord Simon de Codynton, knight, taken 12th April, 48 Edward III [1374], on the day he died.

In the Chamber. Bed with tester and ridells, price 26s. 8d; item 1 [*sic*] cloak price 13s. 4d. whereof 1 price 5s.; item 3 tunics and a gown, price 13s. 4d.; item 1 axe, 1 sword with buckler, price 3s. 4d.; item 2 pairs of spoons price 6s. 8d.; item 2 pairs of shoes much worn, price 2s.; item a chest, price 5s.; item 4 other old chests without locks, price 5s.; item a knife price 3s. 4d.; item 2 bows with 12 arrows, price 3s. 4d.; item 2 cross-bows, price 2s.

In the Hall. Item a set of hangings, blue and white, with 3 bench covers and 6 cushions, old and worn, price 6s. 8d.; item 6 bowls with ewers, broken, price 10s.; item a dining table with a trestle and 2 forms, price 3s. 4d.; item 2 andirons, price 6s. 8d.; item an iron fork with an iron rake for mending the fire, price 6d.

In the Pantry and Buttery. Item 5 cloths with 4 savenapes, 2 double towels and 5 single towels, price 20s.; a bread bin, price 6d.; item a chest without cover, price 4d.; item a slicing knife, price 2d.; item 10 spoons, price 8s.; item 4 beer barrels, price 2s.; item 4 mazer[2] bowls, price 40s.; item a cup with its silver cover, and 3 pieces of silver, price 40s.; item 2 pairs of bottles, price 3s.; item a wooden tankard holding a gallon and one tankard holding a pottle,[3] price 3d.; item a salt-cellar with a candlestick of tin and a copper candlestick, price 6d.

In the Kitchen. Item a brass pot and 7 others, broken, with 2 brass dishes, price 33s. 4d.; item a broken cooking-pot, price 12d.; item 2 small iron cranes, price 6d.; item a broken gridiron with a dressing knife, 6d.; item

---

[1] Part of a translation, edited at Surrey County Record Office, from a Latin document in the possession of Dr. B. Lawn.

[2] A bowl, drinking cup or goblet, originally made of a hard wood (mazer wood, possibly maple). Name applied also to bowls made of other materials. O.E.D.

[3] Half-gallon.

12 platters, 12 dishes, 12 saucers of tin, worn and broken, price 5s. 8d.; item a knife, 1d.; item a worn and broken tripod, price 4d.; item a leaden water-tank, broken, price 18d.

In the Bakehouse and Brewhouse. Item 4 large butts, 4 smaller butts and a tun, price 5s.; item 2 troughs, one for kneading and one for larding, price 5s.; item a moulding table, price 4d.; item a ladder, price 8d.; item a pair of trestles and a riddle for preparing beer, price 2d. with tongs; item 10 quarters of malt, price 50s., 5s. per quarter.

In the Grange. Item in the grange 10 quarters of wheat, price £4, 8s. per quarter; a fan 6d.

Live Stock. Item 3 stots[1] taking the place of cart horses, price 26s. 8d.; item 26 oxen, price £13, 10s. per head; item one young bull, 16 cows, 3 heifers, price 10 marks, 6s. 8d. per head; item 9 steers and heifers, price 45s., 5s. per head; item 112 sheep, price £10 3s. 4d., 20d. per head; item 298 rams, ewes and gimmers, price £18 12s. 6d., 15d. per head; item 162 lambs of their issue, £4 7s. 6d., 10d. per head; item 26 pigs and piglets, whereof 2 are boars, price 34s., 16d. per head; item 12 geese and ganders, price 4s., 4d. head.

Sale of corn. Item received from the Prior of Merton £38 16s. 6d. for 194 acres 20 perches of various sorts of corn in the fields, sold to the said Prior after Simon's death, price 4s. per acre.

Receipts in cash. Item received from the Prior of Merton by his own hands of money due to lord Simon, £13 6s. 8d.

[The Inventory is followed by details of all payments out of the estate, including funeral and administration expenses, legacies and debts to tradesmen.]

Extract From
THE VEWE AND SURVEY OF
THE MANOR OF CODYNGTONE
(c. 1537)

(Public Record Office, E315/414)

[The first two pages are devoted to a description of the hunting amenities of the manorial lands and the Downs.]—Page 3 continues:

Item the Scyte standyth one the West parte of the said manor nyghe and adioynynge to the Churche yerde all environede abowte with highe and gret tymber trees. Whervppone standyth a fayre place well buyldede and withoute decay

---

[1] Steers; but the word was also used to mean horses.

The saide Scyet ys buyldede Square abowte a lytell Courte of euery parte, Except parte of the Northe whiche ys inclosyde with a stone wall and conteynyth in length. Cxl foote and in bredeth. C Fote.

Item at the Entre into the saide Scyte ageynste the North standyth A gate housse wherin ys oone chamber and adioynynge to the same A chamber aboue and beneth the walles of tymber and coueryde with tyle.

Item the hall standyth of the Southe parte of the saide Scyte Northe and Southe and conteynyth in length xxiiij foote and in bredeth xviij foote. And thre parlers and Chambers buyldede square at the endes of the saide hall with oute Castes of bey wyndowys above and belowe, very plesaunte in the vewe and Shewe at the entre into the same and in the saide parler and Chamber be Chymneys very goode and wythin the same be vij Chambers for seruauntes. And in the parler standynge at the west ende of the hall ys a portall and the walles partely Sealede with waynestott. and the Chamber aboue with a goodly bey wyndowe newly caste owte of the same and well glasyde. extendynge aboue and belawe.

Item at the Northe ende of the hall adioynynge to the saide parler ys thre housses wyth ij small Cellers whiche vsually seruede For the pantre, and botrye. Neuerthelesse at the neyther ende of the saide hall towarde the Southe ys twoe housses that were vsually for the saide offyces and at the same ende of the hall ys ane entre ledyng to the Kechyne, whiche ys of a meane quantyte with a doble Chymney, wherof the one ys decayde and adioynynge to the same pastre and twoe larder housses and in the same foure ovyns, and the well for water whiche is very goode and Clere standyth at the Kechyne dore ageynste the west with the gardene and woodyerde for the Coke.

Item one the Southe Syde of the saide hall and newe parler ys A gardene and adioynyng to the same ane orcharde wherin be trees of Dyuers fruytes conteynynge by estimacione with the Cokes gardene one Acre Di' the walles of the saide housses of tymber and coueryde with tyle.

Item at the West ende of the saide Courte standyth A lytell berne with a Stable well buyldede and for vj horsses inclosyng of the northe parte of the saide courte, whiche ys seueryde with a close payle frome the forsaide innercourte. all whiche housses be edyfyede and buyldede with tymber and Coueryde wyth tyle.

Item one the Est parte of the saide Scyte ys a base yerde inclosyde wherin stondyth A berne that ys large and grete conteynynge by estimacione vij^{xx} and xv foote in lengthe and in bredith xxxvj fote. The walles of tymber and coueryde with tyle newly and lately buyldyde the moste parte therof.

Item within the vewe or xl Rode of the saide Scyet and Manor standyth Foure Ferme housses wyth barnes and Stables well buyldede with tymber and Coueryde with tyle and in goode Repare wherin dwellyth and inhabiteth foure honest mene and tall persones mete and able to do the Kynges seruice whiche houses be parcell of the said manor and lettyne to Ferme wyth landes to the saide Fermers for yeres whiche Dothe lyve welthely vppone the same.

Item in the southe felde whiche ys a highe Dry grounde ys A spryng of water that issuyth owte of ane hyll foure Furlonges frome the Scyte whiche ys estemyde to be the hede of A sprynge that ys curraunte at Ewell a quarter of a myle frome the same, Wherbye ij mylles goyth. And because the grounde ys not Caste Rounde abowte the same to oppyne the Sprynge it ys not Curraunte. And the water by estimacione of the leyvell of the grounde myghte be conveyede in Cundyth to the saide Scyte for the fall and Curraunte of the water shall dystende directly Downe the hyll to the Scyte.

[The remaining twenty pages give details of the occupiers of the land, the rents paid, the crops grown and their value.]

NICHOLAS MODENA AT NONSUCH
1542–1544

(Loseley MSS 837)

The Last daye of September
Anno Regis H. viij, xxxiiij°

Nonesuche
Payd vnto Nicolas Modenna the daye and yere aboue wrytten For mastyke vernyshe and oyle with other necessaryes for the pollishing settyng and vernyshing of all those sayd guylte peces to preserue them from wether— viij^{li}

The ij^d Daye of September anno xxxv
Item to Nicolas modenna in Full contentacion and payment aswell for the guylding and hatching of dyuers peces of the kynges armes badges Roses batons and other devyces cutte and kervyd in slate for the garnyshing of tymber worke of the kynges manor of Nonesuche as also coulors mastyke vernyshe patrons and all other his demaundes and requestes and then A clere rekenyng and payment to and with the saide Nicholas made in the endyng of the ij^d Daye of September Furst for the guyldyng of xlviij batons cont. xviij fote square Item for the guyldyng of xxxj^t grete Roses cont xxx^t fote square Summa totalis lxiiij fote at xvj^d the fote—iiij^{li}v^{s}iiij^d

The Last payment was made vnto the kervers of Slate the xxij^ti of Decembre in the xxxv^ti yere of the reigne of owr sayd soueregne Lorde the kyng

The First daye of Nouember Anno
Regis xxxvj^to

Nicolas Modena and dyuers other workmen in Slate wrought some iiij dayes and some vj dayes in the paye endyng the daye and yere aboue wrytten

And they wrought there from the said Furst Daye of Nouember vntill the xxiij^ti Daye of Maye A° xxxvj^to conteyning in all vij monethes makyng ij^c iiij Dayes.

Modenayes byll Noensuch

to be d'd to mr marten

[in a later hand] Nicolas Modena carver and gilder at

Nonesuch 34. 35. 36. Hen. 8

THE KING'S MAJESTY ON THE WARPATH
1545

(Public Record Office, S.P.1/201/784)
(extract)

HENRY   By the king

Right trustie and right welbiloued and trustie and right welbiloued we grete you well. Whereas Giles Geringes overseer of certain of our white workes[1] hath syne our comyng hither brabeled[2] much to vs of his working at whiche tyme as our Surveyor and others hadd secretely reaported, we laide to his chardge. that he haue not been here past twise syne Cristemas last to oversee the workemen vnder his chardge and yet haue taken our wages all thatyme aswell as if he hadd dailie contynued among theim Yea and when our officers asked him the cause of his being awaie so long. and howe our workes went forewarde, his aunswer was that he wolde tell theim nothing therof; but when he shulde see his tyme he wolde make the counsail privey who had tolde him what he shulde do, with many such bragges. Forasmuch as he alledgeth for himself that ye knowe well ynough the cause of his absence and were contented that he shulde be allowed his wag here all the saide tyme of his being awaie. Adding therto that he hath in tymes past shewed you many great and notable faultes of dyuerse of our oficers whiche toucheth vs specially wherwith he is and wilbe alwaies redye to chardge theim. Saiing by expresse

---

[1] Plasterwork.
[2] Brabble—squabble, dispute obstinately.

wordes that if we knewe all as ye do we wolde marvaill thereat. Like as we do not a litle marvaill in cace these his wordes ar true that ye haue not made vs privey therto all this while.

So these shalbe to require you that vppon the receipt hereof ye doo aduertise vs first if ye did appoinct the saide Gyles to be in any place else then at our manor of Nonesuch and to shewe his doynges onely to you and not to our saide officers. Secondely whether ye allowed him his wages here notwithstanding his absence as he saieth vppon your heddes ye did and fynally what thinges he hath at any tyme disclosed to you of any persons that shulde deceyve vs To thintent that nowe at our being here we maie as occasion shall rise chardge booth him and others that haue so offended.

Eftesones praieng you to be playn with vs herein bicause he is a fellowe that glorieth much in himself and his doinges and trusteth in the favor and bearing[1] that he loketh for at your handes

yeven vnder our privey Signett at our manor of Nonesuche the xxj[th] daye of Maie

the Kinges majestie to the counsaill xxj° may 1545

Endorsed   To our right trustie and right welbeloued the Lordes and others of our privy counsull

Giles Gering

ELIZABETH ACQUIRES NONSUCH—
THE NEGOTIATIONS IN PROGRESS, *c*. 1591

(B. M. Lansdowne 103 f. 47)
(Lord Burghley)

privat   A Memor. of matters to be
                                          communicated unto the Q. Majestie

L. Lumley	The howss of Nonsuch. vallewed at ij[c]		ij[c]		
	The litle park vallewed at j[c]xij[li]				
	The Gr pk	j[c]lx[li]	iij[c]xxxiiij[li]	V[c]xxxiiij[li]	
	The meadows	lx[li]			
	a close without the park	xl[s]			

To be assured to hir Majesty with a regraunt of the landes to the L. lomley without rent duryng the Q. raign.

[1] Support.

The L. Lvmley, to have in recompence landes to the vallew of vC^li. payeng the rentes to hir M only dvryng hir reign.

Nota. if he shall have the Grovndes of Nonsuch. only duryng his own liff. and than not to tak the proffittes of the Q. landes, vntill his deth. Than it may fall out that he dyeng afor hir Majesty. the Q. shall be answered only ij^cxxij^li for the Gr park and medoes for that the howss. and litle park will answer no rent, but a chardg of kepyng

(B. M. Lansdowne 66 f. 88)

(Mr. Justice Popham)

After that the lease wich is to be made by her majestie vnto the L. Thresorer and Mr. Fortescue toching the landes wich are to passe in exchaunge for Nonesuch. And that the graunt of the Revercion wich is to passe vnto the behoof of the L. Lumley of the same landes. And her majesties part of the Indentures of Covenauntes are all signed by her majesti

It shalbe Convenient, that all those Bookes doe remaine in my L. Thresorers handes vntill such time as the L. Lumleys assuraunce vnto her majestie of the Mansion house of Nonesuch, and the landes therto belonging be inrolled and the fyne thervppon knowledged.

And such Bondes entred into by the L. Lumley for performauns of the Covenauntes, as the L. Thresorer shall assigne

J. Popham

A Survey of

NONSUCH HOUSE AND PARK

1650

(Public Record Office, E317/Surrey/41)

Surrey

Nonsuch house and Parke cum Pertinenciis

A Survey of the Cappitall Messuag and Royall Mancion house commonly called Nonsuch and of the Parke Wherein it stands and of all the houses and lands therevnto belonging scytuate lying and being in the County of Surry late parcell of the possessions and joynture lands of Henrietta Maria the relict and late wife of Charles Stuart late King of England, made and taken by vs whose names are herevnto subscribed in the Month of Aprill in Anno Domini: 1650: by virtue of a Commission grounded vppon an Act of the Commons assembled in Parliament for the sale of the honors Manors and lands of the late King Queene and prince vnder the hands and seales of fiue or more of the trustees in the said Act named and appoynted,—

Nonsuch *All* that Cappitall messuage or Royall Mancion house with the appurtenances commonly called Nonsuch scytuat standing and being in or neare the midle parte of the litle parke of Nonsuch in the said County of Surry consisting of one fayer strong and large structure or building of free stone of two large stories high, well wrought and batteled with stone and covered with blue slate standing round a Court of: 115: foote long and 132 foote broad paved with stone commonly called the outward Court. The lower of which stories conteynes severall necessary and very vsefull roomes formerly vsed for severall offices as the buttery, the wineceller, three roomes belonging to the ladie Hollands servants, six roomes for the housekeeper, three roomes for the Gentlemen vshers, and quarter wayter, two roomes for the groome porter, and one roome for Mr. Henry Jermin. The higher storie conteynes three roomes formerly the Lady Denbighs groome of the stoole: twoo roomes for the mayds of Honour: three roomes for the Ladie Holland: a dyning roome a withdrawing roome and a bedchamber for the Ladie Carlisle: two roomes for her servants: two roomes for the queenes almner: fower roomes for the lord Dorsett Lord Chamberlayne, and two roomes for the housekeeper.

the outward Gatehouse *Memorandum* that the gatehouse leading into the outward Court aforesaid is a building very strong and gracefull being three storyes high leaded ouer head, batteled and turreted in euery of the fower Corners thereof, the highest of which stories conteynes a very large and spatyous roome very pleasant and delectable for prospect.

the Inner Court *And* allsoe consisting of one other fayre and very curious structure or building of two stories high, the lower story whereof is of good and well wrought free stone and the higher of wood richly adorned and sett forth and garnished with variety of statues pictures and other Antik formes of excellent art and workmanshipp and of noe small cost: all which building lying allmost vppon a square is covered with blue slate and incloseth one fayer and large Court of one hundred thirtie seuen foote broad and one hundred and sixteene foote long all paved with free stone: commonly called the Inner Court. The Lower of which stories conteynes one roome called the guard chamber, two roomes for the ladie Cary, two roomes for Madam Nurse, one roome called the Queenes backstayres, two roomes for

Madam Vautlet the queenes dresser, two roomes for docter Myerne, two roomes for Madam Conget, two roomes for the queenes preists, two roomes for the Master of the horse, two roomes for the queenes robes, two roomes for Madam Cyvet, two roomes for the queenes Querries, the queenes privie Kitchen, one room for the Master Cooke, and one other roome for the Queenes Wayters: The higher storie conteynes certeyne roomes called the presence chamber the privie Closet the privie chamber, the privy gallery, the queenes bedchamber, the queenes backstayres, the Kings bedchamber, the Kings backstayres, the queenes chappell and two roomes for the ladie marquess Hambleton.

Lights *Memorandum* that all the roomes comprised within the said last mencioned building are very fayre and large many of them being waynscoted round and matted and adorned with spatious lights both inwards and outwards guarded with Iron barrs and all of them fitt for present vse.

the inner gate-house *Memorandum* allsoe that the Inward Court aforesaid stands higher then the said outward Court by an assent of eight stepps leading therefrom through a gatehouse of free stone three stories high leaded and turreted in the fower Corners in the midle of which gatehouse stands a clock case turreted and leaded all ouer wherein is placed a clock and a bell this last mencioned gatehouse standing as aforesaid in the midle betwixt the said outward and inward Courts is of most excellent workmanship and a very speciall ornament to Nonsuch House.

Lead battle-ments *Memorandum* allsoe that the said inner Court building is batteled on the outsides thereof with frames of wood all covered with lead and supported with strong barrs of Iron allsoe covered with lead and fixed to the master pannes of the building, which battlements are a very greate grace and a speciall ornament to the whole building, on the east and west corners of which sayd inner Court building there are placed two large and well built turretts of fiue stories high each of them conteyning fiue roomes, beesides theire staire cases, the highest of which roomes together with the lanthorns aboue the same are covered with lead and battled round with frames of wood couered with lead, theise turretts command the prospect and view of both the parkes of Nonsuch, and of most of the Country round about, and are the cheife ornament of the whole house of Nonsuch.

Turret
Cisterne

Memorandum allsoe that in the second storie of the said west turrett there is placed a very large cesterne of lead fed and maynteyned with severall pipes of lead conveying water thereinto from a conduit a good distance from the same standing in the side of a rising ground within Nonsuch litle Parke; this cesterne is of singuler vse to the whole house many pipes being branched from thence for the supply of the offices of the whole house and ought not as wee conceaue to bee remoued thence.

Marble
fountayne

That in the sayd inner Court and neare about the midle thereof there is placed one fayer fountayne of whyte marble supported with two brass dragons vnder which is a large square cesterne of lead sett within a frame of whyte marble, vnto which cesterne is an assent of three stepps: ouer agaynst the South side of which fountayne the foresaid privie gallery doth lie being a roome waynscoted and matted and very pleasant in the midle of which is a balcone of very good workemanshipp placed ouer agaynst the said fountayne.

the
Livery
Kitchen

And allsoe consisting of one other structure or freestone building with two little shedds belonging to the same standing in a litle Court called the Kitchen Court and adioyning to the east side of the said outward Court building conteyning seuerall vsefull roomes to witt one fayer and large liuery Kitchen, a pastry roome a boyling house a botle house a Cole house and seven roomes for officers of the Kitchen and pastry.

the
woodyard
buildings

And allsoe consisting of certeyne other buildings standing and being in the yard called the woodyard and commonly called the gardiners house, the rush house, the privie buttery and the botle house.

bowling
greene

Memorandum that the frontespeece of Nonsuch house is rayled in with strong and handsome rayles and ballasters of free stone adding much to the beautie of the house before which and about 8 yardes distance from the same is a neate and hansome bouling greene well ordered lying much what vppon a square and rayled with good postes rayles and lattices of wood from whence doth lead a fayer and streight path betwixt two fayre rancks of trees vnto the parke Gate which being very high well built and placed in a direct lyne opposite to Nonsuch first gatehouse renders it a good ornament therevnto.

privie
garden

And allsoe consisting of one large garden commonly called the privie garden lying round and adioyning vnto the three outsides of the said Inward Court building compassed round with a brick wall of 14 foote high, and cut out and devided into seuerall allyes quarters and rounds set about with thorne hedges all which though for the present in a condicion of some neglect: yet with a litle labor may answeare the expectatyon of a very hansome garden plot: It being a ground large and spatious enough for such a purpose: to the North end whereof adioynes one Kitchen

Kitchen
garden

garden very vsefull and commodious lying to the east side of the said outward Court building and compassed round with a wall of brick of :14: foote high and on the west side of the said privie garden there hath beene a wilderness growing and severed with a hedge from the said litle parke but the wood of the same

Wilderness

willderness is within three Months last past cutt downe as wee are informed by order of one Mr. Bond one of the Contractors for the sale of the late kings goods but for whose vse or how converted wee cannot discouer on the North side of which wilderness there is one ould orchard or kitchen garden, the contents and number of acres of which said privie garden Kitchen gardens wilderness and orchard and of the scite of the foremencioned buildings and of the said Courts and yards wee estimate to amount to tenn acres of land but the contents thereof are comprised within the totall of acres of the said Nonsuch Parke herein hereafter particularly expressed.

Garden
materialls

Memorandum that in the said privie garden there is one piramide or spired pinacle of marble set vppon a basis of marble grounded vppon a rise of free stone neare vnto which and in the west side of the said west turret there is placed one large marble wash boule or bason ouer which stands a marble pellican fed with a pipe of lead to convey water into the same. There are allsoe two other marble pinacles or piramides called the Fawlcon perches betwixt which is placed a fountayne of whyte marble with a lead Cesterne which fountayne is sett round with six trees called Lelack trees which trees beare noe fruit but onely a very pleasant flower. There are in the said privie garden one hundred and forty fruit trees, two ewe trees, one Juniper tree, six lelack trees, and in the sayd Kitchen garden and ould orchard, seventy two fruit trees, and one fayre lyme tree, all which materialls of the said privie garden and premises are comprised within the grose valewes of the materialls of Nonsuch house as apperteyning therevnto.

the
banqueting
house

And allsoe consisting of one structure of tymber building of a quadrangular forme plesantly scituated vppon the highest parte of the said Nonsuch Parke commonly called the banqueting house. being compassed round with a brick wall the fower corners whereof represent fowre halfe Moones or fortified angles this building being of :3: stories high conteynes three fayer cellers for the first storie, one large hall waynscotted and three other roomes for the second story and fiue roomes for the 3rd story, most of them all waynscotted and lighted quite round the whole house; the stanchions and outposts of which banqueting house are all covered with lead, ouer the third story there is a lanthorne placed covered with lead and in euery of the foure corners of the whole house a balcone placed for prospect.

Memorandum vnto this banqueting house belongs one litle building conteyning a bakehouse and a roome wherein is placed a fayer well with a wheele for the winding vp of water: and one other litle house vsed for a washouse both which buildings stand in the said Nonsuch Parke opposite to the gate leading to the said banqueting house.

Vnder
house-
keepers
lodgings

And allsoe consisting of one other pile of tymber building tyled ouerhead neare adioyning to Nonsuch house on the east side thereof vsually belonging to the vnder housekeeper and inhabited by Mr. Powell vnder housekeeper (de bene placito) conteyning a hall a kitchen a buttery a milkhouse a parler a celler and six roomes aboue stayres. one litle garden and one litle orchard.

Saucery
house

And allsoe consisting of one litle tymber building tyled ouer head neare adioyning to the said vnder housekeepers house commonly called the saucery house conteyning fower litle roomes vsed by the yeomen of the sauces.

Well
house

And allsoe consisting of one brick building neare adioyning to the said saucery house commonly called the well house within which house is a fayre well of a greate depth a large cesterne of lead and a wheele for winding vp the water with two large and strong buckets well bound with Iron.

Stable
buildings

And allsoe consisting of one other pile of tymber building tyled ouer head standing allsoe in the said Parke a litle remote from Nonsuch house vppon the North east vsually called the stable buildings conteyning 8 roomes below stayres two whereof weare vsed for the bakehouse for Nonsuch and ten roomes aboue stayres all of them formerly vsed as lodgings for groomes of the stable and other inferior officers of the Court and one litle garden lying on the backside thereof.

the
greate
stable

And allsoe consisting of one fayer and large building parte wood and parte stone tyled ouer head conteyning a stable for 32 horse to stand a brest posted into stalles, planked and paued, with two litle roomes in the midle thereof for sadles to hang in, vnto each end of which long stable adioynes a severall building the one conteyning a stable for .6. horses to stand a brest ordered as aforesaid and the other conteyning two roomes below and two aboue vsed for lodgings and two other roomes formerly a smiths forge.

litle
stable

And allsoe of one other tymber building adioyning to the said stable buildings conteyneing a stable for eight horses to stand a brest ordered as aforesaid and a roome ouer to lay hay in.

barnes

And allsoe consisting of two barnes standing neare vnto the said long stable on each side thereof one: one of them conteyning 7 bayes of building with a porch and two shedds and the other of them conteyning fiue bayes of building and both of them tyled.

Keepers
lodge

And allsoe consisting of one other tymber building tyled ouer head standing in the said Nonsuch parke a pretty distance remote from Nonsuch house commonly called the keepers lodge consisting of a hall a parler a Kitchen a buttery a larder a skullery a milke house a bolting house a deere house a Cole house and ten chambers or roomes ouer head a stable a litle barne of three bayes a hay house and a barne of fiue bayes thatched a garden or orchard very well planted and two litle yardes.

Valew
of
Materialls

The sayd Cappitall messuage or royall Mancion house and all the said other houses and buildings belonging to the same scytuate and being within the said Nonsuch parke are generally in very good repayre and not fit to bee demolished or taken downe yet in regard wee haue made noe yearely valew of the same wee haue proceeded to a full and perfect view of all the materialls thereof both within and without the same as they stand respectiuely and hauing particularly apprised the same wee doe find that the materialls of all the houses and premises before mencioned are worth to bee sould aboue all chardges to bee allowed for taking downe the same in stone tymber lead slate tyle bricks Iron glass waynscot Cesternes fountaynes fruit trees and other the before mencioned vtensills and premises vppon the place the sum of 7020^{li} :00^s :00^d

Nonsuch litle Parke *All* that Parke or impaled ground commonly called and knowne by the name of Nonsuch litle Parke lying and being betweene the parishes of Ewell and Cheame in the County of Surry bounded with the towne of Ewell vppon the west, the Common feilds there vppon the South, the towne of Cheame vppon the east, and the greate Parke of Nonsuch vppon the North, conteyning in the whole vppon admeasurement six hundred threescore and eleuen acres of land worth in the whole per annum

acr.   val. per ann.

671:00:00   402^{li} :12 :00^d

And all wayes waters passadges liberties priviledges easements Franchises profits commodities advantages immunities Jurisdictyons and appurtenances whatsoever to the said Nonsuch house and parke and premises belonging or apperteyning or therevnto vsed occupied or enioyed or accepted reputed or taken as part parcell or member thereof or of any parte thereof.

Deere *There* are in the said Nonsuch litle Parke one hundred and eighty fallow deare male and female or neare thereabouts which at present wee value to be worth

240^{li} :00^s :00^d

Trees vnmarked *The* tymber trees and other trees now standing and growing within the said litle Parke of Nonsuch being in number two thousand fower hundred twenty sixe ouer and beesides such as are marked out for the vse of the Nauy being for the most part ould decayed pollards or very young spring wood good for litle saue the fier are worth vppon the place aboue all chardges for converting them into mony the sum of 3s. 5d. q^a and 13s. 4d. ouer at all one tree with another in toto

407^{li} :10^s :00^d

Vnder wood *There* are allsoe growing in diuers places of the said Parke diuers bushes of Thorne and other vnderwood which wee valew to bee worth vppon the place aboue all chardges the sum of

050^{li} :00^s :00^d

Tythe free   *Memorandum* that the said Nonsuch house Parke and premises are tythe free as hauing never beene chardged therewith.

Marked trees   *The* trees within the Parke aforesaid allready marked forth for the vse of the Nauie are found to bee in number two thousand eight hundred and fiue, two hundred whereof growe soe neare vnto Nonsuch house and in such a decent order being a speciall ornament therevnto that the cutting downe thereof will not onely very much impayre the magnificence of the structure, but will allsoe exceedingly detract from the pleasantness of the seate, which wee humbly make bould to certifie.

Wee haue not made any reprise for the fencing or keeping vp of the pales of the said parke in regard wee haue valewed the same as it may bee improued and not in relacion as to haue it maynteyned for deare.

	Acres	Vall. per ann.
Totall of acres and Annuall valewe	671	402^{li} :12^s :00^d
Totall of grose valewes of Materialls		7020^{li}
Totall of trees and woods		0457^{li} :10^s
Deere		0240^{li} :00^s

Examined per Will. Webb
   Supervisor General. 1650

Hu. Hindley
John Inwood
John Wale
John Webb

On Cover: 207. Nonsuch house and Litle Park. Car' regis. Surrey. Received this 6th of Aprill. Transmitted to the Serveyor Generall the same day. Returned the 8th of Aprill. Hindley. 17

A Survey of
NONSUCH GREAT PARK
1650

(Public Record Office, E317/Surrey/39)

Surry.
Worcester
Hous
and
Nonsuch
greate
Parke
cum
pertinenciis

A Survey of the greate Parke of Nonsuch and of all the houses lands and hereditaments belonging to the same scytuate lying and being in the parishes of Nonsuch Ewell and Maulden in the County of Surrey late parcell of the possessions and joynture lands of Henrietta Maria the relict and late queene of Charles Stuart late King of England made and taken by vs whose names are herevnto subscribed in the month of Aprill Anno Domini 1650 by virtue of a Commission grounded vppon an Act of the Commons assembled in Parliament for sale of the Honors Manors and Lands heretofore belonging to the late King queene and prince vnder the hands and seales of fiue or more of the Trustees in the Sayd Act named and appoynted.

Nonsuch
greate
Parke

All that Parke or impaled ground with the appurtenances commonly called and knowne by the name of the greate parke of Nonsuch lying and being within the parishes of Nonsuch Ewell and Maulden in the County of Surry or in some of them and all that one parcell of meadowe or impaled ground adioyning to the said Parke vppon the southside thereof and severed therefrom with a pale for the better enioying of the same commonly called the greate parke meadowe which sayd parke and meadowe are bounded with the lane that devides the litle parke of Nonsuch from the said meadowe and greate parke vppon the south and east and with Maulden Common vppon the North east and with Maulden towne and parish lands vppon the North and with Ewell Common vppon the west containing on the whole vppon admeasurement one thousand acres of land worth per annum

Acr	Rods	Perches	valew per ann
1000	–	–	550^{li} :00^{s} :00^{d}

Worcester
House

All that fayre and large Messuage Mancion house or lodge with the appurtenances scytuate and being vppon the highest ground within the said greate parke commonly called and knowne by the name of Worcester house or lodge consisting of one intire pile of very good brick building fower stories high covered with tile well built and ordered. The first storie conteynes a kitchen a beare celler a wyne celler a pantrie roome a dry larder a wett larder a passage roome a dayry roome and a washouse. The second storie conteynes a fayre hall waynscoted and tiled with a foote-pace of boards a parler waynscoted and boarded a withdrawing roome waynscoted and boarded, one great chamber waynscoted and two other chambers two closets and two roomes for servants: the third storie conteynes a large and fayer dyning roome waynscoted, a withdrawing roome and fower bed chambers and two closets. The fourth story conteynes six garrets all boarded and well lighted And allsoe consisting of a very handsome garden plot lying on the North east part of the said house much what vppon a square being compassed with a brick wall of : 10 : foote high on all the sides thereof And allsoe consisting of one handsome greene Court lying before the frontespeece of the said house being seuered from the said park with a brickwall of ten foote high from which Court to the said hall doore is an

The Race   assent of ten stepps and from which Court a race or way is sett forth betwixt two rowes of well growing trees set in a direct line answering the body of the sayd Worcester House which extends it selfe a measured halfe mile in lenght from the same and is a speciall ornament both to the house and parke and allsoe consisting of one Kitchen garden allsoe walled round and of one back court rayled with hansome rayles and of one yard wherein stand one Coach house and pigeon house and some sheds for poultry all very vsefull and necessary

The Keepers Lodge   And all that one messuage or lodge neare adioyning to the said worcester house vppon the North commonly called the Keepers lodge being a tymber building consisting of a hall a parler a kitchen a cellar a buttery a milk house and a washouse and seuen roomes over them three stables one barne of fiue bayes with a porch and a shed all tyled one other barne of fiue bayes thatched one garden one orchard well planted a greene Court and two yards

Ould lodges and Haybarnes   And all those two ould and decayed lodges allsoe standing in the said parke remote from the said worcester house and lodge aforesaid and all those two hay barnes allsoe standing in the said parke the one called sparrowe feild barne and the other haystack barne and all that litle brick building standing neere to the said keepers lodge heretofore vsed for a waterhouse.

And all wayes waters liberties easements profits priviledges and commodities to the said great parke of Nonsuch meadowe and premises belonging or apperteyning or to or with the same vsed or inioyed

Materialls The said messuage called worcester house and the said keepers
lodge and all the said houses barnes and premises except the said
two ould lodges are in very good repayre and not fit to bee
taken downe or demolished yet in regard wee haue not returned
any yearely valew of the same wee haue proceeded to a full and
perfect view of all the materialls thereof both within and without
the same and hauing particularly apprised the same as allsoe the
the said two ould lodges doe find the same to bee worth aboue
all chardges to be allowed for taking downe the same in stone
lead Iron glass waynscot tymber and other the before mencioned
premises vppon the place the sum of

1820^{li} :oo^s :oo^d

fallow There are in the said greate parke of Nonsuch three hundred
deare fallow deare male and female as neare as wee can discouer which
at present wee valew to bee worth

0400^{li} :oo^s :oo^d

Red deare There are in the said parke eight red deare male and female
which wee valew to bee worth

0020^{li} :oo^s :oo^d

trees The tymber trees and other trees now standing and growing
unmarked within the sayd greate parke of Nonsuch being in number one
thousand eight hundred and nineteen ouer and beesides such as
are marked out for the vse of the Navy being for the most parte
ould decayed pollards or very young spring wood good for litle
saue the fier are worth vppon the place aboue all chardges of
converting them into mony the sum of

0280^{li} :02^s :oo^d

springs There are in the said greate parke of Nonsuch several springs
and groues and coppices of young wood conteyning vppon ad-
coppices measurement one hundred and eighteene acres two roodes and
twenty perches the soyle and herbage whereof is valewed with
the said parke as being comprehended within the measure of one
thousand acres aforesaid but the vesture thereof being of
seuerall growths and all the best trees thereof marked out for the
Navie wee valew to bee worth aboue all chardges of converting
the same into mony the sum of

1084^{li} :18^s :oo^d

bushes and vnderwoods
There are allsoe growing in the said greate Parke of Nonsuch diuers bushes of Thorne and other vnderwoods which wee valew to bee worth aboue all chardges as aforesaid the summ of
66^{li} :13^s :4^d

Fishponds
Memorandum that in the said greate parke there are severall fishponds very well imbanked ordered and fitted for preservation of fish and foule and if stored may bee much improved

tithe free
The said greate parke of Nonsuch and the said meadowe and all other the premises are tythe free as hauing neuer beene chardged therewith

marked trees
The trees within the foresaid greate parke allready marked forth for the vse of the Navy are found to bee in number fowre thousand two hundred and eighteene most of them very small tymber

Wee haue not made any reprise for the fencing or keeping vp of the pales of the said parke in regard wee haue valewed the same as it may bee improved and not in relacion as to haue it maynteyned for deare

	Acres	Roods	Perches	valew per annum
Totall of acres and annuall valew	1000 : oo	: oo		0550^{li} :oo^s :oo^d
Totall of grose valewes of Materialls				1820^{li} :oo^s :oo^d
Totall valew of trees Coppices and vnderwood				1431^{li} :13^s :4^d
Deare				0420^{li} :oo^s :oo^d

[Then follows a memorandum regarding the Keepership rights of George and Charles Kirke, and a Report of the Committee for Removing Obstructions dealing with the tithes payable to the Rector of Long Ditton.]

THE SEVERAL DIVISIONS OF
NONSUCH GREAT PARK, 1650

(Public Record Office, E317/Surrey/40)

The seuerall deuisions
of
Nonsuch Great
Parke

1. gouge gate
2. west corner
3. hay stacke
4. gouge gate
5. great Meade

Wee the Surueyors for the Countie of Surry appoynted by authoritie of parliament for the surueying of the Honors Manors and lands of the late King Queene and prince hauing receiued an order from the honorable Trustees dated the 16ᵗʰ of this instant September : 1650 : requiring vs to make an equall diuision of Nonsuch greate parke alias worcester parke in the said county of Surry into fiue distinct parts or diuisions of equall valew and to sett out the bounds thereof according to which order wee haue proceeded accordingly:

And for the first part or diuision wee begin at a gate leading to Ewell common called Gouge gate and as the slow or rill of water runes downe the valley to a greate rew or shaw of thornes and vnderwoods thence leauing the said shaw of thorns on the north directly per the side thereof to the south corner of Mr. Turners lodge taking the said lodge and orchards to the North and soe vnder the orchard hedge to the gate at the vpper end of longwood and soe taking the hedge on the North side of longwood following the same hedge to the brick hill gate and thence along as the pale stands westerly till it meetes at the gate first mencioned called Gouge gate

The second parte or diuision beginns at the rayle about two roods from the west corner of the brick wall of the greate lodge per Mr. Turners yard pale and soe by the Corner of his Orchard to the gate at the vpper end of longwood taking in longwood to the south and soe to Brickhill gate thence by the pales to an high Oake in the pale about thirtie rods belowe Cheame gate towards the North thence to sparrowfeild barne leauing the said barne and dung yard to the south and taking in barnewood to the North to a litle pond on the South west corner of the same wood as the bounds of the said ditch goes northerly leauing Lumly lands to the west and soe downe the glade to an oake within ten rods of the North

end of the ould lodge and from that oake as the riding lies to pheasant
nest gate and from that gate leauing Pheasant nest wood and Fox bushes
woods on the east to the corner of the hedge where a hay stack hath beene
paled in and thence as the hedge lies cross the Lawne to the prince his
standing and from thence per the hedge to the west Corner of the brick
walle of the greate lodge

The third part or diuision beginns at the corner of the hedge where the hay
stack was paled in vnder the west side of phesant neast wood to phesant
neast gate thence along the riding to the oake at the ould lodge west
corner taking in mould wood and willow wood and fox bush scrubbs
and soe on the west side of barne wood to the litle pond at the vpper end
of that wood and taking in sparrow feild barne and yard and to the talle
oake in the pale : 30 : rods to the North of Cheam gate and thence per the
pale to the North corner of the greate meade and soe by the pale to the
ditch on the east side of hay stack barne and thence northerly to the halfe
myle gate per the scrubbed hedge and soe by willow wood hedge to
phesant neast gate and thence by pheasant neast wood to the corner of
the hedge per the hay stack

The fourth part or diuision beegins at Gouge gate per the pale agaynst Ewell
Common to the west corner of the greate meade and thence per the
North side thereof to the east ditch of hay stackbarne and soe by the
scrubed thorne hedge to halfe mile gate thence to phesant neast gate per
willow wood hedge thence to the Corner of the hedge per the hay stack
thence per the hedge that parts the lawne to prince his standing thence
per the thorne hedge to the west corner of the wall of the greate lodge
thence per the south side of the shaw of thornes to the Rithe at the lower
end thereof and thence to Gouge gate as the Rithe lieth

The fifth part or diuision wee conceeue the greate meade as it is now impaled
will bee a fifth part of an annuall profit of the great parke proportionablie
to any of the rest

JOHN INWOOD
JOHN WALE
JOHN WEBB

Sources and Select Bibliography

(INTRODUCTION)

page

16 Willis, Cloudesley S. *A short history of Ewell and Nonsuch.* 2nd edition. Epsom, Pullingers, 1948.

16 Clapham, *Sir* Alfred W., *and* Godfrey, Walter H. *Some famous buildings and their story.* Technical Journals, Ltd., *c.*1914.

16 Manning, Owen, *and* Bray, William. *The history and antiquities of the County of Surrey.* 3 vols. White, 1804–14.

16 Transcription of 1650 Survey. *Surrey Archaeological Collections*, vol. 5, pp. 142–9.

17 Turner, Sydney R. *The Palace of Nonsuch, 1538–1670.* Priv. print., 1948.

I (CUDDINGTON)

21 Archaeological finds at Cuddington. *Surrey Archaeological Collections*, vol. 50, p. 19; 47, p. xxv; 56, p. 139.

21 Chertsey Cartulary. British Museum, *Cotton Vitellius* A.xiii, ff. 23, 38.

22 William I. Hearnshaw, F. J. C. *The place of Surrey in the history of England.* Macmillan, 1936. p. 54.

22 Manor. *Victoria History of the County of Surrey*; edited by H. E. Malden. 4 vols. and Index. Constable, 1902–14. vol. I, pp. 289, 304; III, p. 267.

22 Fitznells Cartulary. Bodleian *Rawlinson MS.* B430. Unpublished transcription by Philip Shearman. Nos. 107, 34, 115, 38, 110, 46, 114, 5, 105, 72, 37, 75

23 Walter de Merton. *Ibid.*, Nos. 27, 57, 15, 82, 60, 70, *and* Ross, Kenneth N. *A history of Malden.* Priv. print., 1947. pp. 15, 17.

24 Candle for church. *Fitznells Cartulary*, No. 120.

24 St. Michael, Laurence de. *Ibid.*, Nos. 16, 11, 26.

24 Codington as surname. *V.C.H. Surrey*, III, p. 267.

25 Sparrowfield. Ross, K. N. *Op. cit.*, pp. 36–41.

28   Vicarage. Manning and Bray. *Op. cit.*, II, pp. 607–8, *and V.C.H. Surrey*, III, p. 270.

28   Church, exemption from taxation. *V.C.H. Surrey*, III, p. 271.

32   Surrender of Manor to Henry VIII. Surrey Record Society. *Abstracts of Surrey Feet of Fines, 1509–1558*. S.R.S., 1946. p. 40.

32   Deer. *Letters and papers, Foreign and Domestic, of the reign of Henry VIII*, vol. XIII, pt. ii, 1280.

35   *Survey of the Manor of Nonesuche, 1538*. Guildford Muniment Room, 10/157.

35   Annexation to Honour of Hampton Court. Public Record Office, C65/148.

2 (BUILDING WORK)

37   Field of Cloth of Gold. Lees-Milne, James. *Tudor Renaissance.* Batsford, 1951. pp. 23–4.

39   Wages, Comparative. Brown, E. H. P., *and* Hopkins, S. *Seven centuries of building wages*. In *Economica*, vol. XXII, no. 87. 1955.

39   Hours of work. Knoop, Douglas, *and* Jones, G. P. *Overtime in the age of Henry VIII*. In *Economic history*, vol. III, no. 13, Feb., 1938. p. 13.

42   Merton Priory surrender. Heales, A. *The records of Merton Priory.* Frowde, 1898. Appendix CLI.

46   Robert Lorde accounts. P.R.O. ref. E351/3199.

49   1541 estimate. B.M. *Royal MSS*. App. 89 (*Cotton* App. XXVIII), f. 69.

50   Toto at Hampton Court. Law, Ernest. *The history of Hampton Court Palace in Tudor times*. Bell, 1885. p. 363.

50   Haschenperg. P.R.O., S.P. 1/205/37 (2).

51   Water supply. (1) *Ibid.* (2) Milner, Edith. *Records of the Lumleys of Lumley Castle*. Bell, 1904. p. 51.

51   Aliens. *Letters of Denization and Acts of Naturalization for aliens in England, 1509–1603*; edited by William Page. Huguenot Society, vol. VIII, 1893, *and* Kirk. *Returns of aliens in London, etc.* Huguenot Society, vol. X, ii.

51   Giles Gering annuity. *Letters and Papers*, vol. XX, ii, 418 (91).

51   Sir Ralph Sadler. Guildford Muniment Room. *Loseley MSS*, LM345/150, *and* LM838.

52   Banqueting House, 1550. Historical Manuscripts Commission. *7th Report*. App., p. 606a.

53   Anthony Watson. *Description of Nonsuch*. Trinity College, Cambridge. MS. R.7.22.

3 (CONTEMPORARY ACCOUNTS AND PICTURES)

(Most references are incorporated in the text)

56   *Life of Arundel*. B.M. *Royal MSS*. 17.A.ix, f. 26r. Transcribed in
     Gentleman's Magazine, vol. 103, 1833.

57   Watson. Title—*Magnificae, et plane Regiae Domus, quae vulgo vocatur
     Nonesuch, brevis, et vera Descriptio*.

63   Hentzner. Alternative version of Latin couplet supplied from Lysons,
     Vol 1, p. 151.

63   Platter. *Travels in England, 1599*; trans. by Clare Williams. Cape, 1937.
     pp. 190ff.

67   Map, Nonsuch to Morden. P.R.O., M.P.B.25.

70   *Vetusta Monumenta*, vol. II, 1765. pl. XXIV.

70   *Richmond and its inhabitants*. Crisp, Richard. 1866. p. 104.

70   Theobalds. *In* Richardson, C. J. *Architectural remains of Elizabeth and
     James I*. 1838.

4 (THE OUTWARD COURT AND KITCHENS)

Throughout the chapter much of the information is taken from:

Exchequer L.T.R. Declared accounts. P.R.O. ref. E351/3226–3283,
covering the years 1592–1670. Gaps have been filled in from Audit
Office copies, ref. A.O.1 (various).
Anthony Watson's *Description*.
Parliamentary Survey, 1650. (See Appendix II)

Additional sources not fully described in the text are:

73   *A survey of Nonsuch Park . . . the estate of Joseph Thompson*. 1731. B.M.
     ref. 6B/1/17.

78   Garderobes.   Wright, Lawrence. *Clean and decent*. Routledge, 1960.

5 (THE INNER COURT)

Sources generally as for Chapter 4. In addition:

98   Lumley inventories. Walpole Society. Sixth volume. 1917–18. *Also in*
     Milner, E. *Records of the Lumleys* (see notes on Chapter 2).

102   Arrangement of palaces. Williams, Neville. *The royal residences of Great Britain*. Barrie and Rockliff, 1960.
108   Etienne Delaune drawing.   V. and A. Museum ref. V377, 1541.

6 (THE NONSUCH ESTATE)

Generally as for Chapter 4. In addition:

114   Hampton Court gardens.   Law, E. *Op. cit.* (Ch. 2), p. 371.
114   Gough, R. *British topography*. 1780. vol. I, p. 133.
114   Apples. Taylor, H. V. *The apples of England*. 3rd edition. Lockwood, 1946, quoting Hill, Thomas. *The profitable art of gardening*. 1574.
123   Trick fountains. Wethered, H. N. *A short history of gardens*. Methuen, 1933. p. 141.
123   Oatlands banqueting house. Amherst, A. *A history of gardening in England*. Quaritch, 1895. p. 114.
124   Whitehall banqueting house. Feuillerat, Albert. *Documents relating to the Office of the Revels in the time of Queen Elizabeth*; edited, with notes and indexes. Nutt, 1908. p. 163.
124   Stow. *Chronicles*. 1615 edition, p. 688.
124   Banqueting food. Feuillerat, A. *Op. cit.*, p. 176.
125   Banqueting house for Carew. Halliday, F. E. *Richard Carew of Antony: the Survey of Cornwall, etc.* Edited, with an introduction. Melrose, 1953. pp. 175–6.
125   *Inventory of the Wardrobe at Nonsuch.* Guildford M.R. *Loseley MSS.* LM840/2.
132   *Survey of the Great Park of Nonsuch, c.*1558. Guildford M.R. *Loseley MSS.* LM844.

7 (1538–1558)

135   John Rede of Ewelme. *Letters and Papers, Henry VIII*, vol. XIV, i, p. 195.
136   1539 visit. *Ibid.*, pp. 364–5.
136   Mats. *Ibid.*, ii, p. 156.
136   Queen's visit, 1544. *L. & P.*, vol. XIX, ii, p. 688.
137   Council at Nonsuch, 1545. *Ibid.*, vol. XX, i, 1017.
137   Henry VIII at Horsley. Bodleian *Rawlinson MSS.* D396, 125–7.
137   Carriage of tents. Guildford M.R. *Loseley MSS.* LM1.

137 Contents of wardrobes. B.M. *Harleian MS.* 1419A, supplemented by Kempe, A. J. *The Loseley manuscripts.* Murray, 1835, *and* Guildford M.R. LM840/2.

140 *Ordinances of Eltham.* Law, E. *Op. cit.* (Ch. 2), p. 147.

141 1546 visit. *L. & P.*, vol. XXI, various pp.

141 Sadler appointed Keeper. Preamble to Guildford M.R. *Loseley MSS.* LM345/10.

142 Keeper's accounts, 1541–2. *The accompt and declaracion of John Skynner.* Guildford M. R. *Loseley MSS.* LM838.

142 Cawarden appointed Keeper. Guildford M.R. *Loseley MSS.* LM345/10.

143 Master of Revels. P.R.O. Pat. 36 Henry VIII, p. 14, m. 23, *and* Feuillerat, A. *Op. cit.* (Ch. 6), p. 5. Fee as Master. Kempe, A. J. *Op. cit.*, p. 93n.

143 Life of Cawarden. *Surrey Arch. Collns.*, vol. 28, p. 9ff.

144 Wardrobe issues. Guildford M.R. *Loseley MSS.* LM840.

145 Banqueting House Keepership. H.M.C. *7th Report.* App., p. 606a.

145 Privy Council, 1550. Dasent. *Acts of Privy Council*, III, 122–5, 326.

145 Cawarden lease, 1547. P.R.O. ref. C66/908.

146 Venison warrants. Guildford M.R. *Loseley MSS.* LM846.

147 Arundel acquires Nonsuch. P.R.O. Pat. 3 & 4 Philip and Mary, pt. iii, m. 36/7.

147 Removal of wardrobe. Guildford M.R. *Loseley MSS.* LM843.

148 Cawarden-Arundel dispute. *Ibid.*, LM845.

153 Copley letter. Kempe, A. J. *Op. cit.*, pp. 59–60.

8 (ARUNDEL AND LUMLEY)

For this and the two subsequent chapters a great many specific details, too numerous to list here, have been taken from the following sources:

Calendars of State Papers Domestic, 1547–1675.
Calendar of State Papers Foreign, 1558–89.
Calendar of State Papers Spanish, 1558–1603.
Calendar of State Papers Venetian, 1603–42.
Acts of the Privy Council, III (1550)–XXXVIII (1621–3).
Sydney, *Sir* Henry, *and others. Letters and memorials of state.* 2 vols. 1746.
Historical Manuscripts Commission. *Reports.*

General sources for Chapter 8:

Milner, Edith. *Records of the Lumleys of Lumley Castle.* Bell, 1904.
Life of Arundel. See notes on Chapter 3.
Dictionary of National Biography.

Additional Sources:

156   Countess of Arundel's funeral. *The diary of Henry Machyn* (B.M.
        Cotton MS. Vitellius F. v); edited by J. G. Nichols. *Camden
        Society,* 1848.
156   Erasmus. *Instructions to a Christian prince.* B.M. *Royal MSS.* 17.A.49.
156   Jane, Lady Lumley.   Translations.   B.M. *Royal MSS.* 15.A.i, ii, ix.
157   Arundel at Nonsuch, 1558. H.M.C. *7th Report.* App. p. 614a.
157   Great Park gates.   Ross, K. N. *Op. cit.,* p. 68.
157   Rutland visit.   H.M.C. *Rutland MSS.,* IV, 382, 384.
158   Elizabeth at Nonsuch, 1559. *The diary of Henry Machyn,* as above;
        missing parts supplied from Strype, John. *Annals of the Reformation
        . . .* 1709. vol. 1, p. 191. Progress details from Aikin, Lucy.
        Memoirs of the court of Queen Elizabeth. 2 vols. 1823. vol. I, pp.
        274–6.
159   Sebastian Westcott.   Feuillerat, A. *Op. cit.,* p. 510.
159   Great Park acquired by Arundel. *Cal. Pat. Rolls,* Eliz. I, 439.
161   Letter, Elizabeth to Arundel.   P.R.O., S.P. 12, vol. 42, no. 34.
161   Date of 1567 visit. *Cal. S.P. Spanish,* 1558–67. pp. 613, 615.
161   Return of Arundel. *Gentleman's Magazine,* Dec., 1833.
163   Release of Arundel and Lumley. *Cal. S.P. Dom. Addenda,* 1566–79,
        p. 454, *and D.N.B.*
163   Nonsuch Library.   Jayne, S., *and* Johnson, F. R. *The Lumley library.*
        B.M., 1956, *and Gentleman's Magazine,* Dec., 1833.
165   Jackman and Lambert.   S.P. 12, vol. 83, no. 60.
165   Lumley petition, 1580.   S.P. 12, vol. 133, no. 26.
166   Florentine debt.   S.P. 12, vol. 99, no. 1.
168   Royal College of Physicians.   Pat. Roll 24 Eliz. I, pt. i, m. 8, *and*
        Steer, Francis W. *Lord Lumley's benefaction to the College of
        Physicians.* In *Medical history,* vol. II, no. 4, 1958. pp. 298–305.
168   Lumley letter to More.   Kempe, A. J. *Op. cit.,* p. 161.
169   Delegates of States General.   Letter in possession of C. F. Moysey,
        Esq., of Torquay.
170   *English Mercurie.* Wood, D. T. B. *The true history of the fabrication of
        of the 'Armada Mercuries'.* In *Nineteenth Century and after,* Feb.,
        1914. pp. 342–54.
173   Elizabeth acquires Nonsuch. *Feet of Fines Surrey.* Hil. 34 Eliz. I. P.R.O.
        ref. CP25(2)/227.

9 (1592–1649)

General sources:

Calendars, etc. See notes on Chapter 8.
Building details mainly from *Declared Accounts* (as Chapter 4).
Issues of the Exchequer, James I; edited by F. Devon. 1836.
Gentleman's Magazine, August, 1837.

Other sources:

176 Breunings von Buchenbach. *Relation über seine Sendung nach England . . . 1595.* Stuttgart, 1865. p. 47.
176 Repair of roads, 1599. Nichols, John. *The progresses and public processions of Queen Elizabeth.* 4 vols. 1788–1821. vol. III, p. 440.
179 Essex incident. Main sources—Sydney *Letters and memorials* and H.M.C. *De L'Isle and Dudley MSS.*, vol. II, p. 395, give Rowland Whyte letter. Aikin, Lucy. *Memoirs of the Court of Queen Elizabeth*, vol. II, pp. 445–8. Handover, P. M. *The second Cecil: the rise to power.* Eyre and Spottiswoode, 1959. pp. 196–7.
182 Duke of Stettin-Pomerania. *Diary*; edited by G. von Bulow. *Trans. Roy. Hist. Soc.*, New series, vol. VI, 1892. p. 57.
182 Country dancing. Onions, C. T., *editor. Shakespeare's England.* 2 vols. 1916. vol. II, p. 438.
182 The Lumleys. Milner, E. *Op. cit.*, p. 75ff.
185 Anne of Denmark Patent. B.M. *Add. MSS.* 6693, 105–18.
185 James I. Willson, D. H. *King James VI and I.* Cape, 1956.
186 Prince Henry. Aikin, Lucy. *Memoirs of the Court of James I.* 2 vols. 1822. vol. I, p. 408ff.
189 Duke of Saxe-Weimar. Rye, W. B. *England as seen by foreigners.* Smith, 1865. pp. 163, 167, 243.
192 Cavaliers at Worcester House. B.M. *Thomason tracts*, 1642. E.127/83(39).
193 Herbert *Memoirs.* 4th edition. Shakespeare Press, 1839. pp. 78–9.
194 *Letter of a Great Victory.* B.M. *Thomason tracts*, 669.F.12(67).

10 (1649–1687)
General sources:

Calendars, etc. See notes on Chapter 8, also *Calendar of Treasury Books*, 1660–89.
Madge, Sidney J. *The Domesday of Crown Lands.* Routledge, 1938.

Building details. P.R.O. *Declared Accounts*, E351/3278–3283. *Works* 5/7–13.

Other sources:

195 Sale of contents. B.M. *Harl. MSS.* 4898.

196 Sale of Palace to Smythson and others. P.R.O. ref. E320/R8.

197 Lambert. Dawson, William H. *Cromwell's understudy: the life and times of General John Lambert.* Hodge, 1938.

197 Debentures. Firth, C. H. *Cromwell's army.* 3rd edition. Methuen, 1921. p. 206.

197 Sale to Lambert. Bannantyne Club of Edinburgh. *Letters from Roundhead officers* . . . Edinburgh. pp. 58–9. Also P.R.O. *Close Rolls, 1654,* ref. C54/3816, no. 9.

198 Sale of Great Park to Pride. P.R.O. ref. E320/R45.

200 Lease of Great Park to Long. P.R.O. ref. E317/912, m. 19–21.

203 Pepys. Extracts from the 1918–20 Wheatley edition, 9 vols. and suppt.

205 Return of Exchequer to Westminster. B.M. *Add. MSS.* 6176, f. 26.

206 Demolition of Banqueting House. P.R.O. ref. *Works* 5/10.

207 Barbara Villiers. Grant of dignities. P.R.O., S.P. Dom., Car. II, 277, no. 136a.

208 Grant to Brounker and Grandison. P.R.O. ref. C66/3120, no. 6.

208 Barbara Villiers. Life. *Inter alia*, Sergeant, Philip W. *My Lady Castlemaine.* 2nd edition. Hutchinson, 1912.

209 Long. Petition for extended lease. P.R.O., S.P.29/276/198. Grant, P.R.O. ref. C66/3119/5.

210 Demolition of Inner Court. P.R.O., *Chancery Proceedings (Reynardson's Division)*, ref. C9/87/30.

214 Indictment of Grafton. P.R.O. ref. K.B. 11/13.

214 Indictment quashed. *The report of several cases . . . in the Court of King's Bench, 1 Jas. II–10 Wm. III*; collected by R. Comberbach. 1724.

215 Topham and Bebington. *Feet of Fines, Trinity, 3 Jas. II*. P.R.O. ref. CP25(2)/799, no. 5.

11 (1688–1959)

217 Mortgage, 1693, and Chancery decree. Northamptonshire Record Office. *Grafton (Wakefield) Collection*, G. 2705.

217 Trustees, 1694. *Ibid.*, G.2702.

217 Conveyance to Grafton. *Ibid.*, G.2705, 2704.

218 Mortgage, 1711. *Ibid.*, G. 2703. Mortgage, 1728. *Ibid.*, G.2744.

218 Act of Parliament, 1731. *Ibid.*, G.3179.

220 Death of Joseph Thompson. Manning and Bray, *Op. cit.*, III, App. p. cxxv.

220 Whateleys. Johnson, George W. *A history of English gardening.* Baldwin, etc., 1829. p. 233.

222 Wyatville. *The Farington diary*; edited by James Greig. Hutchinson, 1922. vol. II, p. 162.

224 Marshall, Charles J. *A history of the village of Cheam.* Rix, c.1925.

12 (1688–1959—SITE)

227 Durdans. Aubrey, John. *The natural history and antiquities of the County of Surrey.* 5 vols. Curl, 1719. vol. II, p. 213.

227 Nonsuch stone used in Epsom houses. Toland, John. *A new description of Epsom . . . in a letter to Eudoxa.* 1711.

227 Camden, William. *Britannia*; newly translated into English, with large additions and improvements. Gibson, 1695. p. 166.

228 Robert Lumley Lloyd. Aubrey, J. *Op. cit.*, vol. V, p. 413.

228 Peter Le Neve. *Gentleman's Magazine*, Aug., 1833. p. 123.

228 Levellers. Salmon, N. *Antiquities of Surrey.* Priv. print., 1736. pp. 51–2.

229 Stuccoes used at Durdans. Title quoted appears in Evelyn, John. *Miscellaneous writings.* Colburn, 1825, pp. 349–424. Extract from p. 419.

229 Pococke, Richard. *Travels through England*; edited by J. J. Cartwright. 2 vols. Camden Society, New series, nos. 42, 44, 1888–9. Vol. II, pp. 171, 261–2.

234 Glyn, Anna L. *A pearl of the realm.* Hutchinson, c.1895.

13 (EXCAVATION)

244 1959 Guide. *The excavation of Nonsuch Palace*, by the author. Ewell, Hill Press.

256 1960 Guide. *Nonsuch 1960: the Banqueting House, with an account of last year's excavation of the Palace site*, by the author and Martin Biddle. Ewell, Nonsuch Palace Excavation Committee.

Index